Achilles beside Gilgamesh

It is widely recognised that the epics of Homer are closely related to the earlier mythology and literature of the ancient Near East, above all the Babylonian *Epic of Gilgamesh*. But how should this influence our response to the meaning and message of either poem? This book addresses this question through an experiment in intertextual reading. It begins by exploring *Gilgamesh* as a work of literature in its own right, and uses this interpretation as the springboard for a new reading of the Homeric epic, emphasising the movement within the poem – beginning from a world of heroic action and external violence, but shifting inwards to the thoughts and feelings of Achilles as he responds to the certainty that his own death will follow that of his best friend. The book will be of interest both to specialists and to those coming to ancient literature for the first time.

MICHAEL CLARKE is Established Professor of Classics at the National University of Ireland, Galway. His interests lie in the comparative study of Classical and medieval literatures, especially ancient Greek and medieval Irish, and in the emergence of Homeric epic out of the ancient Near East. He is the author of *Flesh and Spirit in the Songs of Homer: A Study of Words and Myths* (1999).

Achilles beside Gilgamesh

Mortality and Wisdom in Early Epic Poetry

——

MICHAEL CLARKE

National University of Ireland, Galway

CAMBRIDGE
UNIVERSITY PRESS

CAMBRIDGE
UNIVERSITY PRESS

University Printing House, Cambridge CB2 8BS, United Kingdom

One Liberty Plaza, 20th Floor, New York, NY 10006, USA

477 Williamstown Road, Port Melbourne, VIC 3207, Australia

314–321, 3rd Floor, Plot 3, Splendor Forum, Jasola District Centre, New Delhi – 110025, India

79 Anson Road, #06–04/06, Singapore 079906

Cambridge University Press is part of the University of Cambridge.

It furthers the University's mission by disseminating knowledge in the pursuit of education, learning, and research at the highest international levels of excellence.

www.cambridge.org
Information on this title: www.cambridge.org/9781108481786
DOI: 10.1017/9781108667968

© Michael Clarke 2019

First published 2019

Printed in the United Kingdom by TJ International Ltd. Padstow Cornwall

A catalogue record for this publication is available from the British Library.

Library of Congress Cataloging-in-Publication Data
Names: Clarke, Michael (Michael J.), author.
Title: Achilles beside Gilgamesh : mortality and wisdom in early epic poetry / Michael Clarke.
Description: New York : Cambridge University Press, 2020. | Includes bibliographical references and index.
Identifiers: LCCN 2019038343 (print) | LCCN 2019038344 (ebook) | ISBN 9781108481786 (hardback) | ISBN 9781108667968 (ebook)
Subjects: LCSH: Homer. Iliad. | Achilles (Mythological character) – In literature. | Gilgamesh (Legendary character) – In literature. | Gilgamesh.
Classification: LCC PA4037 .C494 2020 (print) | LCC PA4037 (ebook) | DDC 883/.01–dc23
LC record available at https://lccn.loc.gov/2019038343
LC ebook record available at https://lccn.loc.gov/2019038344

ISBN 978-1-108-48178-6 Hardback

For Niamh

Contents

Fig. 1 Westmacott's statue of Achilles (1822).

Fig. 2 Illustration after Flaxman to Pope's *Iliad* (1793).

Preface

Westmacott's statue in London's Hyde Park (Fig. 1) still catches the eye: Achilles naked with sword and shield, depicted with a severe simplicity that recalls Flaxman's illustrations to Pope's translation of the *Iliad* (Fig. 2). The statue, cast from the metal of captured enemy cannon, was set up by public subscription in 1822 to honour the Duke of Wellington's victories over Napoleon.[1] To choose Achilles to commemorate a commander who defeated a foreign tyrant might seem conventional, even obvious: such is the strength of the assumption, both today and two centuries ago, that the central figure of the *Iliad* is essentially praiseworthy, a symbol of patriotic courage. I believe that by taking this perspective for granted we are liable to distort and stultify our response to the *Iliad* as a work of art in its own right. This book springs from the belief that the fundamental business of the poem is less to celebrate heroic ideals than to probe the darkness in the thoughts and values of warlike men.

Despite all the learning and insight that have been applied to the study of the *Iliad* in our time, and despite the growing realisation that it should be approached as a thematically unified discourse rather than a coalescence of diffuse elements,[2] it is still difficult to grapple in clear words with the problem of its meaning – difficult, in a word, to say what it is *about*. Of course that phrase sounds clumsy, but the question remains insistent. It is no accident that the most powerful modern response to the *Iliad* in negative, even anti-heroic, terms is not an academic reading but a philosophical essay: Simone Weil's brilliant *The Iliad or the Poem of Force*, written in a land waiting in the shadow of the most destructive war of our age.[3] A first sign of the difficulty is in the necessary choice of vocabulary: many of the likely key words – *warrior, glory, valour, hero, fame*, even *epic* – are hardly ever heard today in non-academic English except when talking about matters of fantasy and imagination. But this uneasiness points to a deeper problem: the problem of estrangement, the feeling that the vision and values of this poetry may be so distant as to be unknowable.

---

[1] See Busco 1988.   [2] On the history of these opposing approaches see Kim 2000: 1–8.
[3] Weil 2005 [1945].

It has become increasingly widely accepted that the literatures preserved in cuneiform tablets from the ancient Near East, particularly Mesopotamia – roughly modern Iraq, but generally known in the scholarship by the Greek name used by travellers and politicians up to the early twentieth century[4] – have the potential to revolutionise our understanding of early Greek literature and thought. Over the past twenty years or so, a series of increasingly closely nuanced studies have brought this from the level of a polemical assertion to a relatively uncontroversial fact about cultural history. In this book I will focus on one extraordinarily close experience of confluence between Greek and Mesopotamian literature, aligning the story of Achilles and Patroclus in the *Iliad* with that of Gilgamesh and Enkidu in the *Epic of Gilgamesh*. I believe that the relationship here is so close that it has the power to launch an overall interpretation of the *Iliad* – provided that we begin by appreciating *Gilgamesh* as an integral unity, not just a source of individual elements to be cherry-picked and listed piecemeal as parallels for elements in the Homeric poem. The plan of this book, accordingly, is to *begin* with a careful reading of the Mesopotamian epic on its own terms. If this helps us to renew or adjust our perspectives – above all, if it helps us to ask more clearly why Achilles, the 'best of the Achaeans', brings such destruction on his own people – then it will have been worthwhile, whether or not every suggestion made in this book turns out to be sustainable.

Although I hope that aspects of this book will interest specialist scholars, it is addressed primarily to the reader who wants to engage with the ancient epics, perhaps for the first time, as documents in the history of ideas. I have treated the plots of both *Gilgamesh* and the *Iliad* mostly in sequential order, so as to make it possible to dip in and out of the book when working through the primary texts, and I have included as Chapter 5 an 'Interlude' on literary origins which can safely be skipped by anyone already familiar with Homeric studies. Because this is emphatically not a stand-alone textbook – there are many excellent guides to ancient epic already[5] – I have included plenty of speculation in my responses to the often puzzling and ambiguous evidence. I differ from many Homeric specialists in that I do not find it useful to appeal to theories about 'oral poetry', while I believe

---

[4] The prevalence of the name 'Mesopotamia' in academic writing goes back at least as far as the late eighteenth century, when it was customary to refer to the constituent provinces of the then Ottoman Empire by the names of the corresponding Roman provinces. On early encounters with Mesopotamian studies in this period, see Lloyd 1980.

[5] Among recent publications, perhaps the most useful are Powell 2003, Burgess 2014, and Graziosi 2016, all of which have the virtue of expressing a synthesis of opinions rather than pushing for the positions adopted by their authors in more specialist publications. The articles in Finkelberg 2011 are also useful.

wholeheartedly in the value of interpreting themes and allusions in the light of Greek evidence from beyond the Homeric corpus. My approach is much influenced by the Neoanalyst school of Homeric scholarship, which seeks to read the surviving epics against the background of the wider tradition that must have preceded them, reconstructed mostly from our partial knowledge of the other poems of the so-called Epic Cycle (for definitions see Chapter 5). Less conventionally, I sometimes draw in side-evidence from sources in different literary genres: occasionally lyric poetry, including the quasi-epic narrative poetry of Stesichorus,[6] but more often Attic tragedy and responses to the epic inheritance by Plato and other intellectuals. Although these authors are separated from Homer by deep gulfs of time and ideas, they often provide signposts towards historically meaningful readings. In the same spirit I often put the textual evidence alongside the iconography of painted pottery, finding such comparisons more helpful than unguided speculation based on the literary evidence alone.

   All Greek sources are quoted in my own translations. These may seem idiosyncratic – for example, I often try to follow the syntax and word-order of the original more closely than is usual, and I use circumlocutions for words that have no equivalents in English[7] – but I have tried never to impose a translation tilted artificially towards the conclusion that I am trying to draw. Where there is doubt over the appropriate translation of a word that bears on the argument, I often discuss it in a footnote designed (where possible) to be useful even to the reader with little or no Greek. In view of the range and excellence of the resources that have become available for Homeric studies,[8] it seemed unnecessary to swell the footnotes

---

[6] Stesichorus may be the earliest known poet to respond to the poetic detail of Homeric epic rather than merely the outlines of plot: see discussion by Kelly 2015b.

[7] A special difficulty attends the group of Homeric nouns that refer to the locus of mental and emotional life in the innards, principally *thumos* and *phrenes*. I have usually rendered words in this group as 'thought', 'breath of thought', or the like, rather than the conventional 'heart'. In a previous publication (Clarke 1999, esp. ch. 4; cf. Cairns 2003b, 2014), I tried to make sense of these words in terms of metaphor and metonymy, emphasising that the fundamental process referred to is the flow of breath and bodily fluids in the organs of the upper body. In the present book, the issue of metaphorical versus literal interpretation is seldom directly relevant. More importantly, it seems to me essential to avoid the conventional translation 'heart' for *thumos* and related words, not only because the heart is the wrong bodily organ but also because it implies an orientation towards emotional as opposed to rational cognitive activity, and this distinction is foreign to the usage of the Greek terms in question.

[8] By combining the now complete *Lexikon des frühgriechischen Epos* (*LfgrE*) with the resources of the Cambridge commentaries on the *Iliad* and the Oxford commentaries on the *Odyssey*, supplemented by the many excellent commentaries on individual Books that have appeared since those sets were published in the early 1990s, and more recently in the Basel

with lists of parallel passages or long treatments of the secondary scholar-ship, except on issues where doubt and disagreement remain extreme. However, more detailed guidance seems necessary for ancient sources that survive in fragmentary form and are relatively inaccessible, especially the poems of the Epic Cycle, for which my notes are more copious.

So much for Greek. In the case of the Near Eastern literatures, I am largely dependent on translations, having only a halting knowledge of Akkadian and less Sumerian or Hittite. Perhaps I should not have tried to write this book at all without first learning all three languages thor-oughly, but I felt that there were two reasons to regard this as a counsel of perfection and no more. First, the texts and story-patterns of cuneiform culture were so widely disseminated and translated that a possible chain of influence from *Gilgamesh* onto early Greek thought and creativity may well have come by way of a translation out of the Akkadian original into another language – but it is not clear which language was involved, nor is it likely (in my view) that the surviving Gilgamesh texts from the Hittite world were the key intermediaries.[9] Second, and more important, ama-teurs like myself now have the means to appreciate the texts and their interpretative problems on a far more fine-grained level than was possible even twenty years ago. For Sumerian, a decisive move towards accessibility has been provided by the Electronic Text Corpus of Sumerian Literature (ETCSL) project, with the accompanying handbook by Jeremy Black and others, *The Literature of Ancient Sumer* (2004), which is the source of most of the Sumerian material discussed in the early chapters of this book. For Akkadian, Foster's *Before the Muses* (3rd edn., 2005) provides trustworthy translations of a vast range of texts, some formerly inaccessible. Above all, the opportunity to engage with the *Epic of Gilgamesh* has been opened up dramatically by the work of Andrew George. The magisterial presentation in his edition of 2003, and subsequent articles with material from new manuscripts, make it possible to read the diverse tradition of this epic on a level that was impossible in the past. As with the Greek Epic Cycle, the

---

Gesamtkommentar series, it is now easy to locate an up-to-date summary account of virtually every detailed question of Homeric interpretation.

[9] In particular, this means that the argument will have little in common with that advanced in Bachvarova 2016. I conclude (for summary, see the final chapter) by proposing that the version of *Gilgamesh* whose immediate influence is discernible in the *Iliad* corresponds to the Standard Babylonian Version in its twelve-tablet 'edition'. This means that the Greek reception must be placed towards the later part of the second millennium BCE at the earliest – considerably later than the period of the Hittite and Hurrian Gilgamesh texts examined by Bachvarova, and along quite different routes of contact. It is of course quite possible that there is truth in both arguments.

fragmentary and often doubtful state of *Gilgamesh* has led me to annotate my discussions fairly densely, drawing largely on George's commentaries. I hope any specialists in Mesopotamian studies who read this book will be forgiving of my attempts to understand something of their discipline, its extraordinary achievements and its continuing controversies.

Parts of this book draw loosely on material I have published previously, especially in an early article on lion-similes (Clarke 1995), an essay on Homeric ideas of manhood (Clarke 2004), and here and there in *Flesh and Spirit in the Songs of Homer* (1999). The first half of the Introduction is largely based on a Corbett Memorial Lecture that I delivered at the Cambridge Classical Faculty some ten years ago but left unfinished at the time. The main argument of the book, however, is a new venture, and came of teaching Homer in Greek and in translation at several universities in England and Ireland while simultaneously engaged in more austere projects on the medieval development of the Trojan War legend. I am particularly grateful to students in Maynooth and Galway who have had the spirit and determination to engage with the themes of the *Iliad* and *Gilgamesh* alongside those of the Old English *Beowulf* and the Old and Middle Irish *Táin Bó Cúailnge*. With their help I have learnt that 'heroic poetry' as a universal category is often an illusion, and I have come to appreciate more fully the unique thematic configurations between *Gilgamesh* and the *Iliad*.

For images of painted vases and other artefacts I am grateful to the museums referenced in the Figures, and also to Jonathan Burgess, Mario Iozzo, Thomas F. Carpenter and Alan Shapiro for help with sourcing elusive images. At NUI Galway I owe thanks to the School of Languages, Literatures and Cultures for teaching relief at the crucial stage of preparation, to Edward Herring for helping me to assess painted pottery, and to other colleagues and graduate students for their encouragement and insights, especially Grace Attwood, Jacopo Bisagni, Sarah Corrigan, Ioannis Doukas, Charles Doyle, Micheál Geoghegan, Ann Hurley, Aidan Kane, Peter Kelly, Enrico Dal Lago, Pádraic Moran, Elena Nordio, Dáibhí Ó Cróinín, Jason O'Rorke, Mark Stansbury, Mary Sweeney, and Nick Tosh.

Long ago when I first studied ancient poetry I had the kindest of guides in John Dillon, Jasper Griffin, Stephanie Dalley, and the late Christiane Sourvinou-Inwood, and to them I will always be grateful. I have also gained much from discussions with Jacqueline Borsje, Douglas Cairns, Ashley Clements, Michael Crudden, Bruno Currie, Mikael Males, Brent Miles, Máire Ní Mhaonaigh, Ralph O'Connor, Michael Silk, and Chris Stray.

Bruno Currie in particular read the entire book in draft and made many expert contributions and corrections, while Chris Stray gave me great editorial help as well as personal encouragement. Cambridge University Press's anonymous readers offered invaluable guidance and criticism; Michael Sharp encouraged me to persist with the project, and Nigel Hope provided expert copy-editing. I am of course responsible for all the many errors that remain.

Most important of all, I owe great thanks to my wife Niamh and to our boys Seán, Cormac and Brian: all four of them unfailing in their support, understanding and sense of humour.

Galway, 1 February 2019

Diagrams

Figures

Abbreviations

Aesch. fr.	A. H. Sommerstein (ed.), Aeschylus, *Fragments* (Loeb Classical Library) (Cambridge, MA, 2008)
ANET	J. Pritchard (ed.), *Ancient Near Eastern Texts Relating to the Old Testament*, 3rd edn. (Princeton, 1969)
Apollodorus, *Library* and *Epitome*	J. Frazer (ed.), Apollodorus, *The Library*, 2 vols. (Loeb Classical Library) (Cambridge, MA, 1921)
Atrahasis OBV	The Old Babylonian Version of *Atrahasis*, cited from Foster, *BTM*, pp. 227–80
BTM	B. R. Foster, *Before the Muses: An Anthology of Akkadian Literature*, 3rd edn. (Bethesda, MD, 2005)
CAD	A. L. Oppenheim et al., *The Assyrian Dictionary of the Oriental Institute of the University of Chicago* (Chicago, 1956–), available at www.oi.uchicago.edu/research/publications/assyrian-dictionary-oriental-institute-university-chicago-cad
CEG	P. A. Hansen, *Carmina Epigraphica Graeca Saeculorum VIII–V a. Chr. n.* (Berlin, 1983)
CTH	S. Košak and G. G. W. Müller (eds.), *Corpus des textes hittites/Catalog der Texte der Hethiter*, available at www.hethport.uni-wuerzburg.de/CTH/
ETCSL	*Electronic Text Corpus of Sumerian Literature*, available at www.etcsl.orinst.ox.ac.uk/
Eur. fr.	C. Collard and M. Cropp (eds.), Euripides, *Fragments*, 2 vols. (Loeb Classical Library) (Cambridge, MA, 2008)
GEF	M. L. West, *Greek Epic Fragments* (Loeb Classical Library) (Cambridge, MA, 2003)
GEP	D. E. Gerber, *Greek Elegiac Poetry* (Loeb Classical Library) (Cambridge, MA, 1999)
GIP	D. E. Gerber, *Greek Iambic Poetry* (Loeb Classical Library) (Cambridge, MA, 1999)
GL	D. L. Campbell, *Greek Lyric*, 5 vols. (Loeb Classical Library) (Cambridge, MA, 1982–92)
Hes. Cat. fr. Most	*Catalogue of Women* in G. Most (ed.), Hesiod, *Works*, vol. 2: *The Shield, Catalogue of Women, Other Fragments* (Loeb Classical Library) (Cambridge, MA, 2007)

Hes.Cat. *fr.* M–W	*Catalogue of Women* in Hesiod, *Fragmenta Selecta*, edited by R. Merkelbach and M. L. West in F. Solmsen (ed.), *Hesiodi Theogonia Opera et Dies Scutum*, 3rd edn. (Oxford, 1990)
Hes.*WD*	
Hes. *Th.*	Hesiod, *Works and Days* and *Theogony*, in in G. Most (ed.), Hesiod, *Works* Vol. 1 (Loeb Classical Library) (Cambridge, MA, 2006)
HHAL	M. L. West, *Homeric Hymns, Apocrypha, Lives of Homer* (Loeb Classical Library) (Cambridge, MA, 2003)
IEG2	M. L. West, *Iambi et Elegi Graeci*, 2 vols., 2nd edn. (Oxford, 1989–92)
Il.	Homer, *Iliad*, as edited by M. L. West, *Homerus: Ilias*, 2 vols. (Leipzig, 1998–2000)
LfgrE	B. Snell et al. (eds.), *Lexikon des frühgriechischen Epos* (Göttingen, 1955–2010)
LIMC	*Lexicon Iconographicum Mythologiae Classicae* (Zurich and Munich, 1981–2009)
LOAS	J. Black, G. Cunningham, E. Robson and G. Zólyomi, *The Literature of Ancient Sumer* (Oxford, 2004)
MB Boğ 1, Boğ 2, Boğ 3	Gilgamesh tablets in Akkadian from Hittite sites, edited by George (2003), 1.306–25
MB Ug 1	Middle Babylonian tablet of the opening of the Gilgamesh epic, from Ugarit, as edited and translated by George (2007a)
MFM	S. Dalley, *Myths from Mesopotamia* (Oxford, 1991)
Od.	Homer, *Odyssey*, as edited by H. Van Thiel, *Homeri Odyssea* (Hildesheim, 1991)
OB II	The Pennsylvania tablet of the Old Babylonian *Gilgamesh*, as edited and translated by George (2003), 1.166–92
OB III	The Yale tablet of the Old Babylonian *Gilgamesh*, as edited and translated by George (2003), 1.192–216
OB IM	The Baghdad tablet of the Old Babylonian *Gilgamesh*, as edited and translated by George (2003), 1.267–71
OB Ischali	The Ischali tablet of the Old Babylonian *Gilgamesh*, as edited and translated by George (2003), 1.260–6
OB VA+BM	The tablet 'reportedly from Sippar' of the Old Babylonian *Gilgamesh*, as edited and translated by George (2003), 1.272–286
SBV	The Standard Babylonian Version of the *Epic of Gilgamesh*, ed. and tr. George (2003), 1.531–740

Sources for primary texts

Near Eastern names

Proper names have been standardised, and spellings have been simplified where appropriate with the removal of diacritical marks. Sumerian divine names are used in Chapter 2; their Babylonian equivalents are used elsewhere, with indications of the Sumerian equivalents wherever these seemed useful for clarity.

Gilgamesh texts in Sumerian

These are cited from George's Penguin translation (George 1999: 141–207) except for *Gilgamesh and Huwawa Version A*, which is cited from *LOAS* (pp. 343–52). Significant variations in the translations in the ETCSL database and in the editions by Cavigneaux and Al-Rawi are noted where they arise. For simplicity's sake, the Sumerian form 'Bilgames', used by George, has been replaced by the conventional 'Gilgamesh' throughout.

Gilgamesh texts in Hittite

These are cited from the translation by Gary Beckman in Foster (2001), 157–68, pending the appearance of Beckman's full edition of *The Hittite Gilgamesh*, whose publication was forthcoming at the time this book was finalised.

The Babylonian Epic of Gilgamesh

The Old and Middle Babylonian fragments, and the Standard Babylonian Version of the *Epic of Gilgamesh*, are cited from George's standard edition (2003). The discussion of the Standard Babylonian Version is supplemented where noted by the parallels to Tablet I in the Middle Babylonian text from the Ugarit manuscript *MB Ug 1* (George 2007a) and the new evidence for Tablet V in the Suleimaniyah manuscript (Al-Rawi and George 2014).

I reproduce George's editorial conventions, by which square brackets indicate reconstructed text, italics indicate conjecture, and round brackets indicate an explanatory supplement. In a few instances, for reasons footnoted in each case, I opt instead for the wording of George's Penguin translation, which admits more generous supplements where there are gaps in the transmission. (Note that in some cases the line numbering differs slightly between the two editions.) Occasionally I refer to George's score transliterations, which represent the various manuscript readings in full (www.soas.ac .uk/gilgamesh/standard/). Despite its very different aims and methodologies, Parpola's teaching edition of the Standard Babylonian Version (Parpola 1997) has been extremely useful for cross-checking and comparison.

Atrahasis

This work is cited except where otherwise stated from the translation by Foster, *BTM* 227–80, using the Old Babylonian Version wherever possible.

Other Mesopotamian texts

Sumerian literature is most often cited from Black et al., *The Literature of Ancient Sumer* (*LOAS*) and the associated ETCSL database, and literature in Akkadian from Foster's *Before the Muses* (*BTM*). Where indicated, I have also made use of other works such as Vanstiphout's *Epics of Sumerian Kings* and Westenholz's *Legends of the Kings of Akkade*. For wisdom literature I have drawn on Cohen's *Wisdom from the Late Bronze Age* and Alster's *Wisdom of Ancient Sumer*, as well as Lambert's foundational *Babylonian Wisdom Literature*. For later texts I have made occasional use of volumes in the State Archives of Assyria series, especially Parpola's *Letters from Assyrian and Babylonian Scholars* and Livingstone's *Court Poetry and Literary Miscellanea*. Material from these volumes is available online at www.oracc.museum.upenn .edu/saao/corpus.

Hittite texts

Hittite texts are cited wherever possible from Hoffner, *Hittite Myths*, and the collections of letters edited by Hoffner, *Letters from the Hittite*

Kingdom, and Beckman et al., *The Ahhiyawa Letters*. For the ritual texts discussed in Chapter 11, I follow the standard *CTH* numbering.

Greek

All translations from Greek are my own. Proper names are given in the forms most likely to be familiar to non-specialist readers whose first language is English.

Homer

My translations follow the texts as edited by West for the *Iliad* and Homeric Hymns (the latter in the Loeb volume *HHAL*), and Van Thiel for the *Odyssey*, as in the list above. I have made constant use of the Cambridge commentaries on the *Iliad* and the Oxford commentaries on the *Odyssey*, and of the other commentaries and editions as listed in the Bibliography.

Hesiod

For *Theogony* and *Works and Days* my references follow Most's Loeb edition except where otherwise stated; I have drawn constantly on the commentaries by West (1966, 1978). For the fragments of the Hesiodic *Catalogue of Women*, references are to Most but the numbering followed by Merkelbach and West in the standard Oxford Classical Texts edition of 1990 ('M–W') is also given wherever it differs.

The Epic Cycle

Passages and testimonia are cited wherever possible from West's Loeb volume of *Greek Epic Fragments*, and where this is impossible from West's *The Epic Cycle*.

Apollodorus

I follow the chapter-numbering system of the Loeb edition by Frazer (1921). This work, although old-fashioned, is reliable and also includes invaluable cross-references to other ancient and early medieval sources: a copy of the translation is available online at www.theoi.com.

Other Greek literature

For authors and texts whose numbering systems are not universally standardised – notably lyric poetry – I have usually preferred the Loeb edition where a reliable modern edition exists in this series. In a few cases where this practice fails – as, for example, with verse inscriptions and recently published papyri – I have used the standard numeration from the scholarly editions as indicated in each case.

1 | Introduction

Two sons of goddesses face each other in battle. One of them, Aeneas, is defending his doomed city; the other, Achilles, is part of an alliance fighting for divine justice and the marital rights of its commander's brother, but all such things are now overshadowed by the need to avenge the killing of his friend. He mocks Aeneas for attempting single combat with an enemy beyond his strength; Aeneas in turn mocks Achilles for resorting to mere insult, but then moves on to speak of the past, recalling 'the very famous tales (*epea*) of mortal men' (*Il.* 20.204) about both men's origins.[1] Each is sprung from an elemental power, for Aeneas is the son of Aphrodite, the goddess who presides over sexuality, while Achilles' mother is the sea-goddess Thetis; but on this day, Aeneas foretells, one of them will mourn the death of her son (20.207–12).

So far, these words fit into a familiar cross-cultural pattern of 'flyting', dramatised exchange of self-praise and insult before combat.[2] But Aeneas' tone changes when he traces his father's place in the royal lineage of Troy, picking up Achilles' taunt that he is only a junior cousin of the family:

> Dardanus fathered a son, Erichthonius the king,
> who was born[3] the most wealthy of all mortal men:
> he had three thousand horses that were pastured in the meadow,
> mares who took delight in their gentle foals.
> The North Wind[4] fell in love with them as they were grazing
> and he lay with them in the likeness of a black-haired stallion:
> they conceived and gave birth to twelve foals.
> Whenever those went bounding over the life-giving[5] ploughland,

---

[1] For the following discussion cf. Pucci 1998: 31–48.

[2] On this theme see Parks 1990, esp. 161–78 for a comparative study of the encounter between Aeneas and Achilles.

[3] Or 'became' (*geneto*).

[4] The North Wind Boreas and his brother Zephyrus the West Wind were often held to make horses pregnant: Achilles' horses, for example, were fathered by Zephyrus on a Harpy (*Il.* 16.150).

[5] Or 'grain-giving', this probably being the original meaning; but the meaning 'life-giving' was the standard one assumed by the ancients.

> they ran over the topmost heads of the sprouting corn, nor ever broke
>   them;
> and whenever they went bounding over the broad backs of the sea,
> they ran along the topmost wave-crest of the grey salt water.
>
> (*Il.* 20.219–29)

These are glimpses of the old lore of Troy and its kings, their fabled wealth
and equally fabled untrustworthiness,[6] and their unions with the gods –
Tithonus, brother of the present king, was married to the goddess Dawn,
and Ganymede his great-uncle was taken by Zeus to be his servant or his
boy lover.[7] Aeneas' implication is that his own direct ancestors have no
part in the crimes committed by the royal family proper[8] – but such stories
could be shaped in endlessly varying ways, he says,

> the tongue of mortals can be twisted: in it there are many words
> of every kind, and the meadow of tales is broad this way and that.
>
> (*Il.* 20.248–9)

The word translated here as *tales* is again *epea*, as in the 'famous tales' that
he spoke of earlier, and the 'words' are *muthoi*. Both are ambiguous: *epea*
can refer to the most casual utterances as well as to high narratives, and
muthoi can be simply 'words spoken', not necessarily approaching the level
implied by the modern word 'myths'.[9] Yet the heightened image of the
'meadow of tales'[10] seems to draw each of these terms to the more solemn
and lofty end of its potential range of reference: Homer is alluding to the
endless variation and manipulation that a poet like himself could apply to
traditional materials.[11]

---

[6] This is particularly associated with Laomedon, who cheated Apollo and Poseidon of their
     reward for building walls around Troy, and also cheated Heracles of his reward for killing the
     sea-monster sent by Apollo and Poseidon as a punishment, as a result of which Heracles sacked
     the city. See for example *Il.* 5.638–42, 7.452–3, 14.250–1, 20.144–8, 21.441–57; summary,
     presumably from multiple sources, at Apollodorus, *Library* 2.6.4.
[7] See for example *Il.* 5.265–7, 20.232–5, and on the use of the myth in later homoerotic discourse
     see Davidson 2008.
[8] Cf. Grethlein 2006: 65–70.
[9] On the semantics of the English *myth*, and its uneasy partial overlap in meaning with the Greek
     muthos, see for example Most 1999; Fowler 2011.
[10] Translation is difficult here. 'Meadow' is an established sense for the word *nomós* (see e.g. *Il.*
     18.587), but the word might also be taken in a more abstract way – 'territory', 'realm'. The same
     query arises at Hesiod *WD* 403 and *Homeric Hymn to Apollo* 20.
[11] In the same way, the woman over whom the war is fought, Helen of Sparta, has said earlier in
     the *Iliad* that the evil fortunes of herself and her husband have been ordained so that they will
     become the subject of song (*aoidimoi*) for the people of the future (*Il.* 6.356–8) – almost
     a prophecy of the poem in which the story of those sufferings is taking shape. Cf. De Jong 2006.

I have begun with these words of Aeneas because they sum up the strange beauty of this poetry and the unsettling experience of trying to understand its balance between savagery and elegance, between the brutalities of hand-to-hand combat and the reverberations of myth and pseudohistory: the joys and sorrows of mortals, the loves and quarrels and cosmic powers of gods, all passed through Homer's reflexive awareness of the poetic form itself, the endlessly shifting and self-renewing tradition in which the *Iliad* belongs.

The prehistory of Greek epic

In a sense, the question of the origins of Greek epic is the same as that of the origins of the Greek language. According to the accepted reconstruction, at some time in the Bronze Age its ancestral speakers had come to Crete and mainland Greece from an ultimate place of origin somewhere in west-central Asia, and their speech was one of the family of related languages known as Indo-European.[12] Within that broader relationship the words and phrasal collocations of Homeric verse exhibit many astonishingly close parallels to the poetic language of Vedic, the earliest form of Sanskrit, not only on the micro-scale but often also in more complex details of ideas and imagery. These shared features seem to represent the continuation of elements that belonged in the poetic tradition of the common parent language, Proto-Indo-European, or an early offshoot; and this tradition must have been flourishing already by the time the forebears of Greek and Vedic separated from each other, an unguessably long time before the Homeric poems were composed.

That should be enough in itself to make us treat the precise wording of the poems as a thing of special gravity and depth: but the argument can be pushed further. Some of the phrases shared between Greek and Vedic seem random, no more significant than the stray chunks of Anglo-Saxon phrasing embedded here and there in modern English – *wassail, willy-nilly, so what*[13] – but among them there is a cluster of phrases that suggest a glimpse of the themes of the poetry (or at least the artistic speech) of the lost parent language.[14] One is a collocation meaning something like 'holy strength',

---

[12] For an overview see Fortson 2010: 18–50, with the more bold reconstruction by Anthony 2007.

[13] Notoriously, the collocation of the adjective and verb in Hesiod's advice 'do not urinate upright while facing the sun' (*WD* 727) finds close parallels in early Sanskrit, both lexically and conceptually (see West 2007: 217).

[14] Overview by Katz 2010; see further Schmitt 1967, and among more recent treatments see for example West 2007, with the careful discussion of the methodological problems by Clackson 2007: 187–215.

'god-like vigour': Greek *hieron menos*, Vedic *iṣiréṇa mánasa*. To judge by the attested meanings, the Proto-Indo-European phrase from which both descend would have referred to the energy and vitality of the living body: the force of spontaneous growth and movement that flows in young men and women at the peak of their health and strength, the force that is embodied in the special power and sacredness of kings and resides in the sanctuaries of the gods – in essence, the quality of self-propelled movement and growth that later Greek thinkers would identify as the presence of divinity.[15] Still more telling is the collocation found in Greek as *kléos áphthiton* and in Vedic as *śrávas … ákṣitam*, both of which reach back through a series of well-documented and systematic sound-changes to the formula reconstructed as **klewos ṇdʰgʷʰitom* 'imperishable fame' – fame that will live for ever, fame that will never be worn away like the waning moon.[16] In the Vedic attestations the phrase appears in the context of the reciprocal benefits that flow from devout acts: the worshipper, it is said, will gain 'imperishable fame' in return for offering the sacred drink called *soma*.[17] In Greek we have a verse inscription from the earlier sixth century BCE in which the context is very similar: the making of a dedication to Athene will guarantee *kleos aphthiton* for all time to the man responsible for it.[18] Given the semantic parallel, it is a fair guess that the common ground between these two takes us close to the original associations of the phrase in the parent language, even if this particular Greek example reflects the survival of archaic language and ideas in cultic practice rather than the authoritative literary traditions of the poets.

In Homer, however, the formula belongs in a different thematic config-uration. In response to a public insult, Achilles has withdrawn from the war and embarked on the rage that will lead to the deaths of thousands of his own comrades (*Il.* 1.4–5), and three of his peers have been begging him to re-enter the combat and save them from defeat. His reply is that he is about to abandon the war and sail away home. To him a special choice has been revealed:

> My mother, silver-footed goddess Thetis, says
>   that there are two different demons[19] bringing me to death's fulfilment:

---

[15] Schmitt 1967: 109–12; cf. Clarke 1995b.

[16] See Katz 2010: 361 for a summary; the definitive treatment remains Schmitt 1967: 61–102, esp. 61–9. Cf. West 2007: 406–10.

[17] *Rig Veda* 1.9.7 (where, however, the words are not adjacent to each other). The other instances are in similar contexts (*Rig Veda* 1.40.4, 8.103.5, 9.66.7). On the comparison between Greek and Vedic contexts here see Clackson 2007: 180–2, Volk 2002: 61–3.

[18] Hansen, *CEG*, p. 182, no. 344.   [19] See below, pp. 223–225, for my choice of wording here.

if I stand fast here and fight around the Trojans' city,
my homecoming is lost, but imperishable fame will be mine.
But if I make the journey home to the dear country of my fathers,
noble fame is lost for me, yet for a long time life
will be in me, and death's fulfilment will not be quick to meet me.

(Il. 9.410–16)

Imperishable fame will be mine:[20] this is *kleos aphthiton*, words reaching back to the prehistory of the language.[21] This is the pivotal moment of the *Iliad*, when Achilles rejects everything that the warrior ideal represents; but those who first heard the poem must have known that Achilles would never go home. Looming all along is the certainty that he will stay and die, winning the 'imperishable fame' that is represented by the poem itself. And in Homer's version another level of irony and bitterness will be added, because Achilles will die in the grip of misery and self-hatred that will make fame seem trivial and worthless.

Neither poet nor audience can have sensed in *kleos aphthiton* anything of the prehistory that is revealed by the Vedic correlation. Nonetheless, it is a powerful reminder that the language and thoughts embodied in the epic stretch above and behind any one creative voice, including that of the tradition or intelligence that lies behind the name 'Homer'. This makes it all the more strange that the *Iliad* explores and undercuts the ideals that the men of the Trojan War acknowledge and embody. This tension, as I will try to show, follows from the heightened energy and vitality that characterises men or half-gods like Achilles. Their energy is admirable, it is beautiful, it

---

[20] Volk 2002 shows decisively that the adjective is better to be understood as attributive ('imperishable fame will be mine') rather than predicative ('my fame will be imperishable'). Finkelberg had argued (1986, reprised 2007) that the adjective is predicative, that the collocation therefore fails to qualify as a Homeric formula in the strict sense and that the force of the Vedic parallel is thereby weakened or even invalidated. Even if the syntactic claim were admitted, this argument seems to me extremely narrow: the fact remains that the presence of the same noun–adjective pair in both languages and in such similar contexts points unmistakeably towards a single lexical and semantic configuration in the parent language. In terms of the arguments developed later in this book, however, it remains remarkable that in the Old Babylonian *Gilgamesh* there is a very similar formulation, both lexically and thematically, in which the equivalent adjective is placed in a verbless subordinate clause: *šuma ša darû*, 'a name that is eternal' (*OB* III.148: see below, p. 261). (I owe this observation to Bruno Currie.)

[21] *Kleos aphthiton* also appears in the poetry of Ibycus (fr. 282a.47: Campbell, *GL* 3.223–4), referring to the fame that the poem will give its patron Polycrates (see below, p. 125). Since the context is an evocation of the fame of Homeric heroes, probably Ibycus is alluding to Achilles' words in *Iliad* 9. The same applies to its use in a heroizing verse epitaph from Athens, commemorating dead heroes from the Persian War (Hansen, *CEG*, p. 2, no. 2 (i)), and in the Hesiodic *Catalogue of Women*, where it refers to the fame that will come (to whom?) from Ino's immortalisation (fr. 41.5 Most = fr. 70.5 M–W). These and other doubtful or late examples are also surveyed by Volk 2002.

can bring strength and bravery and wisdom: but potentially it goes too far and becomes wild and ungovernable, and in these final extremes it is to be feared and shunned even when its agents are at the height of their greatness.

The remoteness of Homer

It is no part of this book's aim to try to listen to Homeric poetry via parallel evidence gleaned from living traditions of oral 'composition-in-performance' known from ethnographic fieldwork.[22] It is possible to argue that the poems were composed in an environment where alphabetic writing was the normal tool of the wordsmith, and that the image of the divinely inspired blind singer is itself a myth of self-invention (cf. below, pp. 117–120). But this does not alter the most challenging fact about Homeric poetry: the world-picture and poetics of the epics seem in many ways utterly different from those current in the so-called 'Classical Period' centred on the fifth century BCE, to which the bulk of surviving ancient Greek literature belongs. Just as its language and its poetic resources seem to speak to us from a time more remote and more archaic than (for example) Athenian tragedy, so too its theology and its ethics, its system of social ideals and its conceptualisation of mental and emotional life, seem often to resemble only superficially those of the time of Pindar and Aeschylus, let alone that of Plato. These are writers whom we can hope to know and appreciate as individual creative minds, against a cultural background of which we have straightforward independent knowledge – more remote, certainly, than (say) Tennyson or Shakespeare or even Chaucer, but with a difference of degree rather than of kind. By contrast, every ancient response to Homer that we know of is from outside the speech-community in which the poems originated. This is true in different ways for Theagenes of Rhegium around the 530s BCE, interpreting the Homeric gods as allegories of natural phenomena,[23] for Aristotle explaining the bizarre savagery of Homer's Achilles through a comparison with the equally savage customs of contemporary Thessalians,[24] and for the Alexandrian scholar Aristarchus a century and more later, formulating the principle that Homeric poetry should be interpreted only on the basis of evidence and parallels from within the corpus: as Porphyry would later put

---

[22] A useful introduction to the 'state of the art' on this question is Foley 2002.

[23] On Theagenes see Novokhatko 2013: 31, Lamberton 1986: 32.   [24] Aristotle, fr. 166 Rose.

it, summing up Aristarchus' method, one must 'interpret Homer out of Homer'.[25]

This, more than any other factor, has encouraged the feeling that the Homeric poems are somehow prior to and higher than everything else in the flow of Western literature. As the late antique critic Macrobius put it,

> This is the crowning touch to Homer's glory: though so many authors have watched in wait against him and all have gathered their forces to assail him, 'he stands against them unmoved, like a crag in the sea.' (Macrobius, *Saturnalia* 6.3.1, tr. Kaster)[26]

In this lies the problem. If we are to understand the epics as created works of art, we need a sense of the background from which they emerged: we need a norm or baseline or starting-point against which to locate the messages that they articulate. Whatever those messages are, we can safely assume that they are more than platitudes and truisms. As Christiane Sourvinou-Inwood brilliantly expressed it – thinking of tragic poetry, but the principle applies to any genre characterised by exploration rather than mere celebration – the discourses of serious literature are located at 'the interstices of established belief'.[27] If the conventional world-picture of the community is imagined as a net cast over experience, the points of intellectual interest and creative tension lie in the hollow squares between the lines of fibre – areas of doubt, uncertainty, or contradiction. With the poets of Classical Athens it should be possible (with effort) to distinguish the network from the interstices, because of the wealth of other texts and artefacts and historical knowledge that survive to shed light on the conventional wisdom and 'collective representations' of their time. But with Homer we rely on the same source for reconstructing both. To take examples that will loom large in this book, it is clear that the *Iliad* is exploring themes like the relationship between honour and vengeance, or the intervention of the gods in human thought and action, or the tendency among men of violence for courage to move towards madness: but if we are to try to interpret these explorations, where do we begin? Even our sense of the semantic range of each of the key lexical items – *timē* 'honour', *kleos* 'fame', *moira* 'destiny' – must be built up on the basis of the attestations offered by the Homeric poems themselves. How then can we distinguish

---

[25] Porphyry, *Homeric Questions* 1.56.3–6. On this formulation of Aristarchus' methodology see Montana 2013: 134–6, with Schironi 2018: 75 n. 47.

[26] It may or may not be an irony here on Macrobius' part that the image of the rock in the sea is itself quoted from Vergil (*Aeneid* 7.586), whose intense and allusive engagement with Homer is Macrobius' main theme.

[27] Sourvinou-Inwood 1995: 11.

the unmarked and conventional meanings of those words from the creative, perhaps even anti-traditional discourses that Homer builds up around them?

The hypothesis that Homeric poetry should be heard and contextualised as part of a long pre-existing tradition of oral composition has often seemed to offer the prospect of distinguishing tradition from originality at the level of word-choice, phrasing and poetic diction.[28] However, it has proved harder to find an equivalent opportunity when it comes to matters of ethics, psychology and the thoughts and motivations of Homer's characters. Achilles deploys the resources of Homeric diction and formula on a more heightened, even more creative level than any other character in the *Iliad*,[29] but this in itself offers no direct guidance when we confront the apparent gulf between his words in *Iliad* 9 and what seem to be the default expectations of Homer and his characters about the desirability of a brave death in battle. Again, in *Iliad* 6 when Hector and his wife Andromache confront each other with diametrically opposed images of what a commander in his situation should do – Hector impelled to risk self-destruction for honour and glory, Andromache urging caution and defensive tactics that will save his life and delay the city's fall – it remains an open question whether her advice would have seemed feeble and womanly or deft and subtle when the poem first took shape.[30] As long as the Homeric poems remain our sole useful witness to the world-view of their own author(s) and first audiences, the distinction between tradition and originality remains elusive.

Chasing the heroic age

One traditional response relies on cross-cultural comparison. Running through many responses to Homer are versions of the belief that the epics depict an *heroic age*, something that has emerged again and again at different times and places across the world. The basic principle (or myth) behind this goes back at least as far as Augustine, the idea that the historical development of mankind replicates that of a man growing up.[31] In this scheme the third age of life, roughly the late teens, is the age of youthful ebullience and barely controllable violence, and the corresponding Third Age of the world was the period in which the Trojan War took place. This model reappeared in a new

---

[28] On the cognitive implications of the theory of oral composition, see Minchin 2001.
[29] Classic exposition by Martin 1989: 146–205.
[30] See Graziosi and Haubold 2003, and below, pp. 313–316.
[31] See Burrow 1986 for an overview.

guise among nineteenth-century anthropologists, often in the form of the assertion that the same mentality could be found in peoples at the same stage of development – development typically measured in terms of increasing social and technological complexity. Andrew Lang's enormously popular *Homer and his Age* (1893) declared its credentials with a picture on the frontispiece of Algonquin Indians in battle formation: it is no coincidence that Lang was intellectually close to E. B. Tylor, one of the key exponents of the theory of a universal 'primitive culture' found under parallel forms in societies at the same point in the sequence of development.[32]

A less easily debunked version depends on a cross-cultural model of the epic poet as mouthpiece of an archaic tradition: a blind man with a stringed instrument who sings from inspired memory. The first parallel of this kind to infect Homeric scholarship was provided by the (genuine or bogus) poems of Ossian, which were published by Macpherson from the 1760s onwards with the accompaniment of Hugh Blair's essay systematically comparing and contrasting Homer with the 'Gaelic bard'.[33] As one resurgent national literature after another established its canon, a single work would be selected to fit into the Homeric slot: Beowulf for the English language, the *Song of Roland* for French, the *Nibelungenlied* for German and for Irish the prosimetric saga *Táin Bó Cuailnge* and the so-called Ulster Cycle to which it belongs. Outliers in this group were the heroic songs of the Serbian *guslar* tradition, which were recruited as the national heroic literature of the Serbian nation in the decades of resurgence up to the crisis of 1914.[34] Just as folklorists in northern and western Europe sought living poetic traditions that could be linked to the ancient literatures, so too the equivalent phenomena among the South Slavs were recruited for this role.[35] Moreover, by a strange twist of fortune a surviving offshoot of this tradition in Bosnia was used by Milman Parry as the basis for his newly scientific hypothesis on the oral-formulaic diction of Homeric poetry.[36] When Parry wrote that 'when one hears the Southern Slavs sing their tales he has the overwhelming feeling that, in some way, he is hearing Homer',[37] he was closing a loop that Hugh Blair had begun to construct a century-and-a-half beforehand.

---

[32] Cox 2017.   [33] Clarke 2006.

[34] The classic anthology of Vuk Karadžić is edited and translated by Holton and Mihailovich 1997. For the (re)shaping of the song culture in response to the interference of Parry and others, see Čolaković 2006, discussed by Currie 2012a: 578–9.

[35] On the recruitment of song traditions in Serbian nationalism, see Judah 2010: 17–46.

[36] Parry 1971, with the subsequent scholarly tradition as traced by Jensen 2009.

[37] Parry 1971: 378 (from a paper first published in 1933).

Perhaps the most succinct and elegant expression of the idea of *heroic literature*, at least among English-speakers, was that set out by H. M. Chadwick, first in *The Heroic Age* (1912) and then (with Nora Chadwick) in a more nuanced form in the first volume of *The Growth of Literature* (1932). For the Chadwicks, the model is constructed on the following lines. An earlier, more settled and wealthier civilisation has collapsed; a period of confusion, disruption and impoverishment follows; in that period men of war form an inward-looking and privileged group, relying on strength in physical combat to protect their people or to seize control of other communities; and finally (a stage that was clarified only in the later book) in more peaceful but still impoverished times a poetic tradition enshrines the values of the earlier period as the stuff of legend and song. This model was applied most clearly in the equation of Homeric heroes, seen as a memory of the real-life 'sackers of cities' who throve on the turmoil surrounding the collapse of Aegean civilisation at the end of the Bronze Age,[38] with the legendary warriors of the Celtic and Germanic literatures of medieval Europe, understood as re-evocations of the warlords who came to prominence in Europe after the collapse of Roman hegemony. For scholars working in this framework, it became routine to assume that the ethical values and conceptual norms, and even the details of narrative and imagery, of one such tradition could illuminate those of another.

Sometimes, indeed, the method seems powerful. In a famous passage Chadwick cited the scene in *Beowulf* where the doomed hero tells his followers how he wants to be buried:

> Bid men of battle build me a tomb
> fair after fire, on the foreland by the sea
> that shall stand as a reminder of me to my people,
> towering high over Hronesness
> so that ocean travellers shall afterwards name it
> Beowulf's Barrow, bending in the distance
> their masted ships through the mists upon the sea.
>
> (*Beowulf* 2802 ff., tr. Alexander 2001)

Taking the salient images of these lines – the hero looking to his own death, the memorial mound on a headland of the sea, the perpetuation of his fame in the name of that mound – Chadwick adduced a Homeric passage composed perhaps 1,500 years earlier.[39] Hector, foremost warrior of the Trojans, is about to fight a duel against a Greek champion, and declares to

---

[38] It is useful to compare the modern understanding of this relationship, for which see for example Finkelberg 2005.

[39] Chadwick 1912: 326.

both armies that if he gains the victory he will respect the corpse of his
vanquished opponent, ensuring that it is given the due honours of burial,

> and some day one even of late-born men will say,
> sailing in his many-thonged ship over the wine-faced sea,
> 'This is the grave-marker of a man who died long ago,
> whom once glorious Hector killed, when that man was doing great deeds.'
> So will one say some day, and my glory will never die.   (*Il.* 7.87–91)

At first sight this looks like a perfect case of Chadwick's theory: parallel
cultural values have produced parallel images in two different manifestations of heroic-age ideology.

But there are two problems here. The first is the possibility of indirect
influence. Although it is inconceivable that the poet of *Beowulf* knew
Homeric poetry directly, there is a very real possibility that he or his predecessors were steeped in Virgilian and later Latin epic, and that our lines from
Beowulf look back to a Latin passage which in turn had remodelled the Iliadic
speech of Hector.[40] Second, the very neatness of the comparison risks distract-
ing us from the subtleties of the Homeric passage. We infer that the quest for
fame is the great incitement to bravery and ultimately to defiance of death: to
be remembered, even through a mound and its name, is to win eternal fame.
So far we are on the common ground of the two traditions. But Hector actually
says that the tomb will preserve *his own* name, the name of the man who did
the killing: in effect, Hector will appropriate for himself the glory of the other
man's memorial.[41] The apparent simplicity of the words distracts us from the
fact that when taken on their own terms they have a hard manipulative edge –
this is part of the drama of the warrior's attempt to taunt and overmaster his
enemy before the combat begins.[42]

In this example, we can only speculate about possible indirect reception
of the Homeric passage by the *Beowulf*-poet. Increasingly often, however,
identifiable chains of influence give the lie to universalist readings of heroic
literature. The *Iliad* passage about the 'choice of Achilles', already

---

[40] For the approach compare North 2006, with proposed Classical sources for the image of the barrow (78–80).
[41] For a recent discussion see Clay 2016, esp. 192.
[42] Interestingly, this point was noted by ancient Homeric scholars, among whose remarks is preserved the judgment that Hector's speech is 'self-aggrandising, abusive and barbarously worded' (b-scholia on *Il.* 7.89b). According to the Roman polymath Aulus Gellius, Cicero in his work *De Gloria* ('On Boasting') misattributed the words to Ajax, the Greek fighter in the duel that ensues (Aulus Gellius, *Attic Nights* 15.6.2–3) – which of course removes the combative subtlety of the original.

discussed above, finds an astonishingly clear analogue in the early medieval Irish narratives of the Ulster Cycle, in which the overall forms of society and values so often seem to resemble those of the Homeric world.[43] One day on the plain before the fort where he is being fostered by the king, the boy Cú Chulainn overhears Cathbad the druid prophesying that anyone who takes up arms this day will be famed forever. He tricks the king into letting him do so, and smashes several sets of weapons before he takes up the king's own panoply. The druid reveals what has happened:

> 'It is indeed a day of good omen', said Cathbad. 'It is certain that he who takes up arms today will be famous and renowned, but he will, however, be short-lived.'
>   'A mighty thing!' said Cú Chulainn. 'Provided I be famous, I am content to be only one day on earth.' (*Táin Bó Cúailnge* Recension 1 638–41, tr. O'Rahilly (1976))

Again, whoever framed this story could not have read Homer; so at first the parallelism seems irresistible, right down to the presence in both texts of an adjective for 'short-lived' – Greek *minunthadios*, Irish *duthain*. On such grounds the Ulster Cycle was repackaged as a national 'heroic literature',[44] and it became conventional to identify Cú Chulainn as the mirror image of Homer's Achilles.[45] But everything changes if one posits an author who was conversant with Vergil's *Aeneid* as part of the literary canon of monastic education: glossed and amplified by Servian commentary, which served as one of the principal repositories of encyclopaedic as well as linguistic knowledge.[46] The extended version of the commentary, 'Servius Auctus', which was undoubtedly well known in medieval Ireland, reports as follows in a superficially unrelated context:

> In Homer Achilles recounts that his mother has told him that if he were to remove himself from the Trojan War and return to his fatherland, he would live into deep old age, but without glory; but if he were to continue fighting around Troy, then after winning great glory he would go down to death in his first youth. (Servius Auctus at *Aeneid* 4.696)[47]

If this provided the model for the Irish composer, then the edifice becomes more and more shaky. Homer's Achilles indeed hovers behind Cú Chulainn, but in the form of a Latin summary in a gloss-commentary on a different text altogether. It is even possible that the composer of this

---

[43] The classic statement remains that by Murphy 1955.
[44] For the history of this question see for example Dooley 2006.
[45] For example, Griffin 1980: 39.   [46] O'Sullivan 2018.   [47] Cited by Miles 2011: 166–7.

passage of *Táin Bó Cúailnge* intended his audience to recognise and appreciate the intertextual resonances of the passage and the parallelism that it sets up with the Servian Achilles.[48]

Here again, as with Hector and the grave-memorial, the 'heroic literature' approach tends to blunt the edges of both texts. In Homer, Achilles reveals the choice in order to *reject* the option for death and glory, part of his self-exile from the norms of warrior society and ultimately a step in his movement towards death (see below, pp. 223–225). But Servius does not mention this aspect, and gives only the bare bones of the episode: Achilles was offered the choice of eternal glory, and as a matter of common knowledge he did indeed achieve it. There is no room here for the twists and ironies of the Homeric portrayal, in which Achilles will recognise the futility of glory in the very act of pursuing Hector to the death. But this in turn raises a further problem of interpretation: read as a whole, the Irish saga *also* problematises the fury and potential self-destructiveness of the protagonist, but in very different terms from those in which Homer does so.[49] In context the story is presented as one of several recollections of wild and uncontrollable behaviour voiced by those who knew Cú Chulainn in his childhood, building up to the point that it is 'no wonder' that one who did such things would now be defending the border single-handed with such savagery, planting the severed heads of his enemies in a stream to defy anyone else who might think of facing him.[50] Arguably there is a sense in which *both* traditions are taking a pre-existing tradition of heroic celebration and using it to explore the underlying darkness of the warrior's way of life.

When we allow for the power of secondary and subliterary texts to mediate influence from one literary tradition to another, the echoes between Homer and the later European analogues look less like evidence for human universals and more like subtle and creative reception of the Classical inheritance. All the more reason to avoid the temptation to admit those traditions as comparanda that might shape or distort our understanding of the Homeric poems in their own right.

The eastward look

When the established modes of interpretation are destabilised in this way, they lead at first towards despair. If the cross-cultural comparanda are

[48] Compare the essays in O'Connor 2014.
[49] Key treatments are Radner 1982, O'Connor 2016.
[50] Full discussion in Clarke (forthcoming (a)).

tainted and cannot be credibly used to model the relationship between the created poem and the background tradition, how can we build the framework for a meaningful interpretation? The route out of this impasse begins from the awareness that epic did not arise autonomously from the collective unconscious of the early Greek people, nor simply from the cultural baggage that went along with their Indo-European linguistic inheritance. In a fundamental sense it is embedded in the creativity of a continuous ancient culture-area that stretched across south-west Asia from what is now Iran in the east to the fringes of the Mediterranean westward. The confrontation between Greeks and the Persian imperial power from the late sixth century, though depicted traditionally (and already by Herodotus within a few decades of the events) as a clash between alien and mutually uncomprehending cultures, can be better understood as the erection of a new and artificial barrier over a pattern of fluid merger and interchange that had continued uninterrupted since the remote past.[51] Since the Homeric poems took shape generations *before* that transformation, it makes sense to break down the barrier and accept the consequences.

Until quite recently, however, many Classical scholars would have seen this as a perverse departure from common sense rather than a practical response to the attested realities. Partly, of course, this was because of the belief that all things Asian are alien to European civilisation; but more insidious still, perhaps, was the tendency to erect a barrier between Greek and West Semitic 'worlds' on the assumption that there should be a one-to-one identity between a language and a culture, especially at the remoter levels of antiquity, setting up the Hellenisation of Rome as a unique exception. In this case, indeed, the fact that the principal languages in question belong to different *families* – Akkadian is Semitic, Greek is Indo-European – can only have hardened the sense of radical separateness.[52] Only within the past two decades or so has it begun to be recognised that the cultural boundaries between ancient language-communities were always permeable, and that this facilitated the movement of ideas and even literary genres between languages in every period. Added to this is the growing recognition that multilingualism was the

---

[51] For thoughtful general assessments, see Pelling 2013, Romm 2010; and on the war of 480/479 BCE as the pivotal moment for the establishment of the divide, see Hall 2002: 172–228, with Cartledge 1993: 36–62. See also the brilliant, experimental case study by Morris in her *Daidalos*, where the present general question is explored in the concluding essay (Morris 1992: 362–96, and see further below).

[52] On the history of this dualistic theme in the scholarship, see Burkert 2004, esp. 49–57.

norm, not the exception, in all periods of human history other than those (like our own) in which linguistic uniformity has become an expected characteristic of the nation-state.[53]

The starting-point of this book, therefore, will be the hope that we can gain a newly authentic perspective on Homeric epic by situating it in relation to what scholarship still, clumsily, calls the ancient Near East. Throughout our period the epicentre of this culture-area was Mesopotamia, corresponding roughly to modern Iraq, and its lore and literature are witnessed by the substantial (if invariably fragmentary) remnants preserved on cuneiform tablets in the Sumerian and Akkadian languages.[54] Some of these are from scribal schools and private houses, others from temples and royal archives, the latter dominated by collections from the period of the Neo-Assyrian empire, lasting into the 600s BCE. Beyond the Mesopotamian hub, the culture of cuneiform textuality was deeply multilingual and internationally diffused – in one direction as far as the Hittite realm ruled from what is now central Turkey,[55] and in another towards the Mediterranean coast opposite Cyprus, including the pivotally important case of the city of Ugarit (modern Ras Shamra, Syria),[56] along with the wider Levantine horizon of the 'Phoenicians', peoples who continued to interact and mingle with Greek-speakers for centuries after the destruction of the city of Ugarit itself.[57] The fundamental fact, then, is that the cuneiform world physically touched the world of the Greek language through the course of centuries. Even to refer to it as 'the Near East' or 'south-west Asia' in contradistinction to Greece or 'the world of Greek-speakers' is to impose an opposition that finds little basis in the geographical or cultural realities of the creation and initial reception of the Homeric poems.

By the same token, this perspective means that in the study of later periods, postdating the erection of the barrier between Greek and Persian

[53] On multilingualism in antiquity as a recurring phenomenon and an interpretative problem, see essays in Mullen and James 2012. The question continues to be debated: Greek fluency in Near Eastern languages is treated as an exception rather than a norm in sources of the 'Classical' period following the Persian wars, but this does not necessarily apply to other periods. See further references at Currie 2016: 218 n. 380.

[54] The conventional division of Akkadian into Babylonian (earlier) and Assyrian (later) is not important here, and in practice the later literary tablets exhibit a mixed variety.

[55] Standard survey of the Hittites by Bryce 2002; on the literature, Haas 2006, with anthology of translations by Hoffner 1990. On the Hittite adoption of cuneiform scribal culture, see Van de Hout 2010, 2011.

[56] Useful survey of material from Ugarit in Schniedewind and Hunt 2007: 5–30; see also the anthology of texts by Parker 1997.

[57] López-Ruiz 2010, *passim*; cf. Morris 1992, esp. 101–24.

spheres, we should attach a new significance to those scholars and word-smiths who explored and renegotiated discourses stretching across that gulf between east and west. This includes not only the cross-cultural studies of Greek intellectuals like Herodotus in the *Histories* and Ctesias in his *Persica*,[58] but also later Hellenistic intellectuals who asserted the antiquity and authority of their own civilisations for an audience whose language and orientation were dominated by Greek. Here the key figure is Berossos, the Babylonian priest of Bel whose *Babyloniaca* bore witness to repositories of Mesopotamian wisdom that claimed (rightly, in a sense) to be both more ancient and closer to the divine level than anything that his Alexandrian peers and patrons could claim to have inherited from their Greek forebears.[59]

Greece and Mesopotamia: continuity or external influence?

Since the rediscovery of cuneiform literature began in earnest in the mid-nineteenth century, a recurring adventure has been the pursuit of correspondences between its texts and vocabulary and those of what the discoverers and their public (invariably European and American) regarded as familiar documents of their own heritage. A decisive moment was the recognition in 1872 of a cluster of detailed parallels between the Mesopotamian Flood story recounted in the *Epic of Gilgamesh* and the Flood of Noah from the Hebrew Bible.[60] This made headlines at the time, because of the challenge it laid down to contemporary assumptions about the status of the Bible: the Flood was no longer a unique revelation but part of a continuum of ancient narratives shared with the pagans. In retrospect, one can see that this insight was not strictly new at all, because information about Berossos' version of the Mesopotamian flood myth had been preserved in the chronicle tradition, right up to the ninth-century Byzantine scholar George Synkellos.[61] But such continuities played little part in the conception of literary history that

---

[58] For the fragments of Ctesias translated and put in context, see Llewellyn-Jones and Robson 2010.

[59] On Berossos see Haubold et al. 2013; Haubold 2013, esp. 142–63. The discussion by Haubold is crucial for emphasising the continuity of Greek-Mesopotamian interaction all the way from the pre-Homeric stage to the Hellenistic period, when cuneiform textuality continued under the Seleucid kings in the same period as Berossos was incorporating Babylonian lore into the culture of Ptolemaic Alexandria.

[60] Lloyd 1980: 44–57 remains the best general account.

[61] See Synkellos, *Chronography* ch. 30–32, translated with notes by Adler and Tuffin 2002: 40–41.

prevailed at the time of the discovery: hence the shock of the realisation that the Biblical Flood is only part of a series of linked myths shared between a bewildering variety of neighbouring languages and religious systems.

If theologians were slow to accept the implications of this new contextualisation of the Genesis story (and, ultimately, of much else in the Hebrew Bible), the corresponding step in Classical scholarship was equally hard to take. Despite a number of bold but isolated comparative essays in earlier decades,[62] it is only since the later 1990s that the issue has begun to enter mainstream debate in English. It is a curiosity that although ancient epic has become accepted outside the academy as a transnational category, with *Gilgamesh* comfortably installed there among its peers,[63] many professional Hellenic scholars remain uneasy with the notion of a literary history that roams back and forth across the Hellespont. Throughout this book we will draw on the increasingly eloquent and incisive comparative studies of Homer and Near Eastern literature that have been produced over the past twenty years;[64] but the status of this kind of work remains controversial outside a small group of specialists, and the question of basic orientation remains insistent. Does Greek culture in general – and Homeric poetry in particular – remain rooted in and defined by its emergence from a world centred on Mesopotamia, or is it an essentially different – and essentially *European* – creation with an admixture of Near

---

[62] Such works as Petriconi 1964, Walcot 1966, Penglase 1994 and the earlier contributions to the debate by Martin West (see below) continued to be regarded as marginal or esoteric, at least in English-language scholarly circles, until the questions were given new vitality by the series of contributions discussed in n. 64.

[63] Ziolkowski 2011.

[64] The fundamental survey works are Burkert 1992 [1984], with light revisions of many of its individual arguments in Burkert 2004, and the exhaustive collection of examples by West 1997. Among the many more tightly focussed case studies, generally relying on a narrower range of evidence and a more nuanced sense of methodology, crucial contributions for our purposes are those of Morris 1992 on artistic iconography; López-Ruiz 2010 on Greek reception of Ugaritic and subsequently Phoenician myth and literature; Louden 2011, especially valuable for its exploration of Biblical comparanda; Haubold (see next note) on cosmogonic mythology and *Enuma Elish* in particular; Metcalf 2015, offering a cautious comparison of conventions and imagery in hymns to the gods from Mesopotamian and Greek traditions; Bachvarova 2016 positing Hittite and Hurrian versions of the Gilgamesh narrative (among others) as a conduit for the reception of Mesopotamian lore in pre-Homeric Greek tradition; Currie 2012a, 2016 on issues of thematic analogy, intertextuality and (possible) direct allusion between Mesopotamian and Greek poetic narrative. A useful set of perspectives on the corresponding issues by Near Eastern specialists is provided by the essays in Whiting 2001. An important expression of the 'state of the question' will be offered in Kelly and Metcalf (eds.), *Divine Narrative in Greece and the Near East*, in course of publication as the present essay is being written. I thank Adrian Kelly for sharing advance details with me.

Eastern cultural forms imposed externally upon it?[65] This question needs to be clarified before we can proceed.

In any comparative study of a pair of literatures traditionally regarded as distinct, a simple pattern of activity repeats itself: the demonstration that such-and-such a phenomenon in one literature resembles a phenomenon in the other more closely than can be explained by random coincidence, 'convergent evolution', or the human mind responding independently in similar ways to similar problems. The challenge is to reach from the particular to the general, from the individual case study to a new grand narrative embracing it.

One approach is simply to repeat the demonstration so many times that the cumulative effect becomes overwhelming.[66] Exactly this is done by Martin West in *The East Face of Helicon* (1997), where the array of correspondences gathered between Greek and Near Eastern mythologies and literary corpora is so vast that the reader has no choice but to submit to their onslaught and accept that Greece and Mesopotamia are fundamentally the same cultural world[67] – a decisively important insight, but one that requires further work to be translated into a new interpretative strategy.[68] For a moment on his first page, West moves towards building a framework into which his observations could be fitted:

> Culture, like all forms of gas, tends to spread out from areas where it is densest into areas where it is less dense. (West 1997: 1)

---

[65] On the methodological basis of the search for literary parallels and cross-influences, among many other more or less polemical contributions see in particular Kelly 2008; Van Dongen 2008; López-Ruiz 2010: 1–22, 2014; Rollinger 2014, 2015 and other publications by Rollinger listed in the bibliographies there; Currie 2012a, 2016: 200–22. A series of publications by Johannes Haubold represent successive refinements of a nuanced response to this problem. See esp. Haubold 2000 on the basic methodology; Haubold 2006 on the cultural and political agendas of the scholarly movements involved in the 'oriental turn' in Classical Studies; and above all Haubold 2013: 18–72 with Haubold 2014 and 2015, positing common genre categories between the two literatures as the context for possible cross-influence and the framework for one's own comparative reading. Haubold's basic model tends to privilege fluctuating oral transmission over the transmission of fixed texts, a difference of emphasis that underlies the contrast between his reconstructions and those of Currie in particular.

[66] On the technique of 'argument by accumulation' see the critique by Metcalf 2015: 2–3.

[67] In this sense West 1997 is no less – and no more – than an infinitely variegated restatement of his extraordinarily bold assertion made thirty years earlier: 'Greece is part of Asia; Greek literature is a Near Eastern literature' (West 1966: 31, on which see also Haubold 2013: 5; Currie 2016: 213–22, esp. 216).

[68] It is a curious feature of West's book that his speculations on 'the question of transmission', which in fact anticipate many of the insights of subsequent scholars that are treated in the present chapter, are presented at the very end of his book (West 1997: 586–630) and only loosely related to the detailed exposition.

Anywhere in the relevant period, the 'place of greatest concentration' would be identified among the great urban power-centres to the east: Hattusa, Ugarit, Babylon, Nineveh. Greece in the west, relatively marginal and impoverished by comparison, would be the place whose thinner atmosphere made it especially receptive to influences and ideas from the eastern horizon. This ostensibly straightforward image masks serious difficulties. The model of diffusion from centre to periphery works best with art-forms that encode ideas of social and political power and prestige: monumental sculpture, richly decorated artefacts, the self-laudatory inscriptions and images set up by kings as memorials to themselves. When matches in form and imagery between Greek and Mesopotamian or Levantine artefacts are explained in terms of the periphery emulating the centre,[69] this makes intuitive sense in terms of 'peer polity interaction': the cultural forms and even the ideologies of the more prestigious culture will be imitated or emulated in the lesser. An indigenous ruler in Cyprus is buried with funerary monuments resembling those of contemporaneous Neo-Assyrian princes, the design of a Greek pottery vessel mimics Levantine vessels in precious metals: such dynamics are easy to read.[70] But the movement of literary ideas, poetry and mythological thought may well be more complex. Contact and interpenetration on both levels must have provided endless opportunities for the absorption and exchange of poetry, songs, stories, motifs: one could speculate forever about what might have happened when two traders spent an evening by the fireside, or when a foreign slave used the stories she had heard as a child to entertain her master's children,[71] or when two poets from different traditions competed with each other through an interpreter or via the functional bilingualism referred to earlier. The chances of survival are biased against precisely the types of evidence that would best bear witness to this kind of flux.[72]

Patterns of interaction

A broad historical distinction may be useful here as a starting-point. On any reasonable view, Greek culture in general and the epic tradition in particular had been taking shape for hundreds of years before the surviving

---

[69] See Gunter 2009 and compare Martin 2017.

[70] Gunter 2009, esp. 17–49 on the Cypriot artefacts; cf. Morris 1992, esp. 124–49.

[71] See López-Ruiz 2010: 23–47 for a strong argument for the importance of women slaves in this kind of intercultural transmission, emphasising the role in this process of the Levantine people(s) referred to by the Greeks as Phoenicians. Cf. West 1997: 609–11.

[72] For a valuable corrective from the methodological viewpoint, see Ulf 2014 on the importance of 'open contact zones' for cultural transfer.

monuments of the literature came into being. Hence the origins and
context of something that we encounter in Homeric poetry – a myth, an
ethical theme, a motif – might be located anywhere between the depths of
the Bronze Age and the likely date of composition of the epics *c.* 700 BCE:
and there are grounds for arguing that the context of cultural interaction
differs radically between the earlier and later parts of that wide span of
time.

For much of the second millennium BCE – conventionally, the Bronze
Age – the space defined by the Tigris and Euphrates rivers was the centre of
a nexus of kingdoms and territories stretching to what is now Turkey,
Palestine and Egypt, and thus to the shores of the Mediterranean in the far
west.[73] Interconnections were close, not only through trade and migration
but through high-level political contacts. From Ugarit, pivotally located,
there survives a particularly rich archaeological record of intimate contacts
with the Aegean world.[74] Official and diplomatic texts from the Hittite
capital of Hattusa (modern Boğazköy in central Turkey) include many that
mention a people across the sea called *Ahhiyawa* with whom the Hittites
and their kings had contact both hostile and friendly. Such contact even
involved matters of religion: one of the texts, probably from about 1310
BCE, concerns an oracular enquiry made when the Hittite king is sick, and
one of the prescribed rituals is that gods of the Ahhiyawa are to be sent to
the king, presumably in the form of statues.[75] It is a virtual certainty that
Ahhiyawa is the same as Greek *Akhaiwoi*, which would later be one of the
many Homeric names for all or part of the people of Greece itself.[76]

As examples of such contact multiply, it becomes possible to argue that
Greece in this period should fundamentally be seen as a western outlier of
the Near Eastern world. In the so-called 'palaces' of the materially sophisticated communities that flourished on Crete and then in mainland Greece
in the second millennium BCE, we can see an offshoot of the city civilisation that flourished further east, with the same emphasis on centralised

---

[73] An excellent survey is provided by the articles in Aruz et al. 2013, especially Cline 2013, with the
essays in the associated exhibition catalogue (Aruz et al. 2008).

[74] For Ugarit as a point of transfer between the Mediterranean peoples and the Fertile Crescent in
the second millennium BCE, see Broodbank 2013, ch. 8, esp. 404–15. Van de Mieroop 2013 is
a valuable survey essay emphasising the evidence from Ugarit for reconstructing a picture of
cultural unity and cultural transfer in this period. Cf. also López-Ruiz 2014 for a comparative
study emphasising Ugaritic correlates with Greek myth. For her model of the mechanics of the
transference, see esp. 23–47, 171–204.

[75] Beckman et al. 2011: 183–209, at pp. 192–5, §§23–25.

[76] I leave open the question whether the peoples *referred to* by the two names are identical in
bloodline and collective identity: this is more tricky. Cf. Bryce 2006: 100–6; Beckman et al. 2011:
1–7, 267–84.

kingship and a system of worship in which the king mediates between men and gods, and localised points of contact endlessly suggest themselves. To take a few token examples, the human–animal hybrid known as the centaur originates in Mesopotamian iconography, where it has celestial associations as the constellation nowadays still known as Sagittarius; the image reappears in the archaeological record in small clay images from Ugarit and then re-emerges fully integrated into Archaic Greek myth and art, where the celestial associations are lost or marginalised and the creature's symbolic associations are with barbarism, drunkenness and lack of self-control. The intermediary stages can be disputed in detail, but the overall continuity is not to be doubted.[77] Again, it cannot be a triviality that a large cache of cylinder seals (see p. 38 below) from many places in the Near Eastern world, including Babylonia, has been found in a site dated to the fourteenth century BCE at Thebes in mainland Greece, many of them bearing complex mythological images.[78] The great difference, of course, is that we lack evidence of the dissemination and reception of cuneiform *literature* – or its oral correlate – in Greece or among Greek-speakers abroad; but that does not take away the likelihood of mingling and even fusion in other media of communication.

As a locus of interconnection nowhere, perhaps, is more crucial than Cyprus, poised between the Aegean world and the mainland of what is now Syria, and it is here that we find the only clear exception to the absence of Greek engagement with cuneiform literacy. Evidence for contacts between Cyprus and the great states of the mainland is plentiful in the letters surviving from El-Amarna in Egypt, which are significant not only for the window they open on elite interactions but also for the fact that they are written in Akkadian, then the international language of diplomacy. The letters show that in Cyprus there must have been skilled cuneiform scribes, capable of writing as well as reading in Akkadian.[79] Eloquent testimony of another kind is provided by the excavated wrecks of trading ships, most famously that from Uluburun (*c.* 1325 BCE), on the sea-road between north and south along the Syrian coast just opposite Cyprus. The cargo of this ship includes a vast array of goods, not booty or random accumulation but organised trade, bearing witness to voyages with trading-stops among many peoples and language-communities, and including – crucially for

---

[77] Padgett 2003, esp. 129–55; Childs 2003; Shear 2002, with Pilafidis-Williams 2004.

[78] Kopanias 2008; Aruz 2013. Are these seals a craftsman's cache waiting to be re-carved, or do they bear witness to higher-level cultural interaction in which their images carried meaning in their new Greek context?

[79] Knapp 2008: 298–347, with summary assessment by Broodbank 2013: 396–9.

our purposes – a number of pottery vessels of Cypriot and Aegean types.[80] The movement of the goods themselves is less important here than the social interaction between groups that is implied: organised commerce depends on the facility to communicate verbally across the peoples along the route, through bilingual interpreters or via a shared *lingua franca*. The latter might well have been a language for which little or no written literature survives.

From a strictly Greek perspective, however, relatively little can be said clearly about the cultural forms that held meaning in the Bronze Aegean world, despite the fact that in Crete and Greece the clerks and administrators of the 'palaces' were keeping their records in an early variety of Greek, preserved as the Linear B tablets.[81] Being practical day-to-day accounts and records, the tablets tend not to shed light on the thought-world of the time. A rare exception is the survival of lists of gods to whom dedications and sacrifices are being assigned: among these are names that would later appear among the gods of the Greek pantheon, even some who figure as characters in the Homeric epics. Even here, however, there is no detailed information to locate these divinities clearly in relation either to their later attestations or their possible models and counterparts in the better-known theologies of the contemporary Near East.[82]

What we do know is that the links drawing these lands and peoples together were severed in a phase of destruction and disarray *c*. 1200 BCE. Many of the Aegean 'palaces' were burned (the heat of these fires baked the Linear B tablets and ensured their preservation), the population shrank dramatically and there was a sudden decline in material wealth and the skills of technical artistry that must have gone with it. It is debated whether this collapse was due primarily to invasion – the contemporary attacks of the 'Sea Peoples' on Egypt are often cited – or to an internal force like disease or civil war, or indeed to a chaotic downward spiral resulting from the unsustainable rigidity of the palace-based system of organisation.[83] Whatever drove the change, the evidence is undisputed that the old patterns of internationalism broke down. For some 450 years after the collapse, our knowledge of the imaginative life of the speakers of the Greek

---

[80] On the Uluburun shipwreck see C. Pulak in Aruz et al. 2008: 289–310; Broodbank 2013: 399–411. Its importance was already picked up by Morris 1992: 103–7. On Aegean connections suggested by the cargo, see Bachhuber 2006.

[81] Duhoux and Davies 2008–14.   [82] See Hiller 2008–14, at 1.183–7.

[83] The crisis can be seen as a phase in a continuing cycle of 'boom to bust' in the history of complex social organisation (see e.g. Broodbank 2013: 460–72), or in terms of a more conventional image of hostile attack and destruction (see Cline 2014 for a recent study inclining more towards this line of analysis).

language is slight, and only gradually does a new artistic identity emerge in vase-painting, stone sculpture and metalwork, and eventually in literature, now facilitated by the craft of alphabetic writing and the resulting diffusion of popular literacy and education.[84]

Although high-level, formal interactions must have been weaker in this post-1200 period, the less formal modes of contact undoubtedly continued, and may even have been facilitated by the smaller-scale and less centralised structures of the regional states that had re-emerged after the collapse.[85] Such contacts can be visualised in three possible ways. First, on a relatively simple cultural level, traders, goods, merchants, workers and (most notably) slaves passed in both directions. This must have led to rich cross-fertilisation of ideas, not least through the agency of captive women, many of whom would presumably have been set to work in child-raising. Second, cultural transfer may have been enacted by members of more exalted professions, practitioners of religious cults or of magic or sacred song,[86] perhaps also scribes with the multilingual training that was still practised for cuneiform writing.[87] Third, the opposition between cuneiform and alphabetic written culture in this period, which can at first seem absolute, masks the ancient reality that the two writing systems overlap in their development and diffusion. At Ugarit in the thirteenth century BCE the scribes used a system of 'alphabetic cuneiform' which represented each consonant with a different sign and included a partial series of signs for vowels. The Greek innovation was simply to pursue a similar system to a higher level of precision: they took an array of five signs standing for Phoenician consonants that lack equivalents in Greek, and assigned them new values to distinguish each of their own five vowel sounds from each other. As such, this was only one (uniquely successful) manifestation of a series of experiments and improvements that took place over hundreds of

---

[84] For an overview, see Osborne 2009: 35–130.

[85] The importance of trade as a mode of contact that must have continued despite (or even encouraged by) the crisis of *c.* 1200 BCE is eloquently argued by Morris 1992: 101–49; for updated reflections on the theme by the same scholar see Morris 2006 and Carter and Morris 2014; cf. West 1997: 614–21. The exhibition catalogue edited by Aruz et al. 2014 provides an unrivalled survey of the material evidence for interactions in the period, implicitly contrasted with the Late Bronze Age situation studied in Aruz et al. 2008 and 2013.

[86] Burkert 1992 [1984]: 41–87; West 1997: 609–11; cf. the essays in Hunter and Rutherford 2009 – where, however, the evidence for cross-cultural transfer is not substantial enough to draw relevant conclusions here.

[87] Again, the classic statement is by Burkert (1992 [1984]: 88–127). However, the possibility of Greek-speakers working as cuneiform scribes in this period remains speculative, as (so far as I am aware) there is no direct evidence for anyone who did so.

years across the eastern Mediterranean horizon.[88] When Herodotus says that the alphabet was introduced by Phoenician immigrants accompanying Cadmus, the founder-hero of Thebes (*Histories* 5.58), his account matches the known facts about the origins of Greek textual culture.[89]

As we have noted, there is no direct evidence for the cross-over between cuneiform culture and Greek alphabetic literacy, but this gap may well be a function of the materials used: if (as is generally agreed) literary texts in alphabetic Greek were set down from the start on perishable materials like leather or later papyrus rolls, then it is inevitable that these things have disappeared when the clay tablets of the cuneiform scribes have survived in their thousands. Even within the cuneiform world itself, many texts were recorded and archived on perishable boards, which were inevitably destroyed when clay tablets might survive: there are, for example, many references to such boards in the surviving documentation of the collecting activities of the Assyrian king Ashurbanipal.[90] Tantalisingly, even as early as the Uluburun shipwreck there is found a writing-tablet with traces of wax: is this a glimpse of the setting in which one or other of the Levantine writing systems became the model for the invention of the Greek alphabet?[91]

From the modern perspective, in short, any sense of a radical separation between eastern and western worlds of text-transmission may largely be a side-effect of the skewed evidence: the cuneiform survivals are necessarily dominated by the 'official' languages of the Mesopotamian tradition, while the survival of texts in Greek is overwhelmingly biased towards those that formed part of the school curriculum from the Alexandrian period onwards. Somewhere in the gap, perhaps in a West Semitic language in which none of the relevant texts survive at all, lies the fluid centre in which the creative world that we are studying could be seen in formation.

Modelling parallels

If we were to regard the watershed of 1200 BCE as an absolute division between a world of flux and a world in which Greece was a place apart, we would face a choice between two basic strategies for explaining a given point of parallel between a Greek and a Near Eastern text. Either the similarity reflects the fact that on both sides the most basic forms of thought and

---

[88] Nuanced assessment by Lam 2010; for a broad overview in the context of the grand narrative of cultural history, see Burkert 2004: 16–20.

[89] Willi 2005, and below in Ch. 5.   [90] Fincke 2017: 385–6; cf. Parpola 1983, esp. 2–4.

[91] On the writing-tablet see Bachhuber 2006: 354, Powell 2002: 81–2; cf. already Morris 1992: 105–6.

tradition are rooted in the same ancestral culture and world-view, inherited from the international Bronze Age, or it shows that among Greek-speakers at the time of composition (or shortly before) there was an opportunity, even a desire, to absorb and emulate learning and thought coming as novelties from other lands and languages. In assessing a given instance, it may be useful to think in terms of *depth* versus *specificity* when distinguishing between these two extremes. Broad thematic parallels are more likely to bear witness to shared continuities from the common international culture of the Bronze Age, while small-scale verbal equations may be due instead to more recent, more localised and perhaps more superficial transference of images and motifs.[92] For example, one guesses that the conceptualisation of Aphrodite as a powerful goddess of fertility and sexuality resembles that of Ishtar because of a shared background in Bronze Age religion and myth across the entire Near Eastern culture-area,[93] but that Archilochus (writing in the later seventh century BCE) alludes to the Sumerian or Akkadian proverb 'the hasty bitch gives birth to blind puppies' because he knew this as a saying, perhaps specifically as a foreign turn of phrase.[94] A pervasive and deeply embedded parallel, perhaps difficult for us to formulate precisely, is more likely to be archaic: an atomistic, isolated one is more likely to be recent. The parallel with Ishtar may be of fundamental benefit when we try to make sense of the cults of Aphrodite, but the proverb may not help us much to understand Archilochus as a poet beyond the elucidation of the single line in which it appears.

The possibility then arises that in a single instance both kinds of linkage may be active at the same time. If Homer or Hesiod, 500 years after the destructions of 1200 BCE, is putting verbal form on an image or concept or story-pattern that has already been passed on within Greek confines for generations, then it may well derive ultimately from the cultural and con- ceptual repertoire that the poet's forebears had shared with their eastern neighbours many generations before. For the same reason, when a Greek- speaker listened to words and thoughts coming directly from Mesopotamian

---

[92] For a similar perspective see the thoughtful essay by Noegel 2007.

[93] For example, Teffeteller 2010 powerfully compares the Song of Ares and Aphrodite in *Odyssey* 8 with a Hittite text concerning El and Ashertu (the text is translated (with some different interpretations) by Hoffner 1990: 90–2). Although the Canaanite affinities of the myth invite speculation that the influence on Homer may have come much later via a lost West Semitic intermediary text, perhaps Ugaritic, the parallels presented by Teffeteller depend upon the late Bronze Age evidence of the Hittite text.

[94] Archilochus, fr. 196a.39–41: Gerber, *GIP*, pp. 214–15. See Moran 1978, Hallo 1990: 208, Burkert 1992 [1984]: 122–3, West 1997: 500. Bruno Currie points out to me that the definite article in *hē kuōn* 'the bitch' implies that the proverb is being cited as something already well known to the poet's audience.

or Mesopotamian-influenced sources, he may have been especially receptive precisely because what he heard was *already* akin to what was familiar from his own native language and cultural heritage.[95] The 'borrowing' may be deliberate and overt, or it may be so well integrated into the receiving language – so thoroughly naturalised or 'nativised', one might say – that its eastward affiliations are submerged and invisible to us and to the ancients alike. In the case of more explicit literary forms, this kind of interaction can only have been facilitated by a shared sense of genre and significant form. Hence it makes sense that hymns to the gods, didactic expositions of cosmogony and theogony and heroic narrative offer particularly strong evidence for transfer and even convergence between the literatures.[96]

In contrast with this approach, many of the existing studies in this area follow the strategy of seizing on a specific parallel or suite of parallels in order to localise them at a specific point in space and time, on the hypothesis that a theme or image of alien origin has been transposed into a new context in the receiving culture. This method is applied, for example, by Walter Burkert in his *Orientalising Revolution*, which repeatedly invokes the agency in the eighth and seventh centuries BCE of cross-national and cross-language practitioners of the kind that histories of elite literature tend to marginalise. So Burkert speculates about wandering diviners and magicians as well as artists,[97] arguing (for example) that the story of the assault of the seven champions on the seven gates of Thebes is underlain by Babylonian or Assyrian myth and even ritual built around the pattern of an attack on a house by seven evil spirits.[98] Burkert's implication is that the transference was not *within* a continuously varying culture-area but from

[95] Compare Metcalf's study comparing Ishtar material with the depiction of Aphrodite in Hesiod's *Theogony* (Metcalf 2015: 171–90 and summary conclusion, 225). In practice Metcalf is cautious as to the extent or depth of this influence, but his underlying model posits general thematic similarity between the goddesses as the stimulus to localised borrowing. Across Metcalf's monograph the closest analogy to the mode of influence that I propose here is in fact in his interpretation of the *Hittite* reception of Mesopotamian god-lore: '[T]ranslation and adaptation could take place particularly easily where a basis for comparison already existed' (6, cf. 79–103 *passim*, esp. 83–4). For a quite different case study in comparison that invites the application of the same model, cf. Karahashi and López-Ruiz 2006.
[96] See esp. Haubold 2013: 51–72 for narratives of theogony and divine politics; Currie 2016: 147–222, proposing common strategies of allusion in Greek and Mesopotamian narrative poetry; contrast the more cautious juxtaposition of hymns to the gods in the two traditions in Metcalf 2015, which tends to emphasise local and relatively superficial influence on Greek hymnody (see also previous note).
[97] Burkert 1992 [1984]: 41–87.
[98] Burkert (1992 [1984]: 107–14) links the myth of the Seven Against Thebes to the Akkadian narrative *Erra* and the incantation series *Bīt mēseri* (on which see below in a different context, p. 99 n. 25).

an alien, eastern cultural world into the essentially distinct world of the Greeks. New articulations of the same model, positing something like an 'orientalising period', are implicit (for example) in Ann Gunter's study of influence on Greek art from the Neo-Assyrian empire in the early first millennium BCE,[99] and in Carolina López-Ruiz's study of West Semitic motifs and themes in the Greek lore associated with the cult of Orpheus.[100] But if close interaction was fundamental to cultural and linguistic life *throughout* the stretch of time and space from which our texts emerged, an exclusive emphasis on the mechanics of transmission becomes a distraction. For us, as readers and interpreters separated from the ancient voices by millennia, the search for localised avenues of cross-influence may be less fruitful than the open-ended experience of reading the two litera-tures alongside each other, using the one to shape the questions that we address to the other, and by the comparison entering (with luck) into a more nuanced and historically authentic reading of both.[101]

Gods playing dice: a case study

Let me try to clarify the potential of this approach by looking at a case study from the *Iliad* and *Atrahasis*, the Babylonian narrative of the creation of man and the Flood, which has become a classic problem of interpretation in the scholarly literature.[102] Zeus has sent a messenger to command his brother, the sea-god Poseidon, to withdraw from the battlefield, where he has been supporting the Greeks against the Trojans. Poseidon answers with defiance, saying that the order is unacceptable because his own status is equal to that of Zeus (*homotimos, Il.* 15.186), and to explain this he describes how the gods' powers over parts of the world were assigned to them:

> We three brothers are sons of Kronos, borne by Rhea,
> Zeus, and myself, and the third is Hades who rules over those below.
> It is all divided three ways, and each one was given his due honour:
> I was assigned the grey sea to dwell in forever
> when [the lots] were being shaken out; Hades was assigned the murky gloom,

---

[99] Gunter 2009.

[100] López-Ruiz 2010: 130–70. Distinguish the study of Ugaritic parallels earlier in her book, on which see notes above. It needs to be clarified that for her model there is a decisive difference between the periods before and after the destruction of Ugarit *c.* 1200 BCE.

[101] Cf. Haubold 2013: 10.

[102] Burkert 1992 [1984]: 88–96, cf. Burkert 2004: 29–38; see also West 1997: 109–11. Despite the obvious difference of emphasis, Kelly 2008's tenacious critique of 'orientalising' scholarship has been of great help for framing the present discussion.

> and Zeus was assigned the broad heaven, among the high air and the clouds:
> but the earth is common to us all, and great Olympus.   (*Il.* 15.187–93)

The participle translated here as 'being shaken out' (*pallomenōn*) is unambiguous: the implied image is that three tokens were shaken around in an
urn, and the sequence in which they rolled out determined the share of the
world given to each brother. From this we turn to the opening movement
of *Atrahasis*, composed perhaps a thousand years earlier in Mesopotamia
and widely copied thereafter. The narrative is describing the governance of
the world exercised by the seven great gods, the Anunnaki:

> They had taken the [] ... by its sides,
> they cast lots, the gods took their shares:
> Anu went up to heaven,
> [Enlil too]k the earth for his subjects,
> [the bolt], the trap of the sea,
> [they had gi]ven to Enki the leader.
> (*Atrahasis OBV* I 11–16: Foster, *BTM* 229–30)

Here again we have three senior male gods who draw lots, presumably
from a jar,[103] in order to assign a part of the physical universe to each one.
The similarities between the two passages are not only numerous and
individually salient, they follow a structurally coherent pattern, which
one could express as Diagram 1 (see p. 29).

    This is of course an abstraction, and is not a fully satisfactory account of
either text: in particular, the phrase 'watery realm' glosses over the fact that
Enki does not have the same direct power as Poseidon over the visible sea,
and the phrase 'chthonic realm' splits the difference between Enlil's power
over life *on* the earth and Hades' power over life *below* the earth.
Nonetheless, the fact that the diagram gives an adequate account of the
salient content of both passages suggests that the relationship between
the two is underpinned by something more than mere coincidence or the
tendency of human beings at different times and places to tell similar
stories about the order of the world.

    How, then, are we to make sense of this feeling of confluence? Burkert
argued that the story of the gambling gods is out of place in its Homeric
context, and that it might have been introduced into the *Iliad* (or pre-
Homeric tradition) by someone who had been trained as a cuneiform scribe
and memorised the *Atrahasis* passage from transcribing it in Akkadian as

---

[103] For references on this question of interpretation for lines 11–12, see Foster, *BTM*, p. 278, note
on line I 11.

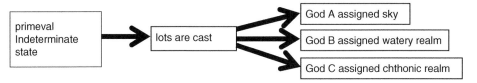

Diagram 1 Schematic representation of parallels between 'gods playing dice' passages in *Atrahasis* and the *Iliad*.

a school exercise or a professional commission.[104] Against this, it has been convincingly argued that the motif of casting lots for an inheritance is in fact typical of early Greek practice, and that the story is consistent with other Greek lore on the origins of the rule of the gods over the world; even if Poseidon's image originated from a Mesopotamian model, it is fully integrated and fully meaningful in its Homeric context.[105] Characteristically, each hypothesis locates itself at a different phase of literary history: the former argument posits a borrowing process at or very close to the time of composition of the *Iliad*, while the latter guesses that if the Mesopotamian motif made its way into Greek storytelling it did so back in the period of fluid interaction before the collapse of *c.* 1200 BCE – so early, in other words, that its eastern affinities are at best a matter of historical curiosity.

But if we are willing to break down the wall between east and west in the way suggested above, the contiguity between the two passages ceases to be a problem that requires explanation: instead, it becomes a route to reading either of them with a more nuanced sense of context. In each case we have the same fundamental world-view, in which the universe can be imagined as divided into physical zones or levels; one god or another can be named (or pictured as naming himself) as having personal lordship over one or other of the levels; but the relationships between the power-zones of the individual gods are open to dispute, and this becomes especially fraught in the context of their relationships with mortals – relationships of protective affection, detached governance, or even cruel indifference as the case may be.

The comparative reading can then be pursued further. An obvious objection to the claim that Poseidon's speech 'translates' the opening of *Atrahasis* is that its meaning in context is so different: in the Greek text the poet is not simply narrating the story, it is spoken by a participant in a dispute in order to press his own claim to rights equal to those of his brother, the supreme sky-god Zeus. It turns out, however, that later in

---

[104] For references see n. 113 below.
[105] For the construction of these alternatives cf. Kelly 2008: 262–73, with detailed references.

Atrahasis the image is redeployed in exactly this way, when the god Enlil reprises the pattern of the opening narrative in a speech of his own.[106] At this point in the story the great gods have agreed a plan to use their powers over nature to bring about the destruction of the human race; but Enlil realises that Enki, the god of the waters below the earth, has secretly been providing them with food in the form of fish. On realising what has happened, he sends a messenger to convey his complaint to Enki, here given his alternative Akkadian name of Ea:

> [   ] the broad sea
> repeated [the message of] Enlil to Ea:
> '[I commanded] that Anu and Adad watch over
>   the upper regions,
> [that Sin and Nergal] watch over the earth between,
> [that the bolt], the trap of the sea,
> [you should] stand guard over,
> together with your hairy hero-men.[107]
> [But you let] loose abundance for the peoples!'
>   (*Atrahasis*, Late Babylonian Version, 'VI' 6′–13′: Foster, *BTM*,
>   p. 266)

The god who sends the message is complaining because the god of the waters has disobeyed the arrangement that they made with their powers, precisely in order to intervene to help his favourites – first the human race as a whole, and later his protégé Atrahasis himself (see pp. 50–54 below). In this way the passage comes again into close alignment with that from the *Iliad*, in terms of rhetorical strategies as much as the bare bones of the story.[108] Again the parallel is inexact, in the sense that the distribution of powers between the gods is being cited by the god making the complaint, not the one defending himself. Nonetheless, the vital point remains that in both cases the scene is developed in terms of a very similar discourse and world-view. The great gods squabble over each other's cosmological roles, while mortals suffer and die: against that background the images in the two narratives take on their meaning, and the common insight underpins any local correspondences in narrative detail, plot-development or verbal

[106] I cite from the Late Babylonian text, where the fullest surviving version of this scene is preserved. In the Old Babylonian Version, see II v 16–19, II vi 28–30: Foster, *BTM*, pp. 244–6, with George and Al-Rawi 1996: 175–83.

[107] The word is *laḥmu*, a demonic attendant of Enki. The word is related to the verb *laḥāmu* 'to be hairy', and in the iconography of cylinder seals these beings are depicted as shaggy humanoids or human–animal hybrids: hence the confusing array of conventional translations – 'hairy hero-man', 'water-monster', etc.

[108] This point is touched on already by Kelly 2008: 272–3, drawing in turn on West 1997: 385.

imagery. Generalised affinity encourages and motivates localised borrowing and cross-fertilisation.[109]

Implications for the reading strategy

The lesson here is that if we agree to treat the two poems as related but
distinct manifestations of a single literary and cultural nexus, then our
reading will be deepened and enriched by the habit of constant comparison, identifying and exploring commonalities and also contrasts between
them as we proceed. Each text serves as a foil to the other, a source for
contrasts as well as comparisons within an overall critical framework that
respects their close interrelation as product of traditions that, although
each rooted in its own language and compositional norms, were nonetheless bound together by shared inherited norms and ongoing currents of
cross-influence. In principle this works the same way whether we hypothesise that *Atrahasis* directly influenced the composition of the *Iliad*, or that
we are dealing with common inheritances from the Bronze Age, or even if
we suspect (as suggested above) that both may be true simultaneously.

The key critical term here is *intertextuality*. It is common in Classical
scholarship to think of intertextuality as a debatable phenomenon of
literary history, encompassing both the modelling of new texts on older
forebears and the more overt kind of allusion in which the younger text
actively evokes the older. Although this approach is conventionally applied
to relationships within Greek or Latin or between those two, it can equally
be posited for those that we find between Greek and Mesopotamian works.
Any version of the hypothesis that Poseidon's image of the 'gods playing
dice' is related to the *Atrahasis* passages might be plotted somewhere on
a scale like that in Diagram 2 (p. 32).

At the right-hand extreme the receiving poet has embedded in his poem
an image or motif from an extraneous source, and his audience may even be
sufficiently versed in 'cultural bilingualism' to recognise this as an *allusion* to
the earlier work – in this case, a work in one of the Mesopotamian

---

[109] Here I draw closely on Currie's argument that the 'allusive art' of Homeric epic is closely
paralleled in Mesopotamian narrative composition: specifically in the techniques of cross-
referencing between story-patterns analogous to each other, and of building a monumental
narrative sequence by combining and remodelling shorter narratives from a pre-existing oral
or written corpus (Currie 2012a; Currie 2016: 147–222 *passim*). See in particular his proposal
(Currie 2016: 174–6) of a triangular relationship of generic resemblance, borrowing, and
intertextual allusion between Gilgamesh's rejection of Ishtar in Tablet VI of the Standard
Babylonian Version of the *Epic of Gilgamesh*, Anchises' reaction to Aphrodite's seduction
attempt in the *Homeric Hymn to Aphrodite*, and Diomedes' attack on Aphrodite in *Iliad* 5.

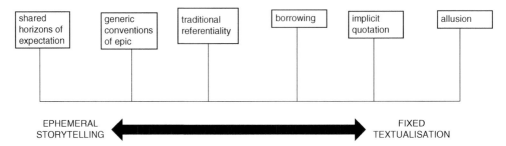

Diagram 2 Graded scale of intertextual relationships.

languages.[110] If the affinity is less meaningful and the relationship more passive, it may simply be a case of *implicit quotation* or *borrowing*, lifted from one text and embedded in another. Less overtly, and pointing less closely towards fixed textual reception, the poet and (potentially) the audience may recognise that the new creation embodies, or varies, or even transforms or subverts the conventions of generic composition or narrative myth-making in the established tradition. This (to reapply terminology normally used for Greek-to-Greek interconnections) would be classed as *traditional referentiality*.[111] Finally, at the most generalised level of comparison and at the left-hand end of our scale, the Greek and Mesopotamian narratives can be treated as parallel but separate responses to a set of recognised traditional norms and expectations – a world-view and a literary imagination – that was shared, with inevitable variations, by the speech-communities (or poetic elites) of the two languages in question. These *horizons of expectation*, to use the now standard term coined by H. R. Jauss, will never be precisely fixed and rigid, even between two contemporary Greek poets or two members of a single listening or reading audience; and because nothing survives in Greek from before the composition of the Homeric poems, the surviving witnesses to this background from the pre-Homeric period are all framed in one or other of the cuneiform languages.

In this book I have tried to avoid pushing my readings wilfully towards the right-hand end of the scale depicted above, and I depend upon

---

[110] An important challenge is posed by Currie's proposal that Greek epic may at times be alluding openly, even intentionally, to material in Near Eastern poems including the Gilgamesh epic (Currie 2016, esp. 200–22). In the case of the materials central to this study, I have not found grounds for advancing anything on the lines of the latter argument, but the question remains a valid and important one for every case study.

[111] The term was originally applied to intertextual relationships *within* Greek - usually relationships between the attested written texts and their (hypothetical) forebears in oral-epic traditions of 'composition in performance'. See the useful discussion of the terminology, and the models it implies, by Currie 2016: 4–22, and compare Burgess 2012.

a working definition of intertextuality that is concerned much more with reshaping our perspectives as readers. In other words, to stay with our last example, my creed is that by juxtaposing the *Iliad* passage with *Atrahasis* we will be brought deeper into the patterns of social ideology, theology and poetics that informed the creative projects of both literary traditions. Such a reading will (I hope) enrich our attempts to bridge the gulf of time and world-view between ourselves and the ancients, if only because it helps us to redefine our sense of the basic business of epic by beginning from the closest cousins or predecessors of the Homeric poems, rather than the disparate European and world literatures that are linked to them by the uneasy mixture of typological analogy and indirect literary influence that we observed in the first half of this chapter.

This approach will take us in directions different from those in much of the specialist scholarly literature in this field. In particular, we will have no reason to deploy one of the key criteria that have been applied to the search for Near Eastern influence on Greek literature: the 'argument by isolation',[112] by which one identifies a motif as 'oriental' because it is seen to be anomalous or unparalleled elsewhere in Greek sources. In the case of the 'dicing for the world' passage in the *Iliad*, as we saw above, Burkert argued for taking this as a quotation from *Atrahasis* partly because it seemed to conflict with other Homeric lore about the distribution of powers among the gods; he even argued, from the location of the source text at the beginning of *Atrahasis*, that a Greek student of scribal cuneiform would have recalled the passage because of the universal habit of retaining the clearest memories of the opening passage of a text studied in the classroom.[113] Our approach, in contrast, will be to use the Near Eastern comparanda as a route towards grasping the key central themes and ideas of the Greek epic tradition, for the simple and fundamental reason that reaching towards the forebears of our Greek artefacts may be the best way to move one's thinking towards their centre and essence. In this case, correspondingly, Kelly's demonstration that Poseidon's image, read with due sensitivity, may in fact be *consistent* with other ideas in Homer and Hesiod[114] serves to strengthen, not to weaken, the usefulness of an intertextual reading – provided that we are willing to learn from contrasts, no less than equations, between the two.

---

[112] For a review and searching critique of the 'argument by isolation', especially as practised by Burkert, see Kelly 2008: 260–1 and *passim*, with Kelly 2014, esp. 30; cf. Haubold 2013: 31–3.
[113] Burkert 1992 [1984]: 89–91, 2004: 34–7; cf. West 1997: 109–11.   [114] Kelly 2008: 262–73.

The task of this book is to explore one specific juxtaposition, between *Gilgamesh* and the *Iliad*.[115] The protagonist, Gilgamesh in the one case and Achilles in the other, is ambiguously poised between the status of a mortal and of a god. In the course of his striving for an immortal name and quasi-divine status among the living, he brings about the death of his best friend – Enkidu or Patroclus – and turns from this towards the certain prospect of his own death. So stated, the confluence in theme and story-pattern begins at the general level of shared *horizons of expectation*, and extends (particularly in the portrayal of the friend's death) towards *traditional referentiality* between kindred story-patterns in the two traditions of heroic narrative. But there is more. Among the episodes from the death to the protagonist's response we will find a series of precise correspondences in motif, imagery and wording that are far more closely enmeshed, and that occur in the same linear sequence in the two poems. At crucial points, focussed on the mourning sequences for Enkidu and Patroclus, we will find instances of what begs to be identified as borrowing, even *implicit quotation*, from *Gilgamesh* within the *Iliad* (below, pp. 269–274).[116] However, the material associated with *Gilgamesh* is seamlessly, even perfectly integrated into the Homeric portrayal of Achilles and Patroclus: there is no tension, no disparity, and this provides the strongest indication of all that the poetic modes of the two languages are part of a single cultural and expressive phenomenon.

Nonetheless, it will be implicit throughout that the comparison across the Hellespont can and should serve to point up differences as well as correspondences. Gilgamesh returns from his encounter with mortality to reintegrate into the life of the city, but Achilles' movement towards his own death finds no such lasting resolution.[117] Our final task will be to make sense of this disparity while remaining faithful to the comparative method, which at that stage will direct us towards a conclusion in which the comparative reading of the two epic traditions will be concerned as much with wisdom literature as with heroic narrative.

---

[115] So far as I know, the first sustained attempt to draw *Gilgamesh* and the *Iliad* together in this way was that by Petriconi 1964; for later developments and refinements see below.

[116] West 1997: 341–3, Haubold 2013: 22–3, López-Ruiz 2014: 169–71, Currie 2012a: 550–2 and 2016: 216–17, Rollinger 2015: 17.

[117] For a structurally comparable reading of the two epics cf. Haubold 2015, showing that the concept of the ruler as 'shepherd of the people' is explored in parallel ways in the *Epic of Gilgamesh* and the *Iliad*, but that in *Gilgamesh* the power of the king is curbed by the gods whereas in the Greek epic Agamemnon is allowed to bully his followers unchecked.

2 | Divinity, humanity and wisdom

Civilisation is a tired word, but if it means anything it means a sense of communal social identity with the rule of law, systematic government, and public order rising above the uncontrolled forces of the natural world, and with a place for visual and verbal artists to respond creatively to those issues. In antiquity, those things were expressed above all in the life of the city: a centre of population and power surrounded by walls and typically asserting itself as the head of a state or polity, led by a king and protected by its own gods.[1] Our concern here is not with the historical realities but the artistic responses. Cities in some form had existed for millennia already in south-western Asia – Çatalhöyük in what is now south-central Turkey was a concentrated population centre as early as the 7000s BCE[2] – but it seems to have been in Mesopotamia from the later third millennium onwards that literature was first committed to writing and preserved as a public possession from generation to generation and from city to city.

The formative stages in the growth of this literature are witnessed by texts in the Sumerian language, which survive largely because they were passed on in the schools of the learned scribes from the Old Babylonian period of the early second millennium BCE.[3] These scribes were much more than secretaries or copyists: as the learned class of their cities, they owned and transmitted a corpus of literature which grew and transformed itself over more than a thousand years, while maintaining and developing the basic tenets of worldview, ideology and even of detailed literary content.[4] In our texts the Sumerian language is significant not as a living speech but as the repository of ancient

---

[1] For approaches to the definition of 'civilisation' for the grand narrative of antiquity compare Wengrow 2010, focussed on the rise of city culture in the Near East, with Meier 2011 on the ideological and creative innovations of the early Greek *polis*. For the case of ancient Mesopotamia see esp. Van de Mieroop 1997, with the survey by Leick 2001.

[2] Survey at Broodbank 2013: 172–8; see further Hodder 2011.

[3] The standard source for the key texts is *LOAS*, in which many of the Sumerian texts discussed in this chapter are translated; the complete corpus is encompassed by the Electronic Text Corpus of Sumerian Literature.

[4] On the role of the scribal profession in the dissemination of the literary tradition, and in particular on the importance of the curriculum used in training the scribes, the collection of essays in Radner and Robson 2011 is invaluable. For the Old Babylonian period, crucial for texts in Sumerian as well as in the Old Babylonian language, see esp. Tinney 2011. On dissemination

knowledge and wisdom, the medium of written scholarship and training in
the scribal school (*eduba*) among people whose primary spoken language was
different, typically Akkadian or one of its family. This means that when we
write of Sumerian literature or a particular Sumerian text, we are dealing not
necessarily with the remoter beginnings of the textual tradition, still less with
the voices of the Sumerian *people* as such,[5] but with the foundational resources
of the learned caste throughout the world of cuneiform scribal culture.
Translation, renewal and dissemination in other and less archaic languages,
especially Akkadian in its Babylonian and Assyrian varieties, extended the
reach of the tradition as far west as the Mediterranean coasts in one direction,
and in the other to the Hittite kingdom in what is now central Turkey, right up
to the watershed of *c.* 1200 BCE and beyond.[6] When the great kings of the
Neo-Assyrian period, above all Ashurbanipal (reigned 669–627 BCE) at
Nineveh, established 'libraries' stocked with copies of canonical texts, they
were enshrining and fixing a literary succession that had already been developing for at least a millennium and a half.[7] Nor did this mark the end of
cuneiform transmission: scribal training and the making of archives continued
into the neo-Babylonian period and beyond,[8] overlapping in time with the
development of alphabetic Greek textuality. Even among the manuscripts of
the Standard Babylonian Version of the *Epic of Gilgamesh* there are survivals
from late in this age: one tablet, for example, marks its own date of transcription by the regnal years of the Greek-speaking kings Seleucus and Antiochus
in the period 292–281 BCE.[9]

King, city and gods

To judge by the textual evidence, a public ideology bound up with ideas of
divine kingship first emerged into prominence in the later third millennium
BCE with Sargon of Akkad and his successors, especially Naram-Sin,[10] and

of scribal culture in the later second millennium BCE, with special reference to wisdom texts,
see Cohen 2013: 3–77 *passim*.

[5] Cf. Cooper 2010.   [6] Particularly useful here is Foster 2007.

[7] Parpola 1983; Fincke 2003–4, 2017; Zamalová 2011. On the systematic gathering of texts for the
royal library of Nineveh see also Frame and George 2005.

[8] For a useful survey of the survivals from the Neo-Babylonian period at Babylon, Sippar,
Borsippa and elsewhere, see Jursa 2011. A striking case study of the fourth-century BCE library
collection found in a house at Uruk is presented by Robson 2011: 565–9. Compare Haubold
2013: 127–42.

[9] George 2003: 1.740, MS f of *SBV* Tablet X.

[10] For the principal texts on these kings, see Westenholz 1997.

was recast with renewed emphasis on the sacral aspects of kingship during the supremacy of Ur under Ur-Nammu and his successor Shulgi. In this schema the king stands over his people like a shepherd, and he mediates between them and the gods; his attributes are poised between those of mortality and those of divinity.[11] Beyond the individual city-state, this ideology embraced the concept of a higher hegemony over the region as a whole, including many cities, and in the text known as the *Sumerian King-List* the title 'King of the Land' was assigned first to one city's dynasty and then to another under the sanction of the god Enlil.[12] As the focal point of power or prestige moved from city to city, Babylon eventually became supreme and the divine authority over the kingship moved from Enlil to its patron god Marduk.[13] Later again, under the Neo-Assyrian empire, this role was assumed by the eponymous god Ashur. For the purposes of this book, it does not matter how well the image of Mesopotamian kingship answers to the realities of statecraft at this or that point in space and time, or to what extent the imagery is to be understood purely as figured language. What matters is the representation itself, placing the king at a shifting intermediate point between the high society of the gods and the low lives of the mass of the people.

Cosmology on the Seal of Adda

What defines a god as a god? Immortality is only part of the answer,[14] and the gods' freedom from the prospect of death is an aspect of a more fundamental uniqueness that separates them from humans: their more-than-mortal abundance of life and of energy, bound up with the quality of self-generating and self-propelling movement. Correspondingly, the gods are in and of the physical universe and the visible landscape, and they may

---

[11] Although the association between kingship and divinity is widespread throughout ancient Near Eastern literature, it is first clearly expressed in the case of Naram-Sin and is exceptionally heightened in the texts concerned with Ur-Nammu and Shulgi of Ur. For its expression in connection with this group of rulers, see Michalowski 2008; Cooper 2008.

[12] See Glassner 2004: 117–55, for the various recensions and expanded versions of this text. The relationship between the king-lists and the Flood narrative discussed later in this chapter is examined by Kvanvig 2011: 83–106.

[13] Kuhrt 1995: 1.53–5, 63–70; Leick 2001: 89–98, 123–35; Van de Mieroop 2007: 59–79.

[14] This point is linked to the fact that in the mythology certain gods undergo death, most obviously Dumuzid the consort of Inana/Ishtar (*LOAS*, pp. 63–99) and also (for example) the god in *Atrahasis* whose flesh and blood are used in the making of the first humans (*Atrahasis* OBV I 204–230: Foster, *BTM*, p. 236). For a survey see Black and Green 1992, s.v. 'dead gods'.

embody the mobile forces that propel it – the movements of the sky, the
vitality of living things, the growth of the crops.[15]

To illustrate the implications of this conceptual pattern, impressions from
cylinder seals provide a stock of useful examples. (A cylinder seal is a rounded
stone-carved matrix that would be rolled onto soft clay blanks to form
impressions of words and images, principally for purposes of
authentication.[16]) In the famous seal used by the scribe Adda *c.* 2300 BCE,
the tall many-horned hats of the figures identify them as gods, and their
attributes allow confident identifications (Fig. 3).[17] Right of centre is the god
known as Enki in Sumerian and Ea in Akkadian, god of river-water and of the
cosmic waters below the earth (*Apsu*), and also of human cleverness and the
arts of civilisation. His identity is marked by the fish-filled river around him
and the bull below, representing its voice as the sound of roaring torrents.[18]
Below is the sun-god Shamash (Sumerian Utu), wielding his pruning-saw as
he cuts his way through the forest to emerge over the eastern mountains. The
winged figure above is Ishtar (Sumerian Inana), who presides over or embodies both war and fertility[19] and is identified with the bright star that we still
call Venus,[20] using the Latin version ultimately translated from her name.
(The figures at the edges are lesser divinities.[21]) In a sense this depicts a divine
society of interrelated anthropomorphic beings, their forms shaped in the
image of their human worshippers; but in a different and complementary
sense it is a picture of the morning – Shamash *is* the sun rising over the
mountains, Ishtar *is* the morning star and Ea's presence is manifested in the
visible waters of the rivers.[22] These gods are immanent in the tangible world
around us, and their powers are the powers of nature. Man's subservience to

[15] Bottéro 1992 [1987]: 201–86. Earlier scholarship could be glib about positing a one-to-one
identity between a god and a real-world phenomenon, ignoring the subtleties of metaphorical
language. See the important correctives by Rochberg (esp. 1986, cf. Rochberg 2016 *passim*).
[16] On cylinder seals see Collon 2005, 2007. There is an excellent collection of illustrated
discussions of individual seals from the earlier periods in Aruz and Wallenfels 2003, *passim.*
[17] The iconography of the seal is discussed, alongside others depicting divinities, by Collon 2005:
164–71 with fig. 761.
[18] For the river-aspect of Enki/Ea, see for example the Sumerian hymn *Enki and the World Order*
(*LOAS*, pp. 215–25), esp. lines 250–84.
[19] See for example the Sumerian *Hymn to Inana* at *LOAS*, pp. 92–9.
[20] Westenholz 2007: 335.
[21] The Janus-faced figure on the right is sometimes identified as Usmu (Sumerian Isimud), the
minister or servant of Ea: his name was interpreted in antiquity as 'two-faced'. Flying above is
the Anzu bird (Collon 2005: 178); the identity of the hunting god at the side is disputed.
[22] For theological texts (albeit from the later phases of Mesopotamian literature) articulating this
principle in varying forms and on various levels of literalism versus metaphor and metonymy,
see Livingstone 1986: 71–113.

Fig. 3 Impression of the 'Seal of Adda'.

them is acted out in the daily rhythms of temple, cult and sacrifice, and it underlies the literature that we will examine in what follows.

The self-praise of Shulgi

Evidence for the textual curriculum survives particularly strongly from the city of Nippur (Nibru), which functioned as the epicentre of scribal culture for the wider region. At Nippur, according to an influential analysis of the survivals, central importance was held by a group of ten short texts nowadays known as the Decad.[23] Some of the Decad texts are hymns in praise of the gods, some are narratives about the divine society, one is even a series of meditative riddles around the Sumerian word for 'hoe'; but among them there stands out the work known as *Shulgi A*, which was one of the extraordinary series of 'hymns' of self-praise that survive under the name of Shulgi of Ur.[24] This poem will serve to orientate us towards the themes from which our later analysis of *Gilgamesh* will develop.

---

[23] The Decad texts are assembled at *LOAS* pp. 299–352. The constitution of the group is defined by Tinney 1999, and the implications for understanding copying practices in scribal education are discussed by Delnero 2010, 2012. However, Robson argues (2001, esp. 50–9) that the evidence used by Tinney is heavily weighted towards the evidence surviving from House F at Nippur, which is not necessarily typical; Robson charts evidence for a wider range of texts of potentially canonical status in the schools, including other Lugalbanda and Gilgamesh narratives.

[24] The Shulgi hymns, alphabetically named (*Shulgi A, Shulgi B* and so on) are translated in the ETCSL database, and *Shulgi A* is printed with notes in *LOAS*, pp. 304–8. The fundamental

Shulgi appears in the records as an historical king, reigning in the years *c.* 2070 BCE; regularly in the tradition he is the son of another legendary king, Lugalbanda of Unug (=Uruk), himself the subject of a sequence of heroic narratives,[25] but it is not clear to what extent the poems date from Shulgi's own time or reflect retrospective invention in later times. *Shulgi A*, like others in the series, is voiced by the king himself proclaiming his own greatness:

> I, the king, was a hero already in the womb; I, Shulgi, was born to be a mighty man. I am a fierce-looking lion, begotten by a dragon. I am the king of the four regions; I am the herdsman and shepherd of the black-headed people. I am a respected one, the god of all the lands. (*Shulgi A*, 1–6)

The two sides of his boast make him a hostile lion to his enemies[26] but a shepherd – that is, a guide and a protector against predators – over the multitudes of the people. He claims an otherworldly parentage, 'begotten by a dragon', and takes divine status for himself, an assertion that becomes more precise as the poem unfolds:

> I am a child born of Ninsumun. (*Shulgi A* 7)

When the king is described as a lion or as a dragon's child, such images are presumably to be heard as metaphor:[27] their vagueness suggests an ambiguity over his origins and his nature.[28] However, the claim to be the child of Ninsumun is more concrete and gives him a precisely defined place in the divine society: Ninsumun (= Akkadian Ninsun), whose name means 'lady wild cow', is one of the great deities of the pantheon.[29] The claim to divine parentage can be understood as referring to his birth, or as a mythical projection of his 'adoption' among the gods at the time of his

---

studies are those by Klein (1980, 1981). In the notes below, the cross-references comparing shared images and motifs between the various Shulgi poems are strictly representative examples and are not exhaustive.

[25] For the Lugalbanda poems, see Vanstiphout 2003: 97–165; one of them is included as *Lugalbanda in the Mountain Cave* at *LOAS*, pp. 11–30, and is more extensively analysed by Black 1998, *passim*. See further below, pp. 57–58.

[26] For Shulgi as champion in war and hunting, see for example *Shulgi B* 21–117.

[27] On the interpretative issues with reading Sumerian poetic imagery cf. Black 1998, esp. 9–13, 55–6.

[28] The king's identification with beasts is a recurrent image in the Shulgi poems: see esp. *Shulgi C* 1–31, *Shulgi D* 1–13, *Shulgi Q* 1–11. The warlike characteristics of different kinds of animals are contrasted with each other at *Shulgi E* 202–19, suggesting that the imagery may be more precise than it seems at first sight.

[29] In *Shulgi P* Ninsumun physically takes Shulgi in her arms and confirms in her praises that he is her child: 'You are a good seed of Lugalbanda. I raised you upon my own holy lap' (22–27). See Klein 1981: 23–26, and compare *Shulgi D* 40–52.

accession.[30] The lines that follow make him the companion of many in the divine community:

> I am the choice of holy An's heart. I am the man whose fate was decided by Enlil. I am Shulgi, the beloved of Ninlil. I am he who is cherished by Nintud. I am he who is endowed with wisdom by Enki. I am the powerful king of Nanna. I am the growling lion of Utu. (*Shulgi A* 7 ff.)

An is the supreme god of the high sky; Enlil is the father of the divine family with Ninlil as his wife; Nintud presides over childbirth; Enki as we have seen is lord of water and of cunning; Utu is the sun-god. This, says Shulgi, is the company in which he moves. The last of these claims is the most profound:

> I am Shulgi, who has been chosen by Inana for his attractiveness. (*Shulgi A* 15)

Inana is the greatest goddess: mistress of animals, of the fertility of the earth and the sexual power of women.[31] Shulgi's most ambitious declaration is that she desires him as a sexual partner, and this implies that he also claims lordship over the fertility of the city and the land.

But after setting himself on this high divine level, Shulgi suddenly returns to earth and the poem becomes a celebration of swift travel in the realm:

> I am a mule, most suitable for the road. I am a horse whose tail waves on the highway. I am a stallion of Shakkan, eager to run. (*Shulgi A* 16–18)

This formulaic image[32] sets the scene for the achievement that forms the centre of the poem: Shulgi 'strengthened the roads, put in order the highways of the land' and built rest-stops and lodging-houses along the way for travellers. To celebrate this imposition of order on the landscape he performed a heroic feat of travel[33] by running in a single day between the cities of Nippur and Ur and back again, a distance of about 300 kilometres:

> I, the lion, never failing in his vigour, standing firm in his strength, fastened the small *ninglam* garment firmly to my hips. Like a pigeon anxiously fleeing from a . . . snake, I spread my wings; like the Anzud bird lifting up its gaze to the mountains, I stretched forth my legs. (*Shulgi A* 42ff.)

---

[30] A distinct version of the divine parentage of Shulgi is recounted in *Shulgi G*, where the moon-god fathers him on the temple priestess (15–20, with Klein 1981: 9).

[31] Westenholz 2007.

[32] For the image of a runner as 'donkey of Shakkan', compare for example *Enmerkar and Ensuhgirana* 45–7, at Vanstiphout 2003: 31.

[33] For the king as runner between festivals compare for example *Shulgi B* 118–30, *Shulgi V* 13–29.

This king's strength is superhuman, he is united with the gods by kinship and friendship, but the roads are a tangible embodiment of the rule of law and social harmony. His role is to regulate and control the realm, and the multitudes gaze up at him:

> The inhabitants of the cities which I had founded in the land lined up for me; the black-headed people, as numerous as ewes, looked at me with sweet admiration. (*Shulgi A* 46–7)

As shepherd of these people, when Shulgi has reached Ur he leads the sacrifice of oxen and sheep in the temple of Nanna the moon-god. There is no tension or contradiction in the fact that he has two such different roles at different times – leader of the people facing distant and untouchable gods, yet also peer and companion of the gods themselves. Through storm and rain and hail he runs back to Nippur to join in its own corresponding festival:

> I drank beer in the palace founded by An with my brother and companion, the hero Utu. My singers praised me with songs accompanied by seven *tigi* drums. My spouse, the maiden Inana, the lady, the joy of heaven and earth, sat with me at the banquet. (*Shulgi A* 79–83)

The sheep-like people praise their king, who has displayed his godlike strength in his feat of running, while he sits with his divine lover, who in turn personifies sexual energy and fertility.

Is the sexual union with Inana merely a figure of speech? It can be understood as an allusive self-identification with her consort Dumuzid, and the imagery might be seen as merely conventional: for example, within the Decad corpus there is very similar phrasing in the *Praise Poem of Lipit-Eshtar*.[34] But the claim to congress with the goddess remains vividly physical: it is instructive to compare another of the Shulgi hymns, *Shulgi X*, which visualises the same theme in still more dramatic terms. Here Shulgi enters the temple of Inana with beasts for sacrifice, then the goddess calls on him to have intercourse with her: 'When he treats me tenderly on the bed, then I too will treat my lord tenderly.'[35] The question over the literal or metaphorical meaning of the claim is broached explicitly in the narrative *Enmerkar and Ensuhgirana*, in which two kings vie for

---

[34] See *LOAS*, pp. 308–11, esp. lines 98–104, and compare the *Hymn to Inana for Iddin-Dagan*, *LOAS*, pp. 262–9. Similarly Sargon of Akkad boasts that he is 'beloved of Ishtar' in the fragment *I, Sargon* (Westenholz 1997: p. 34 at line 2), and likewise in the *Sargon Birth Legend* (Westenholz 1997: p. 41 at line 12).

[35] *Shulgi X* 14–35. See. There are close parallels here with the union of Inana and Dumuzid (Klein 1980: 149–50; see also Klein 1981: 13–14).

supremacy. One asserts himself against the other by claiming to be the only one with whom Inana has sexual intercourse in person:

> He may lie with her on a flowery bed,
> he may meet with Inana in his dreams at night,
> but I shall converse with Inana between her gleaming thighs!
> (Enmerkar and Ensuhgirana 29–32, sim. 60–3)[36]

For this contrast to be possible, the motif of the sexual encounter between king and goddess must be understood in concrete bodily terms.

Although all this seems to happen on a remote and timeless plane, the Shulgi poems show an intense awareness of the multilingual world in which they were composed and transmitted.[37] One of the signs of civilisation embraced by the king is the scribal art:

> I, Shulgi the noble, have been blessed with a favourable destiny right from the womb. When I was small, I was at the academy (*eduba*), where I learned the scribal art from the tablets of Sumer and Akkad. None of the nobles could write on clay as I could. (*Shulgi B* 11–20)

The lines that follow these show that the highest skill was in mathematical arts rather than working with narrative texts, but the latter would have been understood as part of the training, as in the real-life scribal curriculum. Later in the same poem the king is portrayed as skilfully making music and also presiding over the preservation of older literature,[38] and this will be replicated in the celebration and recitation of the Shulgi cycle itself in the future:

> At some time in the distant future, a man of Enlil may arise, and if he is a just king, like myself, then let my odes, prayers and learned songs about my heroic courage and expeditions follow that king in his good palace . . . He should exalt the power of my odes, absorb the exuberance of my songs, and value highly my great wisdom. (*Shulgi B* 281–96)

In this way, the Shulgi poems acknowledge a sense of their own afterlife and, by implication, their role as models of kingly excellence to be emulated in the future.[39]

---

[36] Translation from Vanstiphout 2003: pp. 31, 33. See also lines 78–87 (p. 33), with Vanstiphout's notes explicating the distinction in the imagery between imagined and personal encounters with the goddess; cf. further Vanstiphout 2010.

[37] On Shulgi as polyglot speaker of many languages, including Sumerian, see Rubio 2006.

[38] Shulgi as musician: *Shulgi B* 154–74, cf. *Shulgi C* 75–101; preserving the literature of the past, *Shulgi B* 270–80.

[39] The future recitation of the poems about Shulgi is also described at *Shulgi E* 14–52.

Such is the image of kingship in this society – or, to be more precise, the paradigm of primeval kingship, heroic and close to the gods, to which the more prosaic realities of real-life statecraft would be assimilated. Such images lie close to the thematic starting-point of the epic tradition, which looks backward to a vanished time, when the men who dominated society were poised between gods and mortals and embodied a level of energy to which the lesser humans of later times can only aspire in vain.

The Sumerian *Gilgamesh and Huwawa*

Genealogy is one of the abiding organisational structures of myth-making, distributing the cast of the narratives across remarkably fixed and stable frameworks, so it is reasonable to turn from Shulgi to the one he claims as a brother: Gilgamesh, who is likewise a son of Ninsun and Lugalbanda.[40] (The variant tradition in the *Sumerian King-List*, that Gilgamesh's father was a 'phantom', is another way of articulating the concept that he belongs in the doubtful territory between myth and knowable history.[41]) Among at least five Sumerian works that survive about his life and exploits, the narrative known as *Gilgamesh and Huwawa (Version A)* is included in the Decad.[42] Its theme is Gilgamesh's desire to find and kill the terrifying demon Huwawa: Gilgamesh here is the young king, 'lord of Kulaba' (a name of part of the city Uruk), but the starting-point is not his divine aspect but the certainty that he will die. At the beginning he has decided to go to 'the mountain where no man lives', and he explains the reason to his slave and companion, Enkidu:

> Enkidu, since a man cannot pass beyond the final end of life, I want to set off into the mountains, to establish my renown there. Where renown can be established there, I will establish my renown; and where no renown

---

[40] Gilgamesh is mentioned as Shulgi's brother at (e.g.) *Shulgi D* 288–94, and *Shulgi O* centres around a dialogue of mutual praise between the brothers. See Klein 1981: 10, with Klein 1976.

[41] George 2003: 1.101–4; Sallaberger 2008: 43–58.

[42] See *LOAS*, pp. 343–52; George 1999: 150–202. I quote from the translation in *LOAS* except where otherwise stated. The annotated translation by Fleming and Milstein 2010: 182–207 differs significantly at certain points, but their notes do not always explain the editorial decisions made. Version A, 'The Lord to the living one's mountain', is better attested than Version B, and the latter is relevant to the present discussion only for occasional motifs unique to it (see below). Fleming and Milstein argue that Version A developed in the earlier second millennium BCE, in tandem with the Akkadian version that was incorporated into the Old Babylonian version of the *Epic of Gilgamesh* (summarised at Fleming and Milstein 2010: p. xv, Table 2). This is an important reminder that a given text in Sumerian does not necessarily represent a more archaic stage of development than a related text in Akkadian.

can be established there, I shall establish the renown of the gods. (*Gilgamesh and Huwawa* A 4 ff., *LOAS*, p. 344)

Man cannot pass beyond the final end of life: the knowledge of his own mortality drives him to action. He sacrifices to Utu the sun-god, and when Utu wonders what he is planning he explains more fully what has prompted him to this exploit:

> In my city people are dying, and hearts are full of distress. People are lost: that fills me with dismay. I craned my neck over the city wall: corpses in the water make the river almost overflow. That is what I see. That will happen to me too – that is the way things go. (23 ff.)

The corpses in the river are neglected, anonymous, denied their proper honours and due ritual commemoration to preserve their name and memory. This brutal everyday sight makes him think about mortal limitations, and this takes shape as a maxim:[43]

> No one is tall enough to reach heaven, no one can stretch over the mountains. (28–9)

Why does this awareness of human powerlessness push him to great deeds – what consolation will it be to 'establish his renown' in the mountains that he cannot encompass?[44] The underlying connection, it seems, is that fame is a substitute version of immortality: even if the self perishes the name will live on, and this second-best is the victory to strive for.

Significantly, one Sumerian source associates the quest to seek out Huwawa with another, even more visceral version of Gilgamesh's encounter with the thought of mortality. *Gilgamesh, Enkidu and the Netherworld* is a superficially simple narrative, in which Enkidu becomes trapped in the Underworld and returns as a phantom, recounting the comforts enjoyed in the afterlife by those who are honoured by their living descendants:

> 'Did you see the man with six sons?' 'I saw him.' 'How does he fare?'
> 'Like a man with ploughs in harness his heart rejoices.'
> 'Did you see the man with seven sons?' 'I saw him.' 'How does he fare?'
> 'Among the junior deities he sits on a throne and listens to the proceedings.'
>   (*Gilgamesh, Enkidu and the Netherworld* 264–7, George 1999: p. 188)

In contrast, the man with no heir has poor food in his afterlife, the eunuch is inert and useless, the childless woman is cast aside 'like a *defective* pot', the childless man weeps (269 ff.): cultic commemoration among the living

---

[43] On the correlates in proverb compilations see Hallo 1990.
[44] For the interpretation followed here, see also Taylor 2010: 351–6.

is the only hope, and it depends on the maintenance of one's memory among the community.[45] The copy of this text found at Meturan ends with a linking line indicating that the tale of the combat with Huwawa is to follow immediately afterward in the sequence of texts. This suggests that the editor or redactor used the vision of the afterlife in the same way as the sight of the corpses in the river in *Gilgamesh and Huwawa A*, as an image of the immediacy of death that triggers Gilgamesh's decision to set out on his quest.[46]

In *Gilgamesh and Huwawa* we are far away from the security and bombast of the Shulgi hymns: if Gilgamesh too is the son of a god, then that only makes the sight of the corpses more horrifying and the impulse to seek glory more intense. Gilgamesh's plan is to fell the greatest of the cedar trees on the mountain, which in turn awakens the forest's guardian, Huwawa, who attacks them with his divine powers ('auras')[47] so that Gilgamesh and Enkidu fall into unconsciousness. Enkidu returns first to reality and wakens Gilgamesh, who steels himself for the combat by reminding himself of his parentage:

> By the life of my own mother Ninsumun and of my father, holy Lugalbanda! Am I to become again as if I were slumbering still on the lap of my own mother Ninsumun? (90–1)

Enkidu still warns him of the hostile power of Huwawa and begs to be allowed to return home, imagining how Gilgamesh will be remembered after the exploit, whether in life or in death:

> His pugnacious mouth is a dragon's maw; his face is a lion's grimace. His chest is like a raging flood; no-one dares approach his brow, which devours the reed-beds. Travel on, my master, up into the mountains! – but I shall travel back to the city. If I say to your mother about you 'He is alive!', she will laugh. But afterwards I shall say to her about you 'He is dead!', and she will certainly weep over you. (98ff.)

But Gilgamesh cannot be discouraged, convinced that the two of them together will defeat their enemy; and the sequence of events becomes fraught and complex. Gilgamesh first quails before Huwawa, assailed by

---

[45] On the importance of the commemoration of the dead in Mesopotamian society, see for example Bottéro 1992 [1987]: 279–82, with the case studies in Hermann and Schloen 2014.

[46] George 1999: 189–90; Cavigneaux and Al-Rawi 2000a: p. 19 line 29, with discussion, p. 5. This passage is a key piece of evidence for the theory that the Sumerian Gilgamesh poems were built into a unified sequence or 'cycle' (Gadotti 2014).

[47] A fuller account of Humbaba – the Akkadian form of Huwawa – and his 'auras' is given in Ch. 3 in our account of the corresponding episodes of the Standard Babylonian Version.

the power of the 'auras'; gradually, however, by feigning friendship he tricks Huwawa into abandoning them, speaking of offering him first his own sisters and then rich gifts to solemnise the alliance. When Huwawa has been stripped of his powers, under pretence of a kiss Gilgamesh knocks him down with his fist; then, it seems, he starts to express pity but Enkidu persuades him against sparing him, and finally the enemy is beheaded by one or both of the assailants.

Here in essentials are many themes that will reappear in the subsequent development of heroic narrative, both east and west. The hero's mixed parentage poises him between mortal and divine worlds; the awareness of mortality impels him to do things that will never be forgotten, so that his name will live on after him; his companion and friend is at his side, advising him; he knows fear, he knows indecision, pity cuts across his more urgent quest for fame; and finally he succeeds and wins the glory which, implicitly or explicitly, is represented by the text itself.

But there is a further twist in the plot. Gilgamesh and Enkidu lay Huwawa's severed head before the god Enlil as an offering – effectively a dedication in his temple, such as any ordinary mortal might present – but Enlil is angry, declaring that they should have spared Huwawa and treated him with honour:

> Why did you act in this way? . . . He should have sat before you! He should
> have eaten the bread that you eat, and should have drunk the water that
> you drink! He should have been honoured . . . <by> . . . you! (187 ff.)

The text does not explain exactly why the god is angry – in the Babylonian retellings it is clarified that Huwawa was Enlil's own son, but this is not stated here[48] – nor is it spelled out what the consequences will be; but plainly this moment is ominous, and it suggests that unlooked-for evil will come of the exploit.[49]

This last concept will become crucial in the later articulations of heroic action, in both Mesopotamian and Greek sources. In striving towards an everlasting name something goes wrong, and the wisdom that *no-one can reach heaven* is fulfilled in a more bitter way than through the simple fact that literal immortality is denied. Even those as close to the gods as Gilgamesh are at the mercy of their mysterious and often petty rivalries and favouritisms. If Enlil

---

[48] See below, p. 72.

[49] The notion that the hero would dedicate his defeated enemy to that enemy's master is paralleled at the end of *Gilgamesh and the Bull of Heaven*, when Gilgamesh and Enkidu seem to dedicate the horns of the Bull to Inana herself, the goddess who sent it against them (Cavigneaux and Al-Rawi 1993: p. 126 line 139, with note on p. 100). George, however, leaves the interpretation more open at this point (George 1999: 174).

has reason to be angry at the killing of Huwawa, then equally one must ask why Utu the sun-god encouraged Gilgamesh to perform the exploit in the first place. An additional complexity is suggested by a passage known only from the independently developed Version B of the text,[50] where a further aspect of the involvement of the gods comes into play.[51] When Gilgamesh awakens from the stupor into which he has been thrown by the first of Huwawa's auras, he prays to Enki (= Ea) as his personal protector:

> [may] my god [Enki, the lord Nudimmud,]
> [inspire my words!]
> > (*Gilgamesh and Huwawa* B 82–3, George 1999: p. 164)

Enkidu repeats the invocation in his own words of advice (94), and Gilgamesh again asks Enki to '*inspire* [my words]' (104) when he begins the speech that will enable him to get the better of Huwawa. Huwawa himself then echoes the line, weeping in his defeat:

> O warrior, you deceived me, you laid your hand on me, though you swore an oath to me.
> By the life of [the mother who bore you], the goddess Ninsun, and your father, pure Lugalbanda,
> [your] god [Enki]-Nudimmud *inspired* your words !
> > (lines 130–2, George 1999: p. 165)

Enki is the source and author not only of Gilgamesh's courage in achieving fame, but also of his lies and deception against the son or favoured servant of another of the great gods. Between the members of the divine family there are resentments, rivalries and alliances, the hero looks helpless and insignificant below their mysterious politics.

Consolations after death?

In this way, the fact of the mortal condition is in tension with the heroes' high aspirations. This problem is present even in the Shulgi hymns:

---

[50] George 1999: 161–6.

[51] For the analysis of the addresses to Enki in Version B followed here see George 1999: 161, with Edzard 1993: 11–12. The matter is somewhat doubtful because of the fragmentary state of preservation of the lines in question. As Edzard's edition with interlinear translation shows (Edzard 1993: 16–34), the verb rendered 'inspire' is an editorial restoration; Edzard's translation and that in the ETCSL database are more conservative and leave a gap here. Fleming and Milstein 2010 consistently use an indicative verb, 'inspires my plans' etc., so that Gilgamesh is making an assertion rather than a prayer; but they seem not to give grounds for this choice.

I bestow joy and gladness, and I pass my days in pomp and splendour. But people should consider for themselves – it is a matter to keep in one's sights – that at the inescapable end of life, no-one will be spared the bitter gall of the land of oppression. But I am one who is powerful enough to trust in his own power. He who trusts in his own exalted name may carry out great things. Why should he do less? (*Shulgi B* 175 ff.)

The interrupting mention of 'the bitter gall of the land of oppression' seems to acknowledge the same problem as in *Gilgamesh and Huwawa*, where the hero was driven to action by the sight of corpses in the river. The abiding problem is the impossibility of escaping from mortal limitations, even for king and demigod.

The Sumerian text *The Death of Gilgamesh* explores this theme in a different way, with an inset narrative emerging from a lament addressed to the hero.[52] Gilgamesh is seized by sickness from Namtar, who represents death, and in a vision or dream he sees the gods debating his fate. They recall that among his feats was a journey to Ziusudra, the man who survived the great Flood and achieved immortality, and that he restored the ancient religious rites of Sumer from before the Flood;[53] but this will not be enough to save him from the universal fate of humans. Ea reminds his fellow gods that they have long ago laid down the law that men must die:[54]

> From that time we swore by the life of heaven and the life of earth,
> from that time we swore that mankind should not have life eternal.
> And now we look on Gilgamesh:
> despite his mother we cannot show him mercy!
> (*Death of Gilgamesh* M 76–9, sim. M 166–9: George 1999: p. 199)

Despite his mother: Gilgamesh has divine blood in his veins but still he will die like other men. As Enlil himself puts it: 'I made your destiny a destiny of kingship, but I did not make it [a destiny] of eternal life' (*Death of Gilgamesh* N 1 v 13–15: George 1999, p. 203).

---

[52] I cite *The Death of Gilgamesh* from George 1999: 195–208, a composite version from various manuscripts, close to the edition of Cavigneaux and Al-Rawi 2000b. The translation in the ETCSL database presents the various manuscript fragments individually in sequence. The modified interpretation proposed by Veldhuis 2001 does not, so far as I can see, affect the points made in my discussion here.

[53] M52–8 and later repetitions at George 1999: 198. It has been argued that *Gilgamesh and Huwawa* in its full form included the episode of the journey to Ziusudra (cf. Chen 2013: 165–8, with George 2003: 1.97–8).

[54] The translation of the second line here is particularly doubtful (cf. Cavigneaux and Al-Rawi 2000b: p. 41).

Consolation, such as it is, is offered in two forms. The first is the special status he will enjoy in the Underworld:

> Be not in despair, be not heart-stricken,
> for you will be accounted one of the lesser gods,
> you will act as governor of the Netherworld,
> you will pass judgement, you will render verdicts.
>
> (M 120–3: George 1999: p. 201)

A privileged role awaits him: he will preside over the dead as a judge. The later fragments of the poem linger on the great works made for his tomb and funeral, and one of two surviving endings combines earlier parts of the dialogue to look forward to the perpetual extension of this commemoration:

> Men, as many as are given names,
> their (funerary) statues have been fashioned since days of old,
> and stationed in chapels in the temples of the gods:
> how their names are pronounced will never be forgotten!
> The goddess Aruru, the older sister of Enlil,
> for the sake of his name gave (men) offspring:
> their statues have been fashioned since days of old, and (their names still)
>   spoken in the land.   (M 298–304: George 1999: p. 207)

Although the dominant image here is of cultic statues in the temples, there is a suggestion that the continuation of the family line is what sustains it all – just as in *Gilgamesh, Enkidu and the Netherworld*, when Enkidu told how the honours and food-offerings made by one's living descendants bring solace to the dweller in the Underworld.

The epic *Atrahasis*

All this lore of human suffering and mortality is bound up with the fundamental event of the remote past: the Great Flood. As mentioned above from *The Death of Gilgamesh*, part of the early tradition about Gilgamesh was that he went on a journey to Ziusudra, the survivor of the Flood who escaped death. A version of Ziusudra's own narrative is partially preserved in Sumerian,[55] but it is found in more elaborate form as the poem *Atrahasis*. The Old Babylonian Version of this work is preserved in a manuscript dated

---

[55] For the Sumerian version see *LOAS*, pp. 212–15; Lambert and Millard 1969: 138–45. The surviving fragments begin with the creation of mankind, and there is no indication whether this version included the earlier episode of class warfare among the gods.

to the 1600s BCE,[56] and a somewhat later version is attested on tablets from a number of sites, including Ugarit[57] – particularly suggestive in view of the role of Ugarit as a possible site for mediation between Greek and Mesopotamian tradition. In the present context, however, the importance of *Atrahasis* is as a document of the disjuncture that was imposed between the lives and prospects of humans and those of the gods.

The starting point of *Atrahasis* lies in the deep background of mythical time, before humans came into existence. Social strife arises among the gods, because the more powerful Anunnaki – among them Anu, Enki/Ea and Enlil – have forced the lesser divinities (*Igigi*) to toil as their slaves, working in the fields and digging irrigation ditches.[58] The Igigi rebel and assail the palace of the great god Enlil, the overseer of their labours, threatening to depose him. The confrontation seems about to escalate; but the master gods take counsel, and Ea[59] proposes that new slaves should be made to bear the burden that has been carried by the Igigi:

> Ea made ready to speak,
> and said to the gods [his brethren],
> 'What do we denounce them for?
> Their forced labour was heavy, [their misery too much].
> Every day the earth was . . .
> The outcry [was loud, we could hear their clamour].
> There is [a task to be done],
>
> . . . . . .
>
> '[Mami, the birth-goddess], is present,
> let the mother-goddess create a human being,
> let man assume the drudgery of god.'
>
> (*Atrahasis OBV* I.174–97: Foster, *BTM*, p. 235)

[56] I cite *Atrahasis* from Foster, *BTM* 227–80, using the Old Babylonian Version wherever possible. In the standard edition by Lambert and Millard 1969, the main sequence of line numbers corresponds exactly to Foster's *OBV* text, and except where noted I can see no differences between the two translations that materially affect the interpretation offered here. The same applies to the translation by Dalley, *MFM* 1–38. The edition of the Sippar tablet by George and Al-Rawi 1996 contains much helpful commentary on the work as a whole. There is a useful review of scholarly debate on *Atrahasis* in Kvanvig 2011: 13–82.

[57] See Lambert and Millard 1969: 34, 131–3.

[58] The opposition between the two groups is ambiguous: it may be understood as a contrast between senior and junior (cf. Bottéro 1992 [1987]: 222), between celestial and chthonic, or (as argued by Lambert and Millard in their note on the passage, pp. 146–7) it may simply be between the seven major named deities of the pantheon and an indeterminate group of other deities.

[59] Later manuscripts have a passage in which these same words come from Anu rather than Ea, but it is not clear whether this is a variant version or a repetition – one god making the initial suggestion and the other repeating it (see Foster, *BTM*, p. 259 for *Atrahasis* Late Babylonian Version II 61ff., with Lambert and Millard 1969: 54).

Mami or Belet-ili, the birth-goddess of many names, mixes clay with the flesh and blood of a minor god who has been murdered, most likely understood as the leader of the rebellion;[60] a word-play or implied etymology perhaps associates the *ṭēmu* 'intelligence, cunning, mind' of this slain god with the *eṭemmu* 'spirit, ghost' that is now present in the mixture.[61] From this she takes fourteen pinches of moistened clay and brings about the birth of seven men and seven women. So the new race of human slaves is born; but trouble returns, because as their population grows they in turn annoy the gods and especially Enlil, just as in the earlier strife between Anunnaki and Igigi:

> [Twel]ve hundred years [had not gone by],
> [the land had grown numerous], the peoples had increased,
> the [land] was bellowing [like a bull].
> The god was disturbed with [their uproar],
> [Enlil heard] their clamour.
>
> (*Atrahasis* OBV I.353–9: Foster, *BTM*, p. 239)

Several times this happens, and each time the gods send an affliction to curb mankind: first plague, then drought, then famine. Each time Ea is sympathetic to the human plight, and his special favourite among them, the sage or king Atrahasis (corresponding to Ziusudra in the Sumerian version),[62] is given the resources to thwart the destruction. When the plague comes, Ea encourages him to respond by making the people suspend the regular sacrifices on which the gods depend for their sustenance;[63] when the drought comes, Atrahasis sacrifices to Adad the rain-god and induces him to relent and send moisture; Ea saves humanity from famine by an inundation of fish.[64] So each time the people survive and return to prosperity. Finally, it is decided that Enlil will send a flood to destroy the human race once and for all; but Ea secretly commands Atrahasis to build a survival vessel, here apparently a sealed cube in which he will descend into the waters over which

---

[60] On this suggestion see Lambert and Millard 1969: 153, note on line 223, with Foster, *BTM*, p. 236 n. 1; cf. discussion of the issue and subsequent controversy by Kvanvig 2011: 44–6.

[61] The reconstruction of the etymological play by Abusch 1998 remains doubtful, above all because it is not clear whether the word *ṭēmu* in line 223 refers to 'intelligence, mind' in general or to the 'plan, scheme, cunning' of the rebellion that he has led against the great gods.

[62] The Flood hero is not explicitly described as a king in the Old Babylonian *Atrahasis*, but this is clear in the earlier Sumerian accounts (Kvanvig 2011: 66–8, 99–106).

[63] For the same principle in the Babylonian *Epic of Creation* see Foster, *BTM*, p. 473, at *Enuma Elish* 5.115–17.

[64] Foster, *BTM*, p. 245 n. 1.

Ea presides.[65] When the flood comes, Nintu – another name or identity for the birth-goddess – weeps for the destruction of the people that she has brought to birth, railing against Anu for abandoning them:

> As mayflies[66] a watercourse, they have filled the sea.
> Like rafts they lie against the river meadow (?),
> like rafts capsized they lie against the bank.
> I saw and wept over them,
> I have exhausted my lamentation for them.
> > (*Atrahasis OBV* III.iv.6–11: Foster, *BTM*, pp. 250–1)

Dead mayflies in the waters: the same image recurs under shifting forms in what follows, as the gods' attitudes to human suffering become the focus of their dialogue.[67] When the flood subsides and Atrahasis has been saved, he offers sacrifice and the gods gather 'like flies'[68] around the offering (*OBV* III.v.35, *BTM*, p. 251); Nintu in her anger and dismay takes up beads in the shape of flies, possibly gifts to her from Anu himself, and declares that she will wear them around her neck in memory of what has happened:[69]

> Let [these] flies be jewelry around my neck,
> that I may remember it [every?] day [and forever?].
> > (*Atrahasis OBV* III.vi. 2–3: *BTM* p. 252)

The mother-goddess mourns for the miseries of mankind; but Enlil is furious, realising that someone has survived, and at Anu's prompting Ea reveals what he did for Atrahasis. Finally the gods in conference resolve the situation, with Ea collaborating alongside Enlil. Mankind is allowed to survive, but with the certainty that population growth will be stayed because some women will not reproduce at all, and in addition the birth-goddess will ensure that there are miscarriages, stillbirths and other evils in her area of power to keep the population down:

> Let there be (also) among the people the (she-)demon,
> let her snatch the baby from the lap of her who bore it.
> > (*Atrahasis OBV* III.vii.1–5: *BTM*, p. 253)

---

[65] The familiar Biblical term 'ark' masks the abiding question over the shape and nature of the vessel (see esp. *Atrahasis OBV* III.i.25–33): this issue is beyond the scope of the present discussion.

[66] Foster has 'dragonflies' here. However, George 2012 has shown that the word translated as 'dragonfly' (*kulīlu*) properly refers to a smaller insect and should better be translated 'mayfly' or simply 'fly'.

[67] On the imagery of the flies here, I draw on George's discussion of the corresponding passage of *Gilgamesh* (see pp. 102–104 below). See also Kvanvig 2011: 63–4.

[68] The word for 'fly' in these latter two instances is different, *zubbu/subbu*.

[69] Lambert and Millard 1969: 163–4.

The 'she-demon' here (*pašittu*) is identified with Lamaštu, the personification of stillbirth and the destruction of the newborn.[70] Such is the gods' response to the problem of humanity: only by the imposition of sickness and suffering can our rebellious instincts be kept in check.

Uta-napishti and wisdom literature

Rising over all this, however, is the fate of Atrahasis himself, 'All-wise': in the end Enlil grants him a special gift of immortality, and he will live his unending life far away at the ends of the earth.[71] He has many names: Sumerian Ziusudra 'The far distant one', Akkadian Uta-napishti 'He who found life', Hittite Ullu, Hebrew Noah;[72] in later times he would be identified with Deucalion, the survivor of the flood that ends the Silver Age in Greek mythography. He has a close association with the themes and concerns of the Mesopotamian texts that are loosely grouped together as 'wisdom literature'.[73] Indeed, one of the major Sumerian texts of this kind, *The Wisdom of Shuruppak*, was presented in the Old Babylonian period as a body of wisdom handed down to Ziusudra by his father.[74] These texts, whose generic name simply reflects their affinity with the 'wisdom' books of the Hebrew Bible,[75] were a key part of the curriculum of scribal training,[76] and are well attested from the scribal schools of the Old Babylonian period. Many of them are found translated and disseminated in later centuries as far west as Emra in Syria, Ugarit on the Mediterranean coast and the Hittite centre of Hattusa.[77]

---

[70] Wiggermann 2000.

[71] Older translations of *Atrahasis* lacks this final episode, which until recently was known only from the Sumerian Flood text, the *Epic of Gilgamesh* (Tablet XI, see Ch. 4 below), and the secondary account transmitted in Greek from the *Babyloniaca* of Berossos (Lang 2013; Haubold 2013: 157–63). However, the more recently published New York fragment of *Atrahasis* preserves an account of Enlil escorting the sage and his wife out of the ark, much as in the *Gilgamesh* version. In the *Atrahasis* fragment and the *Gilgamesh* account, Enlil touches their foreheads in a gesture of blessing or as if freeing slaves. (See W. G. Lambert at Spar and Lambert 2005: 195–201, translation at 199–200; George 2003: 2.892–3, note on line 200.)

[72] On these names and traditions see George 2003: 1.152–5, with the (inevitably speculative) reconstruction of the historical development by Chen 2013, esp. ch. 3.

[73] The key text collections are Lambert 1960, Alster 1997 and especially Alster 2005a, with the extremely useful editions and study, focussed on the later development and dissemination of the tradition, by Cohen 2013.

[74] For full exposition of the text see Alster 2005a, 56–102; translated text, Alster 2005a, 284–91. Chen (2013: 8–9 and ch. 3 *passim*) argues that the wisdom tradition represented by this text was drawn into the traditions of the Flood hero in the Old Babylonian period.

[75] Cohen 2013: 7–21.   [76] Veldhuis 2000.

[77] On the dissemination of these texts see Alster 2005a: 18–30; Cohen 2013: 3–77.

Broadly, there are two distinct discourses in the wisdom corpus: on the one hand practical, concrete advice about down-to-earth details of good practice, and on the other hand a strain of pessimistic, even nihilistic declarations about the limitations of human endeavour and the inevitability of death. On the pessimistic side, the central message is summed up in the Akkadian language in *Ludlul bēl nēmeqi, The Poem of the Righteous Sufferer*:

> He who was alive yesterday is dead today;
> for a minute he was dejected, now he is exuberant.
> One moment people are singing in exultation,
> another they groan like professional mourners.
> Their condition changes like opening and shutting (the legs).
> When starving they become like corpses,
> when replete they vie with the gods.
> In prosperity they talk of scaling heaven,
> in adversity they complain of going down to hell.[78]

The proverbial statements add up to a deeper and more general lesson. Life is unstable; prosperity does not last, death awaits; people forget this too easily. One classic statement of the more abstract or purist level of this wisdom is the text known as *Níŋ-nam*, 'Nothing is of value', which is attested in many languages on the basis of the original Sumerian version:[79]

> Nothing is of value, but life itself should be sweet-tasting.
> Whenever a man does not own some piece of property, that man owns
>   some property.
> . . . .of mankind . . .
> . . . ..
> (Even) the tallest one cannot reach to the sky;
> (even) the broadest one cannot go down to the Netherworld.
> (Even) the strongest one cannot [stretch himself] on Earth.
> The good life, let it be defiled in joy!
> Let the 'race' be spent in joy!
> A man's good house is the house in which he has to live!

The first line, shared with the *Instructions of Shuruppak,* encapsulates the theme that is expounded in what follows: the futility of human endeavour and the instability of prosperity prompt the need to take comfort in ordinary everyday things. The second line sums up another paradox:

---

[78] Lambert 1960: 41. See also Foster, *BTM*, pp. 392–409, where these lines appear with a slightly different translation at p. 392, Tablet II 39–47.

[79] See Alster 2005a: 266–87. I cite from Alster's Version A, from Nippur (pp. 270–1).

wealth is illusory, simplicity is wisdom, 'poverty is really riches'.[80] The resolution of the problem is the resigned acceptance of one's own limitations, 'the house in which he has to live'.

The extraordinary text *Shima Milka*, or *The Instructions of Shupe-Ameli*, is framed as a dialogue between a father and a son.[81] The father's advice is the old simple proverbs – work with friends, avoid bad company, do not desire other men's wives, do not jump over a wide canal – but the son replies in terms of a more austere wisdom:

> My father, you built a house,
> you elevated high the door; sixty cubits is the width of your (house).
> But what have you achieved?
> Just as much as [your] house's loft is full so too its storage room is full of grain.
> But (upon) the day of your death (only) nine bread portions of offerings
>   will be counted and placed at your head . . .
> Few are the days in which we eat (our) bread, but many are the days in
>   which our teeth will be idle,
> few are the days in which we look at the Sun, but many will be the days in
>   which we will sit in the shadows.
>   (*Shima Milka* 133'–137', 140'–141')[82]

The pessimism of certain death is the beginning of a sequence of thought that leads to the necessity of accepting and enjoying the small consolations of life while they last.

As we will see in the next chapter, the Babylonian *Epic of Gilgamesh* follows a comparable sequence on an infinitely larger scale. Its narrative enacts a movement from the half-divine self-projection of the king, via his confrontation with the certainty of death, to the point where he is presented with the simpler wisdom that comes of accepting human limitations and allowing them to guide one's life. The immortalised Uta-napishti will be the mouthpiece of this wisdom, framed as a response to the inadequacy of the heroic quest for a name that lasts forever.

---

[80] Alster's formulation (2005a: p. 271, note at line 1).
[81] See Cohen 2013: 81–128; also Foster, *BTM*, pp. 416–20, and discussion by Sallaberger (2010), emphasising the text's implicit rejection of (the practical strand in) the Sumerian wisdom literature tradition.
[82] Translation from Cohen 2013: 99.

3 | Gilgamesh and glory

In contrast to later Western traditions that are classed as heroic epic, great deeds done in battle are *not* the central focus of the early cuneiform literature that we are studying. Sure enough, excellence in battle is one of the characteristic glories of the great king, and this finds its place (for example) in the lamentation in *The Death of Gilgamesh*:

> The great wild bull is lying down, never to rise again,
> the lord Gilgamesh is lying down, never to rise again,
> he who was perfect *in combat* is lying down, never to rise again,
> the warrior girt with a shoulder-belt is lying down, never to rise again,
> he who diminished the wicked is lying down, never to rise again . . .
>
> (*Death of Gilgamesh* M 1–6: George 1999: 197)

Paradoxically, however, among the narrative texts the battlefield is seldom the place where the central issues are explored and put to the test:[1] the real arena of action is within the protagonist or between him and the gods.

Lugalbanda and the gods

This principle is well exemplified in the narratives concerned with Lugalbanda, the father of Shulgi and Gilgamesh.[2] *Lugalbanda in the Wilderness* (also known as *Lugalbanda in the Mountain Cave*)[3] begins in military mode, with Enmerkar the king declaring war against Aratta and mustering his army:

> The levy of Unug marched out with the all-wise king;
> the levy of Kulab followed Enmerkar.
> The levy of Unug was a flood;

---

[1] Even in *Gilgamesh and Akka*, which is concerned with siege warfare, the plot is more concerned with negotiations than combat (George 1999: 143–8).

[2] *Lugalbanda in the Wilderness* and *The Return of Lugalbanda* are best seen as successive episodes of a single narrative sequence.

[3] The name *Lugalbanda in Hurrumkurra* is also used. See Vanstiphout 2003: 99–131; Black 1998: 176–84 and *passim*; useful discussions by Alster 1990, 2005b.

> the levy of Kulab was a storm cloud.
> Hugging the earth like a heavy fog
> their thick dust reached to heaven.
>   (*Lugalbanda in the Wilderness* 26–31, Vanstiphout 2003: 104–7)

In the host march seven champions, who are brothers; Lugalbanda follows them at the rear. The narrative seems to be leading towards battle, but instead Lugalbanda is taken ill on the march and is left in a mountain cave to live or die; his brothers promise that after the war they will return to bring him home or, if he has died in his sickness, to bury him. In the cave, Lugalbanda struggles against fever and death; he prays in his agony to Utu the sun-god, Inana the great goddess, and Suen (= Akkadian Sin) the moon-god, and they grant him their help. Emerging from the cave, Lugalbanda does great deeds in the wilderness – he finds water, makes fire and bakes bread, and brings down wild animals for food. After he has honoured the gods with due sacrifice, there follows a cosmic battle (poorly preserved)[4] after which he is exalted with divine favour:

> From that time, Utu, the . . . of Enlil
> granted to him (Lugalbanda) the great office of herald of heaven,
> and he added the . . . jurisdiction over all the countries.
>   (*Lugalbanda in the Wilderness* 429–31, Vanstiphout 2003: 126–7)

Lugalbanda has become almost an equal of the gods, and (by implication) he is now destined for kingship. In the sequel, *The Return of Lugalbanda*, he returns to the war to help Enmerkar with Inana's support; even there, however, the siege of Aratta is described only for a few lines,[5] and Lugalbanda overcomes Aratta not by fighting but by using a magical fish granted to him by Inana. The essential theme is the relationship between the king, gods and people, and the challenge of mortality that attends the king's movement to success and divine status. The same bundle of themes will be the centrepoint of the development of the epics concerned with his son Gilgamesh.

Development and dissemination of the Gilgamesh epic

From the beginnings represented by the Sumerian poems on Gilgamesh, a single large-scale narrative was gradually developed in the course of

---

[4] For a review of the difficulties of interpretation, see Alster 2005b.
[5] *The Return of Lugalbanda* 254–65, at Vanstiphout 2003: 156–7.

the second millennium BCE.[6] It is possible – even likely – that oral song and storytelling drove much of the development,[7] but it is also certain that a major driver was the transmission of narratives in Sumerian and other languages through the scribal schools. It is agreed that there were two decisive stages in the development of an integrated Gilgamesh narrative, and that both of these show signs of the influence of artistic design rather than merely editorial compilation. The first of these stages was reached with what is known as the Old Babylonian Version, perhaps *c.* 1700 BCE. After a period of complex and less clearly delineated stages, yielding the Middle Babylonian texts, there was further expansion and development into what is now known as the Standard Babylonian Version of the *Epic of Gilgamesh*.[8] The ancients themselves ascribed this latter work to a single master intellect: 'from the mouth of Sîn-lēqi-unninni'.[9] At some stage in the later period of development, possibly the period in which Sîn-lēqi-unninni worked, there was a further (and comparatively inorganic) addition of the Twelfth Tablet, a direct prose translation of part of the Sumerian poem *Gilgamesh, Enkidu and the Netherworld*. The epic is artistically complete without this addition, and the rationale behind its inclusion remains obscure,[10] although it will turn out to be vital to our argument as it develops.

---

[6] For an overview see George 2003: 1.22–33 and his summary accounts, George 2007c and 2010a. Sallaberger 2008 is largely consistent with George; cf. also the foundational earlier work of Tigay 1982. In my discussion I am concerned principally with the Standard Babylonian Version, and I cite the Old and Middle Babylonian tablets only when they provide corroborating evidence for passages for which the evidence in the Standard Version is fragmentary, or where they offer unique evidence for motifs that are important for the Greek reception. I follow George's wide-ranging and thematically inclusive analysis, and try to avoid dependence on one or other limiting hypothesis on the developing *meaning* of the epic (cf. e.g. Foster 1987; Abusch 2001).

[7] For example, Wasserman argues (2011: 4–5, cf. George 2003: 1.143–4) that references to Gilgamesh in Old Babylonian incantations for babies – 'lullaby' texts – bear witness to oral circulation of a kind normally lost from the scribal record. As George (2003: 1.7) mentions, there is a suggestion of a possible mode of oral transmission within the textual tradition itself: in *Gilgamesh and the Bull of Heaven*, his musician Lugalgabagal plays and sings while Gilgamesh drinks beer (see further George 2010b: 113–14), and similarly the song of the same musician Lugalgabagal plays a pivotal role in the plot of the *Tale of Gudam* (Gadotti 2006). It is tempting to see this as a reference to *heroic* song in courtly circles. However, as with the equivalent lore in Homer, there is no way of telling whether this reflects social realities or a fictive back-projection by the makers of the very texts that we have before us.

[8] The text presented in George 2003 is supplemented by evidence from tablets subsequently published with episodes corresponding to Tablets I and V (George 2007a, Al-Rawi and George 2014). An extremely helpful supplement to George's exposition is the extended review by Wasserman 2011, especially the diagram facing p. 2.

[9] George 2003: 1.28.

[10] Vulpe 1994 presents a strong, but necessarily speculative, argument for seeing the Twelfth Tablet as 'a necessary and elegant conclusion'. See further below, pp. 108–110, 289–292.

In the monumental epic, the themes that we have seen in the various Sumerian poems are melded into a vastly more complex and many-faceted unity. The distribution of manuscripts shows that the text achieved canonical status: most date from the seventh century BCE or later, but they must bear witness to a long-established process of codification, study and recopying.[11] Along with numerous fragments from such a wide range of cities as Babylon, Borsippa, Nimrud, Ashur and Sultantepe, and even from Gilgamesh's own city of Warka (Uruk), there are substantial remains of several separate sets of tablets from the royal collection of Ashurbanipal at Nineveh, and these still represent the largest group of witnesses to the epic.[12] Recent work has shown that this archive was the product of a systematic campaign of collection and compilation from sources in pre-existing libraries attached to temples and other scribal centres: it represents, in effect, the codification under Assyrian royal power of the Babylonian textual canon.

Vitally, however, the epic was not merely an archived possession of kings and temple officials. The lore of Gilgamesh was disseminated right across south-western Asia, and the many fragments that survive are no doubt only a small trace of the original spread. Crucially for the comparison with Homer, several fragments in Akkadian have been found at Ugarit,[13] which was to be a major point of contact between the worlds of Mesopotamia and the Greek Aegean up to time of destruction *c.* 1200 BCE, and whose wider region continued in that role into the time when its people were known to the historical Greeks as Phoenicians (above, pp. 16–27). Although little is known of the narrative culture of Levantine languages in this period, it is significant that artistic survivals from the eastern fringe of the Mediterranean in this period include many scenes that invite identification with the two major combats of the epic, those with Humbaba and the Bull of Heaven.[14] From the Hittite empire, whose capital at Hattusa has yielded textual archives in international languages as well as Hittite itself, there is evidence for multiple channels of reception. In Akkadian from this horizon there are three fragments from the Middle Babylonian stage, of which two (*Boğ 1*, *Boğ 2*) differ from each other linguistically and are unlikely to be derived from a single exemplar (the third, *Boğ 3*, is too slight for any

---

[11] George 2003: 1.379–91.   [12] Cf. p. 40 above.

[13] For edition and translation of the Ugarit fragment (now listed as *MB Ug 1*) see George 2007a. In George's view the four pieces all come from the same recension of the epic, one that is closely related both to the Middle Babylonian and the Standard Babylonian Version but distinct from either (George 2007a: 253–4).

[14] Ornan 2010; cf. Lambert 2010.

inferences to be drawn).[15] Alongside the Hittite-language prose paraphrase of the entire story, known as the *Song of Gilgamesh*,[16] parts of which will be considered in detail below, there are also fragments in Hurrian.[17] When the Hittite work calls itself a 'song', this is in keeping with Hittite generic convention and does not necessarily indicate that an oral version has been transcribed;[18] at the same time, however, there can be no doubt that the story of Gilgamesh was known, *as a story*, in many forms in central Anatolia in that period. Variations between the Hurrian fragments – as, for example, in the spelling of proper names – have encouraged the hypothesis that they belong to at least three separate recensions or 'textualisations'. Although the Humbaba episode looms largest across the fragments surviving from the Hittite sites, there is evidence that Hurrian versions as well as the Hittite prose summary also included the journey to Ziusudra/Uta-napishti (under his name of Ullu[19]), corresponding to the story-line of the final tablets of the Standard Babylonian Version.

The question remains open as to how much thematic and poetic unity was maintained through the process of diffusion, and it would be unnecessarily limiting to begin this enquiry with a fixed hypothesis as to how much was due to professional scribes and how much to oral exchange between poets and singers or, indeed, more casual retellings in less artistic forms. In what follows I will present a reading of the Standard Babylonian Version, nuanced in the light of the model of intertextuality and reception outlined in the Introduction. It is not my aim to reconstruct the discourses that drove its composition and original reception – that task belongs to the specialist cuneiform scholars, on whose work I lean throughout – but instead to suggest how the poem in this or a similar recension might have been heard (or read, or encountered at second hand, or otherwise

---

[15] George 2003, 1.306–26.

[16] The surviving texts of the Hittite paraphrase are collected in an authoritative translation by Beckman 2001.

[17] The Hurrian fragments are discussed in detail by Bachvarova 2016: 72–6, arguing speculatively for the survival there of a version of the story in which Gilgamesh spared Humbaba.

[18] For the latest study of the Anatolian reception see Bachvarova 2016: 54–77. Bachvarova's argument is often hard to pin down, because she routinely posits diversity of oral transmission to explain any or all variations between surviving written versions of a given text (see esp. 54–77). Beckman (2003: 45) shows convincingly that the prose *Song of Gilgamesh* calls itself a 'song' in keeping with Hittite generic convention (compare e.g. the 'Song of Kumarbi'), and should not be regarded as a direct reflection of an oral tradition. On the formulaic nature of the 'Let me praise . . .' opening see also Metcalf 2015: 102–3.

[19] Hittite *Ullu* is a loan-translation with the meaning 'the distant one' (George 2003: 1.25; Beckman 2001: 165; Bachvarova 2016: 72–6).

assimilated) somewhere between south-western Asia, the Aegean Sea and mainland Greece up to the time when the Homeric creation came together in the early centuries of the first millennium BCE.

The ruler between human and divine

The poem opens with the praise of Gilgamesh for the wisdom that he achieved on his journey to the immortalised survivor of the Flood, whom we met in the previous chapters as Ziusudra and Atrahasis:

> He who saw the Deep, the country's foundation,
> who knew the proper ways, was wise in everything!
> Gilgamesh, who saw the Deep, the foundation of the country,
> who knew the proper ways, was wise in everything!
> He explored everywhere the seats of power,
> knew of everything the sum of wisdom.
> He saw what was secret, discovered what was hidden,
> brought back a tale of before the Deluge.   (I 1–8)[20]

In the Sumerian texts that mention this journey, what Gilgamesh learnt seems to centre on the correct mode of sacrificing to the gods, a skill that had vanished with the Flood itself.[21] This achievement continues to be specified in the Standard Babylonian Version – he 'established the proper rites for the human race' (I 44)[22] – but it seems to become something more general and more profound: the achievement of the one 'who saw the Deep' was to bring back wisdom, a more basic or intangible truth, keyed to the deep waters over which Ea presides.[23] Just what that truth was will become the focus of the journey's unexpected conclusion.

For the moment, however, this theme looms less prominently than the praises of the king, whose glory presides over the city. The city in antiquity is not the necessary evil that it has become in our world, a place of pollution and overcrowding: rather it is where vitality and

---

[20] The text printed here is George's (2012: 228–9) revised translation of the opening, incorporating supplements from the recently discovered Ugarit tablet *MB Ug 1* (George 2007a: 241).

[21] Recalled in *The Death of Gilgamesh* (M 57ff.: George 1999: 198–9).

[22] The theme may also have been recalled in a now poorly-preserved part of *SBV* Tablet X (George 2003: 1.505), and it is noteworthy that Uta-napishti's account of the Flood includes a description of the sacrifices that he instituted at its end (*SBV* XI 156–63).

[23] On *naqbu* here, indeterminately 'the deep, the cosmic waters' or 'the totality (of wisdom)', see George 2003: 1.444–5.

abundance are concentrated.[24] The hero's achievement is summed up in
the sight of the walls of Uruk themselves, which he built:

> He came a far road, was weary but at peace;
> all his labours were set on a tablet of stone.
> He had the rampart built of Uruk-the-Sheepfold,
> of holy Eanna, the sacred storehouse.
> See its wall like a strand of wool,
> view its parapet that none could copy!   (I 9–14)[25]

It is here that the imagined audience of the poem is to lift up a tablet of lapis
lazuli and read of his glories: this can perhaps be heard as a reflexive
allusion to the epic itself, in which those glories will now be recounted.[26]
The notion that the king's achievements are physically represented in the
city walls is paralleled in the *Song of Bazi*, a poem of praise to another
divinized king from the remote past – whose death, coincidentally or
otherwise, we will also see remembered alongside that of Gilgamesh in
wisdom poetry.[27] Then his greatness is recounted in a paean of praise,
derived from the Old Babylonian sources and looking back ultimately to
the Sumerian texts.[28] He was a warlord, shielding his men and leading their
assault:

> A mighty bank, the protection of his troops,
> a violent flood-wave that smashes a stone wall!   (*SBV* I 33–34)

Like Shulgi, he asserted order over chaos, opening the mountain
passes and digging wells for fresh water, just as he restored the cult
places and their rituals. At the same time as being the 'violent flood-
wave' in wars against his people's enemies, he is master of order and
pattern in his own city, and this in turn is an image of the divine
ordinances that guarantee and embody the order of the world as
a whole. The tension between these two excellences will loom larger
as the narrative proceeds.

---

[24] This principle is explored by Van de Mieroop 1997: ch. 3. For the corresponding idea in the
early Homeric depiction of the city, see Scully 1990.
[25] Text from George 2012: 229.
[26] A similar motif is used in the *Cuthean Legend of Naram-Sin*, where the relevant lines are
substantially preserved in the Late Assyrian Version (Foster, *BTM*, p. 348: see Foster 2007:
16–17).
[27] For the *Song of Bazi* see below, pp. 107–108, and for Bazi and Gilgamesh in the *Poem of Early
Rulers* see p. 86.
[28] Compare esp. the opening lines of *Gilgamesh and the Bull of Heaven* (George 1999: 169) and the
opening and closing of *The Death of Gilgamesh* (George 1999: pp. 197, 208).

Gilgamesh is human, but not in the way that we lesser mortals of later times are human. There is divinity in his parentage; he is the 'wild bull' of his father Lugalbanda and the calf of his mother Ninsun, the Wild Cow Goddess, and its proportion is precisely defined: 'two thirds of him god but a third of him human' (*SBV* I 48). This image of an ambiguous relationship between mortality and immortality locates Gilgamesh at a pivotal moment in the sequence of cosmic history. The *Sumerian King-List* and subsequent texts in the same genre record the gradual shortening of the lives of the kings since primordial times,[29] and this progressive loss of vitality is mirrored in the decline of the human race in general. There is an instructive parallel in the incantation text *Bīt mēseri* – attested in tablets of Neo-Assyrian date, but drawing on older traditions – which gives a list of the succession of divine primeval sages (*apkallu*), who were said to have transmitted and protected the ordinances of cosmic order and harmony.[30] They are identified with the protective deities of whom images are to be placed in the house to ward off demonic attacks, and who are also represented on a more elaborate scale among the human–beast hybrid figures carved in relief in the royal palaces of the Neo-Assyrian period.[31] The first seven of these sages are divine beings, named as carp-fish 'born in the river'; they are followed by four sages 'of human descent', of whom the last, Lu-Nanna, is described as 'two-thirds *apkallu*'[32] – in other words he is at an intermediate point between the divine sages of ancient times and the purely human scholars thereafter, in the same way as Gilgamesh is two-thirds god and one-third human. Lu-Nanna 'expelled a dragon from the temple of Ishtar and Shulgi', and the chronicles also specify that he lived at the same time as Shulgi – who, as we have seen, is represented as calling himself the brother of Gilgamesh.[33]

The ruler as sexual tyrant

If the near-divine vitality of Gilgamesh makes him a potent leader of men and a defender of civilisation, in another sense this very abundance of energy makes him dangerous to human society. This is the pivot on which

---

[29] Glassner 2004: 3–33, with Kvanvig 2011: 83–105.

[30] The text was first published in partial form by Reiner 1961, then with evidence from further tablets by Borger 1974; see further Wiggermann 1992: 105–18, and Borger 1994 with analysis updated from Borger 1974 but a less full presentation of the text; cf. Kvanvig 2011: 107–58.

[31] Ataç 2010.   [32] *Bīt mēseri*, Tablet III, 26–9. See Borger 1994: 230–31; Kvanvig 2011: 108–9.

[33] Glassner 2004: 288–9.

the action now turns. After the opening eulogy, the narrative of the first tablet is set in motion by a more sinister expression of his kingly power, for which the Ugarit tablet provides a startling image, emerging out of context among the opening images of his glorious achievements:

> Gilgamesh lets no young bride go free to her husband,
>> he is their wild bull, they are his cows. (*MB Ug 1* 12–13, George 2007a: p. 241)

The problem comes into clearer focus as the people's complaints grow: he fights his companions endlessly, he harries the young men and 'lets no son go free to his father'; he keeps men busy through labour service or his constant demands for wrestling contests; and he comes between the young women and their mothers and also, more ominously, their husbands (*SBV* I 76).[34] The form taken by this bullying is not made explicit here, and is perhaps deliberately left doubtful. However, a well-preserved section in one of the Old Babylonian texts[35] states clearly that he is claiming the right to have sex with each marriageable girl before she can be united with her husband, and sexual aggression was part of his story even in the Sumerian *Gilgamesh and the Bull of Heaven.*[36]

The same kind of sexually dominating behaviour would become a dark rumour in medieval traditions about the self-assertion of lords over their underlings – *ius primae noctis* in legal Latin, *droit de cuissage* or *droit de seigneur* in French.[37] As we will see in a later chapter, in the *Iliad* too a related problem of the overlord's sexual appropriations sparks off the conflict in the Greek camp. In its conflation of social dominance with privileged access to females, Gilgamesh's behaviour is an expression of the violent, even beast-like extremes to which male power and self-assertion can extend.[38] As such (though this is never stated in so many words) it expresses the uncomfortable truth that heroic energy is dangerous to social order at the very same time as defending and guaranteeing that order – the theme that will be brought into still clearer focus in the *Iliad.*

---

[34] The restoration *muti-ša* 'their husbands', conjectural in George's 2003 edition, is confirmed by the Ugarit tablet (George 2007a, at *MB Ug 1*, line 12), although the line appears there at an earlier point in the passage.

[35] See the Pennsylvania tablet, *OB II* 154–63, with George's note (2003: 1.187–8, cf. 448–9).

[36] George 2003: 1.7, citing Cavigneaux and Al-Rawi 1993: 101–3. On the developing image of Gilgamesh's sexual tyranny between the Sumerian texts and the Standard Babylonian Version, see further Cooper 2002.

[37] Boureau 1998.　　[38] This strategy for interpreting the *Iliad* is explored by Gottschall 2008.

The energy of the 'wild bull' is surging unchecked, and the people suffer. They complain to the great goddess Ishtar,[39] and the gods respond by means that may at first seem strangely indirect: at the prompting of Anu[40] they make a counterpart for him, one who will ultimately become his companion and '*equal to the storm* of his heart' (*SBV* I 97).[41] This is Enkidu, who is made first to live wild among the beasts of the wilderness but is tamed through his sexual initiation with Shamhat (the translators' 'harlot'), a woman whose professional sexual agency is probably to be understood in terms of membership of the group of women consecrated to one of the great goddesses, perhaps Ninsun herself.[42] He learns of Gilgamesh's tyranny; he goes to the city to face him down, barring his entry to a house in which there is a new bride; they fight and, his anger subdued by the combat, Gilgamesh becomes firm friends with Enkidu.[43]

If the behaviour of Gilgamesh and Enkidu reminds the modern reader of adolescent youths, this is perhaps more than a trivial throwaway thought: there may be a sense in which they are moving through changes modelled on the movement of a man from youth to maturity. On an alternative or complementary level, their relationship can be understood in terms of physical sexuality, though this becomes fully explicit only once, in the Twelfth Tablet appended to the epic at a late stage of its development (see below).[44] Wherever we locate the episode of the initial encounter

[39] The name of the god appealed to is not preserved here in the Standard Babylonian Version. George proposed Anu in his supplements (at *SBV* I 80, 93), but his subsequent edition of the Ugarit tablet names Ishtar as the deity who hears the people's complaint (George 2007a, *MB Ug 1*, line 14).

[40] The idea may be understood as coming originally from another god, possibly Ea as George (2003: 2.788, on line 96) suggests. One manuscript at line 100 ascribes the idea to Enlil (George 2003: 1.545 n. 14), which may be significant in view of Enlil's role later in the narrative, when the two heroes kill his son Humbaba.

[41] One unusual tablet preserves a version of the coming of Enkidu in which the names of Gilgamesh and Enkidu have been replaced, respectively, by Sîn the moon-god and Ea, suggesting perhaps that the story has been reinterpreted in terms of a cosmological allegory (George 2007b). This bears comparison with the lines of the Standard Babylonian Version in which Ninsun predicts that Gilgamesh will travel the sky (*SBV* III.102–3, discussed below, n. 53). So far as I can see, however, none of the materials unique to this tablet are relevant to the present discussion.

[42] The usual translation 'harlot' for Akkadian *ḫarīmtu* is potentially misleading. Although the word can refer to prostitution as a profession and as such can be used insultingly (for examples see *CAD* s.v.), it is also used for other classes of women whose lives are independent of men, including the consecrated sex-workers attached to the temples of the great goddesses, including that of Ninsun herself at Uruk (*SBV* III.42 with George 2003: 1.148). Cf. Steele 2007: 305–7.

[43] Most of this section is missing from the Standard Babylonian Version and is supplied from the Pennsylvania tablet.

[44] There are three key passages for this question. First, in Tablet I the symbols of Enkidu's coming that appear in Gilgamesh's dreams seem to be erotically charged: for discussion of the evidence

between the pair in emotional terms, its import in the narrative is clear: Gilgamesh is no longer alone in the expression of his energies. In a sense, the gods have responded to a weakness inherent in the notion that the king should be supreme and unrivalled (*SBV* I 45–6, sim. I 82–7, 95–8, etc.): if his supremacy is unchecked and unmediated, his forcefulness tends towards tyranny. Friendship, perhaps even love, is the instrument the gods use to temper the king's ebullience.[45]

The assault on Humbaba: triumph and peril

In response (it seems) to Enkidu's misery at Gilgamesh's mother's disdain at his uncouth appearance, the two decide to go to the cedar forest to attack its guardian. This episode draws closely on the Sumerian *Gilgamesh and Huwawa* discussed in Chapter 2: but the context is very different, above all because Enkidu was a mere slave in the Sumerian version, but now he is bonded with Gilgamesh as an equal, in companionship and esteem if not in social status.[46] When it becomes clear that Gilgamesh needs Enkidu's help to succeed, Ninsun welcomes him into the community of her temple, and declares him her adoptive son and thus, implicitly or explicitly, Gilgamesh's adoptive brother (*SBV* III 116–28).[47]

Fundamentally, then, it is as a pair bonded together that the two set out to win glory, through exploits that draw them away from the confines of the city and into the wider world beyond. In the discussion that follows, many of the details will inevitably be similar to those that have already been traced in the Sumerian texts examined in Chapter 2; but there are subtle differences, making it important that we trace the development of the story in the Standard Babylonian Version carefully on its own terms.

---

see George 2003: 1.452–4. Second, when Gilgamesh in his mourning for Enkidu veils his face, the simile 'like a bride (*kīma kallati*)' is used (*SBV* VIII.59). The third is in the Twelfth Tablet, when the phantom of Enkidu refers to 'the penis that you touched' (*SBV* XII.96). As noted elsewhere (p. 216), this replaces a reference to *heterosexual* intimacies in the Sumerian forerunner text, suggesting that the relationship between the two friends became more sexualised in the later stages of the tradition. For varying interpretations of the relationship between the Sumerian and Akkadian texts on the issue of the sexuality of the friendship, see Abusch 2001; Cooper 2002; Nissinen 2010; and cf. Halperin 1990, associating the friendship with that between Achilles and Patroclus.

[45] See further Haubold 2015: 248–50.

[46] This theme is already present in the variant text of the Sumerian *Gilgamesh, Enkidu and the Netherworld* in the fragments from Meturan (George 1999: p. 186 at Mt 1 22; Cavigneaux and Al-Rawi 2000a: 4–5).

[47] The phrase 'in brotherhood' (*ana aḫḫūti*) at *SBV* III.128 is conjectural.

Humbaba, guardian of the cedar forest in the far west, on the mountains of the land that we call Lebanon,[48] is a monstrous or demonic being, a terror to men, but is also a divinely sanctioned protector of the forest. Such ambiguity is typical of the lesser divine beings in Mesopotamian thought: a general comparison can be made, for example, with a relatively late newcomer to the array of divinities, Pazuzu the wind-demon, who is a being of terror but is also invoked to ward off evil.[49] With his ominous appearance – his bizarre face, with coiled patterns like entrails, figured as an evil sign in divination – and the supernatural weapons known as his 'auras' or 'terrors', which can also be reified as his cedar trees or anthropomorphically as his sons,[50] Humbaba is an enemy beyond mortal strength: 'His voice is the Deluge, his speech is fire, his breath is death' (*SBV* II 221–2, etc.).

Why do they decide to make the long journey to attack him? The surviving evidence suggests that, despite the more complex dramatisation, the motivation is essentially the same as in the forerunner of this episode, the Sumerian *Gilgamesh and Huwawa* (see pp. 44–48 above). The key lines in which he first explains the plan are missing from the Standard Babylonian Version, but references later in the text confirm that the guiding purpose is that victory over such an enemy will be enough to guarantee unending prestige – 'a name [for] future [*time*]' (*SBV* IV 248) – for them as a pair and for Gilgamesh in particular.[51] In the Old Babylonian version found in the Yale tablet, he makes the same declaration to the assembled people of Uruk:

> I will conquer him in the Forest of Cedar,
> that Uruk's offshoot is mighty I will have the land learn.
> Let me start work and chop down the cedar,
> a name that is eternal I will establish for ever!
>
> (*OB III* 184–8, George 2003: 1.203)

---

[48] On the location see George 2003: 1.20, 93–4.

[49] Pazuzu is described as 'king of the evil wind demons' in the inscription on his famous statuette in the Louvre, Paris; but his image was used for its apotropaic power of driving *away* the pestilential winds, especially the west wind. See Black and Green 1992: 147–9; Wiggermann 2007.

[50] The weapons are various called *melemmū* 'auras', *pulḥiātu* 'terrors', *namrirrū* 'radiant beams' (George 2003: 1.144 with n. 24; Al-Rawi and George 2014: 74–5; Fleming and Milstein 2010: 56–8).

[51] There are indications in the text that Enkidu knew Humbaba in the wild days of his youth (see esp. *SBV* V 89). Among the older versions this is explicit in the Yale fragment (*OB III* 106–7, George 2003: 1.198–9) and the Ugarit fragment *MB Ug 2* (George 2007a, translation at p. 252: 'When Enkidu lay asleep with his animals . . . '). The new fragment from Suleimaniyah has fragmentary lines in which Humbaba may be referring to the same thing (Al-Rawi and George 2014: p. 79, lines 61–72, with their commentary). However, there is no indication that past dealings between the two play any part in motivating the expedition to seek combat with Humbaba.

Yet there is a pessimistic twist behind this ambition. Enkidu, voicing the warnings of caution, tries to dissuade Gilgamesh from seeking out an enemy whom even the gods could not defeat (*SBV* II 226). To this Gilgamesh responds with a fragment of proverbial wisdom:

> Why, my friend, [do you] speak like a weakling?
> And your mouth went limp, you [vex] my heart!
> As for man, [his days] are numbered,
> all that he ever did is but [*wind.*]   (*SBV* II 232–5)

The logic of the sequence can only be that an eternal name is worth seeking because life itself will slip away in death: the quest is to preserve one's name through fame, extending to a more abstract and perhaps more meaningful level the hope of the preservation of one's name through cultic commemoration. Already the urge to heroic achievement is underpinned by pessimism about the limitations of the human condition. This theme is clearly enunciated in the Yale tablet, where the lines equivalent to those cited above are preceded by another proverb, which we have already encountered in its Sumerian form:[52]

> Who is there, my friend, that can climb to the sky?
> Only the gods have [dwelled] forever in sunlight.
>   (*OB III* 140–1, George 2003: 1.201)

So the pair prepare for their expedition; but an ominous note sounds even now, when they pray to Gilgamesh's mother Ninsun. When she hears of the plan her response is one of sorrow (*SBV* III 35), and she turns in complaint to Shamash the sun-god:

> Why did you assign (and) inflict a restless spirit on [my] son Gilgamesh?
> For now you have touched him and he will travel
> the distant path to where Humbaba is.
> He will face a battle that he does not know,
> he will ride a route that he does not know.   (*SBV* III 46–50)

On the face of it this is no more than the mother's worry for her son undergoing such toils: but does it look further, foreshadowing the epic's later theme of the disasters that follow on his exploits? Is it because of the same foreboding or foreknowledge that Ninsun in a later prayer reminds Shamash that Gilgamesh's destiny is to spend his afterlife alongside

---

[52] See above, p. 43.

Ningišzida, the vizier of the Underworld (*SBV* III 104–6)?[53] Here, even in
the fragmentary state of the surviving text, we can trace a theme that will
also loom large in our later study of Achilles: the hero's divine mother has
an intimation that his deeds will lead to his death, so her response even to
their beginning is to lament in anticipation of what will happen in the
end.[54] For Gilgamesh the causal chain that will lead from his present
undertaking to his death remains obscure when she speaks of it, and in
this too the present scene will be paralleled in the Iliadic scenes between
Achilles and his mother Thetis (see below, pp. 207–209).

When the pair are on their journey, the foreboding is repeated in
Gilgamesh's ominous dreams. In one dream a mountain falls on him, in
another storm and lightning ravage the earth, in another he is taken by
a monstrous thunderbird, in another he undergoes combat with a bull; but in
some or all of the dreams a mysterious stranger saves him from the danger.[55]
Each time Enkidu interprets the dreams favourably, as predictions that they
will defeat Humbaba with the help of Shamash; and he reassures him[56] with
praise derived from the formulaic traditions of the Sumerian poems.

In Tablet V they begin to draw near to their enemy.[57] As they climb the
mountain Gilgamesh is smitten by 'stiffness' and terror,[58] under assault
from Humbaba's 'auras', and Enkidu urges him to courage and strength:

> You have been smeared in [blood], so you need not fear death:
> [wax] wrathful, and like a very dervish go into a frenzy.
> Let [your shout] boom loud [like] a kettledrum!
> Let stiffness leave your arms and feebleness arise [from] your legs![59]

---

[53] Ninsun also speaks of Gilgamesh becoming a deity who travels the sky (*SBV* III. 102–3);
elsewhere, however, if he has a glorious afterlife destiny it is as an Underworld deity who judges
the dead (George 2003: 1.129–36, 461, and see above, pp. 48–50).

[54] See Currie 2016: 110, with further parallels.

[55] The dreams, five in all, are only partly preserved in the Standard Version. The group mentioned
here is a synthesis based on George's comparison between what survives of the Standard
Version and a number of other tablets containing earlier variant versions (George 2003:
1.464–5).

[56] This depends on George's partly hypothetical reconstruction of how the surviving lines
originally belonged in the narrative (George 2003: 1.465).

[57] Since the publication of George's standard edition in 2003, the sequence of the text has been revised
by the incorporation of material from the new Tablet V manuscript from Suleimaniyah (Al-Rawi
and George 2014). As well as the entirely new material, the Suleimaniyah manuscript allows much
that was formerly published as the latter part of Tablet IV (from the manuscript denoted AA) to be
reassigned to Tablet V. More recently, Jiménez 2014: 99–100 has published a further fragment from
one or other of the sequences in which Enkidu urges Gilgamesh to kill Humbaba, who then weeps
'before Shamash' (sim. Al-Rawi and George 2014: pp. 80–81, lines 265–75).

[58] See esp. Al-Rawi and George 2014: pp. 76–7, lines 27–30.

[59] Al-Rawi and George 2014: pp. 78–9, lines 39–44.

As Humbaba realises that the intruders are approaching, he speaks aloud to himself in anticipation of the meeting, and Enkidu again reassures Gilgamesh, reminding him of the strength of their partnership: 'One friend is one alone, but [two are two].'[60] When they face Humbaba at last, he rails in mockery against Enkidu and declares that he will kill Gilgamesh: 'I will feed his flesh to the "locust" birds, the ravening eagles and vultures!' (V 94). The weird contortions of his face again terrify Gilgamesh until Enkidu urges him back to the combat (V 95–107). The force of the ensuing battle divides the mountain range in two; but at last Shamash sends winds to bind Humbaba, and he is overcome. In a scene dramatically developed from the earlier Sumerian texts, Humbaba three times begs for his life to be spared, first pleading with Gilgamesh himself and then begging Enkidu to intercede (*SBV* V 144–155, VI 79–80, 238–9);[61] he weeps, offering to become Gilgamesh's slave;[62] but each time Enkidu urges Gilgamesh to kill him and fulfil their purpose, in lines that have been reconstructed conjecturally as follows:

> Establish for ever [*a fame*] that endures,
> how Gilgamesh [*slew ferocious*] Humbaba!   (*SBV* V 188–9, 244–5)[63]

So the guardian of the forest is slain by the two heroes acting together: Gilgamesh cuts his throat and Enkidu rips his body open (*SBV* V 263–5).[64]

This, then, must be the pinnacle of the two heroes' achievement, the deed that will win them their immortal name. But over it hangs the curse that Humbaba utters before he is killed:

> May the pair of them not grow old,
> apart from his friend Gilgamesh may Enkidu have nobody to bury
>   him!   (*SBV* V 256–7)

At the moment of triumph comes the foreboding of disaster. In the immediate context, the danger seems to come from the way the two heroes have become caught among the personal loyalties and enmities of the gods.

---

[60] Al-Rawi and George 2014: pp. 78–9, line 75.

[61] An earlier version also survives in the Ugarit tablet *MB Ug2* (George 2007a: 250–4).

[62] None of the surviving texts of the Standard Babylonian Version preserve the specific point that Gilgamesh feels pity and is about to yield, as in the corresponding Sumerian texts (see *Gilgamesh and Huwawa A*, lines 158–62, at *LOAS*, pp. 347–8, sim. George 1999: p. 159 at lines 158–62; *Gilgamesh and Huwawa B*, George 1999: pp. 165–6 at lines 135 ff.).

[63] Here I include George's conjectural supplements from the Penguin translation; the translation in the standard edition is more conservative and the lacunae are left empty (cf. also Al-Rawi and George 2014: p. 81).

[64] In the Sumerian text Enkidu alone performs the *coup de grâce*, but this should not be taken to mean any lesser responsibility for Gilgamesh, whom Enlil then blames for the killing.

They have been protected throughout by Shamash, as Gilgamesh's mother had arranged: Ninsun reminds Shamash that he hates Humbaba, the enemy of mankind and the 'Evil Thing' of the land (*SBV* III 54).[65] Yet at the same time Humbaba is the son and servant of the great god Enlil. The heroes are aware of the prospect of his wrath, and in the dialogue before the killing, Enkidu has already hinted at the danger:

> finish him, slay him, do away with his power,
> before Enlil the foremost has learned (about it)!
> The [great] gods could be angry with us,
> Enlil in Nippur, Shamash in [Larsa] . . .   (*SBV* V 184–7, sim. 241–4)

In the corresponding Sumerian text, as we saw above, the heroes try to appease Enlil by dedicating Huwawa's head to him, and he responds with anger at Gilgamesh for having killed him rather than taken him as a servant (*Gilgamesh and Huwawa A* 187–92, *LOAS*, p. 349). Here in the Standard Version their response is more complex. As soon as the killing has been carried out, Enkidu realises the consequences ahead:

> [My friend], we have reduced the forest [to] a wasteland,
> [how] shall we answer Enlil in Nippur?
> [In] your might you slew the guardian,
> what was this wrath of yours that you went trampling the forest?
>   (Al-Rawi and George 2014: pp. 82–3, lines 303–6)

Driven (we presume) by this fear of retribution, they first slaughter the 'seven sons' of Humbaba, here a personification of the 'auras' that used to protect him;[66] then, as in the Sumerian text, they cut down one of the high cedar trees of the forest to make a great door to be offered to Enlil at his temple, and float it downriver on a raft, Gilgamesh carrying the head of Humbaba with him (*SBV* V 299–302[67]). Enkidu prays that the sanctuary in Nippur will welcome the offering, and (according to a line attested in one of the Old Babylonian fragments) he hopes that Enlil will 'take delight' in the door (*OB IM* 28, George 2003: 1.271).

Is that hope doomed? At this point the story of the killing of Humbaba concludes, and (to judge from what survives) nothing was said in the epic

---

[65] See George's note on the meaning of this phrase (George 2003: 2.811–12).

[66] Al-Rawi and George 2014: pp. 82–3, lines 307–8. This identification of the 'sons' depends on complementary evidence from the Old Babylonian fragment from Ischali, in which the 'auras' are personified and described as 'escaping in the wood' (*OB Ischali* 12–17 at George 2003: p. 263: see discussion, Al-Rawi and George 2014: pp. 74–5).

[67] Supplemented by Al-Rawi and George 2014: pp. 82–3, lines 320–4.

of Enlil's immediate response. The implication must be that retribution for what they have done will be worked out in more mysterious and unseen ways, and some such schema seems to be needed to make sense of the follies and disasters that beset Gilgamesh and Enkidu from here on.

Ishtar: crisis after triumph

The turn comes immediately, and it comes through the dangerous power of divine sexuality. Gilgamesh at the opening of Tablet VI has returned to the city as the triumphant king, and the goddess Ishtar (= Sumerian Inana) looks down on him with the 'raised eyes' of desire (*SBV* VI 6). As her husband, she says, he will have great honour, and the land and the animals will be blessed with great fertility: all this looks back to the archaic sacral image of the king wedded to the goddess, as in the Shulgi hymns examined in Chapter 2. In this role he will live with her in her temple at Uruk, ruling her centre of power. But Gilgamesh spurns her and rails against her in vicious metaphors:[68]

> [*Who* . . .] would take you in marriage?
> [(You), . . . that does not solidify] ice,
> a louvre-door [that does not] block breeze and draught,
> a palace that massacres [(. . .)] warriors . . .   (*SBV* VI 32–5)

The long catalogue of sinister images culminates in 'a shoe that bites the feet of its owner' (*SBV* VI 41), an image that recurs in omen texts as a harbinger of death.[69] He recounts the tales of other lovers of hers whom she maimed or ruined: most famously Dumuzid (*SBV* VI 46–7), the archetypal 'dying god' who serves as her consort but is sent down to misery in the underworld, but also others whose sufferings at her hands are not known from elsewhere:

> You loved the shepherd, the grazier, the herdsman,
> who regularly piled up for you (bread baked in) embers,
> slaughtering kids for you every day.
> You struck him and turned him into a wolf,
> so his own shepherd boys drive him away,
> and his dogs take bites at his thighs.   (*SBV* VI 58–63)

---

[68] A somewhat fuller version of the present speech is also attested in the Middle Babylonian fragment from Emar (George 1999: 136–8, 2003: 333–6).
[69] George 2003: 1.473.

The pathetic fate of the wolf is akin to that of Dumuzid, in one of the Sumerian articulations: he is a shepherd, and he is transformed into a gazelle to escape the demons sent to take him to the land of the dead.[70] But the story of metamorphosis here is different, and it resembles the many Greek tales of a mortal turned into an animal by a goddess who has used him for sexual gratification.[71] Whoever composed these lines seems to be setting story-patterns in parallel with each other, moving through analogous old tales or poems about Ishtar to give form to Gilgamesh's rejection of the goddess.[72] In context, however, the verbal artistry of the speech makes it all the more startling as an enactment of heroic overconfidence and bravado. This movement of mind begs to be characterised as something like arrogance, pride, recklessness: words that, once we use them, immediately look towards the Greek theme that the hero's highest point of triumph is the moment when he moves to disastrous excess (below, pp. 193–197).

Ishtar goes to Anu her father, the sky-god, to weep for the 'abuse' and 'insult' (VI 84–6) that have been brought against her; he suggests (like a human father to a wilful daughter – a startlingly realistic touch) that she may have begun the trouble by provoking the man, but she persists and demands that he give her the Bull of Heaven – that is, the celestial beast identified with the constellation Taurus – to send against Gilgamesh in revenge, here reprising the Sumerian *Gilgamesh and the Bull of Heaven*. In face of his reluctance she threatens to overturn the cosmic order by wrecking the Underworld so as to release the dead among the living (*SBV* VI 96–100), just as she also threatens in *The Descent of Ishtar to the*

---

[70] See *Dumuzid's Dream* 174–80, *LOAS*, p. 82. On the general question of Mesopotamian analogues for the myths referred to in the list of Ishtar's lovers, see George 2003: 1.473–4, and note possible resonances with the *Tale of Gudam* (on which see Gadotti 2006).

[71] In Greek there are exceptionally close parallels in the *Homeric Hymn to Aphrodite*, whose centrepiece is the sexual union between Aphrodite and the shepherd Anchises, and there are repeated references to the prospect of the maiming, castration or punishment of the mortal lover (*Homeric Hymn to Aphrodite* 187–90, 286–90), while the goddess herself recounts the story of Tithonus, who became shrivelled up and (in later-attested versions) was changed into a cicada after his union with the goddess Dawn (218 ff.). If the story of the cicada transformation is alluded to in this passage (cf. *Il.* 3.150–2), it finds a further close parallel in Gilgamesh's series of ruined lovers: Ishullanu the gardener tries to reject her and is punished by being turned into a *dallalu* (VI 76), a mysterious word which is attested only here, but presumably derived from *dallu* 'small, stunted': it is variously explained as referring to a spider, frog, mole or dwarf (George 2003: 2.838 favours 'dwarf'). On Near Eastern motifs in the *Hymn to Aphrodite* see further Faulkner 2008: 18–22; Currie 2012a, with Currie 2016: 173–83.

[72] Cf. Currie 2012a: 557–62, on the allusive strategies here and their Greek analogues.

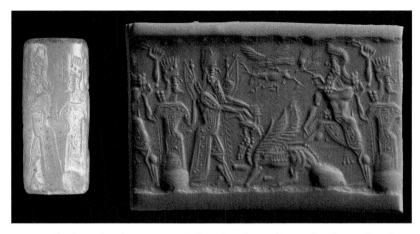

Fig. 4 Cylinder seal with impression believed to show Ishtar with Gilgamesh and Enkidu as they attack the Bull of Heaven.

Underworld.[73] Anu is thus persuaded to release the monstrous Bull for her to inflict on Uruk. Gilgamesh and Enkidu wrestle with the Bull. This scene is almost certainly depicted on several cylinder seals which are dated to the Neo-Babylonian period,[74] postdating the canonisation of the Standard Babylonian Version and therefore belonging to the period when the epic was being widely copied as a classic. One of these images seems to represent the two heroes killing the Bull while Ishtar looks on in dismay (Fig. 4).

Why do they behave like this? There is a clue when, at a difficult point in the combat, Enkidu seeks to strengthen Gilgamesh's resolve by reminding him of the need to preserve the prestige they have won:

> My friend, we vaunted ourselves [(. . .) *in our*] city,
> how shall we answer the dense-gathered people?   (*SBV* VI 130–1)

These lines show clearly that they are still driven by the need for glory that led them to assault Humbaba: to draw back from the present challenge would be to put their prestige in doubt. The aftermath of the exploit repeats and amplifies the problems that they faced after that earlier killing, when they tried to appease the coming anger of Enlil. The heroes first take out the beast's heart and offer it to Shamash (*SBV* VI 148);[75] but his response to the

---

[73] See *The Descent of Ishtar to the Underworld* at Foster, *BTM*, pp. 498–505; also Dalley, *MFM* 154–62. Ereshkigal makes the same threat in the longer and later version of *Nergal and Ereshkigal*: see *BTM*, p. 520, at C v 11′–12′.

[74] Collon 2005: 179–81. See further Ornan 2010.

[75] This seems to have been a customary act after the killing of a bull: see George 2003: 1.476.

offering is not mentioned, and instead Ishtar herself appears on the city wall, wailing for the death of the Bull and (seemingly, though this is a doubtfully attested passage) calling down a curse upon Gilgamesh.[76] Enkidu answers her with insolent violence:[77]

> Enkidu heard this speech of Ishtar,
> he tore a haunch off the Bull of Heaven and threw it down before her.
> 'You too, had I caught you, I would have treated you like it!
> I would have draped its guts on your arms!'   (*SBV* VI 154–7)

After abusing her in such terms, they take the horns of the Bull and decorate them to be used in the veneration of Gilgamesh's deified father Lugalbanda. Significantly, this replaces an episode of the earlier Sumerian poem *Gilgamesh and the Bull of Heaven* in which they dedicated the horns to Inana (= Ishtar) herself, an act that seems to parallel their hapless dedication of Humbaba's head to Enlil.[78] In the newer version, their urge to honour those above them has shifted to the hero's own bloodline: does this heighten the sense of their disregard for the great goddess and, by extension, for the celestial divinities as a group?

So the pair return to the city in triumph, and the people are gathered to admire them (*SBV* VI 169–70). Gilgamesh asks a question of the serving-girls in the palace,

> 'Who is the finest among men?
> Who is the most glorious of fellows?'   (*SBV* VI 172–3)

and they answer with due adulation:

> 'Gilgamesh is the finest among men!
> [Gilgamesh is the most] glorious of fellows!'   (*SBV* VI 174–5)

Ostensibly they have preserved the supremacy with which they 'vaunted themselves in the city', but the implicit foreboding is unmistakeable. The women's praise is the most potent sign that the heroes have reached the pinnacle of success, but that success has been won by rejecting and belittling the goddess as well as by triumphing over a creature who

---

[76] This interpretation is uncertain, and what she says could be simply an expression of grief (George 2003: 2.842, at line 153).

[77] In the Sumerian version Gilgamesh not Enkidu throws the haunch (George 1999: p. 174, at Ma 130 ff.): the change perhaps reflects a redeveloped understanding of the relationship between the two heroes.

[78] See pp. 47, 72 above.

embodies part of the celestial order of the world. Are they now at risk of ignoring or forgetting the old pessimistic wisdom of human limitations, in a magnified version of the false optimism against which the *Poem of the Righteous Sufferer* was a warning? Gilgamesh has climbed to a high place, and he is about to totter.

The death of the friend

Intuitively – or with an unacknowledged memory of the Sophoclean or Shakespearean 'tragic hero' and the critical baggage that hangs around that term – we might expect to hear now of Gilgamesh moving into 'error', *hamartia*.[79] But there is no such easy progression. Instead, the story twists again, and evil comes along a sidelong path. Enkidu has a troubling dream: its details are lost from the Standard Babylonian Version, but clues survive elsewhere, principally in the Hittite prose paraphrase named by its ancient scribes as the *Song of Gilgamesh*. The passage is translated as follows by Beckman, with Enkidu describing his dream to Gilgamesh:[80]

> Anu, Enlil, Ea and the Sun-god of Heaven [were seated in council]. And Anu spoke before Enlil, 'Because they have killed the Bull of Heaven, [and because] they have killed Huwawa, who [made] the mountains thick with cedars' – so said Anu – 'between them [one must die]!' And Enlil said, 'Enkidu shall die, but Gilgamesh shall not die!' (*Song of Gilgamesh* III §1, Beckman 2001: p. 163)

Here, as in the Flood narrative, it is Enlil who inflicts harsh and even arbitrary punishment: why has Enkidu been singled out for death? Is it because – in the Hittite as in the Babylonian version – he had urged Gilgamesh not to spare Huwawa when he begged for mercy (*Song of Gilgamesh* I §22, p. 161)? By asking that question we are trying to fit the poem to a pattern of theological norms that might make sense in our own world; but as the debate continues in the text itself, it depends on a simple exchange of blame and counter-blame among the gods themselves:

---

[79] For Aristotelian *hamartia* see *Poetics* 1453 a 7 ff.; measured discussion by Halliwell 1998: 202–37.

[80] Discussions by Beckman 2003; Bachvarova 2016: 63–72, and on the present passage in particular Stefanini 1969: 41, with George 2003: 1.478.

> Then the Sun-god of Heaven responded to heroic Enlil, 'Didn't they kill them (!) at my (!) behest[81] – the Bull of Heaven and Huwawa? And should innocent Enkidu now die?' Enlil became angry with the Sun-god of Heaven, 'Why do you accompany them daily like a comrade?' (*Song of Gilgamesh* III §2, p. 163)

The dream ended, Enkidu awakens knowing that he will die. It is of course possible that this brief and bald account is a Hittite invention, but this is unlikely to be the case. Another episode of the Hittite text, one that is demonstrably independent of the Babylonian model, reveals its innovative character by using gods from the Hittite rather than the Mesopotamian pantheon; in contrast, the present passage revolves around Anu, Enlil and Shamash the sun-god in just the way that we would expect from the source text.[82] It may or may not be coincidental that from elsewhere at the same find-site there survives a fragment of a Middle Babylonian version telling of the gods gathered in judgment, and one string of words is tentatively reconstructed as the wish or command that Enkidu should not 'acquire descendants'.[83] It is an inviting possibility that this fragment is from a version akin to the source that was summarised and adapted by the composer of the prose text in Hittite. Even without that, however, the Hittite evidence allows us to hypothesise with some confidence about what would have happened in the original Babylonian version of the dream. Enlil spoke out in complaint against the doings of Enkidu; Shamash argued that the heroes were acting at his prompting[84] – at the relevant point in the Hittite version the Sun-god speaks words of encouragement when they first encounter Huwawa, as well as rousing up his winds against the enemy[85] – and Enlil, seemingly, closed down the discussion by accusing Shamash of being meddlesome.

In this partisan bickering among the individual gods, was there any room for a discourse of high justice?[86] Nothing here or in the Babylonian

---

[81] See n. 84 below.

[82] Beckman 2003: 43. On the other hand, Bachvarova (2016: 68) argues that the scene resembles the configurations seen in Hittite prayers and substitution rituals, consistent with the hypothesis that it is not necessarily derived from a passage in the Mesopotamian source.

[83] *MB Boğ 1*, fr. (f), as printed by George 2003, 1.314–17; cf. Bachvarova 2016: 68. For overall surveys of the Akkadian fragments from Boğazköy, see George 2003: 1.306–25, Bachvarova 2016: 60–63.

[84] The transmitted text here is doubtful, and 'your behest' has been emended to 'my behest'. A contrary view was advanced by Stefanini (1969: 43), arguing for retaining the MS reading – which, however, necessitates positing an earlier intervention by Enlil for which there is no evidence.

[85] Tablet I, §§19, 21, Beckman 2001: p. 161.

[86] I am grateful for the comments of the anonymous Cambridge University Press reader, which have done much to clarify the present section.

versions survives to explain or justify why Enkidu alone must atone for the deeds that they both committed in unison. It is possible, however, to speculate that the debate might have worked itself out as a decision to *reverse* an earlier divine plan. The gods, having created Enkidu to help divert Gilgamesh's violence away from his fellow humans, have now found themselves faced with a still greater threat from the pair of them in unison; they decide simply to undo the problem by cancelling the existence of Enkidu. This would then be an instantiation of a pattern repeated across many Mesopotamian narratives of the gods: they have solved a problem by an act of creation, and when that creation becomes troublesome they sweep it away. In the Epic of Creation *Enuma Elish*, for example, Apsu's response to the annoyance caused by his younger descendants is to plot to destroy them, 'to put an end to what we have created'.[87] *Atrahasis* offers an even more precise parallel, giving Enlil the leading role in the reversal: there, as we have seen, it was at his prompting that the entire human race was to be swept away when it had become a nuisance to the gods (above, pp. 52–54). But for Enkidu's death nothing in our texts gives direct support to such a reconstruction, and it remains a guess. From what we can see, this moment in *Gilgamesh* simply expresses one of the abiding strangenesses of all ancient depictions of the gods: their motivations are unknowable, and the sufferings of mortals are only heightened by our ignorance of their decision-making. This problem will recur again and again when we consider the *Iliad*, and we will look in vain in Homeric epic for a more optimistic solution than that offered by the Mesopotamian narratives.

When the Standard Babylonian Version resumes, Enkidu has awoken from his dream, and in anger (perhaps in a fever or delirium, with the sickness of his death already coming upon him) he speaks out against the temple-door that they set up after killing Humbaba as an offering to Enlil, saying that he wishes he had dedicated it instead to Shamash, who had given him help (*SBV* VII 37–64).[88] Enkidu seems to have taken the dream as a certain prophecy of death; Gilgamesh promises to pray to Shamash and the other gods, even Enlil, and to dedicate a votive statue on his behalf, presumably in order to beg them to have mercy; but Enkidu replies that this would be useless, apparently quoting a proverbial saying:

---

[87] Tiamat's indignant description of what Apsu proposes to do: *Enuma Elish* I 45 at Foster, *BTM*, p. 440.

[88] Following George's tentative reconstruction of Enkidu's words about the door (George 2003: 1.478 with n. 120).

> [*What Enlil*] commanded is not like that of the gods of [. . .]
> '[What he] commanded, he did not [erase] again,
> [what] he *proclaimed*, he did not erase again.'   (*SBV* VII 85–7)

Does this refer to the role of Enlil as holder of the 'tablet of destinies', where the order of things is fixed or determined in writing,[89] or to a more mysterious and intangible sense of the causes of death? Either way, Enkidu's death is now certain:

> My friend, [*my destiny is*] drawn,
> people do go prematurely to their fate.   (*SBV* VII 88–9)

'Fate', 'destiny', the order of things, in Akkadian *šīmtu*:[90] the sense of the second line, on George's interpretation, is literally that people go down to death even when it is not *šīmtu* for this to happen so soon.[91] Enkidu curses the hunter and the woman Shamhat, the people who brought him from the wilds to civilisation: he seems to hate the life that he has led in Gilgamesh's company. Shamash replies from heaven with words of consolation, urging him to turn away from this hatred, but as his speech develops it dwells on more grim things:

> Now Gilgamesh, your friend and brother,
> [will] lay you out on a great bed.
> [On] a bed of honour he will lay you out,
> [he will] set you on a restful seat, the seat to (his) left,
> [the princes] of the earth will kiss your feet.
> [He will make] weep for you the people of Uruk, he will make them sob
>   for you,
> the people [so bonny] he will fill full of grief for you.
>   (*SBV* VII 139–45, cf. VIII 84–9)

He will have a great funeral, Gilgamesh and the people will mourn him: but what solace, one wonders, is it to think of these things that will come after death? Is there any blessing in being honoured by 'the princes of the earth' – that is, by the gods who inhabit the land of the dead?[92]

---

[89] See Black and Green 1992, s.v. 'tablet of destinies'. For the significance of the Tablet of Destinies see esp. the poem *Anzu*, in which the Anzu-bird steals the Tablet from Enlil (Foster, *BTM*, pp. 555–78; Dalley, *MFM*, pp. 203–27).

[90] On *šīmtu* there is a very useful summary treatment by Rochberg 2010: 19–30. On the relationship between *šīmtu*, prediction and divination, see also Rochberg 2004: 50–51, 196–7, and cf. Rochberg 2016: 170–6.

[91] George 2003: 2.846, note at line 89.

[92] For this as the meaning of 'the princes of the earth', see George 2003: 2.848, note at line 143.

Enkidu next describes another dark dream, where he was attacked and seized by a demonic man, with the features of the ominous *Anzu* bird and limbs like those of lion and eagle (*SBV* VII 165 ff.). In the dream, Gilgamesh in terror failed to help him, and the assailant turned him into the form of a bird and brought him in this shape to the land of the dead:[93]

> [*He struck*] *me*, he turned me into a dove.
> [He bound] my arms like (the wings of) a bird,
> to lead me captive to the house of darkness, the seat of Irkalla ...
> (SBV VII 182–4)

The dream develops into an account of the Underworld and its miseries, drawing on imagery that was already a set-piece when the epic was composed:[94]

> the house whose residents are deprived of light,
> where dust is their sustenance, their food clay.
> They are clad like birds in coats of feathers,
> and they cannot see light but dwell in darkness.   (*SBV* VII 187–90)

The imagery of this mythical death-world shades into that of the grave itself: it is 'the House of Dust', a place of darkness, misery and absence. Here Enkidu saw the multitudes of the dead:

> I looked and (saw) the crowns stowed away;
> there sat [kings], the crowned heads who had ruled the land since days of
>   old ...   (*SBV* VII 194–5)

Kings, priests and figures of earlier legend[95] were there, gathered before the queen of the Underworld, Ereshkigal, and her scribe: in death, the vision seems to tell, all men will be reduced to the same level of abnegation.

---

[93] George notes the suggestion of a link between the bird-form into which he is transformed in the dream, and the bird-forms traditionally taken by the inhabitants of the Underworld (George 2003: 1.481).

[94] As George notes, the same formulation describes the Underworld in near-identical lines in *The Descent of Ishtar* 4–10 (*BTM*, p. 499), *Nergal and Ereshkigal* (Late Version, ii 1'–7', *BTM*, p. 516). See further below, pp. 253–254.

[95] The text names the legendary king, Etana, who in the surviving portion of the eponymous poem flies on an eagle's back in his quest for the 'plant of life' (see also below, p. 86), and the shepherd god Shakkan. Etana is attested elsewhere as a senior official of the Underworld, and this role has obvious thematic resonances with the later fate of Gilgamesh himself (George 2003: 1.128–9, and below in Ch. 4), but Shakkan's presence is more mysterious (cf. George 2003: 2.850–2, note at *SBV* VII 202). Presumably the thematic significance of both would be clearer if Enkidu's vision survived more fully.

As the days pass after this dream, Enkidu's sickness worsens, he lies in bed; and so he slips away into death, begging Gilgamesh to remember him (*SBV* VII 251–2). Much of the account of Enkidu's dying words is lost, but on the basis of what survives the following restoration has been proposed:[96]

> [*My god*] has taken against me, my friend, . . .,
> [*I do not die*] like one who [falls] in the midst of battle.
> I was afraid of combat, and . . .
> My friend, one who [falls] in combat [*makes his name*],
> but I, [*I do not fall*] in [*combat, and shall make not my name*].
> (*SBV* VII 263–7, following George 1999: p. 62)

This is the final bitterness: he will not now achieve the glorious name that endures, the name for whose sake he and Gilgamesh faced Humbaba, and for whose sake they became supreme in the city. This inglorious death from sickness will cheat him of the very prize that they had sought as consolation in face of the certainty of death.

Enkidu as substitute for Gilgamesh?

'Enkidu shall die, but Gilgamesh shall not die!' The implication seems clear that in some sense Enkidu dies in Gilgamesh's place, as a proxy or substitute for the hero who led the assault on Humbaba and who rejected the advances of Ishtar. That would remain no more than a vague suspicion, a possibility for adding literary shape beyond the realities of the text itself,[97] were it not for a curious crux in the manuscript transmission of Tablet II. Where Enkidu is about to encounter Gilgamesh for the first time to prevent him from intruding on a wedding, the key sentence is translated:

> For Gilgamesh, like a god, a *substitute* was in place.   (*SBV* II 110)

---

[96] Here I print the reconstructed text offered by George in his Penguin edition of 1999: George 2003 gives a more conservative translation where the sequence of ideas is left incomplete, but in his analysis (George 2003: 1.484) he suggests a reconstruction of the same train of thought as is reflected in the more bold restorations in the Penguin edition.

[97] Cf. the psychoanalysis-based interpretation by Van Nortwick 1992, 8–38. Van Nortwick's reading depends on the intuition (or conceit?) that the principal heroes in *Gilgamesh* (as also in the *Iliad* and even the *Aeneid*) are to be understood in allegorical terms, as representing processes of disavowal and integration within a single personality. Although this finds parallels in authentic ancient responses to the Graeco-Roman works (as, for example, in Fulgentius' interpretation of the *Aeneid*), nothing of this kind is attested for *Gilgamesh*, either in ancient responses or within the text. See my review, Clarke 1993.

The problem is the last word of the line in Akkadian, *pūḫu* 'substitute' (the final syllable -*ḫu* is restored by the editor to supply a gap in the tablet, but the reading seems certain). This word has peculiar ritual associations, being one of the key terms associated with concept of the ritual substitute installed in place of a king (*šar pūḫi*).[98] This custom is reconstructed as follows. When the life of the rightful king (*šarru*) was threatened by an evil omen, an insignificant person would be chosen to replace him during the time of danger and to take the evil upon himself, wearing his robes and insignia while the king himself took refuge in pretended obscurity, disguised as a 'farmer' or 'gardener'; and surviving texts leave no doubt that the substitute could be put to death when the peril had passed. For example, a series of letters survive in the name of Mar-Issar, representative in Babylon of the king Esarhaddon,[99] which report the installation of a substitute king in response to the evil portent presented by an eclipse, followed after one hundred days by the termination of the substitute's mock reign:

> [Damqî], the son of the prelate of Akka[d], who had ru[led] Assyria, Babylon(ia) [and] all the countries, [di]ed with his queen on the night o[f *x*th day as] a substitute (*dinānu*)[100] for the king, my lord, [and for the sake of the li]fe of Šamaš-šumu-ukin. He went to his fate for their redemption. We prepared his burial chamber. He and his queen were decorated, treated, displayed, buried and wailed over.[101]

This text dates from as late as the early seventh century BCE, and indeed almost all direct evidence for this custom of royal substitution belongs to the Neo-Assyrian and later periods. However, the role of the 'master scholars' in this period, using knowledge of omens and apotropaic rituals to protect the king and maintain order in the state, stretches back into the longer history of Mesopotamian kingship and should be seen as an expression of an authentic tradition.[102]

[98] The standard study is Bottéro 1992: 138–55; see also Parpola 1970: xxii–xxxii, Rochberg 2004: 78, 222–3.

[99] Parpola 1993: 285–9, nos. 350–352. See also pp. 4–6, nos. 1–4; p. 12, no. 12; pp. 67–8, no. 90 (the substitute's death is explicit here); p. 155, no. 189; p. 157, no. 193; pp. 172–175, nos. 219–221; p. 254, no. 314; pp. 120–124, no. 160 (see here line 4, where the death of the substitute is again explicit). Lambert 1957–8, 1959–60 examines evidence for the ritual itself, including the death of the substitute.

[100] This term is used interchangeably with *pūḫu* in this group of letters from Esarhaddon's servant Mar-Issar and elsewhere: see for example no. 350, line 1'; no. 351, line 5, and cf. p. 121, no. 160, line 4.

[101] Parpola 1993: p. 288, no. 352, lines 5ff.

[102] On the continuity of divinatory traditions see Parpola 1993, xiii–xxx, and cf. Rochberg 2004: 43–97, esp. 63–4; Van de Mieroop 2016: 87–112. The surviving direct evidence for the substitution ritual is assembled by Parpola 1970: xxii–xxxii. The chronicle entry about king

It must be emphasised, however, that the textual evidence suggests that the use of this motif in Tablet II does not extend back to the remoter origins of the Gilgamesh tradition. The complete text of the line where *pūḫu* appears survives in only one manuscript, from the archives of Ashurbanipal at Nineveh;[103] in the equivalent passage of the Old Babylonian Pennsylvania tablet the order of the lines is more logical and the word is *meḫru* 'rival, equal', which yields a simpler meaning.[104] The new wording suggests that at some stage in the transmission, perhaps identifiable with the composition of the Standard Babylonian Version proper, it made sense to at least one editor or redactor to conceptualise Enkidu as a substitute yielded up to death in place of Gilgamesh.[105] If this is right, the motivation may have been connected to one of the pervasive themes visible in *Gilgamesh* and in Akkadian literary tradition as a whole: a concern with *aetiological* narrative, the construction of plot-events to serve as origin-stories for the familiar cultural phenomena of later times.[106] Potentially, at least, Enkidu as a 'substitute victim' would serve as a model or pattern for the royal substitution rituals of the world of the redactor's own time.[107] This one-word allusion cannot be allowed to overshadow our overall understanding of the death of Enkidu, which speaks to the universal sorrow of the death of a loved one, but it remains significant as a strand in the ancient interpretation of what happened between them, and it will reappear when we consider the equivalent crisis in the Greek epic when Patroclus dies in place of Achilles.

The *Poem of Early Rulers*

The miseries of Enkidu's last days, and the sorrows that he expresses before he dies, are firmly rooted in the oldest traditions about him and Gilgamesh. His account of the miserable sights of the Underworld

---

Erra-imittī and his substitute Enlil-bāna, often cited as evidence for the existence of the custom in the earlier second millennium BCE, has recently been reinterpreted as an allusion to problems with the custom in its later form, projected back into the remote past (Glassner 2004: 79–80, with texts at pp. 268–73).

[103] See the full diplomatic edition at www.soas.ac.uk/gilgamesh/standard/file39590.pdf. Of the two manuscripts for this line, one is lacunose for the line-ending.

[104] *OB II* 194, George 2003: 1.178–9.

[105] George suggests that the word *pūḫu* was introduced by 'a Middle Babylonian editor', who misunderstood the original significance of the 'rival' motif and replaced it with 'something he knew: the ritual of the substitute king' (2003: 1.455–6).

[106] Cf. George 2003: 1.92–9.

[107] I am grateful for the suggestions of one of the anonymous readers on this point.

draws on the traditions represented by the Sumerian *Gilgamesh, Enkidu and the Netherworld*, discussed in the previous chapter, and the line reconstructed above as 'I do not fall in combat … ' draws on a line spoken in the Sumerian text by Gilgamesh, albeit in the context of a different kind of descent to the Underworld on Enkidu's part.[108] Clearly, it was always central to the tradition that Gilgamesh was forced to confront these grim truths. As we saw, the Sumerian *Death of Gilgamesh* centres on a dream in which Gilgamesh sees the gods passing judgment on his life and exploits, and deliberating over whether he should be mortal or immortal; they decide he must die, with the consolation of becoming a judge in the Underworld and being commemorated among the living forever.

More widely, the evidence is that the deaths of the heroes of this poem were traditional as paradigms of the universality of death. The key document is *The Poem of Early Rulers*,[109] a text with a remarkably long history and wide dissemination – the original composition in Sumerian led to an Akkadian version and then to a further reworking in Sumerian, and bilingual copies are known from Emar and Ugarit as well as lesser survivals from within Mesopotamia, including a copy from the library of Ashurbanipal. The poem works on the pessimistic wisdom tradition that we have already observed in connection with Uta-napishti, beginning from the absolute fixity of the divine dispensation:[110]

> [The fates are] de[termined] by Ea,
> [the lots are drawn] according to the will of the god.
> > (*Poem of Early Rulers* 1–2)

This, says the poem, is the wisdom of the ancients, 'our predecessors' (4); but they have died and can never return from the Underworld. This thought leads to a catalogue of great names from the past:

---

[108] See *Gilgamesh, Enkidu and the Underworld* line 236, *LOAS*, p. 37; George 1999: p. 187 line 237.

[109] For texts, translations and discussion, see Alster 2005a: 288–322; Cohen 2013: 129–50; Foster, *BTM*, pp. 769–70; George 2003: 1.98–9. The poem is often called *The Ballad[e] of Early Rulers*, and Foster even subtitles it 'a drinking song'. Two factors seem to have influenced scholars in using these terms. First, there is the exhortation to 'let Sirash rejoice over you' (line 23, Alster 2005a: p. 319): Sirash being a goddess of beer, this has suggested to some editors the frame of a drinking-song. Second, the editor Daniel Arnaud called the poem *La Ballade des héros du temps jadis* because of its thematic resemblance to the fifteenth-century poet Villon's celebrated poem of similar name. From the generic point of view, however, the notion of a 'ballad' is potentially misleading for what is essentially a scholarly wisdom text (Cohen 2013: 130, 143).

[110] I cite here from Cohen's edition of the Akkadian text from Emar (Cohen 2013: 133–4), with his secure supplements from the other tablets.

[All life is but a swivel of an eye],
[life of man]kind cannot [last forever].
Where is Alulu [who reigned for 36,000 years]?
Where is [Enten]a who [went up to heaven]?
Where is Gil[gamesh w]ho [sought] (eternal) li[fe] like (that of) [Zius]udra?
Where is Hu[wawa who . . .]?
Where is Enkidu who [*proclaimed*] (his) strength throughout the land?
Where is Bazi? Where is Zizi?
Where are the great kings of which (the like) from then to now
are not (anymore) engendered, are not bo[rn]?

(Poem of Early Rulers 9–18)

Gilgamesh and Enkidu here stand among the proofs or demonstrations that death is inevitable and cannot be escaped. It is worth asking what has led to the selection of this particular list of names, which have close affinities in the *Sumerian King-List* as well as in the Gilgamesh narrative tradition.[111] Alulu, the first king from the time before the Flood, was famed for his great longevity and was associated with wisdom and magical power. Entena is another primal king, better known as Etana: according to the epic named after him, he flew to heaven on an eagle's back in a vain attempt to obtain the 'plant of birth' that would bring about the birth of an heir to continue his line,[112] but he died and his name appears elsewhere as an inhabitant of the Underworld.[113] Bazi and Zizi belong also in the King-List, and may once have been the centre of much other traditional lore – for example, there is a hymn addressed to Bazi, and the tablet in which it survives refers to its public recitation at an annual festival.[114] Gilgamesh is recalled in terms of the story that we have already observed in the Sumerian *Death of Gilgamesh*, his journey to Ziusudra the survivor of the Flood.

One could argue that Etana and Gilgamesh are linked here by the shared theme of a failed quest to reach the divine world (cf. below, pp. 105–108), and speculate that some further factor, unclear to us, creates thematic connections between them and Bazi, Zizi and Alulu.[115] However, the

---

[111] I draw closely here on Cohen's analysis (2013: 146–8, with Cohen 2012); see also Alster 2005a: 308–10.

[112] Foster, *BTM*, pp. 533–54.

[113] References at George 2003: 2.850, note at *SBV* X 202, where Etana is one of those seen by Enkidu in his dream of death. On the wider diffusion of the Etana story in Near Eastern antiquity see Winitzer 2013; Currie (forthcoming).

[114] Cohen 2012: 147, with George 2009: 1–15; and see pp. 107–108 in the present book.

[115] Cohen 2012 suggests that Bazi and Zizi are associated with Gilgamesh and Huwawa because they were held to have ruled in territories to the west of Mesopotamia, and Gilgamesh's quest to kill Huwawa is located in the west.

remaining names suggest a different approach. The Sumerian translation – accompanying the Akkadian in the same manuscripts – allows the following reconstruction of the line about Huwawa:[116]

> Where is Huwawa who was subdued when bowing down (*to*
>   *Gilgamesh*)?   (14)

Huwawa (= Humbaba) is *not* included here because of some glorious achievement, but because of the event that makes him famous in the narrative tradition: his defeat in the combat on the mountain. Listed as he is *between* Gilgamesh and Enkidu, the implication is that for them too the point is that despite their celebrated roles in myth and epic they have faced the same doom as other mortals.

In this way, the burden of the list becomes simply that all fame leads inevitably towards the grave. The implication is that human endeavour is futile, if even the most glorious exploits and the most famous conflicts lead to dust and darkness. But the poem does not simply rest on that bleak thought. Instead, the fact of mortality leads to a new teaching:[117]

> Life without light – how can it be better than death?
> Young man, let me [*teach you*] truly what is your god's (nature; i.e. his
>   eternity).
> Repel, drive away sorrow, scorn silence!
> In exchange for this single [day of h]appiness, let pass a time [of silence]
>   lasting 36,000 [(years)].
> May [Sirash] rejoice over you as if over (her) son!
> This is the fate of humanity.   (19–24)

Although these lines are tantalisingly brief, their import is clear: the right response to death is to defy its bleak reality, to enjoy the 'day of happiness' for which it is the necessary price. Sirash is a goddess of beer (see n. 109): if mortality is the 'fate of humanity', then let there be consolation in the comforts of social life and company while they last.

In the *Epic of Gilgamesh*, as we will see, after Enkidu's death Gilgamesh will be drawn eventually towards a teaching closely akin to that of the *Poem of Early Rulers*. The theme will be worked out progressively, exploring the hero's own sequence of responses to the death of Enkidu – responses that will move from despairing denial towards an acceptance of the truth of the human condition. In the monumental Standard Babylonian Version, as we

---

[116] See composite edition and translation by Cohen 2013: 140–1.
[117] Citing again from the Akkadian text from Emar as edited by Cohen 2013: 134–5.

will see, this message (if that is the right word) is covertly implied rather than stated in so many words; but we will find it explicitly articulated in the Old Babylonian forerunner of that text, and again in the wisdom that Homer puts in the mouths of some of his characters, including Odysseus himself in the *Odyssey* (below, pp. 312–317).

4 | Gilgamesh confronts death

Despite the profound intellectual significance of what has happened between Enkidu and Gilgamesh, to judge from the surviving fragments[1] the poem does not yet move to the inner experiences of the bereaved friend or lover. Instead, Tablet VIII recounts the mourning and commemoration for Enkidu: the external, social manifestations of Gilgamesh's response to the death. When the two men spoke to each other after Enkidu's first ominous dream, Gilgamesh cited a proverbial truth[2] about bereavement:

> To the one who survived grieving was left,
> the [*deceased*] left sorrow to the one who survived.   (*SBV* VII 75–6)

In the enactment of these rituals, lamentation becomes the central thread of the poetry, and from lamentation will emerge the next movement of the action: Gilgamesh's response to the new immediacy of the knowledge that he too will die.

The poetry of lamentation

In his long and richly textured song, 'like a professional mourning woman' (*SBV* VIII 45), he calls on the beasts of the wilderness and the people of Uruk to join him, and he names Enkidu in a series of interwoven images, drawing both on his strange origins in the wilderness and on the intense bond that united them when they were together: donkey of the uplands, panther of the wild, axe at my side, my festive garment, girdle of my delight (*SBV* VIII 46–51). Finally he recalls their greatest

---

[1] The final portion of Tablet VII is lost: here, presumably, the death of Enkidu was narrated.

[2] George points out that the past tense verbs in the lines cited here are examples of the 'gnomic preterite', used idiomatically for general and proverbial truths (George 2003: 2.845, note at lines 75–6, with 1.24–5, note at lines 255–6 of *OB III*). There is a close parallel with the 'gnomic aorist' used in similar contexts in Greek, possibly pointing to a *Sprachbund* phenomenon in the shared history of the two wisdom traditions.

exploits, their victories over Humbaba and the Bull of Heaven and speaks
directly to the corpse:

> '... Now what sleep is it that has seized [you?]
> You have become unconscious and cannot hear [me!]'
> But he, he would not lift [his head;]
> he felt his heart, but it was not beating any more.   *(SBV VIII 55–8)*

Is the attempt to find a heartbeat simply another ritual gesture, or the
enactment of a psychological reality, the refusal to accept that the beloved
form before him is nothing but a corpse? Either way, it seems uncanny. The
overall account of the mourning and funeral period emphasises its extension over several days, and later Gilgamesh will describe how he refused to
relinquish the corpse until it was rotting:

> [I did not give him up for burial,]
> [until a maggot fell from his nostril.]
> [Then I was afraid ...] ... [... ,]
> [I grew fearful of death and so roam the wild.]
> *(SBV X 59–62, sim. X 136–9, 235–9)*[3]

In the earlier version of these lines found in the Sippar tablet (see
below), there is a parenthesis between them – 'Maybe my friend will
rise at my cry!' – in which Gilgamesh seems to be recalling his own
defiant refusal to accept that Enkidu is dead.[4] Is the refusal an
abandonment of sanity? The syntax is ambiguous, and an alternative
translation makes the sentence merely an expression of regret – 'If
only my friend had risen ... .!', so this suggestion cannot be pushed
too far.[5] Whatever the right interpretation on this, there is no doubt
that the images that immediately follow in the Standard Babylonian
Version use figured language to signal an extreme and otherworldly
state of mind:

> He covered (his) friend, (veiling) his face like a bride,
> circling around him like an eagle.
> Like a lioness who is deprived of her cubs,
> he kept turning about, this way and that.   *(SBV VIII 59–62)*

---

[3] These lines are poorly attested for the Standard Babylonian Version and were restored on the
basis of the fully preserved text of the equivalent lines in the Old Babylonian Sippar tablet (*OB
VA+BM* ii 6′ ff.): see George 2003: 1.278–9.

[4] For this interpretation of the parenthetical line, see George 2003: 1.283, note at lines ii.0′–9′.

[5] Wasserman 2011: 13.

Consistently through the history of Near Eastern literature, the gesture of walking back and forth is associated with mourning, grief and misery.[6] Here, if it is formally a ritual practice it is also the acting-out of a state of inner trauma. 'Like a bride': whether or not this implies that the friendship between the two is to be taken in sexual terms, it certainly signals the intense and visceral nature of the relationship, something deeper than ordinary companionship.[7] Accordingly, Gilgamesh in his present state of mind is associated with beasts and birds of prey, with eagle and lion. The lion-image here is particularly revealing: it has affinities with a more conventional image in which Inana in her mourning is 'like a faithful ewe forced to leave her lamb',[8] but this runs much deeper – Gilgamesh's response to his loss will lead him beyond the limits of human civilisation, and on that journey he will be clad in a lionskin.

Gilgamesh wanders the wilderness

The ritual actions continue, and the poem dwells in elaborate detail on the statue of Enkidu that Gilgamesh makes as he had promised from gold and precious metals, with rich offerings for the great gods and the divinities of the Underworld,[9] so that they will 'welcome my friend and so walk at his side', and he will not 'become sick at heart' (*SBV* VIII 132–203). But after these outward gestures, vital though they are, there is a more dramatic thing to be done:

> And I, after you have gone [I shall have] myself [bear the matted hair of mourning,]
> I shall don the skin of a [lion] and [go roaming the wild.]
>
> (*SBV* VIII 90–1)

Shamash himself had already promised Enkidu that Gilgamesh would do this (*SBV* VII 146–7); it seems initially to be treated as an additional gesture of mourning *per se*, continuing the ritual of 'pacing to and fro' but facing

---

[6] See Barré 2001: 179–80, citing this passage; Kselman 2002 for further Biblical examples.
[7] Cf. above, Ch. 3 n. 44.   [8] George 2003: 2.857, note on *SBV* VIII 61.
[9] George 2003: 1.487–90 compares the account of funerary ritual in the *Death of Ur-Nammu* (see *LOAS*, pp. 56–62) and in the prescriptions for a real-life royal funeral listed in a Neo-Assyrian text concerned with the funeral of king Esarhaddon, showing that customarily the grave-goods were first displayed for the sun-god and then assigned to the Anunnaki of the Underworld. This explains why in our text Enkidu's grave-goods are 'displayed to Shamash'. The references to Ishtar 'welcoming' Enkidu perhaps allude to his assimilation in death to the pattern provided by Dumuzid.

outwards and away from human society. Implicitly, however, it represents a more profound movement, towards his awareness of his own coming death. There is an instructive analogue in the Sumerian text *Dumuzid's Dream*,[10] which begins with Dumuzid, the lover of Inana, awakening from a dream full of presentiments of death:

> His heart was full of tears as he went out into the countryside. The lad's heart was full of tears as he went out into the countryside. Dumuzid's heart was full of tears as he went out into the countryside. He carried with him his stick on his shoulder, grieving all the time:
>   'Grieve, grieve, O countryside, grieve! O countryside, grieve! O marshes, cry out! O . . . crabs of the river, grieve! O frogs of the river, cry out! My mother will call to me, my mother, my Durtur, will call to me, my mother will call to me for five things, my mother will call to me for ten things: if she does not know the day when I am dead, you, O countryside, can inform my mother who bore me . . .' (*Dumuzid's* Dream 1 ff., *LOAS*, pp. 77–8)

For Dumuzid here, to go into the 'countryside', that is the wild lands beyond the city, is to lament the approach of his own death. It is possible also to hear an allusion within the poem, to the catalogue of the sufferings of Ishtar's lovers that Gilgamesh invoked when he rejected her sexual advances:

> To Dumuzi, the husband of your youth,
>   to him you have allotted perpetual weeping, year on year.   (*SBV* VI 46–7)

Gilgamesh in that speech was picturing Dumuzid's fate in order to reject it, defying the goddess; yet now, despite all his efforts, the chain of events has brought him to the same conclusion, wandering lost in lamentation in the wilderness. But his journey will take him beyond lamentation to something new, something that looks to a psychological truth as much as to a mythical story-pattern: he will act out an inner transformation, in which his 'pacing' will be transformed into an expression of terror at the universal fact of mortality.

   Gilgamesh is about to embark on a journey whose ostensible purpose is to escape from death; its result, however, will be to bring him to new understanding about death's inevitability, and the lessons that that fact teaches about the right way to live. A sidelight, however distant and indirect, may be thrown on this by the story recorded much later of

---

[10] For this parallel see Rendu 2008, citing the text from *Dumuzid's Dream* discussed here.

a king of Babylon, Nebuchadnezzar in the Biblical Book of Daniel (dated to perhaps the second century BCE, but emerging from older traditions). The king, who has refused to listen to dreams of warning, has walked high on the roof of his palace, confident that it was built for the sake of his own majesty and glory; but he is driven out of the city by the divine will, and a voice is heard from heaven:

> Of you, King Nebuchadnezzar,
> it is decreed:
> the empire has been taken from you,
> you will be driven from human society
> and will make your home
> with the wild animals:
> you will feed on grass, as oxen do,
> and seven times will pass over you
> until you have learnt
> that the Most High
> rules over human sovereignty
> and gives it to whom he pleases.
>
> (Daniel 4: 28–9, translation from the New Jerusalem Bible (1985))

While in the wild 'he was drenched by the dews of heaven; his hair grew like an eagle's feathers, and his nails became like a bird's talons' (Daniel 4: 30); but at the end of the seven years he has indeed learned the truth about the One God and his own place in the scheme of things, and he returns to kingship and supremacy in the city. The story is of course framed as a vindication of the power of the God of the Hebrews, but it is striking that it is set in the context of the Jewish exile in Babylon in the sixth century BCE, and it seems at least a likely possibility that the motifs seen here draw ultimately on story-patterns linked to those of the present movement of *Gilgamesh*.[11] Through his exile in the wilderness, Gilgamesh will move into a new quest, one that runs deeper than heroic action and will lead from despair to new and unlooked-for understanding.

The immortalised survivor

As we saw above, the earlier traditions about Gilgamesh included his journey to Ziusudra/Atrahasis/Uta-napishti – the hero who survived the Flood and was immortalised. In the international dissemination of the epic,

---

[11] Cf. Hays 2007; Stökl 2013: 259–62.

this episode was certainly known as far west as the Hittite world, and it is attested in the Hittite-language paraphrase as well as in the Hurrian versions of the Gilgamesh narrative. Nonetheless, it remains difficult to specify the motivation and purpose of the quest, and one wonders whether it remained constant throughout. The Sumerian *Death of Gilgamesh* remembers that from Ziusudra he brought back the knowledge of rituals from the antediluvian era.[12] So stated, this sounds as if it belongs among his cultural achievements, like digging wells and building the city walls and killing wild beasts, but as the poem goes on the gods invoke Ziusudra's story to state the principle that mortality is the portion of all later men, including Gilgamesh himself.[13] When the journey to Ziusudra is mentioned in the *Poem of Early Rulers* the theme is that he 'sought life' – meaning presumably that he sought the same immortality that Ziusudra had been granted after the Flood.[14] In the remarkable Old Babylonian Sippar tablet, as we will see in more detail below, Gilgamesh is engaged in the journey to Uta-napishti[15] when he is counselled and comforted by Shamash and Shiduri the 'ale-wife' with words of wisdom – but the surviving text does not explain his reason for seeking Uta-napishti in the first place. It is fair to conclude that it was always part of the tradition about Gilgamesh that the outcome of the journey was a revelation above and beyond the ostensible purpose for which it was undertaken.

In what survives of the Standard Babylonian Version,[16] the movement to seek Uta-napishti comes at the opening of Tablet IX, when there is a dramatic turn in Gilgamesh's words (either in real life or in a dream – the text is debated) as he wanders the wild, mourning for Enkidu:[17]

> For his friend Enkidu Gilgamesh
> was weeping bitterly as he roamed the wild:
> 'I shall die, and shall I not then be like Enkidu?
> Sorrow has entered my heart.
> I became afraid of death, so go roaming the wild,
> to Uta-napishti, son of Ubar-Tutu . . . .'   (*SBV* IX 1–6)

---

[12] *Death of Gilgamesh* M 57–60 (George 1999: pp. 198–9, and see above).
[13] *Death of Gilgamesh* M 75–9.
[14] See Alster 2005a: 301–4, at verse 11, with George 2003: 1.19.
[15] Named explicitly at *OB VA+BM* iv: George 2003: 1.280–1.
[16] Note again that the last thirty-odd lines of the closing section of Tablet VIII, the end of the account of the mourning for Enkidu, are almost entirely lost (George 2003: 1.664–5). Was the motivation for the journey clarified in this section?
[17] The relationship between dream-description and straight narrative here is very unclear (discussion: George 2003: 1.491–2).

From a modern perspective, it would be tempting to say that at this point the theme of the poem moves from the heroic to the existential, and that Gilgamesh goes to Uta-napishti specifically in order to seek wisdom about the *meaning* of death (and thus of life). As we will see, however, the evidence suggests that such a reading would be anachronistic. The immediate motivation of the journey is not intellectualised in this way. The driving idea is that since Uta-napishti escaped mortality, Gilgamesh hopes that if he goes to the end of the earth and finds him he will be able to do the same.

The journey takes him first to the uttermost east, to the mountain 'which daily guards the rising (of the sun)' (*SBV* IX 39), and beyond it by mysterious paths – apparently those traversed by the sun at night[18] – to the distant Ocean, which he must cross to reach the home of Uta-napishti. On the way he meets a series of divine or otherworldly beings. The first two, in the mountain of the sunrise, are the terrifying scorpion-people who guard the sun. They recognise that he is partially divine, one of them repeating the line from the first tablet of the epic, 'Two-thirds of him are god but a third of him is human' (*SBV* IX 51, cf. I 48), and they marvel at his achievement in reaching this place. It is here that he gives the fullest surviving account of what he is trying to do, words which in their fragmentary state have been reconstructed as follows:

> [*I am seeking*] the [*road*] of my forefather, Uta-napishti.
> He who stood in the assembly of the gods, and [found life,][19]
> of death and life [*he will tell me the secret*].   (*SBV* IX 75–7)

Assuming the supplement in line 77 is correct, just what is the 'secret'? It remains unclear; and the scorpion-people seem not to comment on the goal of the quest, speaking only of the terrors of the journey. From that ordeal Gilgamesh emerges at the sea, and there meets a mysterious woman, Shiduri the 'ale-wife', who dwells by the shore, and she in turn sends him to Ur-Shanabi, the boatman of Uta-napishti, with whose aid Gilgamesh eventually embarks on the journey across the sea and comes face to face with the survivor of the Flood.

Each of these three meetings repeats the same conversation in varying contexts. When Gilgamesh emerges and approaches Shiduri's house, his appearance is terrifying:

[18] On the physical and symbolic meaning of the path followed, see Horowitz 1998: 96–106, esp. 99–100; Heimpel 1986, esp. 140–3.
[19] The word for 'life' here is *balāṭu*, as in the speeches of Shamash and Shiduri in the Sippar tablet; in context it becomes an etymological paraphrase of the sage's name, which incorporates another word for 'life', *napištu*.

> He was clothed in a pelt, [he was *imbued with*] menace.
> He had the flesh of gods in [*his body,*]
> but there was sorrow in [his heart.]   (*SBV* X 6–8)

The word translated 'sorrow' (*nissatu*) might also be rendered as 'wailing, lamentation':[20] this is still the violent and vocal grief of the mourner. Shiduri, thinking him a dangerous hunter of wild bulls, first tries to bar the door and hide from him; but they speak together and, learning that he is one of the two who overcame Humbaba and the Bull of Heaven, she asks how this great one has come to such a state of misery:

> [Why are your] cheeks [hollow,] your face sunken,
> [your mood wretched,] your features wasted?
> [(Why) is there sorrow] in your heart,
> your face like one [who has travelled a distant road?]
> [(Why is it) your face is burnt [by frost and sunshine,]
> [and] you roam the wild [got up like a lion?]   (*SBV* X 40–45)

The answer sums up the inner terror that has overcome him – terror that we can now, perhaps, come closer to calling existential:

> (For) I, [how could I stay silent?] How could I stay quiet?
> [My friend, whom I love, has turned] to clay,
> my friend Enkidu, whom I love, has [turned to] clay.
> [Shall not I be like] him and also lie down,
> [never to rise] again, through all eternity?
> (*SBV* X 67–71, sim. X 144–8, X 244–8)

In this way his wildness and his restlessness are bound up with his despair, and the 'menace' that terrified Shiduri reappears when he attacks Ur-shanabi and destroys the 'stone ones' on whom Ur-shanabi depends for travelling in his boat.[21]

Gilgamesh will admit later (*SBV* XI 5–6) that his purpose was also to fight Uta-napishti himself, presumably imagining that he could take the means to immortality by force. However, when he finally achieves the journey across the 'Waters of Death' and the two come face to face, Gilgamesh goes on to confront him with a question that has not been heard before:

---

[20] Cf. the verb *nasāsu* 'lament, wail, moan', from the same root (Black et al. 2000, s.v. for each).
[21] The identity and significance of the 'stone ones' remains doubtful (George 2003: 1.501–2).

> I passed time and again over arduous mountains,
> and I crossed time and again all the seas.
> My face did not have enough of sweet sleep,
> I scourged myself by going sleepless.
> I kept filling my sinews with pain;
> what have I achieved by my toil?   (*SBV* X 252–7)

The next lines are fragmentary, but enough survives to show that he ended his appeal by begging to be released from his misery, to return to the carefree entertainments of the past:[22]

> May they bar the gate of sorrow,
> *may* [*they seal its doorway*] with bitumen and asphalt!
> Because of me [*they*] *shall* not [. . .] the dancing,
> because of me, happy and carefree, *they will* . . . [. . .]'   (*SBV* X 262–5)

This at last is the central problem of the *Epic of Gilgamesh*. Gilgamesh has gone from the life of heroic action through loss and grief to isolation and the consuming fear of death: is there any way now of escaping this misery, the misery to which every mortal falls victim?

Uta-napishti's answer

In what survives of Gilgamesh's words, he never says clearly that his goal is to escape from mortality, and when he appeals to Uta-napishti he speaks only of the abandonment of sorrow; but his larger purpose seems to be implicit throughout, and the sage's answer speaks in effect to both sides of his problem. First he reminds Gilgamesh of the blessed good fortune of his part-divine birth, '[built] from the flesh of gods and men' (*SBV* X 268), and goes on (in lines that are only poorly preserved) to describe how much luckier he is than more lowly men: 'the fool', says Uta-napishti, is humiliated and given wretched food and clothing, whereas Gilgamesh is honoured by the people (*SBV* X 270–5). The next lines suggest a further consequence of this contrast, as Uta-napishti adds to his picture of the unfortunate one:

> Because he has no *advisers* [. . . ,]
> (because) he has no words of counsel [. . . . . . ,]

---

[22] For this interpretation of these lines, see George 2003: 1.504.

> have thought for him, Gilgamesh, [. . . . . . ,]
> [. . .] their master, as many as [.. . . . .]   (*SBV* X 276–9)

The thought is hard to reconstruct in the fragmentary state of the lines, but
the sage seems to be imagining one of the ordinary people of Uruk, helpless
without Gilgamesh's advice and guidance because he has abandoned his
people for his journey of misery or (as we might say, translating into
today's cultural terminology) of self-absorption.[23] Neglecting these
responsibilities for his quest to escape death, Gilgamesh has only shortened
his count of days on earth:

> [*You,*] you kept toiling sleepless (and) what did you get?
> You are exhausting [*yourself* with] ceaseless toil,
> you are filling your sinews with pain,
> bringing nearer the end of your life.   (*SBV* X 297–300)

At this point, Uta-napishti's answer might seem complete in itself,
putting final shape on the reduction of Gilgamesh to his mortal
limitations: his quest is futile, and mortality must be accepted. But
for Uta-napishti this is only the starting-point, and he moves on from
Gilgamesh's personal troubles to a didactic meditation on death,
drawing on the older resources of Mesopotamian proverbs and wisdom literature. The question with which he began has close affinities
with the wisdom text *Shima Milka*, discussed above (pp. 55–56),[24] in
the words with which the son challenges his father's homely practical
advice:

> My father, you built a house,
> You elevated high the door; sixty cubits is the width of your (house).
> But what have you achieved?
> (*Shima Milka* 133′–134′, Cohen 2013: 98–9)

Just as the son in that text moves from this sense of futility into thoughts of
the meaning of life and death, so Uta-napishti will move from Gilgamesh's
wasted toil to the fact of his mortality, the prospect from which he has been
fleeing.

The sequence of thought must be traced closely. First, death is universal
and untimely; people pass away like growing plants:

---

[23] The fragmentary lines that follow here concern the gods, celestial phenomena and temples,
perhaps mentioned here as another part of the world-order that it is the king's duty to maintain
(George 2003: 1.505).

[24] This connection is pointed out by Cohen 2013: 121–2.

> Man is one whose progeny is snapped off like a reed in the canebrake:
> the comely young man, the pretty young woman,
> *all [too soon in]* their very *[prime]* death abducts (them).   (*SBV* X 301–3)

Death, here intensely personified,[25] is unseen but cannot be escaped:

> No one sees death,
> no one sees the face [of death,]
> no one [hears] the voice of death:
> (yet) savage death is the one who hacks man down.   (*SBV* X 304–7)

This yields in turn to images of shifting impermanence – at one time or another households and families are built up, inheritances are divided among heirs, quarrels arise among men (X 308–11) – and here again the pattern is crystallised through an image from the natural world:[26]

> At some time the river rose (and) brought the flood,
> the mayfly floating on the river.
> Its countenance was gazing on the face of the sun,
> then all of a sudden nothing was there!   (*SBV* X 312–15)

This draws upon, and perhaps actively alludes to, a passage that we have already observed in *Atrahasis*, where the birth-goddess mourned for mortals who have 'filled the sea' like flies filling a watercourse (see above, p. 53). But Uta-napishti's word-picture is also vivid in its own right: omen texts refer to the swarming of mayflies (Akkadian *kulīlu* in the singular)[27] on the rivers of Mesopotamia, followed by their sudden disappearance, and in modern times the same thing has been observed as a real-life phenomenon.

---

[25] The implicit personification of 'Death', *mūtu*, in anthropomorphic form is attested in texts from as early as the Old Babylonian period (see *CAD* s.v. *mūtu*, (c)), but the examples suggest that this may be a matter of figured metaphorical language and no more. Later, especially in the Neo-Assyrian period, the evidence is stronger. Among the sinister and uncanny beings seen by the dreamer in *The Underworld Vision of an Assyrian Prince* is Death with 'the head of a dragon', human hands and (human?) feet (verse r 3 3 at Livingstone 1989: 68–9). Closer to cultic practice, *mūtu* is treated as a personified divinity in the ritual incantation text *Bīt mēseri* (Meier 1941–4, pp. 144–5, line 80, cited by George; cf. Wiggermann 1992: 110, 116, with Wiggermann 2011). There is no guarantee that this idea would have been articulated in the period when the present passage of *Gilgamesh* was originally composed, but there is a further echo of this text in Gilgamesh's later evocation of the personified Death at *SBV* XI 244–5 (see below).

[26] In my discussion of these much-analysed lines I draw largely on Lambert 1980, Kilmer 1987, and George 2012, which extends the ideas suggested at George 2003: 1.505–6 with n. 20.

[27] George distinguishes the mayfly here from the 'dragonfly' favoured by earlier translators (George 2012: 238, with 2003: 2.875–6, note at 311).

In Uta-napishti's words the traditional image from *Atrahasis* is transformed into a symbol of the abruptness of mortality and the futility of human striving:

> The abducted and the dead, how alike is their lot!
> They cannot draw the picture of death.
> The dead do not greet man in the land.   *(SBV* X 316–18)[28]

This in turn draws on a motif pervasive elsewhere in Mesopotamian literature, the conceptualisation of death in terms of imprisonment: the separation is absolute, and the dead can never cross back into the world of the living.[29]

The keynote, then, is the wavering instability of the human condition, set against the absolute certainty that death lies at the end. If there is room for some more positive consolation in this discourse, it is implicit in the image of the mayfly. The individual comes and goes, lives and dies, but the flow of social life continues – a flow which in the present image, perhaps, is signified by the river itself. Looking back to Uta-napishti's earlier admonitions to Gilgamesh about his social role as king, it is implicit that the fears of the individual for his own fate are a lesser thing than the thought of the continuing vitality of society as a whole.

Uta-napishti's account of the Flood

Uta-napishti ends by moving to speak of the world of the gods. The mother-goddess made an agreement with them – literally 'decreed a decree', 'destined a destiny'[30] – so that in their council they 'established death and life' (*SBV* X 321) but left mortals in a state of endless uncertainty: 'the day of death they did not reveal' (X 322). In terms of the discourse of

---

[28] George's translation cited here differs from many older versions in two respects: (a) in 316 the manuscript reading with *šallu* 'prisoner' is followed instead of the editorial emendation to *ṣallu* 'sleeping person'; (b) the text of line 318 is from a pair of very late manuscripts from Babylon (George's MSS *e* and *f*), rather than that from the Nineveh library of Ashurbanipal, which here has a less satisfactory text implying that the gods imposed the distinction between mortality and immortality on mankind only *after* granting eternal life to Uta-napishti. See George 2003: 2.876–7, note at line 318.

[29] See Chiodi 1995.

[30] Here I try to mimic the collocation of the verb *šiāmu* 'ordain, decree' with the noun *šīmtu*, chiming together in a construction resembling what is known in Greek and Latin as *figura etymologica*. The same phrasing can be used of a human being making a will.

the epic as a whole, this can be heard as recalling Enkidu's complaint when he was dying, that people go to death when it is or seems too soon (above, p. 80). Uta-napishti explains, as if in answer, that the uncertainty itself is inherent in the order of things. This is stated as an abiding and permanent principle, as if laid down at the time mankind was first created. In the context of these two interlocutors, however, it inevitably also evokes the other great narrative of myth or pseudohistory in which Uta-napishti played a part. In the Sumerian *Death of Gilgamesh*, as we saw above in Chapter 2, the gods in council decreed death for Gilgamesh in terms of the principle laid down after the Flood:

> After [the assembly] had made the Deluge sweep over,
> so we could destroy the seed of mankind,
> in our midst a single man still lived,
> Ziusudra, one of mankind, still lived!
> From that time we swore by the life of heaven and the life of earth,
> from that time we swore that mankind should not have life eternal.
>
> (*Death of Gilgamesh* M 72–77, sim. M 162–7: George 1999:
> pp. 199, 202–3)

In one and the same meeting, the gods decided that Ziusudra – that is, Uta-napishti – would live forever and that all other men would undergo death. What survives of the final portion of *Atrahasis* is consistent with the same reconstruction of the gods' decisions (above, p. 54 with n. 71), and it explains the underlying logic of the next sequence of dialogue between Gilgamesh and Uta-napishti, at the beginning of the eleventh tablet.

Picking up (one guesses) on Uta-napishti's words about how the gods imposed the rule of mortality, Gilgamesh questions him concerning his own story. Amazed that he looks the same as himself – that is, the same as any living human – he asks him how he alone has escaped death (*SBV* XI 7). Uta-napishti answers by narrating much of the story of the Flood and his own role in it. Here we encounter the compositional strategy that shows how this version of *Gilgamesh* was constructed on a monumental scale, drawing upon the inheritance of other narrative texts. The architect of the epic is using his spoken words – character-text, in narratological terminology – to embed a version of what must already have been familiar as the culminating episode of *Atrahasis*.[31] Through the personal

---

[31] On the compositional technique of absorption, and its implications for intertextual reading, see Currie 2012a, with Currie 2016: 213–22, characterising this as an example of the dynamic of creating a monumental poem on the basis of simpler (oral?) forebears – a practice, according to Currie, that was equally prevalent in both Greek and Mesopotamian poetic traditions in our period.

favour of his divine protector Ea, he has been granted immortality, winning the agreement even of Enlil, who touched his forehead and that of his wife so that they would be liberated from dying like the rest of humanity:

> ' . . . In the past Uta-napishti was (one of) mankind,
> but now Uta-napishti and his woman shall be like us gods!
> Uta-napishti shall dwell far away, at the mouth of the rivers!'
> They took me and settled me far away, at the mouth of the rivers.
>
> (*SBV* XI 203–6)

Enlil's words are effectively a ceremony of renaming, such as might be performed at the release of a slave into freedom and citizenship: his old name of Atra-ḫasīs, 'exceedingly wise', is replaced by the name that means 'he who found life'. The significance of this name is transparent, so Enlil's words have the same import as those he used in the corresponding passage of *Atrahasis*: 'You will become like a god; [you will receive] life'.[32] In this way they lead directly to Uta-napishti's final question to Gilgamesh:

> But now, who will bring the gods to assembly for you,
> so you can find the life you search for?   (*SBV* XI 207–8)

The point of the question is that it cannot be answered: Uta-napishti was released by a unique dispensation, and Gilgamesh can never hope for the same. This bleak truth means that the Flood story is a confirmation of the truths that Uta-napishti taught earlier as gnomic wisdom: death is everywhere and for Gilgamesh there is no escape.

As noted above, Uta-napishti's image of universal mortality as the mayflies on the river echoes the birth-goddess's imagery in *Atrahasis*. It is worth exploring whether other meaningful linkages can be traced between our text and its forebears. In the *Gilgamesh* version the mayfly image is absent from the birth-goddess's lament, but is replaced by a related word-picture:

> It is I that gave birth (to them)! They are my people!
> (Now) like so many fish they fill the sea!   (*SBV* XI 123–4)

Although this image seems more conventional, it perhaps looks back to a further intertext within the *Gilgamesh* tradition: corpses floating in the water were precisely the sight that drove Gilgamesh on his

---

[32] Lambert in Spar and Lambert 2005, translation at p. 100 line 19.

quest in the ancient Sumerian narrative *Gilgamesh and Huwawa A* (above, pp. 44–45). In this case, admittedly, it is impossible to tell whether those associations might still have been meaningful when the Standard Version was composed; but we are on surer ground a little later, when the narrative again matches *Atrahasis*. Just as in the earlier poem, the gods, parched and hungry because of the cessation of human offerings during the Flood, 'gather like flies' around his sacrificial offering (*SBV* XI 163), and Belet-ili the mother-goddess lifts up the fly-shaped beads given to her by Anu, saying that she will wear them in memory of what has happened (*SBV* XI 165–7; see above, pp. 53–54). In this way, the image of the death of the mayfly sets up multiple thematic linkage with *Atrahasis*, implicitly evoking lines of the earlier poem even when they do not appear on the surface.

In the same connection, it is striking that Uta-napishti does *not* recount *Atrahasis*' stories of the earlier destructions visited on humanity by the gods, nor does he explain how the gods imposed disease and sterility as part of the order of things. However, after Belet-ili's speech of lamentation there is an exchange between the gods that seems laden with allusions to this theme. The mother-goddess continues (in lines not known for *Atrahasis* at this point) to attack Enlil in particular:

> Let the gods come to the incense,
> (but) may Enlil not come to the incense,
> because he lacked counsel and caused the Deluge
> and delivered my people into destruction.   (*SBV* XI 168–71)

Here – as before in the aftermath of the slaying of Humbaba, and in the decision to doom Enkidu to death – the apparent vindictiveness of Enlil towards mankind comes to the foreground of the gods' politics. Again following *Atrahasis*, Enlil is filled with rage at the sparing of this one man from death (*SBV* XI 175–6), but Ea in turn fights back against him, speaking now in terms of justice and injustice:

> You, the sage of the gods (*apkal ilī*), the hero,
> how could you lack counsel and cause the deluge?
> On him who commits a sin, inflict his crime!
> on him who does wrong, inflict [his] wrong-doing!   (*SBV* XI 183–6)

This is a call to balance and proportion in retribution, with the implication that the devastation of the Flood has been excessive: so Ea goes on to name other, lesser tribulations that could have come instead – lion, wolf, famine, plague[33] – as if recalling from *Atrahasis* the earlier depredations imposed by the gods. In all this there seems to be room for a discourse of a theological kind, exploring and perhaps questioning the role of divinity in the causes of human suffering; but no solution or consolation is offered in face of these images of cruelty and indifference. The emphasis is all on Uta-napishti's extraordinary escape into immortality, and the implicit contrast with the predicament of Gilgamesh – and, by implication, that of those who hear or read the story in later and more feeble generations.

The mouldy loaves

So far, the pessimistic truth has been voiced through two quite different discourses, one drawn from the traditions of wisdom literature and one from those of mythological narrative. Uta-napishti's teaching continues in two further stages, again contrasting with each other in kind but expressing the same insight. First, he follows up his unanswerable question with a sudden command:

> But now, who will bring the gods to assembly for you,
> so you can find the life you search for?
> Come, for six days and seven nights do not sleep!   (*SBV* XI 207–9)

Gilgamesh tries to meet the challenge but soon slips out of consciousness, and stays asleep for the whole week. At Uta-napishti's command his wife bakes her daily loaf of bread each day and sets them by the wall, so that when he awakens he sees each one successively more stale and mouldy than the last, and understands how completely he has failed. This story sounds simple and homely compared with what has gone before, and that variation seems to be part of the poem's programme: they have physically acted out a proof that a man cannot even defeat sleep, presumably carrying the implication (albeit unstated) that the stronger and deeper power of death must be even further beyond human power to overcome. As Gilgamesh says when he understands the meaning of the loaves before him,

---

[33] At line 195, the affliction in question is referred to by the divine name 'Erra', which as George explains (2003: 892, note at 193 and 195) is paralleled in other texts as a reference to plague. An anonymous reader suggests that this usage may reflect the progressive exaltation of Erra's role among the gods at a late stage of the text's development and transmission: just as he effectively replaces Enlil here, so he takes over the role of Marduk in the *Epic of Erra*, a composition that is as late as the eighth century BCE (see Foster, *BTM*, pp. 880–1, and text at pp. 889–90).

> How should I go on, Uta-napishti? Where should I go?
> The Thief has taken hold of my [*flesh*.]
> In my bed-chamber Death abides,
> and wherever I might turn [*my face*], there too will be Death.
>
> (*SBV* XI 243–6)

The suggestion of personification in the earlier passage has become more heightened, and the use of the word for a thief (*ekkēmu*) leaves no doubt that Gilgamesh is describing Death – who now invites a capital letter in English – as a personal agent, virtually a demon.[34] It is instructive here to speculate in terms of a bundle of ideas found in Greek mythical thinking a few centuries later: from Homer onwards Sleep and Death are brothers (see p. 147) and Death is the elder.[35] The personification expresses a principle equivalent to that underlying the story of the loaves – if you cannot defeat the younger brother, you hardly have a chance against the elder and more powerful.

In this grim certainty Gilgamesh is ready to turn homeward: at Uta-napishti's command his body is washed, his 'matted hair' is made clean and the skins he wore are discarded and replaced by 'a royal robe, the attire befitting his dignity' (*SBV* XI 258, 267), which will stay miraculously clean until he arrives in the city – the city over which he will again assume the role of king, if only a king who is doomed to die.

The lost plant

But when he is about to leave in the boat, a final layer of teaching is laid on. Uta-napishti at his wife's pleading reveals another 'secret matter ... a mystery of the gods', using the same terms as those with which he began his narrative of the Flood (*SBV* XI 281–2, cf. XI 9–10), but in a very different generic idiom, a mode that we might be tempted to call folktale. There is a certain plant, he says, growing deep in the waters below the earth, which has the power to bring rejuvenation to one who has grown old. Having set out with Ur-shanabi the boatman, he dives down and finds

---

[34] Again, the parallels for this level of personification are found closer to the manuscript date than the date of composition. As George notes (2003: 2.893–4 at line 244), 'Death' (*mūtu*) and 'Robber' (*ekkēmu*) are co-ordinated in the list of demonic enemies in *Bīt mēseri* (see Meier 1941–4, pp. 144–5, line 80, and note above); compare the Assyrian 'Elegy on the death of a woman', which includes the image 'death has slunk stealthily into my chamber' (Livingstone 1989: p. 38, at line r.4).

[35] Shapiro 1993: 143–4.

the plant, and turns triumphantly homeward with it towards Uruk, where he plans to use it in the future to 'go back to how I was in my youth' (*SBV* XI 300). Along the way, however, he pauses to bathe in a pool, and something unexpected happens:

> A snake smelled the fragrance of the plant,
> [silently] it came up and bore the plant off;
> as it turned away it sloughed a skin.   (*SBV* XI 305–7)

This is the final enactment of the truth about mortality, through what is effectively a beast-fable: a mere creeping thing has taken the means to win new life, Gilgamesh knows that he will never find such a plant again, and there is no escape from 'the doom of mortals'.

In the retelling, this story again seems simple, even childlike, but this may be deceptive. The motif of the lost plant has a parallel in the myth of Etana, the primal king whom we saw associated with Gilgamesh in the *Poem of Early Rulers* (see above, p. 86): Etana, seeking an heir to continue his line, travels to heaven on an eagle's back in search of the 'plant of life' that will bring about the birth of his child. Etana at first fails, abandoning the flight in terror, but eventually gains the plant and secures a successor for himself;[36] Gilgamesh, on the other hand, is thwarted in his attempt to win the plant of rejuvenation.[37] There are still closer resonances with the story of Adapa of Eridu, attested in a Sumerian version as well as in the Akkadian poem *Adapa and the South Wind*.[38] Adapa is an ancient sage (*apkallu*), possessed of great wisdom and granted magical powers by Ea; after suffering in a storm he uses his powers to curse the south wind and break its wing, upon which he is summoned to heaven by Anu to answer for what he has done. Ea warns him not to accept food or drink from the gods, as these will be 'the food of death' and 'drink of death' (*Adapa* fr. B1, 32–41, *BTM* p. 528); Adapa obeys these instructions, not realising that what Anu has offered him is actually the 'food of life' and 'water of life' (fr. B1, 73–80, *BTM* p. 529). In this way Adapa has unwittingly passed up the

---

[36] The key passages are in the 'Late Version' of *Etana*, Tablet III/A–III/C: see Foster, *BTM* 550–3, with Haul 2000: 44–7.

[37] On this parallelism see Currie (forthcoming). Currie points out that the Greek encyclopaedist Aelian (second century CE) preserves a birth-narrative of Gilgamesh (*Nature of Animals* 12.21), whose imagery appears to derive from a version of the Etana story, independent evidence of cross-over between these two legendary figures.

[38] *Adapa* is edited and translated with an interpretative essay by Izr'el 2001; I cite the modified translation by Foster, *BTM*, pp. 525–30.

chance to taste the food of the gods and (on one possible interpretation) to escape from mortality altogether.[39] The pivot of the whole story, it seems, is that despite all his greatness Adapa could not escape death. As the introductory preamble puts it, the god

> made him perfect in wisdom,
> revealing (to him) the designs of the land.
> To him he granted wisdom,
> eternal life he did not grant him.   (*Adapa* fr. A 2–4, *BTM*, p. 526)

As so often, it is hard to pin down the moral or lesson that is conveyed by Adapa's inability to escape death, but within the narrative Anu responds to his failure both by laughing at Ea's attempted deception (*Adapa* fr. D 5: Foster, *BTM*, p. 530) and also, it seems, by remarking on the feebleness of human aspirations: 'Alas for the wretched people!' (*Adapa* fr. B 83: *BTM*, p. 529).[40] His experience is in some sense a model for that of mankind as a whole, made all the more bitter by the contrast with the special favours he had received from the gods in his life as a sage.

So Gilgamesh returns to his life in the city of Uruk, accompanied still by Ur-shanabi, and when they arrive there he shows his companion the walls of the city:

> Go up, Ur-shanabi, on to the wall of Uruk and walk around,
> survey the foundation platform, inspect the brickwork!
> (See) if its brickwork is not kiln-fired brick,
> and if the Seven Sages did not lay its foundations!   (*SBV* XI 323–6)

His words repeat the opening image of the whole poem, when the narrator urged the listener to look at the mighty walls and to read the story of Gilgamesh's achievements on the tablets that are set there. This could be read without nuance, as a return to the simple celebration of his greatness, as in the closely related wording of the *Song of Bazi*:[41]

---

[39] For the difficulties of this line (*Adapa* fr. B 82: Foster, *BTM*, p. 529) see Izre'el 2001: pp. 31–2, note at 68. Izre'el suggests that the words translated as 'you shall not live' may simply refer to loss of enjoyment of the divine food, or may also refer to 'the loss of the chance to gain immortality'.

[40] I emend Foster's translation 'the wretched peoples', as Akkadian *nišū* as a grammatical plural need not imply a multiplicity of distinct groups or nations. Compare Izre'el's 'Alas for inferior humanity!' (Izre'el 2001: pp. 21, 32).

[41] George 2009: 1–15.

> He rules the sacred people,
> the ram, monarch of his city.
> Behold the king, lord of the throne-dais,
> sharp of horn, gorer of his enemies!
> With his horns he gored the enemy princes,
> two (of them) bow down at his feet.
> Is his dwelling not large (and) well stocked,
> Are (not) the eunuchs of the sea his eunuchs?
> Is his brink not high, a rival to the mountain?
> It pierced the netherworld and abutted the heavens.
> Observe its fortifications, on high it is exalted (?).
> The one that knows not will . . . and go down.   (*Song of Bazi* 34–44)

This is the language of praise and glorification: look at the greatness of Bazi's achievements. Only elsewhere, in the *Poem of Early Rulers*, do we reflect on the fact that Bazi died (above, p. 86). But when Gilgamesh makes the same command, after hearing so many times that death awaits him, the question of meaning cannot be avoided. What does the sight of the city mean at that deeper level? Is the time ahead in its ordered and civilised spaces merely a prelude to death, or can life there in peace bring solace, even happiness?

The wisdom of the Twelfth Tablet

The end of the eleventh tablet is framed as a conclusion, with ring-composition echoing the opening of the first, and the last words to Ur-shanabi leave us poised with a question-mark over the meaning of the final word-picture. However, a hint of a clearer answer can be picked out in the strange addendum that follows as Tablet XII of the Standard Babylonian Version.[42] This is different in style and inconsistent in plot with the rest of the epic, being a prose translation of part of the Sumerian text *Gilgamesh, Enkidu and the Netherworld* (see above, pp. 45–46).[43] Arguably, it is wrongheaded even to try to find a way to insert Tablet XII into the governing themes of the epic. Given that its opening lines make no effort

---

[42] George argues that Tablet XII was added editorially to the poem 'when the Standard Babylonian Version was redacted', and that this may have been part of the project of Sîn-lēqi-unninni himself (George 2003: 1.49).

[43] For the Sumerian text see George 2003: 2.774–7; George 1999: 175–95. The reason for the addition of Tablet XII remains disputed, but it is likely that when Tablet VII was complete Enkidu's dream of the Underworld included a description of various different kinds of people in the Underworld: note esp. the fragment of a line '[.. .. .. I] saw his person' (*SBV* VII 221). If this is right, the materials in the final tablet will have resonated with that earlier episode in the main narrative. For this argument see George 2003: 1.52.

to fit with what goes before, it is possible that it was added purely for its antiquarian interest – a reminder of how Gilgamesh was seen in the now venerable and academic literature of the Sumerian language.[44] But this may be less than the full truth, and we will see that it is possible to draw it into alignment with the wisdom of Uta-napishti.

Its story is located earlier in time, Enkidu being still alive. As we saw when we looked briefly at the original Sumerian work, Enkidu has descended to the Underworld to recover a magical ball and mallet, which Gilgamesh had been given by the goddess Inana; he has neglected the ritual acts needed to protect himself there, and has become trapped among the dead. By special divine favour it is arranged that this lost being, referred to here by the name *utukku* (normally used of an Underworld demon), is allowed to slip out to visit Gilgamesh, 'like a phantom' (*SBV* XII 83, 87).[45] They embrace and kiss one another; after describing in graphic terms the decay and degradation of his own body, Enkidu recounts the fortunes of various categories of people in the world beyond death, showing that everything depends on the number of descendants one has left behind. The man who has left only one son weeps because his house has been lost and due offerings cannot be made there (*SBV* XII 103),[46] but the man who has left two sons eats bread, and those who have left larger numbers of sons are comforted accordingly beyond the grave:

> 'Did you see [the man with six sons?]' 'I saw (him).
> [Like a ploughman his heart rejoices.]'
> '[Did you see the man with seven sons?' 'I saw (him).]
> [Among the junior deities he sits on a throne and listens to the pro-
> ceedings.]'   (*SBV* XII 113–16)

---

[44] There is evidence that one of the surviving copies was made by its scribe Nabû-zuqup-kēnu soon after the death in battle in 705 BCE of his king, the Assyrian Sargon II, whose corpse had not been recovered. Was he concerned with this text because Sargon's fate was that of one of the unfortunates mentioned by the ghost (*SBV* XII 149–51)? Important though this possibility is, it does not explain the original inclusion of Tablet XII as part of the Standard Version, because the wording of the colophon implies it has been transcribed from an older master copy. See George 2003: 1.49, 1.53–4, with Frahm 1999; contrast Rollinger 2015: 15, who repeats the assertion that Nabû-zuqup-kēnu was responsible for adding Tablet XII to the epic for the first time.

[45] The revenant is called here (*SBV* XII 83, 87) by the name *utukku*, more normally used of a demonic being in the Underworld but here – as George shows by comparing a similar usage in an astrological omen text – virtually equivalent to the more usual *eṭemmu* 'ghost', 'wraith', which is the word used within Enkidu's vision to refer to the inhabitants of the Underworld (George 2003: 2.902, note at line 83). The one-word simile 'like a phantom' uses a different word, *zāqīqu*, which denotes something like windy nothingness.

[46] For this interpretation, see George 2003: 2.903, note at line 103.

In contrast, the former palace eunuch, obviously childless, is left idle in the corner (*SBV* XII 117–18); the following lines are lost, but the list presumably continued as in the Sumerian original, with other categories of the childless who are left wretched after death. Enkidu continues with the man who has died in battle and is therefore honoured, while the one whose corpse is left unburied finds no rest:

> 'Did you see the one who was killed in battle?' 'I [saw (him).]
> His father and mother lift up his head[47] and his wife [weeps]
>   over [(him).]'
> 'Did you see the one whose corpse was left lying in the open countryside?'
>   'I saw (him).
> His ghost does not lie at rest in the Netherworld.'   (*SBV* XII 148–51)

Finally, Enkidu points to the wretchedness of the one who has no-one to leave him the customary offerings for the dead:

> 'He eats the scrapings from the pot (and) crusts of bread that are thrown away in the street.' (*SBV* XII 153)

Only by continuing in the memory and veneration of the living – and literally by consuming the offerings that they leave for the dead – can the shade find comfort in the Underworld. In Enkidu's case, it is easy to infer (in the twelve-tablet context) that part of the bitterness of his death is that he died without a family of his own, with no-one but Gilgamesh to leave behind him – the very fate that Humbaba wished upon him with his curse (p. 71 above).

If this emphasis on ritual observance and memory seems reductive and simplistic, then perhaps that is a misapplication of our modern sensibilities to a world that had a different understanding about the effects on the dead of the veneration offered to them by the living. The words of the ghost should be heard as another reminder of the fundamental principle that is taught by Gilgamesh's wanderings: the hero's quest for glory leads to barrenness and isolation unless one is also maintained in respect by community and family.

The wisdom of Shiduri

The didactic meaning of all this is implicit at best. Although it may seem easy to draw the inferences that we suggested in our analysis of

---

[47] Meaning that they honour his memory (George 2003: 2.735 n. 10).

the Uta-napishti scene, in the actual words of the text there is nothing to say how the ethical lessons of Gilgamesh's experience should be applied in practice; likewise, when he sees the city walls there is no open statement of how he is to reinitiate his rule over Uruk, nor at the end of the Twelfth Tablet do we hear his response to the messages brought by the shade of Enkidu.

It is striking, however, that from earlier in the development of the Gilgamesh tradition we have a text in which the further, positive movement of thought is indeed vocalised, albeit at an earlier point in the story. This is the famous fragment from the Old Babylonian period, known as 'the tablet reportedly from Sippar'. This piece, possibly from as early as the eighteenth century BCE, preserves portions of an account of Gilgamesh's travels that is broadly similar to the corresponding parts of the Standard Version, but it includes stretches of poetry that have no surviving counterpart in the later epic.[48] In the first section of this fragment, Shamash the sun-god looks down at Gilgamesh and warns him that what he is doing is futile: 'You cannot find the life you seek' (*OB VA+BM*, i 8′). Gilgamesh answers that the need to escape death compels him, but when he does so he uses an image that we have not seen before in our study:

> I shall lie asleep down all the years,
> but now let my eyes look on the sun so I am sated with light.
> The darkness is hidden, how much light is there?
> When may a dead man see the rays of the sun?   (*OB VA+BM*, i 12′–15′)

The lines that follow are lost, but there is enough here to indicate a significant variation on the theme that we suggested above: in George's words, 'Gilgamesh replies . . . that while he still has life he must use it to the full, against the day when he will see the sun no more.'[49]

This sense not of the purely negative terror of death but of an option for a positive, humane response, a compulsion to be 'sated with light', is expressed more fully in the second part of this tablet. Gilgamesh is talking to the 'ale-wife' whom the Standard Version calls Shiduri. He tells her how he mourned Enkidu till a maggot emerged from him, and how he now wanders in fear of death, and her answer begins with the pessimistic wisdom familiar throughout this tradition:

---

[48] See George's summary treatment (2003: 1.272–5). My references are matched to the edition there (George 2003: 1.276–81), corresponding to George 1999: pp. 122–6, where the siglum 'Si' is used to refer to this text.

[49] George 2003: 1.273.

> You cannot find the life that you seek:
> when the gods created mankind,
> for mankind they established death,
> life they kept for themselves.   (*OB VA+BM*, iii 2–5)

This is a gnomic statement of the same basic truth that was explored and nuanced in the narrative of *Atrahasis*, and which in the Standard Version would be the burden of Uta-napishti's teaching. Here, however, there is a crucial difference, because she continues with a much fuller teaching about how to respond to mortality:

> You Gilgamesh, let your belly be full,
> keep enjoying yourself, day and night!
> Every day make merry,
> dance and play day and night!
> Let your clothes be clean!
> Let your head be washed, may you be bathed in water!
>   (*OB VA+BM*, iii 6–11)

This should be heard not as a counsel of glib hedonism, but as something more profound: she is urging him to revel in the here-and-now, with its straightforward and immediate happinesses. It seems almost like an explication of the thought at the end of the *Poem of Early Rulers*, when man was told to grasp this brief time of life and place himself in the hands of Sirash the beer-goddess (above, pp. 87–88).[50] But her teaching develops in a further direction, because her talk of everyday pleasures dwells on the celebration of home and family:

> Gaze on the little one who holds your hand!
> Let a wife enjoy your repeated embrace!
> Such is the destiny (*šīmtu*) [*of mortal men,*]
> that one who lives [. . . . .]   (*OB VA+BM*, iii 12–15)

Here, then, is our clearest surviving expression of the wisdom that is needed to answer the hero in his torment: the heroic life is nothing compared to the simple everyday life of a man in his household. The tantalising gaps in the last two lines here prevent us from knowing how Shiduri closed her speech, and Gilgamesh goes on simply to repeat his need to travel to Uta-napishti (*OB VA+BM*, iii 17–24). Enough survives, however, to show that the Sippar text takes the theme of the inadequacy of the

---

[50] This parallel with the words of Shiduri is explored by Cohen 2013: 144–5.

heroic life and makes it into the starting-point for a chain of more positive ideas about the right way to live.

To modern sensibilities, this seems to provide exactly the conclusion that one needs to add to the pessimistic truth symbolised by the mayflies in the river: rather than merely dwelling on mortality itself, Shiduri is giving a more rounded and more satisfactory expression of the didactic burden of the entire Gilgamesh legend. Its absence from the Standard Version may of course be an accident of transmission, as it is hardly guaranteed that the ancient editors had the entire existing corpus of Old Babylonian works to choose from. Alternatively, however, it may be the result of a deliberate policy of selection and deselection, perhaps practised by Sîn-lēqi-unninni himself.[51] Such revisions and omissions in textual renewal are known from elsewhere in the Akkadian corpus, and the ancient editors and revisers should be thought of as active creative agents.[52] The omission, if such it is, may be part of a more general tendency to avoid openly didactic discourse, so as to allow the moral and ethical dimensions of the story to express themselves more powerfully by pregnant suggestion. Perhaps also the difference can be explained in terms of dramatic progression. In this Old Babylonian tablet, set as it is during the outward journey, Shiduri is giving the hero reasons to return to the everyday world before coming to the end of his quest; in the Standard Version, by the time he confronts Uta-napishti the chance to do that has been lost, and the wisdom voiced then is all the more bleak and uncompromising.[53]

If there is any truth in these suggestions, we can conclude that the Sippar tablet bears explicit witness to values that run through the *Epic of Gilgamesh* tradition as a whole, right through the course of the second millennium. This will become important when we turn to the Greek materials, because although the main set of parallels with the *Iliad* will come from the Standard Version, nonetheless our final argument will depend on reading a key description of Achilles from the *Odyssey* in terms of a close comparison with the words of Shiduri in the Sippar tablet (below, pp. 312–317).

[51] To my knowledge, the clearest statement of this problem of apparent omission is that by Abusch 2001: 617–18. Cf. Tigay 1982: 95–103, for a valuable survey of the editorial adaptation of earlier Babylonian materials in this section of the Standard Version.
[52] For parallel examples see Foster, *BTM* 509, on variant versions of *Nergal and Ereshkigal*, and Lambert and Millard 1969: 38, on omissions and recastings in the Assyrian version of *Atrahasis*. Similarly, though on a longer time-scale, the latter part of the attested version of *The Descent of Ishtar* defies clear interpretation unless it is compared systematically with the Sumerian *Descent of Inana*: see Lapinkivi's notes in his commentary (2004), *passim*.
[53] This presumes that the design of the Standard Version allowed for just one episode of extended didactic discourse. This is of course entirely speculative.

Prospect

The *Epic of Gilgamesh* encapsulates a tension that will remain with us throughout this study. Its starting-point is the glamour of the hero: his security in his own lordship over the city, the great walls that he built, the undying fame that he achieved. Yet in the course of the narrative he moves to a darker and more down-to-earth self-awareness. At the height of his glory something goes wrong – through folly, through arrogance or simply through a mysterious ethical geometry that means that the very fact of success engenders its own ruin – and his beloved friend dies. From there on the story is no longer one of violent action: only by roaming the desert and crossing the waters of death does Gilgamesh learn the truth about his own mortality and weakness, and only with that awareness can he take his place again in the social life of the city.

In the literature of ancient Mesopotamia, no other narrative about mankind survives with the same depth and complexity as *Gilgamesh*. In what follows, I will try to show how similar and overlapping themes inform the heroic narrative poetry of the emergent civilisation that swims into our records a few centuries later in the westward islands and peninsulas that we have come to call Greece. At the heart of that tradition, the story of rage and mortality built around the friendship of Achilles and Patroclus resonates, both through correspondence and through contrasts, with that of Gilgamesh and Enkidu. Our next task will be to try to use this fact to deepen and clarify our reading of the Greek work, before asking what lessons this teaches about the patterning of literary history.

5 | Interlude on Homer and the Muse

For Mesopotamian literature there are few clues to the relationship between the scribal world of written transmission and the realities of composition, performance and public reception (see above, pp. 56–62). The same question about Archaic Greek poetry finds far stronger materials for an answer, and any study of the *Iliad* or *Odyssey* depends on one's working hypothesis for the interpretation of various different kinds of evidence for the relationship between Homeric words and the identity of the creative agency behind them. In this chapter I will sketch one possible assessment of that relationship, in order to prepare for the close reading of the *Iliad* that will follow.

The voice of Homer

The consensus view is that the poems of Homer, and the associated but distinct tradition under the name of Hesiod, took something like their present form between 800 and 680 BCE, more likely towards the later end of that range.[1] Very little else survives that can be securely dated to that period, and our only significant prior records of the Greek language date from hundreds of years earlier, the Linear B tablets already briefly discussed in the Introduction. From the centuries immediately following the collapse of Aegean civilisation, the cultural life of Greece is represented by relatively slight material survivals and no texts; consequently, the external evidence for Homeric origins is limited to what can be gleaned from much later sources. All we can be sure of is that the *Iliad* and *Odyssey* gradually emerged into prominence out of a larger tradition of poetic composition, becoming established as foundational classics in the schoolroom and the public mind, whereas the other early narrative epics of the Cycle (see below) eventually receded into relative obscurity.

If much later reports are to be trusted, at Athens from the second half of the sixth century BCE onwards it was prescribed that the Homeric poems would

---

[1] The long debate on the relative and absolute chronology of this sequence of poetic composition is outside the scope of this book.

be recited in correct order at the festival of the Panathenaia. This tradition was in the hands of men known as *rhapsōidoi* 'stitchers of song' or 'staff-holding singers',[2] who recited the poems and passed them down from teacher to pupil within their profession. Little is known directly of these rhapsodes and their art,[3] but a sidelight is provided by Plato in his dialogue *Ion*, in which Socrates talks with the rhapsode Ion, portraying his connection to Homer and the gods of poetry through an analogy with a phenomenon from physical geology.[4] Taking the natural (or divine) powers of attraction possessed by the 'stone of Heraclea' (nowadays called magnetite), it is possible to transfer its polarised alignment to a piece of metal – in Socrates' example, a metal ring – and to use this in turn to polarise another ring, so as to create a series of magnets each dependent on the last. The rhapsode belongs in the same kind of series:[5]

> So you know that the man in the audience is the last of these rings, which, as I said, take their power from each other under the influence of the stone of Heraclea. You, the rhapsode and the actor, are in the middle, and the first is the poet himself. The god through all of these draws the soul of men in whatever direction he wishes, suspending their power from each other. (Plato, *Ion* 535e7 ff.)

Socrates' ultimate purpose is destructive – to undermine Ion's claim to personal expertise on the subject-matter of the poetry – but the very fact that the rhapsode accepts the analogy as valid suggests that in real life too such men were seen as divinely inspired intermediaries linking the generations of listeners back to Homer and thus to the Muse, the daughter of Recollection (*Mnēmosyne*) who virtually personifies the poetic tradition.[6]

The tradition of the rhapsodes followed upon, or overlapped with, that revolving around the family or caste known as the *Homēridae*, 'sons of

[2] The word *rhapsōidos* must in origin have been a verbal governing compound, 'stitch-song', 'stitcher of song', its first element corresponding to the verb *rhapto*. However, as Graziosi (2002: ch. 2) points out, the earliest sources for rhapsodes emphasise the staff (*rhabdos*) but have little to say about stitching. Graziosi points out that when the verb *rhapto* is used of poetry the reference seems to be to authorial composition rather than performance. See esp. Hesiod, *Cat.* fr. 297 Most = fr. 357 M–W, and Pindar, *Nemean* 2.2, using the words *rhapta epea* 'woven words, woven epics' for the singing of the 'sons of Homer', on whom see below.

[3] The question of the balance between passive transmission and active (re)creation in the activities of the rhapsodes is beyond the scope of this book: an important recent contribution is Tomasso 2016, arguing that variant surviving versions of the Proem of the *Iliad* represent the creative contributions of rhapsodes in performance.

[4] I survey the evidence in Clarke 1995b.

[5] For an overview on this much-discussed passage see Murray 1997: 8–12, and cf. Pelliccia 2003.

[6] Mnemosyne as mother of the Muses: see Hes. *Th.* 53–61, 915–17. West collects further evidence for the virtual identification of the Muses with beings representing memory or recollection (West 1966: 174, note at *Theogony* 54). On the Muses and personification, see also Murray 2005.

Homer', 'descendants of Homer'.[7] From this background there somehow emerged a book tradition with a relatively fixed and stable text of the poems – stable enough, that is, for an author like Plato in the early fourth century BCE to assume in his readers a knowledge of the content and even wording of individual episodes and even lines of the Homeric poems, with details that often differ little from the editions we use today.

But everything the ancients tell us about Homer himself, his life and his fortunes and his blindness, has the stamp of myth-making, the projection of the later literary reception onto an imagined past.[8] The classic example is the famous passage in the *Homeric Hymn to Apollo* where the singer, in a narrative framed as praise for Apollo as god of song and master of the choir of girls of Delos, turns to a description of himself:

> But come, may Apollo be kind to me with Artemis,
> and blessings on all of you [maidens]: and of me hereafter
> be mindful, whenever some one of earth-dwelling men
> comes here, a wretched stranger, and asks:
> 'Maidens, which man is sweetest to you
> of poets, and in whom do you take most pleasure?'
> You must all answer him with one voice:
> 'A blind man, and he lives in craggy Chios;
> his songs are supreme for the times that come after.'
>
> (*Homeric Hymn to Apollo* 165–73)

But this makes sense only as a retrospective projection: the shadowing out of *future* glory implies that this blind man of Chios was already a famous figure of the past when the words were composed.[9] Combining this with the ancient ascription to Cynaethus, one of the Homēridae, we have here the emerging tradition that such poems have come from the Muses via a blind master whose art was the fruit of their divine influence.

Here and in the ancient *Lives* of Homer, to say that the poet was blind is to put mythical shape on the concept that the inspiration of the Muses gives

---

[7] The evidence for identifying the Homēridae with rhapsodes centres on Pindar, *Nemean* 2.1 ff. and the ancient commentary upon those lines. Additionally, the work known as the *Contest of Homer and Hesiod*, which dates to the second century CE but preserves material of earlier Hellenistic origin, records that the people of Chios use the name 'Homēridae' to refer to the supposed descendants of Homer on that island (*Contest* 1.2: West, *HHAL*, pp. 318–22).

[8] The evidence for the biographical lore on Homer is well surveyed by Graziosi 2002; see also Beecroft 2011. On Homer as a divine or mythical figure, see also Hunter 2018, esp. 2–4.

[9] For the present interpretation of this much-discussed passage of the *Homeric Hymn to Apollo*, cf. Furley 2011: 223–4, Currie 2016: 19–21. For the data on the authorship and dating of the *Hymn*, see also Richardson 2010: 13–15.

insight beyond and above the sight of the eyes.[10] We are on the same level of biographical myth-making with the claim or rumour that Homer's father was a divinity (*daimōn*) who made choral music with the Muses and impregnated a mortal girl,[11] or the more mysterious story that his father was a river and his mother a nymph – ready to be rationalised into the variant version that his mother lay beside the river while giving birth to him.[12]

Poet and Muse

It is perhaps an exaggeration to claim (as many scholars do) that Homer himself is a myth, a personification of a collective poetic tradition, 'a traditional bardic function rather than an individual';[13] but in a sense this claim is consistent with the way poetic composition is pictured within the epics themselves.[14] There are two key figures here: Demodocus in the distant land of the Phaeacians, and Phemius who sings to the 'suitors', the intruders occupying Odysseus' palace on the island of Ithaca during his wanderings. Homer gives a detailed account of Demodocus' practice when the *theios aoidos*, 'godly poet', is summoned to sing,

> for to him the god has given song (*aoidē*)
> to bring pleasure, whichever way his heart urges him to sing
>
> (*Od.* 8.43–5)

The poet is blind, the loss of his bodily sight being balanced by the higher vision that comes from the goddess:[15]

[10] Such traditions, however, do not necessarily correspond to the modern view that Homeric poetry is to be associated with special sublimity (cf. Hunter 2018: 61–2) or taken as the record of a pre-literate tradition of oral composition. See Beecroft 2011 for the point that the ancient *Lives* almost always treat Homer's blindness as *acquired* during life: the poet begins in a literate world and becomes a Muse-inspired singer like Phemius or Demodocus only when his blindness is imposed upon him.

[11] Pseudo-Plutarch *On Homer (I)* 3: West, *HHAL* pp. 406–7. Here, in what seems to be a schoolbook compilation of Roman date, the story is ascribed to the lost third book of Aristotle's *Poetics*, and is combined with the birth beside the river Meles (see note below).

[12] See for example *Contest of Homer and Hesiod* at West, *HHAL*, pp. 318–19; Pseudo-Herodotus *On Homer* 3, *HHAL*, pp. 356–7.

[13] A statement of this approach in its most trenchant form is Nagy 2012: 29–78; among the many more nuanced versions of the theory, see for example those of Foley (1999, esp. ch. 1; 2002), West 1999.

[14] For what follows compare the sensitive treatment by Clay 2011: 14–37.

[15] For an explicit enunciation of this principle, albeit in the case of a blind prophet rather than a blind poet, see Apollodorus on Pherecydes' account of Teiresias: Athene was unable to restore his eyesight when he had been blinded, so she gave him instead the ability to understand the utterances of birds (*Library* 3.6.7).

> From close by came the herald, leading the trusted poet (*aoidos*),
> whom the Muse loved, and she gave him both good and evil:
> she deprived him of his eyes, but gave him sweet song.   (*Od.* 8.62–4)

A lyre is put before him and his hands are laid upon it; when he and his audience have eaten and drunk, he begins to sing. But the agent behind these verses is not Demodocus himself:

> The Muse impelled the poet to sing the fames of men (*klea andrōn*),
> the path[16] whose fame (*kleos*) was reaching heaven at that time,
> the quarrel of Odysseus and Peleus' son Achilles.   (*Od.* 8.73–5)

The voice comes from the Muse, and ultimately from her mother and her association with the god Apollo, who presides over the lyre and the bow and the truth of prophecy. Likewise, in the vengeance at the end of the *Odyssey* Phemius risks being caught up in the slaughter, and he pleads to be spared:

> I am self-taught, and the god has planted in me
> all kinds of paths [of song].   (*Od.* 22.347–8)

Earlier in the action of the *Odyssey*, it has been hinted that this singer has access to truths hidden from others. When the suitors sat in the palace feasting on another man's wealth, Phemius was singing to them of the homeward journey (*nostos*) of the Greeks from Troy, and the pains imposed on them in that journey by the goddess Athene (*Od.* 1.326–7) – an allusive warning, if they could only hear it, of the vengeance coming towards them across the sea with Odysseus' return. His claim, that the 'paths of song' come to him both from a god and from within himself, is not self-contradictory:[17] rather, it is best understood as the pairing of mythical and literal expressions of the idea that he puts perfect metrical form on his thoughts and stories in the very act of singing them. In this single sentence, the skill of 'composition in performance' is being conceptualised equally as the result of a lifelong immersion in the poetic craft, and (on the higher level of language) as the continuous inspiration of the Muse.

Exploring these depictions of singers within the poems, we cannot tell to what extent they reflect historical reality: they may, of course, be the self-

---

[16] On the 'path' (*oimē*) as the plot or sequence of ideas in a poem, see p. 201, with n. 9.

[17] The authoritative account of the 'double plane' of motivation and thought-formation in Homeric epic, with divine intervention inseparable from autonomous human mental activity, remains Lesky 2001 [1961]. On the present passage see esp. pp. 184–7.

representation of a poet or poets who actually composed in an entirely different way but are reimagining an archaic art-form in the same way that they reimagine archaic ethics and battle-tactics. That said, these passages are certainly consistent with the way the art of the primary narrator is conceptualised in the opening line of each epic:[18]

> Of the man sing to me, Muse, the man of many turnings ...   (*Od.* 1.1)

> Wrath – sing, goddess, the wrath of Peleus' son Achilles ...   (*Il.* 1.1)

The Muse is again the agent – the poem's 'I' – and the poet is her mouthpiece. Similarly, when the time comes in the *Iliad* to recall the names and numbers of all the armies that gathered for the expedition, Homer tells us that no strength of mind or body would be enough to achieve such recollection without the Muses' help:

> You are goddesses, you are present, you know everything,
> we hear only fame (*kleos*) and have seen[19] nothing.   (*Il.* 2.485–6)

Since the linguistic forms as well as the sheer complexity of Homeric poetry mean that the tradition must have been in the making for many generations before the likely date of composition of the epics that have come down to us, it is an attractive guess – but no more – that Homer himself composed while singing in something like the manner of the 'divine singers' described within the poems.

Early responses to Homeric poetry

Cutting across this picture is an extraordinary technological development, the invention and dissemination of Greek alphabetic writing. As already noted in the Introduction, the West Semitic method for recording consonantal sounds with a small set of interchangeable signs was a decisive innovation in scribal practice, being far more flexible and precise than the complex arrays of signs used in earlier cuneiform. Arising out of this, the Greek alphabet in its full form permits the recording of the flow of language with radical accuracy and economy: it is so simple that anyone

---

[18] In my translations here I double up the key words 'wrath' and 'man', to mimic the emphatic fronting of these words (*mēnin, andra*) in the original Greek lines.

[19] 'Have seen' here could equally be 'know': such is the ambiguity in the verb *oida*, an archaic stative (perfect) formation of the verb meaning 'see'.

can learn it, and so accurate that the script can be sounded out even by one who does not recognise the words in question. In these qualities it differs from all the earlier writing systems of the ancient Near East, which is why we still use it today with only minor adjustments.[20] Consequently, the very earliest surviving inscriptions include ephemeral and unofficial types of communication, even erotic and scurrilous graffiti.[21] The sheer efficiency of the process opens up the possibility, at least, that the Homeric poems were fixed in writing at or soon after their composition as monumental works, and that written texts had a controlling influence on subsequent transmission.

This last point must remain strictly speculative. It is telling, however, that it is from precisely the kind of context described above, the use of alphabetic writing at a relatively low-status level of social culture, that we glean our first clear signs of the epic genre emerging into the daylight. A battered pottery cup dated to about 740–720 BCE, made as far east as Rhodes but found in a burial mound on the island of Ischia near Naples, carries a scratched alphabetic inscription in Greek script of the type normally associated with Euboea, whose fragments allow the following reconstruction (Figs. 5(a), 5(b)).[22]

> Nestor's cup I am, good to drink from.
> Whoever drinks this cup empty, straight away
> the desire of beautiful-garlanded Aphrodite will seize him.

This is verse, albeit clumsily fitted together, and its compositional technique has much in common with those of the Homeric poems. The second and third lines approach Homeric metrical patterns, and the complex compound adjectives are unmistakeably poetic, perhaps representing a distinct but closely related variety of epic diction;[23] but the content of the verses is still more revealing. When the cup announces – speaking in the first person, as inscribed vessels usually do – that it is the cup of Nestor,

---

[20] The case for relating the origins and canonisation of Homeric poetry directly to the phenomenon of alphabetic writing has been advanced in a series of controversial publications by Barry Powell (see esp. Powell 2002, and cf. Teodorsson 2006). For the data see also Willi 2005, and summary account by Osborne 2009: 101–5.

[21] Powell 1991: 119–86.

[22] The standard edition is that by Hansen, *CEG*, pp. 252–3, no. 454. See also Powell 1991: 163–7, Osborne 2009: 106–10.

[23] On the correspondences and divergences between the language of the cup and those of the Homeric poems, see Risch 1987; Pavese 1996.

Fig. 5 (a) The 'Nestor Cup'.

Fig. 5 (b) The inscription on the 'Nestor Cup' transcribed.

'good to drink from' and with the power to provoke sexual passion, presumably through the potency of the wine that it holds, the most puzzling part is the proper name. *Nestor* is unlikely here as a real-life name, but it is the name of the oldest and wisest of the Greek leaders in the Trojan War, survivor from an earlier generation and an earlier way of life than his peers. In the *Iliad*[24] a captive slave-woman is laying the table in his hut in the Greek war-camp, and on it she places

> a cup, beautiful on all sides, which the old man had brought from his
>   home,
> studded with golden rivets; there were four
> ears [= handles] upon it, and two doves around each one
> were feeding, and below there were two supports.
> Another man would have toiled to lift it from the table
> when it was full, but Nestor the old man lifted it effortlessly.
>
> (*Il.* 11.632–37)

---

[24] On the context see below, p. 237.

Unless we are victims of a remarkable coincidence, the inscription on the Ischia cup is referring to this passage of Homeric poetry, or perhaps to a related episode earlier in the course of the Trojan War: there is evidence that in the lost epic poem *Cypria*, which narrated the beginning of the war, Nestor spoke at length about the divine power of wine over the minds of mortals, and this may well be the key to the allusion.[25] The association with Nestor is presumably ironic, because the Ischia cup so obviously fails to match the glamour of the one he owned in the epics. Here is a hint that some at least of our surviving traditions about Homer's people were known in the second half of the eighth century BCE, and were familiar enough to be the subject of playfully allusive or even comical poetry[26] in the context of the male drinking-party or *symposion*, in which the combination of elegant eroticism with poetic exchange was commonplace.

Beginning with the generation *after* the period of the Nestor Cup, evidence in the same direction begins to accumulate in the artistic record.[27] An elaborate funerary urn from the island of Mykonos, dated not long after 700 BCE, carries on its neck an unmistakeable image of the Trojan Horse, and on its body there is a series of panels depicting warriors attacking women and children, inviting the interpretation that these are the inhabitants of Troy in the fall of the city.[28] Three vases survive from different parts of Greece and Italy, all dated around the central decades of the seventh century and all depicting what we know as one of the climactic scenes of the *Odyssey*, where Odysseus and his men blind the one-eyed Cyclops after making him drunk with the wine they have brought

---

[25] Danek suggests (1994/5) that the verses refer to an orally transmitted forerunner of an episode in the Cyclic *Cypria* concerning a feast at the home of Nestor in the preparations before the outbreak of the war (*Cypria* fr. 18: West, *GEF*, pp. 96–7).

[26] Or possibly the discourse of aphrodisiac magic, as argued by Faraone 1996. Faraone suggests (106–11) that the association with Nestor may refer vaguely to his famed wisdom, rather than specifically to the cup described in the *Iliad*; and he argues for the possibility (elided by most writers on the subject) that 'Nestor' might simply have been the name of the real-life owner of the cup.

[27] For the examples discussed in this section see Snodgrass 1998: 67–100; Osborne 1998: 53–68; Giuliani 2013 [2003]: 53–102, sceptical (perhaps excessively so) of attempts to match visual images to the narrative myths now known to us; compare the nuanced but more positive discourse of Junker 2012 [2005]: 64–95, and the wide-ranging survey of Trojan War images by Carpenter 2015.

[28] See further M. Anderson 1997: 182–91. Giuliani (2013 [2003]: 57–70) argues that of the assemblage of scenes on the Mykonos vase only the image of the Wooden Horse is specifically tied to this particular mythical narrative. The scenes of slaughter and destruction below it, according to Giuliani, are generic images of the fall of a city and do not ask to be linked to particular episodes in the Trojan story as told in the Epic Cycle. (On the methodological issues, see notes later in this chapter.)

Fig. 6 Menelaus and Hector over the dead Euphorbus.

as a visiting gift.[29] Differences of detail make it problematic to argue that these depictions depend directly on our *Odyssey*, but they point irresistibly to the spread of the narrative of the Trojan War and its aftermath; a fourth vase found in Etruria, from a little later in the seventh century, depicts the same scene with imagery precisely matching the Homeric account.[30]

By 620 BCE, the evidence multiplies for artistic iconography tracking the subject-matter of epic poetry. A round plate from Rhodes shows two warriors, labelled as Hector and Menelaus, facing each other in single combat over the fallen Euphorbus (Fig. 6), identical in essentials to the scene in the *Iliad* where Menelaus kills Euphorbus but withdraws when Hector confronts him to claim his comrade's corpse (*Il.* 17.19–110). Puzzles of course remain. In its frieze-like symmetry the plate seems to depict the opening moment of a formal duel over the corpse, whereas in our *Iliad* Menelaus withdraws cautiously on Hector's arrival. Possibly the artist was thinking of a version in which the episode developed in a different way from that known to us from the *Iliad*; equally, he may have been following a compositional scheme that happens to differ from our own default expectations about how such a moment of the action would be depicted.

Cumulatively, such artefacts make it virtually certain that in the period between 750 and 620 BCE the Homeric poems acquired forms very like those in which they come down to us. It is consistent with this that the first surviving poetry in other genres includes phrases and images that not only refer to the narrative outline of the Trojan War story, but also reverberate

---

[29] On the four vases depicting the blinding of the Cyclops see Snodgrass 1998: 89–98; Lowenstam 2008: 13–18; Giuliani 2013 [2003]: 70–88.

[30] Malibu, Getty Museum, 96.AE.135.

with Homeric themes and phrasing. In the work of Alcaeus, a poet whom tradition placed in the decades either side of 600 BCE, there is a mention of the opening word and thematic centre of our *Iliad* – *mānis*, the vengeful anger of Achilles.[31] A few decades later, about 550, the poet Ibycus declares his *refusal* to sing of the 'much-sung strife' of the Trojan War, saying that its heroes, including Achilles, have already received their due celebration (literally 'beauty'): instead, his present song will confer on his patron Polycrates *kleos aphthiton*, 'imperishable fame' (Ibycus fr. 282.47 at Campbell, *GL* 3 pp. 223–4) – the same verbal formulation that we find at the centre of Achilles' bitterness and death in the *Iliad* (see above, pp. 4–6 and pp. 223–225 below).[32] These poets must be looking to Trojan War epics that were closely similar, at least, to those we have inherited.

Correspondingly, from the same historical moment the record begins to include verse epitaphs whose theme and tone coincide with the discourses of Homeric heroism, as in this example from Corcyra *c.* 600 BCE:[33]

> This is the tomb of Arniadas: him blazing-eyed Ares killed
> as he fought beside the ships by the flowing of Arathos
> doing great deeds of war along the battle-clamour of groans.
>
> (Hansen, *CEG*, p. 80, no. 145)

There is an extraordinarily close relationship between this epitaph and the words used by Homer's Hector when he is setting up a formal duel between himself and a champion to be chosen by the Greeks, already cited in the Introduction (above, pp. 11–13). The verb in the participle *aristeuonta* 'doing great deeds of war' is almost a technical term for the essential activity of the warrior in battle. Evidently poetry close to what we see in the Homeric epics gave special meaning to the terms in which Arniadas was remembered. Nonetheless, it is characteristic of such reception across genres that the epitaph lacks the nuanced irony that we observed in Hector's actual words in the *Iliad*: here as elsewhere, the broad outlines of heroic tradition and heroic language have become normative, even clichéd.[34] This will be important later in this book, when we consider evocations of the Homeric inheritance by later authors such as Tyrtaeus, Simonides and Plato (below, pp. 263–267).

As we move forward in time, the range of evidence broadens. Evidence grows for the veneration of ancient heroes, often at sacred sites that were

---

[31] Alcaeus fr. 44.8: Campbell, *GL* 1.258–61. However, compare Kelly 2015b for a sceptical view of this question.

[32] On Ibycus and the Trojan War tradition, see Noussia-Fantuzzi 2015: 440–6.

[33] Discussion by Hunter 2010: 281–2.   [34] Cf. Clay 2016, and above, p. 11.

Fig. 7 Cup by Douris showing a schoolroom scene.

themselves monumental tombs from the Aegean civilisation of the receding past, and surviving artworks include more and more scenes that answer to specific events and characters in the Trojan War legend. In part this is fortuitous: a market developed in Italy for painted pottery, often carrying scenes from myth, and an extraordinary number of these vases have survived in Etruscan tombs and elsewhere for the simple reason that their high firing temperature made them extremely durable and, being made of clay rather than metal or marble, they were not worth recycling in later times. Although it is usually impossible to tell to what extent (if any) the artists were responding to literary sources, nonetheless the sense of an increasing confluence of poetic listening and visual imagination makes it reasonable to admit artistic evidence when reimagining how the ancients might have visualised the events in the poems.[35]

---

[35] The methodological problems of this approach become pressing only if one tries to treat a given vase-painting as a straightforward illustration of a particular literary work. In reality, of course, the relationship between artistic and textual representations is bound to be indirect at best, at worst minimal. Contrast Shapiro 1994 and Schefold 1966 and 1992 [1978], both of whom tend towards the 'illustration' model, with the pervasive scepticism of Small 2003: 8–78. An important contribution to the debate is made by Giuliani 2013 [2003], who posits a movement in vase-imagery across the eighth to fifth centuries from generic, non-specific depiction towards an increasing tendency to assign images to particular mythical characters and ultimately to individual moments in the temporal unfolding of a narrative. Giuliani is arguably over-resistant to the narrative interpretation of iconography in any of these periods: for a sensitive assessment of the issues, see Lowenstam 2008, cf. Lowenstam 1992. In this book I have tried to steer a middle

A cup of *c.* 490–480 BCE by Douris, a vase-painter given to fastidiously exact depictions of real-life events,[36] shows a teacher and pupil with a papyrus roll on which is written a line of poetry: it is a grammatically faulty version of the opening line of a poem about the Trojan War in Homeric style, naming the river that runs across the plain of Troy: '*O Muse, to me . . . I start to sing about well-flowing Scamander*' (Fig. 7). Not much later, to judge by the anecdotal evidence, the epics of Homer were being studied in the schoolrooms: Plutarch preserves a story of Alcibiades mocking his teacher for using a copy of the Homeric poems with variant readings of the text noted in the margins.[37] Already we are close to the philological science of the Alexandrian scholars and thus to the exegetical materials preserved in the margins of medieval Byzantine manuscripts, on which the modern editions are largely based.

Homer, the Epic Cycle and Hesiod

The *Iliad* and *Odyssey* once stood among a much wider array of epics that narrated the sequence of mythical history from the origin of the gods onwards, centred on the two great wars fought for the cities of Thebes and Troy.[38] From at least as early as the Hellenistic period onwards, these epics were arranged schematically in sequence as the Cycle (*kuklos*), a name which implies not circularity but completeness: the sum of the story was contained in this integrated succession of poems.[39] Chance and fashion, and the recognition that the *Iliad* and *Odyssey* possessed unique

course: it seems perverse to refuse to admit artistic evidence into the discussion, but it is also wise to avoid projecting artistic evidence back directly onto the texts.

[36] Charlottenburg F2285, from Cerveteri. Among the very many approaches to interpreting the scroll depicted in this famous cup, see esp. Powell 2002: 138–40; Sider 2010.

[37] Plutarch, *Alcibiades* 7.2.

[38] The current state of research on the Epic Cycle is surveyed in the essays in Fantuzzi and Tsagalis 2015a. Sammons has a useful study of the preservation of plot-summaries via the *Chrestomathy* of Proclus (2017: 225–38). For an accessible edition of the principal surviving fragments and testimonia see West's presentation in *GEF*, with his commentaries on the Trojan War epics in *EC*, and cf. Davies 2014 on the Theban epics. (Note, however, that West's presentation in *GEF* of Proclus' summaries of the Cyclic poems includes additions from Apollodorus, enclosed in angle-brackets: there is no guarantee that these inclusions are authentic.) On the constitution of the Cycle, and the canonisation of the *Iliad* and the *Odyssey* as the supreme representatives of the epic tradition, the authoritative study is Burgess 2001. The secondary evidence provided by the depiction of the action of the Cyclic epics in the miniature reliefs known as the *Tabulae Iliacae* (Petrain 2014) is vital, but in practice does not affect any of the specific arguments addressed in the present book.

[39] On this and other possible interpretations of the metaphor in the term 'Cycle' see Fantuzzi and Tsagalis 2015b: 1–7.

excellences, mean that of the other Cyclic poems we have only stray scraps and bald plot-summaries;[40] but these are vital nonetheless for understanding the overall tradition and the subject-matter of the Homeric poems themselves. Much ink has been spilt on trying to establish which of the Cyclic epics are older and which are younger in origin, and to what extent they respond to the *Iliad* and the *Odyssey* or represent independent reflections of pre-Homeric tradition. There is perhaps no better comment on this than the ancient tradition (or was it a joke?) that Homer himself composed the *Cypria*, the Cyclic epic telling of the opening of the Trojan War, but had nothing else to provide as a dowry for his daughter when she married the poet Stasinus, who in turn was later listed as its author.[41]

In recent decades, Homeric studies have been revitalised by the growing realisation that the Cyclic epics can help to provide contexts for our reading of the *Iliad* and the *Odyssey*, shedding light on the full breadth of the lore of the heroic world. Even if a given poem was composed later, its outline and its fragments may be invaluable as indicators of the traditions on which Homer builds and the norms to which his poetry responds.[42] Such an approach (still sometimes known by the name 'Neoanalysis') is distinct in principle from the question of oral composition, except in the sense that the oral hypothesis has been a powerful reminder of the richness and variety of what must have been composed and heard before and around the coming-to-birth of the surviving epics – all simultaneously embodying established tradition and renewing or even subverting it in the process.[43] In our next chapters, the *Cypria* in particular will provide crucial evidence for understanding the meaning and destiny of the heroic race. The poems that narrated the later stages of the war will be less prominent (if only because of lack of evidence), but our reflections on the death of Achilles will depend largely on the slight evidence surviving from the Cyclic epics – principally the *Aethiopis*, but also

---

[40] The argument that the Homeric epics were seen as *qualitatively* superior is doubtful at best, but the ancient testimonia do indicate a contrast between the depth and complexity of Homeric composition versus the tendency towards plain sequential narration in the non-Homeric poems of the Cycle (see Fantuzzi 2015, with Griffin 2001 [1977]). Sammons 2017 begins by recasting Griffin's formulation in a more modern critical idiom (1–24) but continues throughout his monograph with speculative reconstructions of complex narrative structures in the course of the Cycle poems.

[41] For references see West, *GEF*, pp. 65–7, with Currie 2015: 282–3.

[42] For the question of influence and allusion between the Homeric poems and the Cyclic epics – and/or the forerunners of the attested poems in each case – see for example Burgess 2001: 132–71; Kullmann 2015; Currie 2016: 55–78; cf. Finkelberg 2015.

[43] On the relationship between the oral hypothesis and the approach to the Epic Cycle proposed here, cf. the elegant analysis of the question by Burgess 2006.

the *Little Iliad* and the *Sack of Troy* (*Iliupersis*), in which the fighting ended with the fall of the city.

Alongside this material stand the Homeric Hymns[44] and the poems of Hesiod, whose name was customarily joined with Homer's in antiquity but who fits less easily into modern assumptions about the proper subject-matter of poetry. Where Homer narrates, Hesiod expounds and teaches the nature of the gods and the world, and the wisdom of the good life. Homer (as we have seen) fades as an individual behind the power of the Muse, but Hesiod makes his own personality express itself with stark individuality, despite the prominence of his invocations of the Muses (*WD* 1–2; *Th* 1–22, 36–52). In the *Theogony*, his account of the origins and relationships of the gods, he tells how he was a shepherd until the Muses came and breathed the gift of song into him. His *Works and Days* is cast as a response to a particular moment in his unfortunate life: he presents himself as an embittered farmer who has been cheated by his brother Perses. At the opening he steps forward at once as a personal agent – 'I wish to speak the truth to Perses' (*WD* 10) – and from that desire springs everything that he goes on to teach, moving above and beyond his petty problems to expound universal truths.[45] So described, this man seems quite unlike Homer, the depersonalised agent of the Muses; and, indeed, the scholars who have set Homer up as the representative of a primeval tradition of oral poetry have found it much less easy to apply that model to the poet of the *Works and Days*. Nonetheless the affinity between them in world-view, lore and language is overwhelmingly close, closer than the relationship between either of them and any other texts surviving from antiquity.

The clue to understanding the kinship between Homer and Hesiod is to see that Hesiod's poetry works on a more heightened level of dramatic representation. Though his tone and style seem very different from those of the *Iliad* or the *Odyssey*, they resemble those of many of Homer's wisest and most wordy speakers: Nestor, the representative of ancient ways and wisdom among the Greek leaders at Troy, or Phoenix, the old tutor of Achilles who warns him of his coming self-destruction, or Achilles himself when he sets out a theology of human suffering in his final scene in the *Iliad*. Odysseus himself becomes Hesiodic when, disguised as a beggarman, he takes pity on one of his own enemies and tries to warn him of the vengeance of the gods (*Od.* 18.125–50).[46] In other words, the voice of Hesiod assimilates more to that of a Homeric *character* than to the primary

---

[44] The Homeric Hymns are cited in this book from West's Loeb edition in *HHAL*. I avoid using the shorter hymns, whose origins and dating are insecure.

[45] Overview treatments: Nelson 1998, ch. 4, 5; Clay 2003.   [46] Cf. p. 257 below.

narrator,[47] and on this principle his wisdom will be crucial for us. In the same inclusive spirit we will also draw on a group of more derivative poems attributed in antiquity to Hesiod, notably the *Catalogue of Women*[48] and the bizarre, baroque evocation of the images on a heroic artefact, the *Shield of Heracles*.[49] Even if some of these were composed significantly later than the major Hesiodic poems, they are bound to include themes and images that open doors onto the context or antecedents of the earlier works.

What unites this corpus? To what extent can the works surveyed above be said to represent a single genre with interrelated themes and world-view? Three criteria work together here. First comes the authority of the ancients: as we have seen, Homer, the Cycle and Hesiod were routinely grouped together as witnesses to the most ancient traditions of serious poetry, *epos* or *aoidē*. The second is language: throughout the corpus we find a variety of Greek which (despite diachronic and other variations) is remarkably consistent in the range and variety of grammatical features, vocabulary, syntax and style that are permitted, and no other part of the early Greek literary inheritance can be categorised in the same way. The third and decisive feature is metre. All these poems are composed along the same rhythmical scheme, a scheme that was probably inherited from the remotest antiquity, transmitted and developed in tandem with the rich and specialised linguistic resources that enabled the poets to frame their thought in accordance with its fixed norms and verbal formulae. An analysis of this metre, the *dactylic hexameter*, belongs in a different book from this one, and it will suffice here to posit that this formal structure determines the especially close relationship between the poems that embody it. The voice of the poet, lent flow and authority by the music of the lyre and the higher vision signalled by the Muse, taught the Greeks something about the meaning of life. In Herodotus' simple formulation, Homer and Hesiod established the genealogy and characteristics of the gods for the Greek people for the future.[50] In the following chapters I will try to show how that voice put form on a teaching of wisdom, mediated through the actions and passions of gods and demigods.

---

[47] For a comparable approach see Tsagalis 2006, and cf. Scodel 2012, Canevaro 2015.

[48] The definitive edition of the fragments in Merkelbach and West is best used alongside the (sometimes differently sequenced) edition with translation by Most 2006: 2.40–261.

[49] Edition and translation at Most 2006: 2.2–39.

[50] Herodotus, *Histories* 2.53. See Gould 2013 [1994]: 196; Hunter 2018: 79–81.

6 | The race of half-gods

Wisdom, as we have suggested, is at the centre of the epic tradition overall, and as we move towards the inner discourse of the Trojan War poems, Hesiod's *Works and Days* will provide our initial orientation, beginning from the family dispute that prompts the poet's sequence of teachings. Hesiod's father has died, leaving him and his brother Perses to inherit the farm; but Perses has set up a dishonest scheme with corrupt local leaders (*basilees*, sometimes translated 'kings' or 'chieftains'), trying to leverage greater wealth for himself and in the process ruining his own fortunes.[1] Hesiod's ultimate aim is to show the absolute importance of living in accordance with justice. Counter-intuitively, perhaps, for the modern reader, he begins by reminding Perses (and thus the poem's audience) of the fact of human weakness and lowliness, with the ethical consequences that follow from that truth: above all, the virtue of earning one's own food and livelihood by working the soil.

The wisdom of hard work

'The gods', says Hesiod, 'keep life hidden from mankind' (*WD* 42). Immediately this recalls the words of Shiduri to Gilgamesh in the Sippar tablet: the gods assigned death to mankind but kept life for themselves.[2] Its placing in Hesiod's sequence of thought suggests that for him too it is part of an inherited stock of wisdom.[3] In context, however, there is a subtle difference. Where Akkadian *balāṭu* refers here to life as opposed to death, in relation to Gilgamesh's attempt to escape from mortality,[4] for Hesiod

---

[1] For this view of the overall discourse of the *Works and Days* compare Clay 2003: 31–48, with Clay 2009a; Nelson 1998: 59–81; Canevaro 2015, *passim.*

[2] *OB VA+BM*, iii 4–5, at George 2003: 279. See above, pp. 111–112.

[3] See Naiden 2003; cf. Clarke 2004: 76, the same comparison in a more vague formulation.

[4] Contextually this is clear, as Naiden shows; note, however, that the overall lexical range of *balāṭu* includes 'means of life, sustenance' (see *CAD* s.v. *balāṭu* (substantive) §§ 4, 5, and cf. *balāṭu* (verb) §3(a), (c)), and thus rather closely shadows that of Greek *bios.* This means that the Hesiodic line is extremely close to Shiduri's if each is considered as a fixed maxim, irrespective of context.

the thing that has been hidden – *bios* – can be translated as 'life' but also as 'livelihood', 'the means of life', and this latter sense is uppermost as he continues:

> The gods keep life hidden from mankind:
> for otherwise you would work with ease, even for a single day,
> so that you would have enough to hold for a year in idleness:
> at once you would set up the rudder above the smoke [of the fireplace],
> ended would be the work of the cattle and toiling mules.
>
> (Hes. *WD* 42–6)

Where Shiduri warned Gilgamesh against his barren search to escape from the prospect of death, Hesiod warns Perses and his audience against the hope of escaping from the endless effort to draw a living from the soil. It follows that since the divine powers deny us the prospect of an easy idle life, we must exhaust ourselves if we are to put food on the table with honesty. The toil of the farmer is an expression of conformity to the gods' plan for mankind.[5]

Human decline and the scheme of the five races

Hesiod proceeds to amplify and extend his exposition through a series of reflections on the mythical past. Prometheus the divine friend of humans stole fire to ease our lives, and to restore the balance Zeus arranged for the making of Woman in the form of Pandora; she unleashed evils and sufferings on mankind, with Hope the only good thing left behind:

> Another thousand miseries wander among the human race:
> full is the earth of evils, and full is the sea:
> there are sicknesses among humans during the day, and others by night
> move of their own accord, bringing evils to mortals
> in silence, for Zeus has taken away their voice.   (*WD* 100–5)

Sickness and disease are signs of the divine order, just as in *Atrahasis* with the final dispensations made in the resolution of the class war between humans and gods (above, pp. 53–54). Once again, however, the identity between motifs hides a difference in the wisdom that is taught. The regime that Zeus has imposed on the human race is not like that in *Atrahasis*, designed to prevent us from becoming strong enough or numerous enough

---

[5] Cf. Canevaro 2015: 99–114.

to be a threat. Instead it is a moral stimulus, because it makes us struggle through life in healthy competitiveness – Hesiod's 'good Strife' (*WD* 17–26) – with constant reminders of our weakness and limitations, and of the doomed instability of wealth won easily and crookedly. This leads finally to Hesiod's description of the rhythms and routines of the small farmer's life through the seasons – practical agricultural advice as an application of the fundamental principle that frugality is in accordance with justice.

Hesiod next reveals a different but parallel teaching about the distance between mortals and gods: the story of the five 'races' of mankind.[6] Gods and humans began in unity but parted stage by stage, and the poet traces this movement in the gods' creation of five successive races or births (*genea*) of human beings.[7] The first were golden: under the rule of Kronos, son of the old sky-god Ouranos, they lived without toil or sickness or old age, and after their painless deaths they became lesser divinities upon the earth (*daimones . . . epichthonioi*, 123–4), overlooking the deeds of later men.[8] Then the gods made a silver race, marked by the start of decline and disarray: they neglected the honours due to their divine makers and behaved with ignorant violence (*hubris atasthalos*, 134) against each other. Silver is harder and less perfect than gold, and it takes a tarnish. If this underlies the symbolism of the metals, it helps to explain why Hesiod says that the people of the silver race would remain a hundred years in infancy and then lived as adults only for a short space, suffering pains because of their own folly. After death they passed into the Underworld below, and Hesiod calls them 'blessed mortals' rather than divinities (141). Next was made a race of bronze, the harder metal that turns rough and dull greenish with time: they were men of war and violence and savagery, with untamed hard thoughts in their breasts (147) and with weapons and houses

---

[6] The discussion here represents only one of several possible approaches to the myth of the five races: in particular, there is a case for emphasising cyclical alternation as well as simply decline, and it is a moot point whether it should be interpreted in unison with Hesiod's narration elsewhere of the succession of divine kingships from Kronos to Zeus. Among the countless published studies of the myth of the five races, I have found most help in Most 1998; Clay 2003: 81–95, with Clay 2009a: 78–82; Tsagalis 2009: 144–6; Currie 2012b; Zanker 2013.

[7] Hesiod's term *genos* extends from abstract 'birth, origin' to collective 'kin, race, group of common birth'. The conventional translation 'generation' is thus potentially misleading; even more so 'age', as in 'Golden Age', which is appropriate only to later versions of the myth.

[8] The following two lines (124–5) in which these *daimones* travel unseen through the world, watching over the judgments and crimes of men, are missing from some of the papyri and from citations of the passage by ancient scholars, and it is likely that they are an intrusion here, copied from the later passage (*WD* 254–5) in which the same lines appear in a somewhat different context (see West 1978: 183).

of bronze. The violence and oppression of war was their life, they slaughtered each other and went down to nameless darkness in death. This
sequence of hardness, discoloration and the loss of vitality culminates,
says Hesiod, in the race of our own time, made of iron (180–201). Toil
and trouble are everywhere, imposed upon us by the gods, and the wretchedness and crimes of this race will lead to its own destruction. Men will lose
respect and restraint, oaths will be broken, the goddesses Abashment and
Disgrace (*Aidōs, Nemesis,* 200) will abandon the world, and in parallel with
this the vitality of human beings, and their affinity with their forebears, will
be lost. Children will cease to resemble or 'harmonise with'[9] their parents
or their fellow men, and babies will already be grey-haired when they are
born, their vital energy lost when their time has only begun.

The general theme of human decline is paralleled in Mesopotamian
tradition, as we have seen,[10] but its articulation as a succession of races
linked to metals is unique to Hesiod.[11] It is noteworthy that each of the
races is made separately, whether by Zeus or by the gods as a group, rather
than being linked genealogically to each other as one might expect – and as
later Greek poets assume even when alluding closely to this passage of the
Works and Days.[12] The poet himself seems to present his teaching as
something new, a *logos* (106), perhaps 'account, scheme, principle' – this
is a one-off story designed to express a deep truth,[13] rather than part of an
inherited stock of myth that his audience will find familiar.[14]

[9] The meaning of the Greek adjective *homoiïos* is doubtful here (*WD* 182). The range of meaning
of the word is as broad as (e.g.) English 'alike', 'similar', and the pairing of the parent–child
relationship with that between guest and host or friend and friend (183–4) suggests that the
'similarity' in question is like-mindedness and harmony. However, in an account later in the
poem of the blessings of peace and justice, Hesiod includes the image that 'women give birth to
children who resemble their parents' (*WD* 235), and this seems to refer to physical
resemblance – when children look like their parents it is because the bloodline is running true.

[10] See pp. 62–64.

[11] As is well known, the account of the succession of races finds parallels in Near Eastern
literatures, but only on the broadest thematic level (cf. e.g. Koenen 1994; West 1997: 312–19;
I. Rutherford 2009: 14–16). The use of the imagery of metals to symbolize an historical
succession is closely paralleled in the dream of Nebuchadnezzar in the Biblical Book of Daniel
(ch. 2), but the resemblance seems not to extend to the background concepts – the theme in
Daniel has nothing to do with the idea of declining vitality.

[12] For example the Alexandrian poet Aratus, in a passage closely recalling Hesiod's myth of the
races, has Justice complain to the Silver Race that they are worse than their 'golden fathers', and
that they will produce even worse children (Aratus, *Phaenomena* 123–26). See further Van
Noorden 2015: 168–203.

[13] Cf. Haubold 2010: 25–8.

[14] By the same token the myth of the five races finds no clear equivalent in the Homeric poems,
and even the Hesiodic *Catalogue of Women* seems to follow a simpler structure of contrast
between past and present, contextualising the heroic race as the product of an age of carefree
intercourse between gods and mortals that resembles the Golden race of *WD* 109–20.

As we have described it so far, the sequence seems logical and complete: four metals and four races slipping away from godlike ease towards corruption, feebleness, disarray and death. But among them there is another race, placed between bronze and iron:

> Again another race, the fourth upon the land that nourishes many,
> Zeus Kronos' son made, more just and better:
> the godlike race of hero men (*andres hērōes*), who are called
> half-gods, the previous birth[15] upon the boundless earth.   (*WD* 157–60)

Two great wars brought about their destruction:

> Evil war and the painful battlefield destroyed them:
> some before seven-gated Thebes, the land of Cadmus,
> it destroyed as they fought each other to win Oedipus' herds,
> others by leading them over the sea's great gulf
> in ships to Troy to win fine-haired Helen.   (*WD* 161–5)

Two generations in the stricter sense of that term, the elder who fought over Thebes (the war of the 'Seven against Thebes') and the younger who fought over Troy: these are the subject-matter of narrative epic. Given that this race interrupts the sequence of metals and of human decline, it is likely that it has been introduced from elsewhere, perhaps by Hesiod himself, in order to explain where those who belong at the centre of Greek myth are to be placed in this (newly articulated?) scheme of mythological time.

Heroes and half-gods

In my translations so far I have put 'hero' for Greek *hērōs*, but this is only a placeholder – in practice it is seldom satisfactory to translate an ancient word with the English one derived from it. In today's language *hero* carries a heavy legacy of old assumptions and theories, in tension with the more vague associations that it attracts in popular culture. In the texts under study here, these people are certainly not uniformly admirable or brave or morally upright, and it would be a recipe for political disaster if leaders were to aspire uncritically to their qualities. Although the word *hērōs* is

---

[15] The word translated 'birth' here is *geneē*, the feminine cognate of the neuter *genos*. It is not clear whether there is any real difference between the two words. Presumably the meaning here is that the heroes immediately precede ourselves in the sequence of races.

elastic in its range of meaning,[16] and as an honorific title it can even be used to address a major deity like Dionysus,[17] it clusters more around the veneration given to a minor divinity, one whose presence would be tied to a specific local cult site.[18] Archaeology and traditions recorded in antiquity show that many of the characters familiar to us from the epic poems were named as the objects of such veneration, and heroic status was regularly given after death to eminent protectors and champions of the state and its people.

But Hesiod gives this race another name too, *hēmitheoi*, 'half-gods'. Here as always this is a collective term, a title for the whole race rather than used in the singular for an individual,[19] and the formulation 'they are called . . .' (note the present tense) perhaps suggests an allusion to the honorific title by which they were addressed in poetry[20] or even in cultic devotion.[21] However, the word 'half-gods' also gives a hint of why this race is both glorious and dangerous, admirable and problematic: its members stand in an ambiguous and wavering relationship with the limitations of human vitality and the certainty of mortality – that is, with the fundamental facts of the human condition, for Hesiod's audience as for you and me. To be a half-god is to hover uneasily between the comforts of divinity and the sobering certainties of mortal life. Accordingly, the recurring theme of the heroic race is the sufferings and pains that they underwent, as Simonides in the early Classical period was to put it in a song of lamentation:[22]

> For not even those who lived before us
> and from the gods, the kings, were born as half-god sons,
> completed life without toil, undiminished, without danger,
> and arrived at old age . . .
>
> (Simonides, fr. 523: Campbell, *GL* 3, pp. 418–19)

The word 'undiminished' is *aphthiton*, the word that appeared in the key formulation in the *Iliad*: *kleos aphthiton*, 'imperishable fame'. The half-god's

---

[16] On the semantics of *hērōs*, see Currie 2005: 60–70, and cf. Bremmer 2006.

[17] The word is used in this way in the cult hymn to Dionysus preserved by Plutarch, *Greek Questions* 36 (= *Moralia* 299B). See Furley and Bremer 2001: 2.373 with 374–5, note on line 1.

[18] Antonaccio 1995, esp. 145–97; Antonaccio 2005. Van Wees has an insightful study (2005) of the formation of the idea of the 'race of heroes' against the background of the development of hero cult and the Greek sense of history and mythical pseudohistory.

[19] This feature of the usage of *hēmitheoi* is pointed out by Van Wees 2005: 364–5.

[20] Compare Hesiod's list of the epithets of Aphrodite (*Th.* 195–200), where the formulation 'gods and men call her . . . [by such-and-such names]' presumably refers to the practice of poets.

[21] Cf. Currie 2005: 64 with n. 38 (where, however, this speculation is not explicitly stated).

[22] See Bremmer 2006: 23–24, and Van Wees 2005: 373–4, on this fragment and its relationship to Simonides' heroic praise of the contemporary dead of the battles of the Persian War.

life is subject to slow but certain decay and waning – what lasts is his name and his glory.

Looking back, 'half-gods' also recalls one of the driving problems of the *Epic of Gilgamesh:* he has partially divine origins, 'two-thirds of him god and one-third human' (*SBV* I 48, cf. IX 51), but death takes him all the same. Significantly, in the one instance where Homer calls the men of the Trojan War *hēmitheoi*, he does so in the context of their deaths.[23] After the Trojan War is over, the poet explains, the stockade around the Greek assailants' camp will be destroyed when Apollo diverts many rivers to engulf it,

> . . . Grēnikos and Aisēpos and bright Scamander
> and Simoeis, where many oxhide shields and fourfold helms
> had fallen in the dust, and the race (*genos*) of half-god men.
>
> (*Il.* 12.21–3)

Death will be the central theme of the Race of Heroes: the death that they underwent, like every other mortal, despite their lofty descent and their glories.

The lines so far cited from Hesiod's account of the heroic race are broadly consistent with the Homeric poems. Next, however, Hesiod introduces another prospect for them:[24]

> Then death's fulfilment covered over some of them;
> but others, granting them livelihood and lands apart from men,
> Zeus Kronos' son settled at the edges of the earth,
> and they dwell with breath of life untroubled
> in the islands of the blessed ones beside deep-whirling Ocean,
> heroes secure in wealth,[25] for whom the grain-giving ploughland
> three times in the year bears flourishing honey-sweet corn.
>
> (*WD* 166–73)

This is the oldest surviving depiction in Greek literature of the idea that the misery of death need not be inevitable, if only for these men of the past who were kinsmen and friends of the gods. Homer, indeed, mentions a concept

---

[23] See further Clay 1999.

[24] A variant version of the passage is attested which lacks line 166. Without 166, the words that I translate in 167 as 'but others' lose their contrastive force, and the sense would be that *all* those who died at Thebes and Troy went to the Isles of the Blest. As West points out in his note on the passage, the idea of a universal heroic return to life seems to be unparalleled elsewhere in Greek epic tradition, and I follow West in regarding 166 as authentic. See also Van Noorden 2015: 74–5.

[25] *Olbioi* 'secure in wealth': the concept of *olbos* includes the ideas both of abundant prosperity and of permanence.

like this just once. Menelaus learns the truth of his destiny from Proteus, the shape-changing divinity who lives among seals in the sea, and Proteus tells him that he will not die but will be sent by the gods 'to the Elysian plain and the edges of the earth' (*Od.* 4.563–8), where there is a life of endless ease similar to that in Hesiod's islands; but the exception proves the rule, this is a unique gift to Menelaus because he has married Helen and is thus the son-in-law of Zeus (*Od.* 4.569).[26] This means that there is a stark contrast between the Hesiodic and the Homeric vision of the race of heroes. For Homer's people, as we will see in more detail below, the prospect of death is absolute and unmitigated, no less than for the audience of the poem. This bifurcation in turn mirrors the Gilgamesh tradition: from *Gilgamesh and Huwawa* through to the Standard Babylonian Version, the narratives in which he confronts the fear of death marginalise or bypass the alternative tradition that grants him a blessed afterlife as a judge or king in the Underworld.[27]

Gods and half-gods in the *Catalogue of Women*

Elsewhere in the corpus ascribed in ancient times to Hesiod, the poem known as the *Catalogue of Women* or *Great Ēhoiai* (now fragmentary) is a summary compilation of mythical narratives, grouped according to the kinship relations of the mothers of the male heroes. Its genealogical structure reflects its origin as a continuation of Hesiod's *Theogony*, and the ancients regarded it as equally authentic. Nowadays it is generally held to be later, but still within the ambit of the authentic epic tradition.[28] Rather than a progressive sequence of decline like that seen in the Five Ages, the poem follows a simpler sense of contrast between the remote past and what came later. It opens with a time when gods and mortals mingled, not only in sexual congress – between mortal women and male gods – but also in social life:[29]

[26] Proteus' full formulation 'because you hold Helen and are to them [i.e. to the gods] the son-in-law of Zeus' suggests that the blessed afterlife of Menelaus may be connected to the tradition – not directly attested in Homer – that Helen was herself a goddess (Austin 1994: 73).

[27] See above, pp. 48–50, and for the full range of data, see George 2003: 1.119–35.

[28] On the dating and attribution of the *Catalogue of Women* see Hunter 2005b; Clay 2005: 25–26. A sustained analysis of the *Catalogue* is offered by Ormand 2014, arguing that the poem's overarching theme is rooted in a sense of social change in the late Archaic Period, specifically 'the emerging conflict of elitist and middling ideologies' (p. 50) in the area of marriage. On Ormand's reading, the narrative of a movement away from sexual unions between gods and mortals relates to a real-life threat to the maintenance of aristocratic claims to divine ancestry.

[29] For an analysis of the opening fragment of the *Catalogue*, see Irwin 2005.

> For at that time they held their feasts together, and council meetings
> were in common between immortal gods and mortal humans.
>
> (Hes. *Cat.* fr. 1.6–7 Most, M–W)

So far this sounds like the blessed ease of the Golden Race of the *Works and Days*; but the lines that come next (of which only stray words survive in the papyrus fragment) clearly struck a more pessimistic note:

> and yet not equal-in-life . . .
> men and women . . .
> foreseeing old age in their thoughts . . .
> the one group for a long time . . .
> young men, but the others at once . . .
> immortals . . . youth . . .   (Hes. *Cat.* fr. 1.8–13)

These broken lines seem to have spoken of the prospect of death that lay before these first humans, despite their closeness to the gods.

Subsequently the poem traces the gradual separation of humans from gods along a series of lines of genealogical descent, punctuated by repeated minglings and encounters across the divide. Running through the whole is the prime case of Heracles, the most famous offspring of a union between Zeus and a mortal woman, who has now become a god.[30] But all this belongs in the past, and it will not come again: the fifth Book of the poem tells how the mingling came to end.[31] The progression has reached the time when Helen, natural daughter of Zeus and legal daughter of Tyndareus king of Sparta, has been assigned to a husband and borne a daughter, Hermione, 'against expectation' (Hes. *Cat.* fr. 155.95 Most = fr. 204.95 M–W), whatever that means.[32] Suddenly the poem moves to the divine plane:

> All the gods set their thoughts apart
> out of strife: he was planning wonderful works then,
> high-thundering Zeus, to confuse things along the boundless earth,
> causing turmoil, and now he much desired to remove from sight

---

[30] See Hes. *Cat.* fr. 22.22–33 Most = fr. 25.22–33 M–W, and *Shield of Heracles* 27–56, lines said in the manuscripts to have been included in the *Catalogue* (fr. 138 Most = fr. 185 M–W, also fr. 139). On Heracles in the *Catalogue* see the acute analysis by Haubold 2005.

[31] In the interpretation that follows I draw especially on West 1985, esp. 119–21, and Clay 2005. Cf. also Koenen 1994; González 2010; Ormand 2014: 196–216. Nonetheless, the overall argument presented here is my own and strictly tentative.

[32] The significance of the birth of Hermione in this sequence remains unclear (cf. González 2010: 391–7; Ormand 2014: 202–6).

the race of men who speak with voices – ostensibly (*prophasin*) to destroy
the life-breath (*psuchai*) of the half-gods ...
> (Hes. *Cat.* fr. 155.95–100 Most = fr. 204.95–100 M–W)

Zeus' plans are always deep and are never clearly knowable, even to
the poets or to the other gods, as we will see more clearly later (pp.
170–172). But here it is unambiguously stated that he wished to bring
about their deaths – and also to achieve something more. The key
word is *prophasin*, which I have rendered provisionally as 'ostensibly'.
The noun *prophasis* is easily translated 'excuse, pretext', but it does
not necessarily indicate deceit or lies. To explain it here, where the
form of words is literally 'as regards a *prophasis* ... ',[33] it is useful to
think through a Homeric example of the same word used in the same
syntactic position: when a group of women join in lamentation with
another who is singing at the funeral of a man she loved, they are
singing 'as regards a *prophasis*' of this man's death, but each one is
really lamenting her own troubles (*Il.* 19.301–2). Here, similarly, Zeus
causes the heroes to lose their life or soul or last breath – *psuchē* – in
death, but something else happens that cannot be seen so openly. The
lines that follow introduce the prospect of the war that Zeus was
about to cause. The papyrus is again fragmentary, but the following
reconstruction is likely:[34]

> But the blessed ones .... as in the past
> apart from men should have their [?livelihood] and dwelling-place
> [?so he established] among gods and mortal men
> .... .suffering upon suffering,
> Zeus ...   (Hes. *Cat* fr. 155.103–6 Most = fr. 204.102–6 M–W)

In the first line, which are the 'blessed ones' (*makares*): gods or half-gods?[35]
If the word refers to the latter, the heroes, then these lines correspond closely
to the description in the *Works and Days* of the translation of the heroes to
new lives of ease 'in the islands of the blessed' (*en makarōn nēsois, WD* 171);
but it remains possible that the 'blessed ones' are simply the gods, and that
the poet is explaining that Zeus was about to prevent the continuation of

---

[33] Accusative of respect. See the excellent discussion of the present passage by Clay 2005: 29–31,
and cf. González 2010: 379–82.

[34] The words in square brackets tagged with query marks reflect some of the conjectures printed
by Most in the Loeb edition; Merkelbach and West are more cautious.

[35] Cf. González 2010: 411–413; also Clay 2005: 31 with n. 29, implicitly sceptical of the
reconstruction proposed by West 1985: 119–21 and followed by Koenen 1994: 30. There is
a tentative review of the debate by Ormand 2014: 205–11.

social and sexual intercourse between the two kinds – henceforth the gods would live apart, and mingling would cease.

Even if the latter is right, however, the question remains: if the destruction of the heroes' lives was Zeus' *prophasis*, what was the plan or thought underlying it? Hesiod goes on to describe an enormous storm that arose, perhaps a cosmic signal of the coming destruction or the harbinger of a cataclysmic flood.[36] In the account of this storm a strange riddling image emerges:

> The sea swelled, and everything trembled from this:
> it wore down the strength of mortals, and the harvest was diminished,
> in the spring season, the time when the hairless one gives birth in the
>   mountains
> in the earth's hidden place to three children in the third year.
> (Hes. Cat. fr. 155.127–30 Most = fr. 204.127–30 M–W)

In form, the image recalls an equally mysterious one in Hesiod's *Works and Days*,[37] when he pictures a young virgin moistening her skin with oil:

> on a winter's day, when the boneless one chews his own foot
> in his fireless home and his miserable dwelling:
> for the sun does not show him the meadow to roam in,
> but onto the home and city of the black men
> he turns his path, and reveals himself little to the Greeks.   (*WD* 524–8)

The passages revolve around kennings, riddling names for animals: almost certainly the 'boneless one' (*an-osteos*) is the octopus, the 'hairless one' (*a-trichos*) is the snake.[38] It is hard not to suspect that the octopus is more than merely picturesque here, that it carries some other allusive meaning;[39] the same principle encourages a closer look at the snake. In the poorly preserved lines that follow, Hesiod first describes its behaviour in

---

[36] It is an attractive possibility that this motif is akin to or even directly derived from the Mesopotamian flood myth, just as the motif of the overburdened earth from *Atrahasis* figures in the account of Zeus' plan for the Trojan War in the *Cypria* (see pp. 160–162 below). However, direct textual evidence to support such a theory is lacking, although it is striking that in (later-attested) Greek tradition the flood of Deucalion was located at the end of the third (bronze) age (see Apollodorus, *Library* 1.7.2, with Gantz 1993: 195–6). If this goes back to an early source, we have a (separate) parallel within Greek for the idea of a flood as marker of the end of one of the ages of primordial history. Cf. Bremmer 2008: 101–16.

[37] West 1985: 130 sees the *Catalogue* image as an imitation of this passage of the *Works and Days*.

[38] For the 'boneless one' see West 1978: 289–90, note at *WD* 524; the 'hairless one' is more doubtful, and its interpretation as a snake depends on identifying it with the 'terrible snake' explicitly so named a few lines later. So far as I can see, all recent contributions to the debate follow this line: earlier suggestions are collected in *LfgrE* s.v. *atrichos*.

[39] Cf. Bader 1989: 119–24 on possible sexual symbolism here.

springtime, descending from the mountains and moving under the trees hidden from human sight; then, in lines that are each half-lost, with the coming of winter it lies under some kind of covering (135) and moves into what sounds like a state of death:[40]

> a terrible snake, blood-red along its back . . .
> but it, aggressive and wild . . .
> the darts of Zeus overcome like . . .
> its breath-spirit (*psuchē*) alone remains . . .
> this, around the bedchamber that it has shed itself . . .
> slight . . . below the earth . . .
> goes, sent into darkness . . .
> lies . . . .   (fr. 155.136–43 Most = fr. 204.136–43 M–W)

The snake is overcome, apparently by Zeus' thunderbolts or a force associated with them; only the breath of its life, *psuchē*, remains when it has shed its skin. Although nothing but single words remains of the next lines, it seems certain that they described the snake's return to life in the vitality of its new skin.[41] The match with the earlier image of the *psuchai* of the heroes heightens the suggestion that this word-picture served to crystallise the idea of the prospect of a return to new life after the destruction of the Trojan War: either the revitalisation of the whole world or, as in the *Works and Days*, the renewal of the heroes' lives after their bodily deaths.

As a motif, additionally, the Hesiodic snake recalls the final failure of Gilgamesh, where the plant of rejuvenation is stolen from him by the snake and it sheds its skin as it glides away (above, pp. 105–107), but the Greek fragment is so doubtful that the similarity cannot usefully be pursued here.[42] Looking forward in Greek tradition, the notion that the *psuchē* remains independent of the body seems to foreshadow the uses to which the myth of heroic resurrection was later applied in philosophical religion and cult. From as early as the time of the poet Pindar, the concept of the heroic Isles of the Blest played a formative part in shaping concepts of a happy afterlife of the soul, to which one might aspire through initiation into a special cultic group or body of esoteric learning, most famously those

---

[40] My translation follows the text of Merkelbach and West here.

[41] On further Greek parallels for the symbolism of the casting off of the snake's skin, see Brown 2014, including the passage from Nicander referenced in the next note below.

[42] West has shown that a story related to that of Gilgamesh and the lost herb of rejuvenation is also referenced much later in the *Theriaca*, a poem on zoological lore by the Hellenistic poet Nicander (lines 343–66: see West 1997: 118).

associated with the names of Orpheus and Dionysus.[43] While it would be reckless to interpret this fragmentary poem in terms of such a highly developed sense of dualism, the suggestion remains that the *Catalogue* articulated a heightened image of heroic death and revitalisation, giving shape to what had been more dimly projected for the fourth race in the *Works and Days.*

Fame as surrogate immortality: Sarpedon to Glaucus

In contrast with the Hesiodic tradition, the myth of heroic resurrection is completely absent from the Homeric depiction of the Trojan War. Similarly, although there is good evidence that the other poems of the Epic Cycle had much to say about the burials of the warriors, sometimes specifying sites that are known independently to have been locations of hero cult in historical times, there is little indication that these poems spoke openly of the prospect that the heroes would one day be exalted as the objects of cultic devotion.[44] The notable exception to this is the *Aethiopis*: there is evidence that in this epic Dawn gained immortality for Memnon,[45] and Thetis conveyed Achilles to the White Island (*Leukē*) after his death.[46] But nothing like this is ever mentioned in the *Iliad.* At Troy the demigods have no prospect of anything but the veil of darkness falling over their eyes. Beyond that lies only the sightlessness of the grave and the decay of their flesh, tangible miseries on which is built the mythical image of Hades as a realm of pain and darkness.[47] Possibly this contrast between Homer and Hesiod stems from the fact that the two poets or traditions were in touch

[43] For recent surveys see Edmunds 2015 on the religious aspect, Long 2015: 51–87 on the philosophical.

[44] For Homer this point can be made virtually without qualification, but in the case of the poems of the Epic Cycle the evidence is less decisive. There are certainly indications of an emphasis in Cyclic poems on the burials of heroes at locations that are known to have been sites of hero-cult in later times. Danek observes multiple suggestions that the Cyclic *Nostoi* was concerned with the burials of the heroes, perhaps alluding to cultic commemoration at the same sites (Danek 2015: 375–6). However, nothing that survives suggests that the Cyclic poems made this connection explicit. On the contrast between Homer's near-silence on hero cult, contrasted with the abundance of allusions in later poetry, see Currie 2005: 47–59.

[45] Proclus' summary of the *Aethiopis*, para. 2 (West, *GEF*, pp. 112–13) is the only primary evidence for this. See further below, p. 302.

[46] In Proclus' summary of the *Aethiopis*, para. 4, Thetis takes the remains of Achilles to the White Island. Later sources attest that he was venerated in later times on what was claimed to be this island (see West, *EC* 155–56; Burgess 2009: 110–31).

[47] For a recent survey of the lore of the Homeric afterlife see Martin 2014, and cf. the insightful study by Sourvinou-Inwood 1995.

with different sets of ideas about the nature of the afterlife and the relationship between the heroes of contemporary cult and those of poetic narrative.
Equally, it can be argued that Homeric poetry deliberately avoids invoking
this version of the myth of the heroic race, in order to heighten the bitter
realism of their experience. Mortality and the fears and ethical compul-
sions that follow from it are no less real to the heroes than they were to
a man listening to the poetry with the knowledge that sooner or later he
would have to stand in the battle-line himself in the wars of his own city.
This means that the thoughts and actions of the heroes have a seriousness,
an immediate relevance to real life, for those who were to listen to them and
eventually to study them as venerable classics in the 400s BCE and beyond.

The *Iliad* offers at least one passage that begs to be heard in terms of
exactly this sequence of thought.[48] As so often, it is in the midst of a scene
of extended and inconclusive battle-narrative that the most basic principles of ethics are explored. Sarpedon is a son of Zeus himself, who
impregnated his mother in Lycia in the far south-east, where she in
turn was one of the children of the great monster-slayer Bellerophon
(*Il.* 6.196–9).[49] With the glamour and remoteness of this past behind him,
he fights at Troy alongside his cousin Glaucus. The tale of his parentage is
known among the other warriors – early in the battle-narrative
Tlēpolemos (himself a son of Heracles) tries to *disprove* the claim by
reducing him to cowardice and defeat (*Il.* 5.627–62), but Sarpedon wins
their duel, with Zeus ensuring that Tlēpolemos' spear does not strike
home, and for the time being his son avoids death.[50] Later, when Hector
is leading the Trojans towards what seems like victory, Zeus launches
Sarpedon to attack the Greek encampment, and as he surges forward –
like a lion attacking a homestead, to kill or be killed himself (*Il.*
12.299–308) – he turns to his friend to speak about the reasons why
men fight:

---

[48] For an extended meditation on Sarpedon in text and art, see Spivey 2018.

[49] This summarises the genealogy recounted by Sarpedon's friend Glaucus to an enemy before
combat. Interestingly, there is evidence that in the *Catalogue of Women* Hesiod represented
Sarpedon as one of three sons fathered by Zeus in the form of a bull on Europa, making him
brother of Minos and Rhadamanthus (fr. 89, 90 Most = fr. 140, 141 M–W). In order to
harmonise the two stories, and to remove the problem that Europa's son could not have been of
fighting age at Troy, Homer's Sarpedon was sometimes taken to have been the *grandson* of the
brother of Minos, or alternatively he was said to have been given a life to last three 'generations',
geneai (Apollodorus, *Library* 3.1.2). Cf. Asheri et al. 2007: 194, at Herodotus 1.173.1; Gantz
1993: 210–11.

[50] 'his father still (*eti*) warded off disaster' (*Il.* 5.662). For the sense of *eti* here, see Kirk's note
(1990: 125, note at lines 660–2).

Glaucus, why are we two rewarded more than anyone else
with the seating, and the portions of meat, and the full wine-cups
in Lycia, and all men look to us as to gods,
and we are assigned a plot of land beside the banks of Xanthos,
beautiful with vineyards and corn-bearing ploughland?   (*Il.* 12.310–14)

In return for these honours, they must demonstrate their strength and win
fame where their countrymen can see it:[51]

So now we must stand among the foremost of the Lycians
and hurl ourselves to meet the blazing battle,
so that one among the Lycians in their close armour will say:
'Indeed not without fame (*akleeis*) are they lords of Lycia,
our chieftains, and they eat the fat flocks of sheep
and drink the chosen honey-sweet wine: for there is also noble
strength in them, when they fight among the foremost Lycians.'
(*Il.* 12.315–21)

Honour and good reputation in return for glorious fighting, fighting in
turn as reward for honour: the reciprocal contract is implicit throughout
the discourse. But a deeper and more startling twist comes in what
Sarpedon says next:

O my dear friend, if we two could escape from the war
and we could expect to be ageless and deathless forever,
I would not fight myself among the foremost
nor would I send you out into the battle that glorifies men:
but since in truth the demons of death stand beside us
in thousands, whom it is impossible for any mortal to escape or avoid,
let us go, and to someone we will offer a cause for boasting, or he to us.
(*Il.* 12.322–8)

There is tenderness here, and I have not overtranslated the affectionate
phrase *ō pepon* with which he begins.[52] Driven first by the need for
respect and praise from the men around them, the heroes aspire beyond
that to the everlasting repayment of glory (*kleos, kudos*), in other words
a repetition of one's name and achievements that will last forever. This
need is compelling because death is certain and such commemoration
will ensure a presence, if only a verbal one, among men after death. The

---

[51] Here I supply the logic of the connection of ideas that seems to be bundled up in the single word
tō, 'So . . . ' (*Il.* 12.315).

[52] Cf. *Il.* 16.492, where Sarpedon uses the same term of affection to Glaucus when at the point of
death.

principles that are expressed here were already implicit as early as *Gilgamesh and Huwawa*, when the sight of corpses in the river was the stimulus to deeds that will establish an everlasting name (above, pp. 44–45), but they are here raised to the level of explicit meditation that is characteristic of Homeric discourse. Glory in the form of poetic memory serves the same function as statues and commemorative images: as we saw in the case of the statue Gilgamesh makes for Enkidu, the likeness is a guarantee of surrogate presence in the community after death. Hence it is all the more important that in the Homeric version the grimness of death is unrelieved: any prospect of an escape, such as resurrection in bodily or wraith-form in the Isles of the Blest, would rob these struggles of the imperative need that drives them.

The mortality of Sarpedon

For Sarpedon the certainty of death stands in especially sharp relief because Zeus is his father and he is thus literally of semi-divine parentage, *hēmitheos*.[53] In the ensuing combat Zeus tries to protect him from death, ensuring that he is unhurt when struck by arrow and spear (*Il.* 12.402–3); but in a later battle he finds that he cannot save him. A mysterious attacker has launched a great onslaught against the Trojans, and Sarpedon tells the faltering Lycians to stand firm so that he can face this man in combat and find out who he is (*Il.* 16.419–25) – in fact he is Patroclus disguised as Achilles. Zeus looks down and realises that it is now the 'portion' (*moira*) for Sarpedon to be killed; he wonders aloud whether he can save his son and snatch him out of the battle, sending him home safe; Hera his wife objects, reminding him that this is a mortal man long destined for this share (*aisa*) (*Il.* 16.441), and that many of the gods have sons in this war and would want to help them in the same way if they could.[54] Zeus accepts that his son must die, and makes blood fall to the earth like rain. Sarpedon's end is steeped in poetry. He is like a tree cut down by woodsmen or a bull brought down by a lion (*Il.* 16.482–91), but the brutality is visceral: Patroclus pierces him between heart and lungs (16.481) and stands on

[53] For an insightful study of the death of Sarpedon in terms of his special status as son of Zeus, see Delattre 2006 and compare Clay's argument (2009b; cf. Clay 1999) that Zeus reacts as he does to the prospect of Sarpedon's death because, uniquely among the combatants of the *Iliad*, he is a son of Zeus and thus symbolises the end of the heroic race as a whole.

[54] Homer does not explain why this outcome would be unacceptable to the gods: the question of the relationship between 'fate' and the agency of individual gods is posed but not answered in Homeric discourse. A full discussion of this issue would be beyond the scope of this book.

the corpse after his life-breath has seeped out, pulling out his spear and his innards with it (16.503–5). Zeus gives him such divine honour as he is permitted, and sends Apollo down to clean his dead son's wounds:

> He [sc. Apollo] brought him to be carried by the pair of swift guides,
> twin brothers Sleep and Death, who quickly placed
> him in the rich homeland of broad Lycia.   (*Il.* 16.681–3)

The presence of these two gods represents the idea that Sarpedon's death merges with sleep in its gentleness, and they take him for burial to the homeland whose fertility he himself has remembered on the battlefield. The attendance of these gods prompts us to wonder whether Homer is alluding to the hero-cult that Sarpedon received in Lycia as a matter of historical fact:[55] but here as elsewhere it is not mentioned openly, and it is not yet known whether such cult existed as early as the date of composition of the epic.[56]

Sarpedon lives and dies in the same ethical world as other men, but he is an especially bitter expression of the urgency of the need for honour and fame, both because his parentage means that he came so close to escaping mortality and also (implicitly) because he is dying far from home, fighting in defence of a doomed city that is not his own. His last words to Glaucus are telling:

> Glaucus my dear, warrior among men, now most of all
> you must be a spearman and a courageous warrior.
> Now evil war should be your desire, if you are swift . . .
> For to you afterwards a rebuke and a reproach
> I will be all the days without cease, if the Achaeans strip
> my armour when I am fallen in the struggle by the ships:
> but hold out in strength, and hearten all the people.
>   (*Il.* 16.492–4, 498–501)

He speaks of his own corpse as a token of honour or dishonour, not for himself but for those who will fight to gain possession of it, and he urges his friend to fight because of the fear of disgrace, the mirror image of the quest for glory. So with his last words he returns again to the need for respect, a need that makes sense only because men like him and Glaucus know that they must die.

From *c.* 510 BCE survives the vase known (after its painter's signed name) as the Euphronios Krater, a work of monumental scale and

---

[55] Suggested by Nagy 1983, and also pursued at length in the final chapters of Spivey 2018.
[56] The evidence is reviewed by Currie 2005: 50 with n. 27.

ambition (Fig. 8).[57] On one side is the dead Sarpedon, his wounds still fresh and weeping, as the winged brothers Sleep and Death lift him up under the supervision of Hermes, who belongs here not only because he is Zeus' messenger but also because one of his traditional roles is to guide souls to the Underworld after death.[58] On its own this might look like a glamorous imaginative fantasy, elegant but distanced from contemporary reality; but everything changes when we turn to the other side of the vase.[59] Four young men – barely more than boys, being beardless – are arming them-selves, but nothing in the pose or physique implies that they necessarily belong in the distant heroic past.[60] One might interpret them as other warriors in the Trojan War, perhaps Sarpedon's own Lycians arming themselves; equally, however, they are indistinguishable from ordinary people of the time the vase was made and displayed, arraying themselves for battle or (as some have argued) for military athletics or dancing. The two older men standing to either side of Sarpedon are repeated almost identically in the scene of the arming soldiers: perhaps these are to be read as idealised spectators, looking both on the high world of myth and on the daily realities of military service.

Every battle in the world of the Classical city-state was fought by citizen militias, not by professional soldiers. If this vessel was set up for public display or even if it simply stood full of wine at a *symposion*, the male

---

[57] The vase is now at the Museo Archeologico Nazionale, Cerveteri, having formerly been at the Metropolitan Museum in New York.

[58] See for example *Od.* 24.1–14. This is the only place in Homeric poetry where Hermes takes this role, and it is usually considered a late addition to the text; but it is noteworthy that Homer describes Sleep and Death as the dead Sarpedon's *pompoi* (16.681, translated here as 'guides'), and Hermes as guide of the dead is *psycho-pompos*, 'wraith-guide'. The Homeric wording perhaps invited the addition of Hermes' personal presence. Shapiro compares the Euphronios krater with other vase-paintings of the death of Sarpedon, some of which include a small-winged figure identifiable as his breath-spirit or *eidōlon* (Shapiro 1993: 132–65, 246–50).

[59] Here I assume that we have reason to look for a meaningful thematic relationship between the two images. In principle it remains impossible to tell whether two scenes juxtaposed on a single vase are meant to be read together, and a sense of the correct 'grammar' for such readings can only develop by experiment. For a thoughtful treatment of this methodological issue, see Steiner 2007: 94–170 *passim*.

[60] Steiner argues that the arming figures are Lycians or Trojans from the Trojan War itself (Steiner 2007: 115, with references to earlier scholarship on both sides of the question at 285–6, nn. 60–3). The names labelling the figures ought to be a guide here, but their evidence is equivocal and it remains possible to argue both for contemporary Athenian resonances and for connections to the Iliadic context of the Sarpedon scene. Stansbury-O'Donnell (1999: 105–7, cf. Stansbury-O'Donnell 2006 *passim*) argues that the arming of the warriors is being linked implicitly to the prospect of a heroic death connected to the ideal represented by Sarpedon: this corresponds closely to the interpretation advanced by Spivey in his recent essay (2018: 102–33). For variant approaches to the problem cf. Lowenstam 1992: 175–6; Junker 2012 [2005]: 55–9; Schefold 1992 [1978]: 248–50.

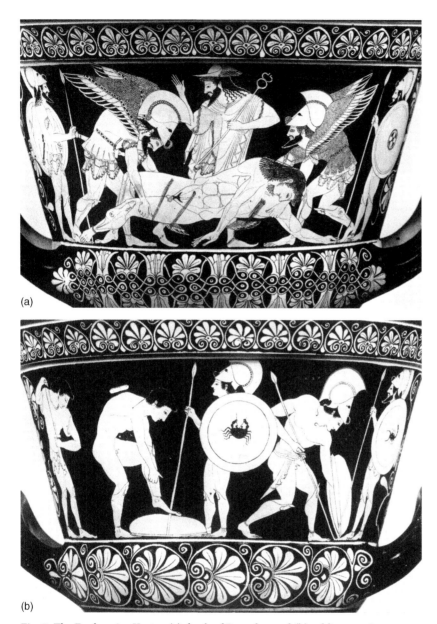

Fig. 8 The Euphronios Krater: (a) death of Sarpedon and (b) soldiers arming.

drinking-party that was central to social life in the period, the conjunction
of the two images would have been a reminder that we all face death with
the same finality as the Lycian demigod: as Aeschylus puts it in a fragment
from a tragedy on the miseries of Sarpedon's mother, 'the war-god always

desires to pluck the best flower of an army'.[61] It is for this reason, fundamentally, that the inner struggles of Homeric warriors are those of any and
every thoughtful human being, with just the same immediacy as the
turmoil that gripped Gilgamesh after the maggot dropped from Enkidu's
flesh.

---

[61] Aesch. fr. 100, well adduced by Spivey 2018: 163. On the verb translated 'pluck', built on the
basic image in the noun *anthos* 'flower, upsurge, best [of the people]', see Clarke 2005: 32.

7 | The plan of Zeus

In the *Works and Days* it is Zeus who makes the heroes and brings about their posthumous translation to the Isles of the Blest, and in the *Catalogue of Women* he establishes the great destruction that ends their time of flourishing on earth. Here, then, the story becomes a matter of theology: What does it mean to speak of Zeus' desires and decisions? And how do they relate to those of the other members of the divine society?[1]

The squabbles of the gods

Although Zeus' name and identity have an obvious Indo-European ancestry and must stem from the same remote past as does the Greek language itself, nonetheless his roles and titles also have strong affinities with the sky-god figures of other religious traditions in the cuneiform world.[2] Both in *Atrahasis* and in the Gilgamesh narratives we have seen a pattern by which the gods respond to a crisis by meeting in council and reaching a decision by debate and cross-argument, presided over by Anu, sky-god and father of gods. So too in Greek epic Zeus, sky-god and 'father of gods and men', presides over the other deities who assemble on Mount Olympus, like an indulgent king over the squabbling and scheming junior members of his extended family.[3]

It is evidently part of the Homeric programme to acknowledge, even to celebrate, the triviality and short-sightedness of this politics.[4] Just as Atrahasis

---

[1] For the background argument of this chapter cf. Versnel 2010: 151–237, who addresses many of the same questions in terms of the overall interpretation of early Greek theology, relying on a posited tension between cosmic order and 'paratactic multiplicity' – the coexistence of several concepts, discourses or divine personalities whose mutual relationships need not be systematised.

[2] See for example López-Ruiz 2015: 376–7, with West 1997: 114–16.

[3] Cf. West 1997: 44–51; López-Ruiz 2014, esp. 66–8; Louden 2011: 16–29, emphasising that in both traditions the sky-god acts as mediator (or 'chairman'?) in such disputes between the gods. In practice Zeus sometimes resonates with Anu and sometimes with Enlil, as in various examples posited in the present book.

[4] For introductory surveys of this question and the long debate on it, see Kearns 2004, with Graziosi and Haubold 2005: 65–75. With regard to the Judgment of Paris, the classic discussion is Reinhardt 1997 [1960].

was supported by Ea and resented by Enlil, just as Gilgamesh and Enkidu brought down the vengeance of Enlil by killing Humbaba and suffered the wrath of Ishtar for rejecting her seductive advances and mocking her in person, so in the world of the Homeric epics each god pursues a personal agenda of reward and punishment. It may seem like a rational theology of reciprocal benefit when a god protects his or her own children, or repays favours for honours previously given, but all too often their motivations seem impossibly petty – most obviously when they promote their children and favourites by inflicting pain on their enemies, or when they repay old debts and punish old wrongs through the descendants of the mortals originally involved.[5]

For our purposes, chief among these quarrels and rivalries is that concerned with the Judgment of Paris, which sparked off the Trojan War. The Latinised mythographic version has become part of our common culture, but it includes many later distortions and modifications,[6] so it will be well to give the outline of the earliest knowable version as told in the *Cypria*.[7] The three great goddesses, Aphrodite, Hera and Athene, driven to rivalry as to which of them was most beautiful, paraded before Paris prince of Troy;[8] each offered rewards to Paris in return for victory;[9] Aphrodite bribed him with the promise of Helen, and won the contest. When she honoured the promise by enabling him to take Helen from her original husband she became the ally of the Trojans in the subsequent war, and the defeated contestants allied themselves with the Trojans' enemies.

The *Iliad* recalls the Judgment of Paris only once,[10] setting it in stark contrast with the human horrors of the war that followed. Achilles has

---

[5] Cf. Ahrensdorf 2014: 25–72.

[6] The versions found in familiar modern summaries usually approximate to that in the Latin mythography of Hyginus (*Fabulae* 92.3), which despite its brevity and corruptions has been deeply influential on the handbook tradition ever since its publication in 1535.

[7] Fragments at West, *GEF*, pp. 68–9, 85–9. Standard discussions are West, *EC* 73–9; Currie 2015; Gantz 1993: 2.567–71. In the *Library* of Apollodorus, this section is preserved only in abbreviated form in the *Epitome* (3.1–2), and it is dangerous to make inferences from its wording when uncorroborated by other sources.

[8] Aphrodite's alluring appearance in the contest is lingeringly described in surviving fragments of the *Cypria*: West, *GEF*, fr. 5–6, pp. 84–6.

[9] Apollodorus records the bribes offered by Hera and Athene, respectively, kingship over all men and victory in war (*Epitome* 3.2), and his account corresponds closely to that given by Helen herself in Euripides' *Trojan Women* (923–34); West as usual inserts the extra words from Apollodorus into his text of the relevant passage of Proclus' summary of the *Cypria* (*GEF*, pp. 68–9).

[10] For a recent study of the literary dynamics of the allusion see Mackie 2013, and cf. esp. Richardson 1993: 276–8; Burgess 2001: 48 with n. 3; Davies 2003 on the origins and affinities of the myth. For most of the major issues about the details of the story, the earliest significant evidence is in evocations of the Judgment in Trojan-War-themed tragedies of Euripides, as for example *Andromache* 289–92. This and other Euripidean passages on the subject are analysed by Stinton 1990 [1965].

indulged his anger against Hector, the killer of his beloved friend Patroclus, by abusing him after he is dead (see below, pp. 287–289). After drilling holes through the tendons of his ankles to attach him to his chariot (*Il.* 22.395–404), he has gone on dragging him again and again around Patroclus' memorial (24.15–18), defiling the corpse and leaving it unburied; it would have begun to rot, were it not divinely preserved by Apollo, Hector's protector (24.18–21, cf. 24.411–15). Most of the gods join Apollo in feeling pity at what is being inflicted on the corpse, urging that Hermes should secretly remove it to safety, but three of them resist the proposal:

> This was pleasing to all the other gods – yet not to Hera
> nor to Poseidon, nor to the owl-faced virgin,
> but they stood as when first holy Troy became hateful to them
> and Priam and the people on account of Alexandros' ruinous folly (*ātē*),
> Alexandros[11] who insulted the goddesses, when they came to the
> sheepfold
> and he approved her who offered woeful promiscuity.[12]   (*Il.* 24.25–30)

Hera and Athene are still bitter at having lost the contest; Poseidon, see-mingly, remembers an older insult, when he and Apollo built the walls of Troy and Priam's father Laomedon refused to pay their wages.[13] In any world-view that I can imagine, these small rivalries and jealousies ought to mean nothing beside the degradation now being inflicted on Hector; yet they are enough to determine the wishes of three gods – gods who somehow also play their parts in presiding over the order of the universe. Apollo reminds the gods of the sacrifices Hector used to offer them in his life; Hera argues against Apollo, not for moral or sacred reasons but on the grounds that Achilles deserves the gods' help because his mother is a goddess and they were all guests at her wedding (*Il.* 24.59–63). When Zeus finally tries to resolve the quarrel he remains within the same narrow circle of reciprocities, appealing to the debt of gratitude that they owe to Hector:

> Never has the altar been without our apportioned feast,
> the poured offering and the sizzle: for that is the reward (*geras*) assigned
> to us.   (*Il.* 24.69–70)

---

[11] Elsewhere in this book I use *Paris*, which has become more usual in subsequent tradition than the Homeric *Alexandros*.

[12] The word translated 'promiscuity' is *machlosunē*, which is unique here in Homer: ancient commentators take it as meaning an insane excess of sexual desire, linked to the adjective *gunaikomanēs*.

[13] Poseidon refers explicitly to this grudge at *Il.* 21.446–57, cf. 7.452–3.

An ancient listener to the *Iliad* would have understood the full horror of the way Hector is being treated: defilement of a corpse brings *miasma*, religious pollution, and it represents a depth to which only beasts or savages would stoop. Yet here, as it takes place before their eyes, the gods think only of their personal allegiances and their due honours: the smoke of the sacrifice that rises to their nostrils and provides their feast, just as the gods in *Atrahasis* decided on the survival of mankind because of their need to be fed through the sacrifices offered by humans in their temples (above, p. 52).[14] The questions prompted by this passage are also those that hang over the overall myth of the Race of Heroes. Why did Zeus cause the Trojan War? Let us turn back for a moment to the wording of the *Catalogue of Women*:

> [Helen] bore Hermione lovely-ankled in the halls,
> unexpectedly. All the gods set their thoughts apart
> out of strife: he was planning wonderful works then,
> high-thundering Zeus …
>
> (Hes. *Cat.* fr. 155.94–7 Most = fr. 204.94–7 M–W)

The phrase 'set their thoughts apart [from each other]' closely echoes a Homeric phrase, which describes the gods' rivalries against each other when they take sides in battle.[15] On the face of it, then, another squabble in the Olympian family was the trigger for Zeus' original plan for the disasters and bloody battles that next arose. The gods' vicious behaviour when Hector lies rotting is part of a pattern that goes back to the ultimate beginnings of the war.

Destiny and justice

Is it an anachronism here to look for something like justice, for a meaningful sense of divine order and principled causation? This question will be insistent for anyone who expects God or gods to be in control of the destiny

---

[14] The pseudo-Platonic *Alcibiades II* (at 149 d) cites as if from the *Iliad* a passage, long accepted into published editions as *Il.* 8.548–53, in which the Trojans offer a hecatomb or sacrifice of a hundred cattle, from which the sizzle rises into the sky; the gods *refuse* to divide it between them (*ou … dateonto*, 550) because they feel enmity towards Troy. This plainly implies that they would otherwise have consumed it as a feast. Only one line of this passage (549) is transmitted in the mainstream manuscript tradition; but the lines seem ancient, and probably simply represent a more crude or literal evocation of a principle that is elsewhere implied but left unstated.

[15] With 'set their thoughts apart' (*dicha thumon ethento*) in the *Catalogue* passage compare esp. 'holding their thought apart' (*Il.* 20.32), and 'the thought blew apart in their minds' (*Il.* 21.386).

of the world, as in the three Abrahamic faiths. Some might point for an answer not to these individual Olympians but to a more abstract force, something that in English might be called Destiny or Fate. Just as with Akkadian *šīmtu*, Homeric Greek has words that invite such translations, but their place in the order of things remains opaque. Each of the two words *moira* and *aisa*[16] may mean simply a share or portion of anything that is divided,[17] but can also name an agency in causation. Towards this end of the range, the poet often seems to draw near to the fully divine image, which takes sharp form in later poetry and art: Moira is a woman who ordains or safeguards the appointed moment of a mortal's death – or, in the most elaborate articulation, there are three Moirai who spin the thread of a life, stretch it out and break it at death.[18] Within Homer there is a hint at least that such a force overrides the will of the individual deity, even Zeus: when Zeus wants to spare his son Sarpedon from death at Patroclus' hands, he is reminded that this man has been 'long ago destined (*peprōmenos*) for his portion (*aisa*)' (*Il.* 16.441 = 22.179). When a duel is about to take place, a Homeric character can assert that the gods already know 'for which man death's fulfilment is destined' (*Il.* 3.309),[19] but Homer does not explore or clarify the relationship between this principle and the will of the individual deity.[20] In later Greek intellectualism, by contrast, the question could be articulated explicitly, as in a celebrated example from Herodotus. Croesus of Lydia, a king who has been defeated and enslaved despite having bestowed great gifts on Apollo's shrine at Delphi, demands that the god explain why he allowed him to suffer disaster; Apollo responds that he did indeed *delay* the king's fall as long as he could – 'but the apportioned destiny cannot be escaped, even by a god' (*Histories* 1.91).[21] The words translated as 'apportioned destiny' (*peprōmenē moira*) shadow the Homeric wording;[22] yet this sense of an

---

[16] For a useful summary of the semantic patterns of *moira, aisa* and related words in Homer see Janko 1992: 4–7. *Moros*, effectively a masculine equivalent of *moira*, is a less common member of this group of virtual synonyms.

[17] This is visible in particularly stark form in the Law Code of Gortyn in Crete, where *moira* is used to refer to a 'share' or 'portion' of property (Gagarin and Perlman 2016, pp. 334–428, text G72 at 3.28–9, 4.41, 4.43). Similarly *aisa* is attested in Cypriot and other Greek varieties as the word for a measure of wine (noted by Pulleyn 2000: 227, at line 416).

[18] See e.g. *Il.* 20.127–8, 24.209–10; *Od.* 7.196–8. Even on this level *moira* can be exchanged with *aisa* as a virtual synonym. For a recent survey treatment of the *moirai* see Pirenne-Delforge and Pironti 2015: 42–3; the most useful longer treatment is that by S. de Angeli, *LIMC* VI.1 636–48.

[19] Achilles uses similar wording of his knowledge that it has been destined, *peprōtai*, that he and Patroclus should die at Troy (*Il.* 18.329).

[20] For a thoughtful overview of this issue, see Eidinow 2011: 66–92.

[21] On the theology of this passage, see Harrison 2000: 225–7, comparing Eidinow 2011: 67–118.

[22] On Homeric allusion in this story cf. Pelling 2006b: 85–7.

ordered relationship is not even hinted at anywhere within the surviving corpus of epic. If there is a theology of fate somewhere in the world-view of the poets, it remains obscure.

Justice, says Hesiod, is Zeus' daughter; when men abuse her by their lies and corruption, she complains to her father and he sends famine and suffering and disaster, but he rewards the honest with peace and prosperity, with fertility in the land and in women (*WD* 213–27).[23] In Hesiod's scheme of the five races, we humans of the fifth race have no knowledge or recognition of the watchfulness (*opis*) of the gods (*WD* 187), and Homer evokes the same idea in a description of a storm:[24]

> As when all the black land is weighed down under a storm
> on an autumn day, when Zeus pours out his water
> in a rush, when he is angry with men and resents them
> because they have made crooked judgments by force in the assembly,
> and they have driven out justice, heedless of the watchfulness (*opis*) of the
>   gods;
> all their rivers run rushing in a flood,
> then the torrents cut through many embankments
> and with great roaring they rush to the swelling sea
> headlong from the mountains, and men's works are diminished …
>
> (*Il.* 16.384–92)

Because Zeus is sky-god as well as father of Justice, it is from the sky that the signs of his anger come. Notice, however, that this passage is not part of the events of the Trojan War: it is a simile-image prompted by a description of the noise and onrush of an army. The simile is implicitly located in the world of the poet and his audience, rather than that of the heroes: within it, those who suffer from the torrents do so because they have disregarded the 'watchfulness of the gods', but in the main action of the *Iliad* the gods seem to watch men only for frivolous and selfish reasons.[25]

The obvious way to find a high divine purpose in the Trojan War is to pin it on one of the more specific manifestations of Zeus' role in the world. One of his titles is Zeus Xeinios, Zeus who presides over *xenia*, the duty of

---

[23] For fertility as a reward for justice see also *Od.* 19.107–114, where it is a reward for the virtue of the king.

[24] On the ethical concepts in this simile in relation to Hesiodic ideas, see Yamagata 1994: 60–92; Allan 2006: 9–16.

[25] In contrast to the *Iliad*, this theme appears explicitly in the *Odyssey*, where both Odysseus and other characters mention that the suitors in their bullying behaviour have had no thought for the *opis* of the gods (see *Od.* 20.215, 21.28). At 14.80–108, Eumaeus the virtuous swineherd speaks at length of their disregard for *opis*, treating it as a divine principle in the same way.

ritualised friendship that confers mutual obligations on guest and host from different communities.[26] As everyone knows, the war began because Paris, prince of Troy, stole or ravished or seduced Helen, the wife of Menelaus king of Sparta, when he was a guest in Menelaus' house. So Menelaus himself cries across to the Trojans in battle that they will suffer the vengeful anger (*mēnis*) of Zeus Xeinios, who will destroy their city (*Il.* 13.620–5).[27] It would be possible to tell the story of the war without going beyond this principle; but there remains the darker question: why did Paris take Helen in the first place?

The *Cypria* and the causes of the war

The story recalled in the *Iliad* passage discussed earlier, where Aphrodite offered Helen to Paris as a bribe, fits into the larger tale whose earliest known narration was in the *Cypria*: at the wedding-feast of Peleus and Thetis, which all the gods attended, the goddess Strife (*Eris*) had made the three goddesses quarrel for the title of the most beautiful. The story has persisted through the centuries, with the detail of the golden apple as the prize becoming more and more prominent,[28] but we need to go further back to explain why the quarrel developed in the first place. Here we depend mostly on Proclus' summary of the plot of the *Cypria*, expanded with the aid of a scattering of more detailed accounts from the ancient and late antique mythographers.[29] Proclus begins simply with the statement

[26] On Zeus Xeinios and the theological understanding of the Trojan War, see e.g. Allan 2006: 3–8. For standard treatments of Homeric *xenia* see Van Wees 1992: 172–82, 229–37; Von Reden 1995: 13–44; cf. Seaford 1994: 1–29.

[27] Menelaus expresses the same principle at greater length at *Il.* 3.351–4. For the *mēnis* of Zeus against those who disrespect *xenia* see also *Il.* 14.283–4, which shares wording with *Il* 13.620–5. *Xenia* and its abuse as one of the recurrent themes of the *Odyssey*, including and contextualising the case of Paris and Helen, is beyond the scope of this book.

[28] The story, subsequently so famous, that Strife provoked the quarrel by tossing down an apple 'for the fairest' of the three goddesses is not found in any of the early written sources, although an apple or something like one is held in Hera's hand in several vase-paintings of the Judgment of Paris from the fifth century BCE (Gantz 1993: 567–71; West, *EC* 75–9; on the difficulty of explaining the motif, see A. Kossatz-Deissmann at *LIMC* VII.1: 176–88, at p. 187). The meaningless and probably corrupt phrase 'an apple about beauty' appears in the relevant passage of Apollodorus (*Epitome* 3.1.2); otherwise the first explicit account specifying Strife's use of a 'golden apple' is in the mythographic papyrus fragment POxy 3829 referred to in our main text here (see West, *GEF*, pp. 80–1). As so often, today's standard popular version is matched in Hyginus (see above, p. 152, n. 6).

[29] For analyses of the sources for the first episode of the *Cypria*, and the relationship between Fr. 1 and the Proem of the *Iliad*, see esp. Currie 2015: 285–7, 295–7; West, *EC* 65–9. Key discussions are Koenen 1994; Mayer 1996; Clay 1999; Burgess 2001: 149; Marks 2002; Graziosi and Haubold

that 'Zeus makes plans (*bouleuetai*) with Themis about the Trojan War',[30] but a text on papyrus of the second century CE, which presents itself as background information for the plot of the *Iliad*, gives a more detailed version of the same statement:

> Zeus, recognising the impiety (*asebeia*) of the heroic race, deliberates with Themis as to how to destroy them entirely.[31]

Themis, the goddess who personifies the divine order of the world,[32] joins with Zeus in planning the war as a punishment. So far this seems consistent with the account we have seen from the Hesiodic *Catalogue of Women*, but with a distinct emphasis on the moral failings of the heroic race – giving Zeus a motive for their destruction similar to that which drove him to destroy the Silver Race in Hesiod's scheme (*WD* 137–9). Zeus, according to the next sentence of the fragment, instructed Hermes to prevent Strife from attending the wedding, at which she then arrived in defiance; Proclus, correspondingly, specifies that in the *Cypria* Hermes was acting under Zeus' command when he led the goddesses to be judged by Paris.[33]

Was all this designed expressly to spark off a great destructive war? The route towards an answer takes us first to the *Iliad*. In the sequence of events the *Iliad* came immediately after the *Cypria*; where its themes and wording interact with what we know of the other epic, this will be either because it influenced the *Cypria* poet directly or (more likely) because both alike subsume and respond to pre-existing traditions of mythical pseudohistory and poetic art. The *Iliad*, ostensibly, is concerned only with a slice of the history: it is set towards the end of the siege years, and takes a single episode, a quarrel between a warrior and his commander and its disastrous aftermath, to stand for all the dark themes of the war. Its opening lines are about Zeus' plan for the deaths of heroes:[34]

> Wrath – sing, goddess, the Wrath of Peleus' son Achilles,
> ruinous, which threw countless pains on the Greeks
> and cast down to Hades many mighty ghosts
> of heroes, and left the men themselves for dogs to seize

2005: 122–5; Scodel 2008; Barker 2008; Allan 2008b.The argument presented here draws on elements of all these papers, built into a tentative synthesis of my own.

[30] *Cypria* Arg. 1: West, *GEF*, pp. 68–9. The manuscripts here have *Thetis*, but it is virtually certain that this is an error for *Themis*.

[31] POxy 3829 ii 9: see West, *GEF*, pp. 80–1, and *EC* 68, 73–5.

[32] For *themis* as an ethical concept, see Yamagata 1994: 72–92; Du Sablon 2014: 135–66. On the personification the best survey remains *LIMC* VIII.1 (Supplementum), 1199–1205.

[33] *kata Dios prostagēn* (*Cypria*, fr. 1.1: West, *GEF*, pp. 68–9).

[34] On the poetics of the proem cf. esp. Redfield 2001 [1979].

and for vultures to divide – and Zeus' plan was coming to fulfilment.

(*Il.* 1.1–5)

Ancient commentators were divided as to the meaning of the words *Zeus' plan was coming to fulfilment.* The mainstream view, following the principle of 'interpreting Homer out of Homer', was that this refers to the plan made by Zeus with Thetis within the *Iliad*, which we will discuss below (pp. 207–209). However, the makings of a more complex answer survive in the medieval manuscripts of the *Iliad* in a chunk of marginal commentary forming part of the D-Scholia.[35] It is believed to be derived from the ancient source known as the *Mythographus Homericus*, whose author or authors took a more outward-looking view of the mythical background to the Homeric poems, often including parallels that respond well to modern approaches to intertextuality.[36] The author of this text records the existence of a darker and more complex explanation of these words, which associated the Iliadic 'plan of Zeus' with Zeus' decision to destroy the heroic race entirely. This will bring us to the deepest level of myth, the level on which gods are present in or identified with the physical forms of the world around us.

Zeus' grandparents are Ouranos, the high sky, and Gaia or mother-earth, gods whose loves and struggles at the world's beginning are expounded in Hesiod's *Theogony*.[37] Although in stories of less remote times they are usually silent and unmoving and may seem marginal, they remain real presences throughout.[38] According to the *Mythographus*, 'some people' allege that Zeus' plan was prompted by his grandmother:

> They say that Earth, weighed down by the multitude of humans, when there was no piety (*eusebeia*) among humans, asked Zeus to relieve her of the burden. (Schol. D on *Il.* 1.5; West, *GEF*, pp. 80–1)

---

[35] Edited by Van Thiel 2000; on the manuscript context see Dué 2009 on the manuscript Venetus A.

[36] The name *Mythographus Homericus* is given to the presumed author of a series of micro-texts elucidating Homeric passages with mythological information taken from other literary sources, often named poets of post-Homeric date. Some of these *Mythographus* texts are preserved in Homeric manuscripts, in the commentary corpus known as the D-scholia, while others survive in papyrus fragments (see Dickey 2007: 20–1). Montanari 1995 remains the standard study (on the present scholion see esp. 161–2). The papyrus survivals from the *Mythographus* are presented by Van Rossum-Steinbeek 1998: 85–118.

[37] There are also ancient references to a Cyclic *Theogony* with material on the origins of the gods sprung from Ouranos and Gaia: see D'Alessio 2015: 199–202.

[38] See for example Sophocles, *Antigone* 337–41, and other sources collected by Clarke 2001a.

The presence of the word *eusebeia*, the opposite of *asebeia*, suggests that this is somehow linked to the account in the other mythographic papyrus cited above (*POxy* 3829) – perhaps both were excerpted from the same lost original. The writer goes on to give a sequence of lines from the *Cypria*:

> There was a time when the countless tribes – roaming ever over the land –
> <of humans were weighing down>[39] on the breadth of the deep-chested
>   Earth.
> Seeing her Zeus pitied her, and in the close thought of his mind
> he decided to lighten all-nourishing Earth of [the weight of] humans,
> by stirring to flame[40] the great strife of the Trojan War,
> so that he would empty the weight through death: and at Troy those men,
> the heroes, were being killed, and Zeus' plan was being fulfilled.
>
> (*Cypria* fr. 1: West, *GEF*, pp. 82–3)

The problem was overpopulation and the annoyance that it caused among the gods; the wholesale destruction of this race of men was the solution. Although this story might have been told at the very beginning of the *Cypria*, it is more likely that it was a flashback later in the poem,[41] perhaps even voiced by a human or divine character. The opening formula 'There was a time when … ' suggests that something new and recondite is being revealed, a narrative previously unknown to the internal addressee and, by extension, to the original audience of the *Cypria* itself.

It has long been recognised that the closest parallels for this story are in cuneiform literature. The motif of human behaviour annoying the gods and prompting vindictive punishment is found repeatedly – an example is the text known as *The Slaying of Labbu*, where the groans and lamentation of humanity prevent Enlil from sleeping and he sends a monster against them[42] – but the *Cypria* story bears an even closer resemblance to *Atrahasis*, and it seems certain that the motif originated in one or other articulation of that myth. The *Mythographus* provides additional evidence for this connection, giving the following summary:

---

[39] The transmitted text is metrically faulty, with several syllables missing; the words in angle brackets represent Greek *anthrōpōn epiedse*, one of several possible restorations that have been proposed. The general sense of what must have been here is, however, clear from the wording of the prose passage introducing these lines.

[40] Greek *rhipissas*, sometimes translated 'fanning' (as in English 'to fan the flames'): the verb *rhipidsō* is built on the noun *rhipis*, which names an instrument used for fanning flames to stimulate a fire (see also Aristophanes, *Frogs* 360).

[41] This is well argued by Sammons 2017: 37–42, speculating that the context may have been an 'analeptic excursus' in the poem's narrative of the Judgment of Paris.

[42] Lambert 2013: 361–5, with Lambert's introductory analysis.

Zeus at first and immediately made the Theban war, through which
he destroyed very many men, and later again the Trojan War, using
as his counsellor Blame (*mômos*) – this is what Homer calls 'the plan
of Zeus' – since he was able to destroy them all with thunderbolts or
deluges; Blame urged against this ...[43]

The reference to thunderbolts *or floods* provides the corroborating clue.
Zeus' thunderbolts are conventional, but the notion of an unfulfilled plan
to send a flood seems redundant for the story.[44] Its presence here can be
explained as influence from the Mesopotamian flood myth, mediated
perhaps through a version of *Atrahasis* itself, which is known (for example)
in a Hittite rendering.[45] It is an attractive possibility that a Greek who
encountered this story linked it to the established image in his own tradition that treated destructive *weather* as a conventional sign of Zeus'
vengeance on the crimes of men, as in the Iliadic simile discussed above
(p. 156), and that in this way part of the plot-line of *Atrahasis* entered what
became the *Cypria*'s account of the destruction of the heroic race.

In terms of its cast of divine characters, too, the story has been fully
integrated into Greek norms. Both Themis, with whom Zeus took counsel
when he planned the war, and the more mysterious figure of 'Blame',[46] are

---

[43] From the D-scholia on *Il.* 1.5. See West, *GEF*, pp. 80–3; Currie 2015: 285–6; cf. Barker 2008.

[44] On the flood of Deucalion see also above, p. 141, n. 36. The earliest surviving reference to this
flood is in an ode of Pindar (*Olympian* 9.41–53), and its Greek context is distinct from that of
the myth under study here. Presumably elements of the Mesopotamian flood story have entered
Greek mythology separately in these two contexts.

[45] Bachvarova 2016: 29–32.

[46] 'Blame' is my best attempt at translating *Mômos*; West uses 'Cavil', which is unsatisfactory
because this word barely exists in modern English. In non-mythological language the word
mômos refers to blaming or fault-finding (*Od.* 2.86), likewise the verbs built on its stem
(*mômaomai*, etc.). In the few surviving relevant passages in Greek literature, there is an
association with envy and jealousy (Pindar, *Olympian* 6.74–6; Callimachus, *Hymn to Apollo*
113). The little-known personification of *Mômos* appears first in Hesiod's *Theogony*, where he is
one of the children of Night (*Th.* 214). Further evidence in early sources is slight (although he is
referred to surprisingly frequently in the Hellenistic and later epigrams of the Palatine
Anthology). Plato refers to the personified Momos as a cliché for fault-finding (*Republic*, Book
6, 487 a); two satyr-plays, one by Sophocles, are known to have been named after him and
presumably included him as a named character; and he has been tentatively identified as a
winged figure departing from the scene of the Judgment of Paris in a vase-painting of about
510–500 BCE (see E. Simon at *LIMC* VI.1: 649–50, and cf. Currie 2015: 285). Burkert
ingeniously proposed that *Mômos* here in the *Cypria* is in origin a borrowing from a different
Mesopotamian source, the Babylonian creation narrative *Enuma Elish*, in which the deity
Mummu, adviser of Apsu the personification of subterranean waters, urges the destruction of
the younger deities who are troubling the ocean-goddess Tiamat (Burkert 1992 [1984], 103; see
Enuma Elish I 48–50, at Foster, *BTM*, p. 441). If this is the case, however, the motif has been
recontextualised, because the *Cypria* is not a cosmogony, and the resemblance between *Mômos*
and Mummu does not extend much beyond the resemblance in sound. Cf. Currie 2016: 205–7,

examples of the mode of personification typical of epic discourse, especially in the rhetoric of speeches and in Hesiodic exposition: an element of
Zeus' deliberations takes on the contours of an active deity who persuades
and manipulates him.[47] The same applies to the point that Earth's complaint is not only at the burden but also at the impiety (*asebeia*) of humans:
the causal explanation, based on her outrage at crimes and immorality,
harmonises with the overall behaviour patterns of the Homeric gods. As
such it provides a motivation more subtly articulated than in *Atrahasis*,
where the gods were disturbed simply by the noise and turmoil of the
increasing human population. Structurally, also, the motif of the weight of
humans upon Earth's back has much in common with Hesiod's primeval
myth in which her husband Ouranos has refused to allow her unborn
children to emerge from her womb, and she groans in pain because she is
'constricted' from within (*Theogony* 159–60).[48] The motif of interior
pressure is re-enacted and redeployed, as it were in a reverse image, by
the external pressure that sparks off the action of the *Cypria*.[49]

Zeus and Nemesis

The *Mythographus* goes on to explain how Zeus took Blame's advice that
he should not destroy humans by 'floods or thunderbolts', but should
instead pursue two more devious schemes, which would lead to the
destructions of war. One was to induce the sea-goddess Thetis – whom
Zeus himself had desired, according to the ancient consensus – to marry a
mortal man, Peleus. At their wedding would begin the quarrel between the
goddesses that Paris would so ruinously judge, and the child of their union
would be Achilles,[50] the most brilliant and (as we will see) the most
problematic warrior of the Trojan War. The other was ostensibly

and note that at the opening lines of *Enuma Elish* 'Mummu' is also represented as a title or
aspect of Tiamat herself (rendered 'Matrix-Tiamat' by Foster).

[47] Compare for example *Ātē* 'Ruinous Folly' (*Il.* 19.90–133), the *Litai* 'Beggings' (*Il.* 9.502–12), and
Mētis 'Planning, Cunning' (Hes. *Th.* 886–900).

[48] Hesiod goes on to tell how Ouranos' refusal to relieve the pressure inside Gaia's womb leads her
to scheme against him so that her son Kronos ambushes his father from inside her genitals,
overthrowing him until he is overthrown in turn by his own son, Zeus.

[49] See Clay 2005: 30–3. Through the *Theogony* narrative the relationship between Zeus and Gaia is
a recurrent theme, and Zeus was said to have succeeded in winning the war against the old gods
by relying on advice from Gaia. See Apollodorus, *Library* 1.2.1, probably derived from the
Cyclic *Titanomachy*, with Hesiod, *Theogony* 617–28.

[50] This point seems obvious, though there is no evidence that it was emphasised explicitly here in
the *Cypria*.

unconnected: to bring about the birth of what the scholion simply calls 'a beautiful daughter'. This of course is Helen of Troy.

The familiar story, implicit in Homer and explicit in later sources, is that Helen was fathered by Zeus on Leda, the wife of Tyndareus. The story that Zeus took the form of a swan to seduce her, and that she gave birth to Helen as an egg, has been notorious at least since the time of Euripides, who makes Helen herself recount it – albeit as an account (*logos*) told by others – in her opening speech in the play that carries her name.[51] However, the *Cypria* included a different and terrifying account of her origins.[52] In this version her mother was not a mortal woman but another personified deity, Nemesis. I will use the translation *Disgrace* for her name:

> Disgrace with her beautiful hair, mingling in lovemaking,
> bore her to Zeus, king of the gods, under violent compulsion.
> For she tried to flee, nor was she willing to mingle in lovemaking
> with father Zeus, Kronos' son; she was oppressed by the thought of shame
>   (*aidōs*)
> and disgrace;[53] and along the earth and the murmuring black water
> she tried to flee, and Zeus was pursuing her – he yearned in his heart to
>   seize her –
> sometimes along the swell of the greatly surging sea,
> as he stirred up the great deep, with her in the form of a fish:
> sometimes up along the river Ocean and the limits of the earth,
> sometimes along the turf-rich land; ever she turned into
> beasts, such woeful creatures as the mainland nurtures, in order to escape
>   him.   (*Cypria* fr. 10: West, *GEF*, pp. 88–90)

This is preserved as a quotation out of context, but (as with the story of the overburdened Earth) it is possible that it originally belonged in a speech

---

[51] The data for the parentage of Helen are lucidly assembled by Gantz 1993: 318–23, suggesting that the tradition has conflated two distinct articulations – one in which Leda is impregnated by Zeus in the form of a swan, the other in which Zeus mates with Nemesis in bird-form. When Helen in the *Helen* recounts the story that Zeus and Leda were her parents, the doubtfulness of her wording leaves open the possibility that the truth of what happened was different (17–21, 256–9, cf. *Iphigenia at Aulis* 794–800). The *Helen* never refers explicitly to the version in which Nemesis is her mother, although she speaks of the war as a response to the overburdening of Gaia, a clear reference to the *Cypria* (*Helen* 38–41, see below).

[52] For Nemesis personified see Hesiod *Th.* 223, *WD* 200. In both cases she is closely associated with *Aidōs*, the personification of the fear of loss of reputation: as West puts it, 'Both are forces that inhibit wickedness, one working from inside, the other, public disapproval, from without' (West 1978: 204, note at *WD* 200).

[53] The curious form of words – the personified Nemesis is full of the thought of *nemesis* itself – is not unparalleled. Homer has a similar collocation when Ares in person, wounded in combat, cries out as men cry out in battle (*arēs*) (*Il.* 5.859–61, see Clarke 1999: 271–2). For a similar polysemy with the deity Lussa, see pp. 282–285.

delivered by a character rather than in the voice of the primary narrator, in which (to judge by the Homeric evidence) personified deities are less likely to be described in such vivid terms.[54] Fundamentally, the Greek word *nemesis* names a social force, the public reproach that comes as retribution in response to openly wicked behaviour.[55] There are other examples in Homer and Hesiod of divine contours given to a phenomenon that subsists in people's talk, such as Rumour,[56] but the present example is unusually vivid. Aristotle would later formalise the definition of *nemesis* as 'feeling pain at someone who appears to be succeeding undeservedly' (see esp. *Rhetoric* 1837 a 9). He writes as follows of the *nemesētikos* or 'person given to *nemesis*':[57]

> What the ancients called *nemesis* is the practice of being angry at failure or success that is beyond what is appropriate, but of being glad at [these things when they are] appropriate: on account of which they consider *Nemesis* to be a goddess. (*Eudemian Ethics* 1233 b 22–6)

In the early epic, the former of these is what most defines *nemesis*: it is the reproach that will be called forth by cowardice or bad behaviour, and the fear of it is a spur to steadfast virtue – for which reason it is often paired with *aidōs*, the fear of loss of reputation that helps men to preserve their courage against the odds.

In what sense, then, is it meaningful that Zeus' union with Nemesis should be the trigger for the creation of Helen? Without more of the *Cypria*, it is hard to say whether anything significant was made of the fact that this was an incestuous rape. It seems to be more important that the child of this ugly union will become the ultimate symbol of scandalous sexual behaviour. When Paris seizes Helen from her husband and takes her to Troy, their so-called marriage[58] will be the classic case of social crime that goes unhindered and unpunished – unpunished, that is, until the coming of the Greeks and the war that will send the race of heroes to their end, as Zeus has planned all along. It may be significant that even

---

[54] Sammons 2017: 43–7 speculates thought-provokingly that the words may have been spoken by Aphrodite.

[55] For *nemesis* as an ethical and social concept in early Greek language and thought see Yamagata 1994: 225–38; Cairns 1993: 51–4, 83–7; and see Konstan 2003; Konstan 2006: 111–13, on post-Homeric usages and the redefinition by Aristotle. On the redevelopment of Nemesis as a personification in later art and cult, see Smith 2011: 41–6, with Smith 2012.

[56] See e.g. the evocation of *Phēmē* 'Rumour' as a goddess (*WD* 760–4), comparing Homeric *Ossa* 'Rumour' (cf. Clarke 1999: 265–7).

[57] Explained lucidly by Konstan 2006: 114–15, with a slightly different translation.

[58] Proclus' summary of the *Cypria* records that they carried out a marriage ceremony on their arrival in Troy (*Cypria* Arg. 2: West, *GEF*, pp. 70–1).

within the *Iliad*, the phenomenon of *nemesis* is twice spoken of in connection with Helen. For example, when her two men fight a duel over her, Aphrodite snatches Paris away from peril and orders Helen to join him in bed. She replies that it would be *nemessēton* 'a cause for reproach' for her to do so now (*Il.* 3.410), but the goddess cajoles her into obeying. Later, when Hector finds the pair there so far from the battlefield, she tells him she wishes she had a husband who understood what reproach (again *nemesis*) and humiliation mean among men (*Il.* 6.350–1).[59]

Euripides, whom we will see repeatedly evoking lore associated with the present narrative sequence,[60] alludes in his *Trojan Women* to the idea that Helen was the daughter of a more amorphous kind of personification. Troy has fallen to the enemy, and amid the atrocities inflicted by the Greeks Andromache, Hector's widow, rails against her:

> Shoot sprung from Tyndareus, you are never Zeus' daughter,
> and I say that you were born of many fathers:
> first the hellish Fury (*Alastōr*), then Envy,
> then Murder and Death and all the evils that earth nourishes.
>
> (*Trojan Women* 766–9)

These essences are conceptualised here as *male* deities, monstrous and sinister fathers, implicitly the counterparts of Nemesis the mother. The disasters that Helen brought are reified in her parentage, and she becomes less a human being than a force of pure evil.

To return to the *Cypria*: Nemesis fled from her father's assault, and (as another fragment tells) she eventually took bird-form and Zeus, now also in the shape of a bird, raped her so that in due course she laid an egg.[61] The poem seems to have told that the egg laid by Nemesis was found and hatched by Leda in the royal palace of Sparta;[62] so Helen was raised there as if she were the king's daughter. The bitter story is now ready to unfold.

---

[59] Note also that when Menelaus and Paris are about to begin their duel, the old noblemen of Troy say that it is 'no cause for reproach' (*ou nemesis*) for the Greeks and Trojans to fight over such a woman (*Il.* 3.156) – as if replying implicitly to the opposing political movement that advocates her return to the Greeks and an end to the war, as urged in the assembly by Antenor (*Il.* 7.345–53). See further Scodel 2008: 219–21.

[60] On Euripides' allusions to Homeric and Cyclic lore about the Trojan War, see Torrance 2013: 218–45.

[61] Philodemus, *On Piety* B 7369, as restored by Obbink: see *Cypria* fr. 11 at West, *GEF*, pp. 90–2. Cf. below, Ch. 8 n. 13.

[62] See also Apollodorus, *Library* 3.10.7. Pausanias, describing a shrine of Nemesis at which there was a carving of Helen, Leda and the goddess, mentions that '[?the] Greeks say that Nemesis was the mother of Helen, but that Leda gave her the breast and reared her' (1.33.7). Conversely, he also tells how at Sparta the egg *laid* by Leda was displayed (3.16.1), invoking the other tradition about Helen's parentage.

When Aphrodite has used the promise of this wondrous daughter of Zeus as a lure for Paris, she fulfils her promise by sending him to the palace where she is now living with her husband, King Menelaus, in Sparta; he leaves with the woman and certain treasures, which he has stolen at the same time as her;[63] the Trojans refuse the Greeks' demands for her return, the war begins, and the heroes go down to their deaths.[64]

The plan of Zeus

All this, says the *Cypria*, was the working of a divine purpose: 'Zeus' plan was coming to fulfilment'. From what we have been able to reconstruct of the *Cypria*, he planned with and manipulated several elemental powers – first Themis, then three children of Night, namely Blame, Strife and Nemesis[65] – to bring about the set of circumstances that would lead to the Trojan War and ensure that it would be devastatingly destructive. Intriguingly, a late fifth-century vase survives on which the main scene of the Judgment of Paris is accompanied on the upper register by Strife and Themis (labelled *Eris, Themis*) in intimate conversation, as if plotting what will come about through Strife's interference (Fig. 9).[66] This vase irresistibly suggests influence from the *Cypria*, whether directly or mediated through more fluctuating and ephemeral forms of narration – as usual with artistic reception, it is impossible to choose firmly between close textual dependence and more generalised *traditional referentiality*, to use the terminology of literary intertextuality sketched at the beginning of this

---

[63] The 'possessions' (*ktēmata*) that Paris took with Helen are mentioned in Proclus' summary of the *Cypria* (paras. 2, 10: West, *GEF*, pp. 68–9, 78–9) and often in the *Iliad*, where their return is paired with the return of Helen herself. Presumably the theft compounded Paris' offence against the rules of *xenia* – no-one could plead that the possessions wanted to be taken away, as was so often suggested about Helen.

[64] There is a curiosity later in Proclus' summary of the *Cypria*, when one of the final items in the sequence of episodes is listed as 'the plan of Zeus so that he may lighten (subjunctive *epikouphisēi*) the Trojans by removing Achilles from the war' (Arg. 12: West, *GEF*, pp. 80–1). The wording here has an obvious verbal similarity with the *Iliad* scholion's account of the plan to 'lighten' Earth's burden, in which the verb is similarly *kouphisthēnai*, aorist passive infinitive. Is there a trace at Arg. 12 of a passage in the *Cypria* in which the Iliadic 'plan of Zeus' was explicitly yoked together with the plan to relieve Gaia? This is argued by Marks 2002: 9–10: however, to metaphorically 'lighten, relieve' the Trojans by removing Achilles from the battlefield is not the same as literally to 'lighten, relieve' Earth of her burden by causing men to die. Perhaps this difficulty would disappear if we had the full text of the putative source that lies behind both the scholion and Proclus' account. Cf. Currie 2015: 294–5; West, *EC*, pp. 125–6.

[65] For these figures among the children of Night, see Hesiod, *Theogony* 214, 223, 225.

[66] St Petersburg, 0.28 (St. 1807) = *LIMC* III 848, s.v. Eris no. 7. See Shapiro 1993: 58–61, 223–4; Smith 2011: 48.

book (see above, pp. 31–33). Either way, however, any construction of this narrative must have prompted the question: was Zeus' plan simply a way of doing away with the burden that annoyed his grandmother, or could it be articulated on a more theologically profound level?

In the surviving mythographic accounts, as we saw, the relationship between the physical weight on the Earth and the 'impiety' (*asebeia*) of the heroic race is left unclear and must be inferred indirectly. Once again, however, we find sidelong evidence in Euripidean tragedy. In the opening speech of the *Helen*, already referred to above,[67] the strange recondite traditions on which Helen draws include Stesichorus' account of Hera's revenge for her failure in the beauty contest, in which she replaced Helen with a false phantom or *eidōlon* at the moment when Paris was taking her to Troy (*Helen* 31–6).[68] This, she says, became part of a larger chain of events:

> For others of Zeus'
> plannings joined together with these evils:
> for he brought war to the land (*chthōn*) of the Greeks
> and to the wretched Phrygians, so that from the host of mortals
> and their multitude he might lighten his mother, the land,
> and make known the mightiest man of Greece. (*Helen* 36–41)

The logic of Helen's words includes the lightening of Gaia's burden, the Judgment of Paris, and the death of Achilles in the sweep of Zeus' plan.

A second example comes near the end of the *Orestes*, a play set in the aftermath of the Trojan War. Apollo comes to save Helen from the vengeance of her enemies and bring her to immortality in the stars, because she is Zeus' daughter and the war she caused was part of the divine purpose:

> For the gods, by means of her loveliness,
> brought Greeks and Phrygians [= Trojans] to conflict
> and established their deaths, so as to draw away from the land
> the oppression of the abundant human population.
> (Euripides *Orestes* 1639–42)

The word translated 'oppression' is *hubrisma*, the abstract noun derived from *hubris*: this is bullying violence as carried out by those who rise above

---

[67] For an excellent summary account of the theological questions raised by this passage, see Allan 2008a: 61–6.

[68] On the background of this (presumably anti-traditional) story, first attested in Stesichorus' *Palinode*, see Austin 1994; and compare the nuanced assessment of Stesichorus' discourse by Beecroft (2006, with 2010: 144–57).

Fig. 9 (a) Vase showing the Judgment of Paris, with detail of Eris and Themis.

their proper station to inflict harm on others. Apollo's wording again suggests that the overburdening of Mother Earth and the scandalous behaviour of the heroic race could be seen as a single evil in the world, manifested both physically by oppressive weight, and morally by oppressive behaviour.[69] Whether that subtle linkage was explicit in the text of the *Cypria*, or whether it represents a later level of interpretation overlaid on the epic (perhaps by Euripides himself), must remain a matter for speculation.

---

[69] Euripides elsewhere says more vaguely that Zeus planned the war in order to cause suffering and death among the Greeks and Trojans (*Electra* 1282–3; Collard and Cropp, Eur. fr. (unidentified plays) 1082).

Fig. 9 (b) Detail of the vase in Fig. 9 (a).

The *Iliad* never explicitly mentions the story of the oppression of Gaia; but there is one intriguing possibility of an allusion to it. We will see in due course how Achilles responds to Patroclus' death by hating himself for being its unwitting cause. Here is the climactic moment when he tells his mother Thetis that he accepts and even wishes for his own death in battle, which is now inevitable:

> Let me die at once, since I was not to defend
> my friend, who was killed: far away from his fatherland
> he died, for he lacked me when I should have been his defence
>   against woe.
> Now, since I will not return to my own dear fatherland,
> nor did I become a light for Patroclus or my other
> comrades, the many who were tamed by bright Hector,
> but I sit here by the ships, a useless burden on the ploughland,
> although none other of all the Greeks is my equal
> in war ...
>   (*Il.* 18.98–106)

In the words 'burden on the ploughland', do we hear a hint of the strange dark story from the *Cypria*? Although this cannot be pushed too far, it is thought-provoking that the image appears at this moment of heightened intensity, when the central theme of the concluding movement of the *Iliad* is first emerging clearly into words. The aftermath of the death of Patroclus will bring Achilles to the point where he will, very literally, play his part in Zeus' plan by ceasing to be a burden on the soil – along with the countless others who will have been sent to death as a result of the plan that his mother instigated on his behalf in the first book of the *Iliad* (on which see further below, pp. 199–201).

Knowing the divine will

Behind any such explanations of war and suffering, the plans of the 'father of gods and men' remain forever mysterious. This is seldom explicitly stated; but it takes shape at one point in the *Catalogue of Women*, when the poet – turning aside from the narration of a particularly strange myth of metamorphosis – states a proverbial or gnomic truth:

> But the mind (*noos*) of Zeus is hidden, and no-one among men
> is able to understand it …
>
> (Hes. *Cat.* fr. 10.97–8 Most = fr. 10a.97–8 M–W)

We can clarify what this means by exploring comparable passages from the tragedians in the generations after the composition of the *Catalogue*. A similar idea forms the background to a choral song in Aeschylus' *Suppliants*, in a dramatic context closely aligned with that of traditional religious devotion.[70] Women fugitives, fleeing from marriages imposed against their father's wishes and their own will, arrive in Argos to seek protection under Zeus – Zeus *aphiktōr* 'the Zeus of refugees', (line 1), Zeus *sōtēr* 'the saving Zeus' who shelters the needy (26). Reflecting on their flight from male aggression, and their ancestral descent from one of the god's sexual liaisons with a mortal woman,[71] they pray for his aid but recognise the chaotic uncertainty that surrounds it:

> Let all come to the good from Zeus in truth:
> what Zeus desires is not easily hunted out;
> the paths of his thinking heart, tangled

---

[70] Sommerstein 2010a: 96–110 sets out a convincing reconstruction of the plot of the *Suppliants* and the trilogy to which it belonged. The hymn to Zeus is discussed and edited by Furley and Bremer 2001: 1.279–85, 2.241–5; on its place in Aeschylus' thought see esp. Parker 2008: 135, distancing himself from the (formerly mainstream) view that Aeschylus is articulating an anti-traditional and implicitly monotheistic concept of Zeus.

[71] Io: see *Suppliants* 15–17, 40–56, etc.

> they stretch out and full of shadows,
>> impossible to gaze through and understand.   (*Suppliants* 86–7, 93–5)[72]

The metaphor is difficult. In English we tend most often to conceptualise an argument or thought-sequence in terms of a building – we construct it, it has foundations, it might collapse – but in Greek there is more often a metaphor of pursuit and hunting: one chases a thought or an understanding and finally brings it to ground like a wild animal.[73] To try to look directly into Zeus' thought is like hunting in a dense forest, becoming confused and lost in the undergrowth. Yet nonetheless hope remains, the expectation that his desires will certainly be fulfilled, and fulfilled for the good:

> It falls in safety, not on its back,[74]
> when a matter is brought to fulfilment by [the nod of] Zeus' head.
> It blazes out on every side
> even in darkness, with black
> fortune for the people who speak.   (*Suppliants* 91–2, 88–90)

The nod of Zeus, the final decision-making of the chief divinity, is full of absolute cosmic significance, even when it is enmeshed in the trivialities of divine politics. For the women, as they continue their song, this calls up the certainty that Zeus will cast down those who rise too high:

> He throws down mortals in utter destruction
> from their high-towering hopes,
> without needing to arm his power with weapons.
> There is no toil in the work of the divinities:
> sitting still, he achieves his thought entirely unaided
> from the sacred seats.   (*Suppliants* 96–103)

There is consolation in the certainty that the instability of human fortunes, the coming fall of those who think themselves secure, is part of the fulfilment of the god's desires.[75]

So stated, this theology represents ideas that were already traditional in Aeschylus' time. But in the probing and even anti-traditional intellectual

---

[72] In this and the following quotation I adopt the rearranged line-sequence as printed in all the major modern editions. With the MS sequence the thought is more interlaced, but remains similar in essence.

[73] See for example Plato, *Republic* 432 b ff.; *Laches* 194 a ff.; *Parmenides* 128 c.

[74] A metaphor of an animal landing safely, as in a fall from a height?

[75] Cf. Sommerstein 2010b [2000], reflecting on the parallels between the hymn in the *Suppliants* and the more famous 'Hymn to Zeus' in Aeschylus' *Agamemnon* 160–83, which can be read in terms of the same intellectualising movement as the hymns discussed in this section.

language of Euripides, the same web of ideas can be seen merging into uncertainty about the very nature of divinity, in language that sounds like that of abstract theism. In the *Trojan Women*, at the moment when Menelaus is about to bring Helen out before the women of the city whose destruction she has caused, Hecuba pushes at the limits of linguistic expression in her prayer:[76]

> You who are earth's support and hold your seat upon the earth,
> whoever you are, impossible for guesswork to understand,
> Zeus, whether you are the necessity of nature or the mind of mortals,
> I beseech you: for moving along your noiseless path
> you bring forward the things of mortals in accord with justice.
>
> (*Trojan Women* 884–8)

The formulae of devotion dissolve into the mist: 'you have invented new addresses to the gods' (889), replies Menelaus, and indeed Hecuba's imagery is close to that of the philosophical speculators of Euripides' own day.[77] Similar ideas take shape in the *Helen*, when the Chorus are singing about the sufferings and deaths of the war and Helen's place in the divine scheme. In the midst of their reflections on these miseries, specifically those of women abused by male violence,[78] they sing of the impossibility of understanding the divine purpose behind the war:

> What is god, what not god, and what in the middle,
> who among mortals can search it out and tell?
> He has discovered the ultimate limit, he who sees that the things of the
>   gods
> leap hither and thither and back again
> with ambiguous, unexpected happenings.   (*Helen* 1137–43)

Although this begins from a reflection on the strangeness of Helen herself, it extends to the unknowability of the plan overall. In a sense, to admit human bewilderment at these things is not to undermine inherited attitudes to divinity, but rather to affirm them and participate in their modes of thought.

---

[76] Later in the same play the Chorus sing to Zeus as 'you who step upon the celestial seat and the high air (*aithēr*)' (1078–9), using more traditional images corresponding conceptually to the ideas behind Hecuba's imagery in line 884.

[77] The formulation 'earth's support' (*gēs ochēma*) suggests a possible allusion to Diogenes of Apollonia, who posited *aēr* 'cosmic mist, air' as the fundamental divine principle. For a thoughtful treatment, see Dillon 2004.

[78] The image of the Trojan women, led away to enslavement, resonates closely with the opening invocation of the nightingale, a symbol of women's lamentation in general and in particular of the suffering women in the myth of Tereus (*Helen* 1107–16, with Allan 2008a: 271, note on lines 1107–12).

Although the words of these choruses speak of an intellectualism that has sought to escape from traditional mythological forms, nonetheless their central reflection is in a line of direct continuity from Mesopotamian wisdom: mortal life is uncertain, the gods are jealous of overweening success, the human who thinks himself secure in prosperity is thrown down. Somewhere in this matrix of ideas lies the truth that the life and death of Achilles, and specifically the destruction and turmoil that dominate the plot of the *Iliad*, were part of the working-out of the will of Zeus.

As we have seen, the marriage between the sea-goddess Thetis and the mortal Peleus would not only spark off the quarrel between the three goddesses but would also lead to the birth of Achilles, the most bitter enactment of the sorrows of heroic mortality. The *Mythographus Homericus* refers to Thetis' 'marriage to a mortal (*thnētogamia*)'[1] – phrasing that suggests this marriage marked a *reversal* of the mingling between male gods and mortal women that characterised the heroic age, at least according to the formulation followed in the *Catalogue of Women*. Only a handful of references survive to suggest how the wedding was narrated in the *Cypria*,[2] but painted pottery will help us to guess at a sharper visualisation and a clearer sense of its momentous significance in the unfolding of mythical time.[3]

The wedding of Peleus and Thetis

Two of the most elaborate surviving black-figure vases, the Sophilos Dinos[4] of *c.* 580 BCE (Fig. 10) and the uniquely ambitious François Vase of perhaps a decade later (Fig. 11),[5] give the wedding of Peleus and Thetis an especially prominent place among their scenes of the heroic race.[6] In

---

[1] *Cypria*, fr. 1: West, *GEF*, pp. 80–3.

[2] For the surviving secondary accounts of the *Cypria* narration see fr. 2–4 (*GEF*, pp. 82–5), with Proclus' summary (*GEF*, pp. 68–9); discussion at Currie 2015: 285–6, and West, *EC* 69–75; cf. Apollodorus, *Library* 3.13.5. Fr. 4 of the *Cypria*, from the D-scholia at *Il.* 16.140 (West, *GEF*, pp. 84–5), on the spear given to Peleus among the wedding-gifts, only makes sense if its author is treating the *Cypria* account as consistent with that implied in the *Iliad*.

[3] Summary discussion, Gantz 1993: 229–30.

[4] Also known as the Erskine Dinos: London, BM 1971, 1101.1.

[5] Firenze, Museo Archeologico Nazionale, 4209.

[6] On the iconography of the wedding in the François Vase and the Sophilos Dinos, see survey by Osborne 1998: 87–95, with Lowenstam 2008: 19–23; Brownlee 1995; Giuliani 2013 [2003]: 110–30. Giuliani downplays the possibility that the scenes on the François Vase constitute a coordinated response to the mythical tradition, and sees their significance in terms of generic design rather than narrative meaning (see esp. p. 118, the wedding procession as 'a wonderful opportunity to populate the frieze along its full length'). For a subtle recent attempt at a cogent and co-ordinated interpretation of the iconography, see Kreuzer 2013, comparing Shapiro's survey in the same volume of varying interpretative strategies applied since the first publication of the vase (Shapiro 2013).

Fig. 10 (a) The Sophilos Dinos, showing Ocean among the wedding-guests.

Fig. 10 (b) Peleus welcoming the wedding-guests.

each case a long continuous frieze shows the gods in procession arriving at
the wedding. They include Zeus, Hera and all the Olympian family, with the
Muses to preside over song and the Graces representing social harmony.

Fig. 11 The François Vase: Dionysus.

Shown here from the Sophilos Dinos is Thetis' grandfather, Oceanos, the god whose serpentine coils embody the great river of water that encircles the inhabited earth, with the lesser rivers that stretch out from him as smaller snaky forms. On the François Vase Cheiron, the wise and ancient centaur who will be Achilles' tutor or foster-father, is at the head of the procession, welcomed by Peleus while Thetis is half-hidden in the house. Further back in the line is Dionysus, looking straight out at the onlooker with an amphora over his shoulder. From the way he hoists it with one hand, we infer that the amphora is empty: it is his wedding-gift, and in the epics it becomes a portent of the fate that awaits Achilles. Facing his death in the closing movement of the *Iliad*, he encounters the ghost of his beloved friend Patroclus, who speaks of the burial that they will receive together:

> So now the bones of the pair of us will be enclosed by one urn,
> the golden amphora, which your lady mother gave to you.   (*Il.* 23.91–2)

The second line is not securely attested in the manuscript tradition, and is perhaps a post-Homeric addition,[7] but the story to which it refers is laid out in a closely related passage of the *Odyssey*, in which the ghost of Agamemnon tells the ghost of Achilles how the two men's bones were mingled in this amphora:

---

[7] Richardson 1993: 176–7, note at line 92.

> ... the gift of Dionysus
> [Thetis] said it was, and the work of famous Hephaestus.   (*Od.* 24.74–5)

Even if (as is likely) the section containing these lines[8] is also a post-Homeric addition to the text, they suggest how the symbolism of the wedding gifts was understood in the earlier stages of the *Odyssey*'s reception.[9] With an integrated reading of the iconography of the François Vase as a whole, we are invited to see a web of connections between this scene and the episodes elsewhere on it that are connected to Achilles' death – the killing of Troilus (on which more below), the funeral games of Patroclus, and the corpse of Achilles himself, carried by Ajax on his back from the battle before the walls of Troy (see below, pp. 308–309).[10]

Within the *Iliad*, too, these wedding gifts serve as reminders of the problem of Achilles' mortality. Thetis has sent him out to war as any mother would send her son, with his father's armour – yet this armour was the gods' gift to Peleus (*Il.* 17.194–7, 18.84–5 etc.), and the spear that no other man at Troy can wield was made for him by Cheiron the centaur from an ash tree of Mount Pelion (*Il.* 16.140–4, 19.387–91, 22.133–4).[11] In later chapters we will see the poet returning again and again to these arms in connection with Achilles' death. The horses, too, that bring Achilles' chariot to battle were Poseidon's gift,[12] and we will hear them prophesying in the *Iliad*.

Thetis is a daughter of Nereus, one of the many variant articulations of the maritime deity known as 'the Old Man of the Sea': why did she marry a mortal against her will, as she puts it herself in the *Iliad* (18.434), and why was their wedding celebrated by all the gods? Two explanations are known from antiquity. According to the first, ascribed to the *Cypria* by

---

[8] The so-called 'Second Nekuia'.
[9] An ancient note (scholion on *Il.* 23.92) gives an extended history for the golden vase, naming Stesichorus as the source. While this suggests the character of early interest in the lore of the wedding gifts, and can be used to support the argument that the artistic depictions are responding directly to whatever account Stesichorus gave, it does not necessarily imply that the Homeric lines discussed here are interpolations composed under direct Stesichorean influence.
[10] In a remarkable paper Andrew Stewart argued (1983) that the overall programme of this side of the François Vase alludes to Stesichorus' version of the Trojan War narrative (cf. previous note). As the surviving relevant details of Stesichorus' account are very slight, Stewart's argument is of limited value for the overall argument pursued in the present chapter. Giuliani (2013 [2003]: 120–4) is sceptical on Stewart's theory, in keeping with his overall tendency towards minimal interpretation; compare the brief review by Osborne 1998: 93–5.
[11] An alternative tradition may also have existed, in which the armour that Achilles brought to Troy was made by Hephaestus and given to him by his mother Thetis. See Ch. 11, n. 15.
[12] On the horses see esp. *Il.* 16.866–7, 23.277–9 and Ch. 12, n. 2.

Philodemus about 60 BCE, Thetis refused Zeus' sexual advances out of respect for his wife Hera, and he punished her by forcing her to marry a mortal.[13] Other poets beyond the early epic tradition supply a more grave reason for its importance: when Zeus desired Thetis and sought to ravish her, it was prophesied that Thetis' son would be greater than his father, implying that he would be a threat to Zeus' power and could overthrow him as Zeus had overthrown Kronos.[14] Reluctantly, therefore, she was assigned to Peleus – either by Zeus himself or by Hera, who says even in the *Iliad* that she personally chose Peleus for Thetis on account of his excellence among mortals.[15] Peleus grappled with her as she tried to slip free, shifting between the many shapes of her watery nature, until at last he mastered her to his will. Whether or not the story of this prophecy was narrated within the epic tradition,[16] it gives food for thought as we consider Achilles. If Peleus is in some sense a stand-in, Achilles' father is *almost* Zeus. Through Peleus, Achilles is literally the great-grandson of Zeus, and his mother is herself a goddess (*Il.* 21.109, with 1.280), but the strange story of his parents' union invests him with a more intimate and unique closeness to the gods: with a slight shift of vowel length and accent, *dîos Achilleus* 'bright Achilles' might become *Diòs Achilleus,* 'Achilles [son] of Zeus'.[17] His heroic excellence – *aristos Achaiōn,* best of the Greeks, and *theois epieikelos,* one resembling the gods – was envisaged in later times as the epitome of masculine perfection, nowhere more clearly expressed than in the poise and balance of his portrayal in a vase of *c.* 470 BCE, by the artist known as the Achilles Painter (Fig. 12). This demigod is defined from the start as one who almost, but not quite, escapes from the limitations and imperfections of mortality: over him as over Sarpedon hangs the inevitable prospect of death in war.

---

[13] This is ascribed to the *Cypria* in the fragmentary text of Philodemus' *On Piety* (see West, *GEF,* pp. 82–3, *Cypria* fr. 2), to which corresponds a briefer mention (without attribution to the *Cypria*) at Apollodorus, *Library* 3.13.5.

[14] This prophecy is recounted by Pindar, *Isthmian* 8.26–51 and is integral to the plot of Aeschylus' *Prometheus Bound* (see *Prometheus Bound* 757–70, 908–27) and the now lost *Prometheus Unbound*: see Sommerstein 2008: 196–210, with Sommerstein 2010a: 204–8. On the relation between this theme and Thetis' portrayal in the *Iliad,* cf. Slatkin 1991: 53–84.

[15] *Il.* 24.60, elaborated at Apollonius of Rhodes, *Argonautica* 4.805–9 (see West, *EC* 70).

[16] It is worth noting that the prophecy comes from Prometheus' mother Themis (Pindar, *Isthmian* 8.31), the goddess of unageing law, whom Aeschylus' Prometheus in another context identifies with Gaia, the Earth (*Prometheus Bound* 209–10). The Plan of Zeus in the *Cypria* was framed under the influence of Themis and Gaia (see above in the previous chapter): was there a variant version in which the two goddesses were one and the same?

[17] Cf. Janko 1992: 158, note on *Il.* 14.75–7.

Fig. 12 Name vase of the Achilles Painter.

Stray hints and recollections allow us to reconstruct the prophecies that were made at the wedding about Achilles' future. A Euripidean chorus reimagines the coming of the companions of Cheiron:[18]

> With pine trees and with greenness for garlands
> the horse-stepping[19] band of the centaurs
> came to the banquet of the gods and to Dionysus' wine-bowl,
> and aloud they cried out: 'O daughter of Nereus:
> the prophet who knows Phoebus' muse,
> Cheiron, announced that you will bear
> a child, a great light for Thessaly,
> who will come with the shieldbearing spearmen of the Myrmidons
> into the famous land of Priam to burn it to nothing . . . '
>
> (*Iphigenia at Aulis* 1058–70)

In this version the prophecy is voiced by Cheiron, the kindly centaur, and seems unequivocally glorious; but other ancient accounts were less straightforward. Plato, discussing examples of the scandalous tales that

---

[18] On Euripides' deployment of traditional material about the wedding in this passage, see Torrance 2013: 88–9.

[19] *Hippobatas*: in this word the verbal element *-batas* is ambiguous, and the phrase could be translated 'band [as if] mounted on horses' or 'band moving like horses' – the strangeness of the centaur is poised between these two senses and they are not necessarily distinct.

poets tell of the gods, quotes a fragment of Aeschylus in which Thetis long afterwards recalls the song that Apollo sang at the wedding:[20]

> And he recounted the fine progeny that would be mine,
>   that my child would not experience sickness and would have great life
>   and vitality:
>   and on completing his account of my fortune, god-loved,
>   he sang out a song of triumph, gladdening me at heart.   (Aesch. fr. 350.1–4)

Thetis trusted the voice of Apollo, believing him incapable of falsehood (5–6), but she was deceived:

> He who was singing, present at the feast,
>   he who said these things himself – it is he who killed
>   my son.   (7–9)

Did Apollo lie in this song? Aeschylus' wording suggests rather that what Thetis is recalling was laden with the ambiguity typical of Delphic prophecy – if Achilles would never decline into sickness, it would be because he had died first in battle.[21] It is impossible to tell how far back the story of the misleading wedding-song stretches into the tradition inherited by Aeschylus; but it is suggestive that within the *Iliad* Hera, attacking Apollo for his enmity against Achilles, recalls that he sang at the wedding-feast and in the same breath calls him 'ever untrustworthy' (*apiste*, *Il.* 24.63). If she is alluding to the deceptive prophecy, this casts a shadow over the whole story of Achilles' life and death, and over the enmity between him and Apollo that comes into ever greater prominence in the closing books of the *Iliad*.

Achilles between divinity and mortality

When we pursue this line further, the question suggests itself: was Thetis misled by Apollo's prophecy into allowing Achilles to go to his death?

---

[20] Plato, *Republic* 383 b. Sommerstein (2008: 309 n. 1) suggests ways in which each element in the song, as worded by Thetis, can be seen as a veiled prediction of Achilles' fate. Burgess (2004a, and cf. 2009: 18) suggests that the portrayal of Apollo's song as deceitful is Aeschylus' innovation; in contrast Hadjicosti 2006 argues that the song of Apollo was treated as deceitful at various stages of the epic tradition, and adduces the remarkable passage of Quintus of Smyrna – much later, but unlikely to be anti-traditional – in which Hera attacks Apollo for his treatment of Apollo, specifying the disjuncture between the song's predictions of glory and the fulfilment of Achilles' death before the Scaean gate (*Posthomerica* 3.117–50).

[21] It is also possible, as Sommerstein suggests in his note on the passage, that the prophecy could have been fulfilled by his translation after death to the White Island (see pp. 307–308 below).

Although the direct evidence in epic is too slight to allow a confident reconstruction,[22] hints survive elsewhere of a story-line broadly akin to this. Clustered around Achilles are shifting versions of the story of his mother's attempts to save him from the prospect of death,[23] by purifying away the mortal part of his nature with fire[24] or by dipping him in the river Styx in the Underworld to make him invulnerable.[25] Likewise, the story is ascribed to 'the Cyclic poets' that one or both of his parents hid him on the island of Scyros disguised as a girl to avoid the call to arms.[26] In every variant the plan fails. Peleus interrupts Thetis before she can burn away his mortality; the water of the Styx does not cover the ankle that Thetis grips, so it remains vulnerable; Achilles' disguise is penetrated by a trick, and he is forced to go to war.[27] The converse idea seems to be explored in the story of the prophecy that the first Greek to land at Troy would be the first to die: Thetis warned her son to hold back, and instead

---

[22] Cf. Burgess 2004a; Mackie 2013. It is of course entirely possible that Aeschylus has invented the episode on the basis of the cue at *Il.* 24.63, or that he has brought together several different suggestions from Homer and/or the Cyclic epics.

[23] On the evidence for these stories see Burgess 2009: 8–25, with the exhaustive collection of evidence and carefully argued reconstructions in Burgess 1995.

[24] The story of Thetis trying to make Achilles immortal in fire is first securely attested in Apollonius of Rhodes, *Argonautica* 4.867–80. As Burgess shows (1995: 219–21), the purpose and context of the procedure with fire remains unclear, but the story stands in a close relationship to others in which she puts her children in water. An ancient note (scholiast on *Argonautica* 4.816, also listed as Hes. *Cat.* fr. 237 Most = fr. 300 M–W) records that in Book 2 of a poem called *Aigimios* it was said that Thetis put her children (plural) by Peleus into a vessel of water 'wishing to learn whether they were mortal', but that 'others [say]' she used fire, as in the Achilles story recounted a few verses later in the *Argonautica*. See further Mackie 1998.

[25] The famous story of the dipping of the infant Achilles in the Styx is not directly attested before Statius' *Achilleid* (1.33–4, 1.268–70, 1.480–1; for other mentions in the scholiasts and mythographers see Burgess 1995: 222). As Burgess points out, the very obscurity of Statius' phrasing suggests that he is referring to an already established tradition, albeit perhaps a relatively recondite one, presumably related to the myths described in the previous note above.

[26] Schol. D on *Iliad* 19.326 (= *Cypria* fr. 19: West, *GEF*, pp. 96–9) attributes the plan to Peleus and says that the story is 'in the Cyclic poets'; Apollodorus (*Library* 3.13.8) says the plan was made by Thetis. West argues that the story of the concealment of Achilles on Scyros was not in the *Cypria*, pointing out that Achilles' visit to Scyros mentioned in Proclus' summary (*Cypria* Arg.7: West, *GEF*, pp. 72–3) fits into a different part of the narrative, and that none of the early epic sources that refer to his marrying Deidamia and fathering Neoptolemus on Scyros actually imply the concealment story (see esp. *Little Iliad* fr. 4: West, *GEF*, pp. 126–7, with *EC* 104). As Currie points out, however (2015: 288–9), the motif in itself appears to be an ancient one (cf. also Heslin 2005: 193–236), and there is no reason to exclude the possibility that it was attested in this or another early epic source. Achilles could of course have visited Scyros twice.

[27] See for example Schol. D on *Iliad* 19.326, where the exposure of Achilles is described. The complete story from concealment to exposure was depicted in a painting by Polygnotus in Athens (Pausanias 1.22.6), and it formed the background to Euripides' play *Skyrioi*.

it was Prōtesilaos ('First-one-of-the-host') who threw his life away.[28] Homer recalls him in the tally of Greek hosts and their leaders:

> Prōtesilaos, Ares' man, had been their leader
> when he lived: but now the black earth held him.
> His wife was left with ravaged cheeks in Phylakē
> and his house half-complete: him some Trojan man killed
> as he was leaping down from the ship, the very first of the Greeks.
>
> (*Il.* 2.698–702)

According to a story attested in later sources, his wife assuaged her grief like Gilgamesh on the death of Enkidu, by making a statue of him, which she embraced – in this case sexually; the gods pitied her and released him from the Underworld for a little while, but when he was sent down again she killed herself.[29]

Although this particular articulation suggests a rather late source, perhaps from tragic drama, the inevitable death of Prōtesilaos is food for thought as representing another acting-out of the fundamental problem of heroic action: why are men so willing to throw away their lives in war? Achilles' destined mortality, set in the sharpest possible relief by his glamorous origins, is an image 'writ large' of this ethical and psychological crux, which is hinted at under many forms in the course of the *Iliad*. As if accidentally, Homer dwells for a moment on two brothers, from the coast near Troy, going down in the surge of battle:

> ... two men, the best of the people,
> the two sons of Merops of Perkōtē, who above all others
> knew the arts of prophecy, and he had tried to forbid his children
> to march to the man-destroying war: but they would not
> obey him, for the spirits (*kēres*) of black death were leading them.
>
> (*Il.* 11.328–32, sim. 2.831–34)

Why did they wilfully turn towards their end, and what does it mean to speak here of the 'spirits of black death'? To see the strangeness of their choice, the full horror represented by the word *kēr* must be drawn out. It is only when Homer describes a battle-scene on a work of art that we see the shape of this being in sharper focus:

---

[28] The main source is Apollodorus, *Epitome* 3.29–30; cf. Gantz 1993: 592–3; Burgess 2009: 17. Davies (1989: 46) and West (*EC* 114–15) suggest that the full story of the prophecy may have been in the *Cypria*; cf. also Currie 2015: 292.

[29] For the sources on varying versions of this myth, see Apollodorus, *Epitome* 3.30.

In [the battle] they were mingling, Strife and Struggle and the destroying *kēr*
who was grasping one man alive but fresh-wounded, another yet
  unwounded,
and she was dragging another man dead by the feet through the fray:
the garment on her shoulders was all gory with the blood of men.

(Il. 18.535–8)[30]

Images of this demon of slaughter are hard to identify in surviving art, but
Pausanias describes seeing one labelled as *kēr* on the Chest of Cypselus,
a decorated box of complex iconography made (probably) in the early sixth
century BCE.[31] In a scene of single combat from the Theban war, one of the
duelling brothers was marked out by the presence of this demon: 'Behind
him stands a woman with teeth as savage as those of a beast, and her claws
are bent like talons.'[32] The Hesiodic *Shield of Heracles*, probably composed
in the same period, has an exuberantly vivid description of a similar *kēr*,
again in the hyper-realised imagery of the description of a figured shield:[33]

And after them
the dark-blue *kēres*, gnashing their white teeth,
terrible-faced, savage, bloodied, unapproachable,
held a struggle around the fallen: all of them were eager
to drink black blood: whoever they seized first,
lying or falling newly wounded, around him
they cast their great talons, and to Hades his wraith went down,
to gory Tartarus: when they had satisfied their thoughts
with human blood, they flung him backward
and rushed again into the surge and press of battle.

(Shield of Heracles 248–57)

The *kēres* roam the battlefield, and they drag away those who are to die:
beyond lies the grave and the darkness of Hades. This is as true for Achilles
as it is for any other men who fight, on the plain of Troy or in the
communities whose members formed the ancient audience of the *Iliad*.

---

[30] These lines occur also in the Hesiodic description of the shield of Heracles, with the characteristic addition of a line that makes the figures virtually come alive: 'she [viz. the *kēr*] was giving a terrifying look and roaring out a clanging sound' (*Shield* 158–60). Given the overall vividness of visualisation in the Shield of Achilles, there is no reason to follow West in regarding the Iliadic lines as an interpolation.

[31] On the problems of interpretation posed by the Chest of Cypselus see Snodgrass 1998: 109–16; on the imagery and inscriptions of the Chest and their literary correlates see Borg 2010, esp. 95–6 on *kēr*.

[32] Pausanias 5.19.6.

[33] On the heightened imagery of the *Shield* and its relationship to the aesthetics and poetics of Homer and Hesiod proper, see Martin 2005; Stamatopoulou 2013.

The death of Troilus

If the battlefield is a place of such horrors, it is also the place where masculine energy is brutalised; and the meagre fragments of surviving knowledge are enough to show that in the *Cypria* and the wider tradition the opening action of the Trojan War was full of savagery.[34] When the Greeks first sailed they did not know the route, and they arrived at Teuthrania by mistake and sacked it in the belief that it was Troy.[35] Assembling again with their ships at Aulis, they were frustrated by contrary winds and were instructed that they could appease Artemis, the goddess preventing them from sailing, only by sacrificing Agamemnon's virgin daughter Iphigenia to her; this they did, deceiving her by pretending that she was to come to Aulis to marry Achilles himself. Although these ghastly things are never mentioned in the Homeric poems proper,[36] they are included in our records of the *Cypria*.[37] The antiquity of the story of the sacrifice of Iphigenia is suggested by the fact that it is found in distinct but parallel versions in the *Cypria* and in the *Catalogue of Women*[38] – in the former she is replaced by a deer at the last moment by Artemis, in the latter (under the variant name of Iphimedē) she is replaced by a phantom (*eidōlon*) and becomes the goddess Hecate when removed from the world of mortals.[39] Here we have two different ways of articulating the basic idea that the goddess saved her miraculously from death at her father's hand.[40]

[34] For the episodes recounted here from the *Cypria* see Proclus' summary, paras 7–8 at West, *GEF*, pp. 72–5, supplemented as usual from Apollodorus; West, *EC* 104–7, 109–11; Currie 2015: 289–91. West argues that the attack on Teuthrania was originally a separate event altogether, which was drawn into the Trojan War narrative by introducing the 'silly story' that the Greeks mistook it for Troy (*EC* 106). This view remains purely speculative in the absence of any real knowledge as to how the *Cypria* articulated the episode.

[35] Kullmann has powerfully argued that the *Iliad* alludes to but suppresses direct mention of the Teuthranian expedition: for a summary statement of his position see Kullmann 2012. Compare Currie 2016: 243–4 on the chronological problems that are introduced if the Teuthranian expedition is combined with the principal Trojan campaign in a single count of years: this certainly suggests the coexistence of several divergent traditions that resisted reduction to a single narrative pseudohistory.

[36] The Homeric poems never mention the sacrifice of Iphigenia, and in the *Iliad* Odysseus says that Agamemnon has three living daughters, one called Iphianassa (*Il.* 9.145). On the assumption that Iphianassa and Iphigeneia are variants for the same person, this has sometimes been taken to imply that Homer does not 'know' the story of the sacrifice (cf. Hainsworth 1993: 77, note at *Il.* 9.145). However, there is every reason to take Iphigeneia and Iphianassa as different people, as seems to have been done in the *Cypria* itself (fr. 20 = scholiast on Sophocles *Electra* 157), in which case the sacrifice may instead be an already established tradition which the Homeric poems actively avoid mentioning. Cf. Burgess 2001: 150–1; Currie 2015: 291–2; West, *EC* 109–11.

[37] Cf. above, pp. 128–129.   [38] Hes. *Cat.* fr. 19.17–23 Most = fr. 23a.17–23 M–W.

[39] On the motif of the *eidōlon* here see West 1985: 134; Clarke 1999: 196; Bremmer 2002: 42.

[40] It is curious that in the *Catalogue of Women* version the sacrificed daughter is called by yet another name, Iphimedē; this adds to the suggestion that the story was widely diffused in variant forms.

But Homer refers to the name, at least, of the victim of another atrocity of the pre-*Iliad* stage of the war, when Priam the old king of Troy names sons of his who have died at Achilles' hands:

> Alas for me and my evil fate, for I fathered the greatest of sons
> in broad Troy, and I say that not one of them is left –
> Mēstor the godlike, and Troilus who delighted in horses
> and Hector . . .   (*Il.* 24.255–8)

The killing of Troilus was narrated in the *Cypria*, according to Proclus' summary,[41] and it is frequent in early Greek vase-painting (Fig. 13). Significantly, in view of our discussion above, among many other examples we find it depicted on the François Vase (Fig. 14).[42] Given the early artistic documentation, it seems reasonable to hypothesise, if no more, that the Troilus story belongs in the formative stages of the epic tradition. If Homer barely mentions it, then that is consistent with his overall tendency to refer to the most terrible elements of the story only through stray hints and covert allusions.[43] Troilus was only a boy when he came on horseback to the sanctuary of Apollo outside the city,[44] where Achilles waited in ambush for him. In later versions the story is often eroticised: the boy is killed when he rejects Achilles' sexual advances, which are then transferred to his sister Polyxena.[45] Although it is unlikely that the erotic aspect was in the early epics, the sources are consistent on the point that Troilus was very young – not yet fully grown, to judge from the vases. In many early examples of the scene, the killing takes place beside the altar of Apollo, on ground sacred to the god who presides over boys about to come to manhood.

[41] Para. 11 at West, *GEF*, pp. 78–9; the corresponding passage of Apollodorus (*Epitome* 3.32) specifies that the killing was an ambush at the shrine of Apollo Thymbraeus.
[42] Gantz 1993: 597–603; Lowenstam 2008, esp. 24–5, 35–9.
[43] The tradition that the Troilus episode is a post-Homeric invention is hard to sustain, and appears to hark back to the theory that the entire story was prompted by the Homeric epithet *hippiocharmēs* (see next note, with Currie 2015: 294). Kullmann argues that Homer in the *Iliad* knows but suppresses the story of the killing of Troilus (Kullmann 2012: 113, 2015: 122).
[44] This is consistent in the primary sources, though one ancient commentator (schol. A on *Il.* 24.257) argues that the epithet *hippiocharmēs*, translated above as 'who delighted in horses', implies that for Homer he is full-grown. So far as I know this view is unsupported elsewhere before Dares and Dictys. See also West, *EC* 121–2. Unfortunately, very little knowledge survives about Sophocles' tragedy *Troilus*.
[45] For the beauty of Troilus, see for example Ibycus fr. 282 (a) 41–5, fr. 282B v (Campbell, *GL* 3, pp. 222–5, 240–3). The principal Greek source for the version in which Achilles killed Troilus after the boy had resisted a sexual advance is in Lycophron's recreation of the prophecy of Cassandra (*Alexandra* 308–13); Hornblower notes that her words make sense best according to the sexualised version of the myth (Hornblower 2015: 186–8, note to lines 307–313; cf. also Servius' commentary on *Aeneid* 1.474). See also Davidson 2007: 281–4. Remarkably, the ambush is depicted in the Etruscan Tomb of the Bulls at Tarquinia (*c.* 550 BCE) alongside explicitly sexual images.

On the François Vase the god looks across to Achilles' attack on the boy, with his hands raised in a gesture of dismay; late sources even attest a tradition that made Troilus Apollo's son.[46] The sheer cruelty of this killing, and the desecration that went with it, is a powerful reminder that the glamour and sheen of *bright Achilles, the best of the Achaeans* are in tension with a nature that tends towards savagery.[47] Within the *Iliad*, the enmity between Apollo and Achilles is a recurrent element in the plot,[48] but its cause is never explicitly stated: nor is its motivation explicable simply in terms of the general principle that it is not destined or apportioned (*aisa, Il.* 16.707) for Achilles to be the one who succeeds in storming Troy. For those who listened to the *Iliad* and depicted the narrative on the vases, if not for Homer himself, the slaughter of Troilus could be seen as the outrage that led the god to pursue him to his downfall.

Read in this way, the murder of Troilus ceases to be a marginal issue, as can too easily be assumed through a reading that focusses only on what is explicitly mentioned in the *Iliad*. Rather, it can be seen as the defining image of the tendency towards unrestrained violence that runs through the life of Achilles. In the François Vase this reading is a potential inference, no

Fig. 13 Vase showing Achilles in wait for Troilus.

---

[46] Apollodorus, *Library* 3.12.5 and the Lycophron scholia on *Alexandra* 313 attest the tradition that Troilus was a son of Apollo. If so, this becomes the first reason for Apollo's hatred of Achilles, implicitly adding to the vehemence with which Apollo pursues him after the death and mutilation of Hector (cf. West, *EC* 122; Burgess 2009: 38–9).

[47] See also Kreuzer 2013, esp. 115; Lowenstam 2008, esp. 139–48.

[48] As a device for structuring an overall interpretation of the *Iliad*, the antagonism between Achilles and Apollo has been invoked many times by Gregory Nagy: for a particularly clear articulation, see Nagy 1990: 7–17. To my knowledge, however, Nagy does not clearly explain the *cause* of the quarrel at the level of personal motivations.

Fig. 14 Troilus and Achilles on the François Vase: (a) detail of Troilus and (b) drawing of the entire scene, made before the vase was further damaged.

more; but it is irresistible (for example) in the pairing of scenes on a vase by Lydos, active in Athens *c.* 560–540 BCE (Fig. 15). On one side Achilles is leaping at the boy Troilus, and the scene is identifiable by the dropped water-jar and the figure of his sister fleeing. On the other side is the final fall of the city with the central atrocity committed by the triumphant Greeks in their rampage: Neoptolemus, the son of Achilles, swings a helpless Trojan child by the leg and seizes the defenceless Priam, dragging him for slaughter from the altar of Zeus at which he has taken refuge.[49] The web of connections, personal and ethical, between the two scenes reads as a commentary on the problematic nature of Achilles and his bloodline.

[49] Berlin, Antikensammlung F1685. For my reading here cf. Steiner 2007: 109–10; Stansbury-O'Donnell 1999: 166–7. Giuliani 2013 [2003]: 173–6 analyses the scene of Neoptolemus and Priam acutely; surprisingly, however, he does not mention that Troilus is on the other side.

Fig. 15 Vase by Lydos, *c.* 560–540 BCE: (a) Troilus and Achilles and (b) Priam and Neoptolemus.

Tydeus and Diomedes

The savagery of Achilles becomes an acting-out of the ethical and psycho-logical problem that characterises the heroic race as a whole: excessive energy tends towards a kind of madness, the madness that makes men of war rush willingly towards their own destruction. This takes on sharp contours in our fragments of knowledge about Tydeus, one of the seven besieging champions in the attack on Thebes, the first of the two great wars of the heroic race.[50] The story survives in the ancient *Iliad* commentaries of the *Mythographus Homericus*, and may well have been narrated in the Cyclic

---

[50] I follow the version of the story preserved among the D-scholia at *Iliad* 5.126 (= *Thebaid* fr. 9: West, *GEF*, pp. 50–3), supplemented by Apollodorus *Library* 3.6.8, which has much of the same wording and evidently comes from a common source. For further sources see Gantz 1993: 517–18. As Torres-Guerra (2015: 233–4) points out, the evidence that this episode was narrated in the *Thebaid* is imperfect: the sources repeatedly give Pherecydes as the authority, and only in one copy of the *Iliad* scholion is the story referred to the Epic Cycle, in an addition made by a second hand after the note had been written. Davies argues (convincingly, in my view) that the weight of likelihood is that the episode circulated before the *Iliad* and that Homer avoids it for aesthetic reasons, 'to avoid grim and grisly stories' (Davies 2014: 37).

Thebaid, which ancient authorities associated especially closely with Homer himself.[51] In the battle before the gates of the city, Tydeus has been mortally wounded by Melanippus; but Athene, for reasons no longer known, wishes to make Tydeus immortal, and goes to bring him a herb or potion that will achieve this. One of his own allies, Amphiaraus the prophet, sees Athene coming, and to satisfy a grudge against Tydeus he cuts off Melanippus' head and gives it to him, upon which Tydeus splits open the head and gulps down the brains in his anger or passion (*apo thumou*). Horrified, Athene turns away, and the dying Tydeus asks her to transfer onto his son the favour he has lost. Tydeus was about to be raised to the level of the gods and escape the circles of mortality; but at that same moment he descended from human decency to become like a wild beast, lion or wolf or monster of fantasy. This image seems more grotesque and extreme compared to anything that we will see in the *Iliad*: but it expresses perfectly the tension in the temperament of the heroic race, and the ambiguity of the future that awaits them.

Tydeus is a looming presence in the most prominent of the battlefield episodes that occupy the bulk of Books 2–8 of the *Iliad*.[52] Agamemnon, as the senior commander, has gone up and down the companies of warriors in his army, encouraging some with praise and trying to shame others into action by mocking them for cowardice or sluggishness. When he reaches Tydeus' son Diomedes, he compares him at once to his father:

> So now, son of war-minded horsebreaking Tydeus,
> why do you cower, why do you look from afar on the bridges of war?
> Tydeus had no liking to cower in this way,
> but always wanted to be fighting the enemies far in front of his friends;
> so they said who saw him at work . . . (*Il.* 4.370–4)

From here on, the image of Tydeus overshadows the thought and actions of his son, a theme made all the more fraught by the fact that Diomedes himself claims – perhaps disingenuously? – to have no memory of him from childhood (*Il.* 6.222–3).[53] Agamemnon continues with a story of Tydeus' wild strength: during the expedition against Thebes he defeated the Thebans single-handed in an athletics contest, and went on to slaughter

---

[51] As West points out (*GEF*, p. 8), Herodotus' story of the banning of Homeric poetry by the tyrant Cleisthenes of Sicyon (*Histories* 5.67) makes much more sense as a reference to the *Thebaid* than to the *Iliad* or *Odyssey*. On the ascription of the *Thebaid* to Homer, see also Davies 2014: 28–33, Torres-Guerra 2015: 217–19.

[52] On the image of Tydeus in the portrayal of Diomedes, see further Pratt 2009; Sammons 2014.

[53] See Graziosi and Haubold 2010: 38, suggesting that Diomedes may be trying to distance himself from the deeds of his father at Thebes.

all but one of fifty men who were sent against him in ambush.[54] Sthenelus, Diomedes' friend, responds angrily against the claim that he is a lesser man than his father, reminding Agamemnon that Diomedes and his companions finally sacked Thebes when their fathers had failed to do so (*Il.* 4.404–10); Diomedes himself responds more mildly, reminding him that it is right for Agamemnon to goad his followers into action.

But what happens next to Diomedes enacts a more dramatic response to the insult. Just as Athene supported Tydeus in his time,[55] so now she gives strength and energy to his son:

> Then to Tydeus' son Diomedes Pallas Athene
> gave force and courage, so that he would become conspicuous
> among all the Greeks and would win noble glory (*kleos esthlon*);
> she made blaze from his helmet and shield an untiring flame,
> like the autumn star that most of them all
> shines bright when it has been bathed in Ocean;
> such a flame she made blaze from his head and shoulders
> and launched him into the midst, where most men were being routed.
>
> (*Il.* 5.1–8)

This is not a simple image of heroic glamour: the star in question is Sirius, the Dog of Orion, 'an evil sign among mortals' and a bringer of fever and death.[56] Diomedes surges against the Trojans like a river in flood as he slaughters them (*Il.* 5.87–94); undaunted by an arrow-wound he prays to Athene, and she makes his limbs light and explains what she has done to him, giving him the power to recognise gods on the battlefield and also filling him with preternatural energy:

> Into your breast I have sent your father's force,
> fearless, such force as the shield-shaking horseman Tydeus held.
>
> (*Il.* 5.125–6)

The word translated as 'force' here is *menos*, the name for the surge of thought or anger or any self-propelled, onrushing motion. The experience is mental and emotional, but in the ancient understanding of human nature it is bound up with the inhalation of breath and the swelling of the chest as a man moves into violent action. His fury is like that of a marauding lion (*Il.* 5.136–43, 161–4), yet he also seems near-divine.

---

[54] The athletics challenge and its bloody aftermath are recalled again by Athene at *Il.* 5.793–813, and by Diomedes himself at *Il.* 10.284–9. See further Davies 2014: 33–8. Other early evidence is slight, but Statius was to make it the centrepiece of Books 2 and 3 of his Latin *Thebaid*.
[55] See *Il.* 4.390, 5.116–17, 10.284–6.   [56] See *Il.* 22.26–31; Hes. *WD* 417 with West's note.

The Trojan Aeneas is not sure whether he is a mortal or a disguised god
(*Il.* 5.174–8), but his companion Pandarus suspects that he recognises him:

> If he is the man I speak of, Tydeus' battle-minded son,
> then it is not without a god that he rages, but near him
> stands one of the immortals, with shoulders wrapped in cloud . . .
> (*Il.* 5.184–6)

'He rages', *mainetai*: the verb is derivationally related to *menos*[57] but
answers only to the more violent and dangerous level of the types of
motion named by the noun – rage and fury and ultimately the extreme
of mental violence that Greek calls *mania*, frenzy or madness. Aeneas is
saved from the onslaught by his mother Aphrodite, the goddess who
presides over or personifies sexual desire and intercourse;[58] Diomedes,
with Athene's encouragement (*Il.* 5.130–2), hurls himself against the goddess and pierces the end of her finger with his spear. Crying out in pain she
drops Aeneas, and Diomedes shouts out against her in contempt
(*Il.* 5.348–51). When Aphrodite withdraws up to Olympus, the action
moves to the level of politics among the gods, with the triviality and
pettiness that we have seen before: she goes to her mother to be comforted
for her wounded finger, and Hera and Athene sneer about her to Zeus
(*Il.* 5.421–5). Just as with the gods' feast at the end of Book 1 (see below, pp.
209–212), the jarring contrast between divine triviality and human passion
makes for a reflection on mortality and its sorrows. When Aphrodite is
wounded, instead of blood there comes from her finger *ichōr*, the essence
of immortality that flows in the gods' veins (*Il.* 5.339–42); but Diomedes is
doomed by his human weakness, as Aphrodite's mother reminds her
among her consolations:

> The fool, the son of Tydeus does not know in his thought's breath
> that the man will not be long-lived who fights against the immortals;
> his children will not be at his knees to call him 'Daddy'
> when he comes from the war and the harsh battling;
> so now let Tydeus' son, however strong he may be,
> take thought lest one stronger than you fight against him,
> lest Aigialeia, Adrēstos' prudent daughter,
> will for long wake the household from sleep with her wailing,
> longing for her wedded husband, the best of the Greeks,
> Aigialeia, the strong wife of horse-breaking Diomedes.   (*Il.* 5.406–15)

---

[57] Cf. below, pp. 194–195.   [58] On the politics of the gods in this episode, see Jackson 2010.

The goddess imagines the scene of widowed misery with startling vividness: Diomedes is courting death by daring to oppose gods with human
violence – a reminder of men's lack of substance compared with the
carefree immortals who toy with them. Traditions beyond Homer worked
out the story in a different way, with Aphrodite punishing Diomedes by
turning Aigialeia to shameless adultery,[59] and it is likely that the wording of
the present passage prompted that story of viciously devious revenge.[60]

    Diomedes goes on to fight other and stronger gods. First he hurls himself
against Apollo, who is protecting Aeneas, and the god warns him of his folly:

> Take thought, Tydeus' son, and withdraw: do not desire
> to set your thoughts on a level with gods, for they are not equal tribes,
> the immortal gods and humans who walk on the earth.   (*Il.* 5.440–2)

Diomedes draws back, but eventually Athene launches him against Ares,
and he wounds the god of war himself:

> A second time Diomedes, mighty in the shout, rushed forward
> with his bronze spear; Pallas Athene thrust it
> into the base of Ares' flank, where he was girt with his lower armour:
> there he struck him and pierced him, and bit the fair flesh,
> then pulled out the spear again; and brazen Ares roared aloud,
> as loud as would cry out ten or eleven thousand
> men in battle, bringing together the strife of Ares.
> Trembling took hold of the Greeks and the Trojans
> in fear, so loud did Ares scream out, insatiable in war.   (*Il.* 5.855–63)

In the fury of combat Diomedes has set himself against the god who
personifies that fury, and the description strains the limits of language
and of visualisation:[61]

> As when a gloomy mist appears out of clouds
> from the heat, when an evil-blowing wind has arisen,
> so to Tydeus' son Diomedes did brazen Ares
> appear together with the clouds, going into the broad sky.   (*Il.* 5.864–7)

---

[59] The story is in the scholia at *Il.* 5.412, and is explicit in Lycophron's *Alexandra* (610–13; see
   Hornblower 2015: 263). Apollodorus mentions her adultery with the son of Sthenelus without
   referring to Aphrodite's intervention (*Epitome* 6.9), but this is not incompatible with the
   account in the *Iliad* scholia. On these sources see Gantz 1993: 699.

[60] The word-family of the verb *goaō*, whose participle I translate as 'wailing' in *Il.* 5.413, is in
   Homer used only in the context of grief and mourning. However, the scholia on the present
   passage tell how she grieved for his *absence* by weeping and lamenting 'even at night', and that
   this led to the adultery.

[61] On the difficulty of following the sense of this simile, see Kirk 1990: 149–50, note on 5.864–7.

Diomedes continues in his wild career, until the Trojans decide that they cannot stand unaided against him, and Hector is sent to ask Athene to intercede for them,

> so she will keep the son of Tydeus from holy Troy,
> the wild spearman, strong master of the rout,
> who I declare has become the strongest of the Greeks.
> We did not fear even Achilles so much, the leader of men,
> who they say was born of a goddess; but this man is raging (*mainetai*)
> too much, and no-one can draw equal to him in force (*menos*).
>
> (*Il.* 6.96–101)

The correspondence between the verb *mainetai* and the noun *menos* accentuates the image of a state of strange intensity. Like each of the other thematic movements that are woven together in the battle-narrative of this section of the *Iliad*, Diomedes' surge does not reach a final conclusion: his onrush is stalled when he discovers that one of his intended victims is a family friend (*Il.* 6.212–36), and thereafter the focus moves away from him.[62] But his assault on the gods remains as an image of the excess to which a hero's strength and will can drive him. As such, it foreshadows the structurally similar sequence that will be followed by Achilles, which we will trace later in this book.

Diomedes and Gilgamesh

Moreover, the episode invites a reading in parallel with the scene in the *Epic of Gilgamesh* where Gilgamesh rejects the sexual advances of Ishtar. The two passages have often been compared, exploring a coincidence of action and imagery so close that it invites the hypothesis of direct influence from text to text.[63] Diomedes' contempt for Aphrodite recalls the way Gilgamesh and Enkidu reviled Ishtar, insulting her and pelting her after killing the Bull (above, pp. 74–77). Ishtar is goddess of war as well as sexuality; Aphrodite, of course, normally embodies only one of those forces, but in certain versions of her cult she was indeed worshipped as a war-goddess, holding a combination of roles precisely reminiscent of

---

[62] He returns to the forefront only after Agamemnon announces that he has despaired of capturing Troy, and Diomedes vows that he and Sthenelus will sack the city on their own (*Il.* 9.45–9).

[63] Burkert 1992 [1984]: 96–9; Burkert 2004: 41–4; West 1997: 361–2; O. Anderson 1997; Currie 2016: 173–8, 195–7; for a sceptical view, Kelly 2008: 289.

Ishtar.[64] Later in our scene Zeus reminds Aphrodite that war is not her concern (*Il.* 5.428–30), as if the poet is alluding to the contradiction inherent in this aspect in the range of traditions about her.

In the denouement, the parallels become still tighter, and the sequences of events in the two texts fall into alignment. When the warrior has assaulted the goddess, Gilgamesh verbally (*SBV* VI.22–91) and Diomedes physically (*Il.* 5.334–430), she takes refuge with her parents and demands that they punish the offending mortal. At this point, crucially, the two pairs of parent deities are named along parallel patterns: the combination of male Anu and female Antu (*SBV* VI 82–3) finds an answering structure in Zeus and Dione (*Il.* 5.370, 381), where the *Dio-* stem of the male name matches *Diōnē* in exactly the same way.[65] This precise correspondence of detail strengthens the suspicion that this may be a case of direct influence from one tradition or text upon the other; for us at this point of our argument, however, this localised match is less significant than the parallel in structure and causation between the two plots overall. Gilgamesh and Enkidu mocked Ishtar when they had reached the point of triumphant success as heroic masters of Uruk, and that mockery led to Enkidu's death and the destruction of Gilgamesh's confidence in his own life. Diomedes, similarly, was driven by his very abundance of strength and vitality towards the self-destructive wildness in which he abandoned all natural limitations and attacked the gods themselves, first Aphrodite and then Ares. Irrespective of any more specific linkages, the two passages embody the same basic story-pattern, the same sense that the abundant energy of the demigod will lead to his undoing.

Just as with Gilgamesh and Enkidu, under the shadow of subsequent traditions we might be inclined towards a psychologically based reading of the story-pattern of Diomedes' attack on the gods: the hero has an inherent 'flaw' that brings about his downfall. But there is no such comforting relationship between cause and effect, between folly and its punishment. The principle is simply that great strength and energy tend towards excess, that *menos* slips towards *mania*.[66] The tendency to go too far can be manifested in action, the wild fury of the hero in battle, or in passion and pride, the exaggerated and insatiable demand for respect and status that drives Achilles (as we will see in the next chapter) to rise up against Agamemnon and take such terrible revenge upon him.[67] Internally it is a swelling and expansion of the stuff of thought and will, the mental energy

---

[64] For warlike Aphrodite, strongly attested at Sparta, see Budin 2010; Pironti 2010.
[65] See the analysis by Currie 2016: 173–8.   [66] Cf. Redfield 1994: 128–59.
[67] I offer a fuller sketch of this way of reading the Iliadic portrayal of heroism in Clarke 2004.

that in the early Greek view of man is identified as – or figuratively linked to – the movement of breath and blood and bodily fluids in the breast.[68] When Athene 'breathes *menos*' into Diomedes she is giving him special energy through the stuff that he has inhaled into his lungs: this is a mythically heightened version of the experience that Agamemnon undergoes in the opening quarrel of the *Iliad*, when he rises up in anger and 'his black *phrenes* were filled all around with *menos*' (*Il.* 1.103–4).[69] Translating from ancient conceptual norms to our own, this can be identified with what you and I know as the physical excitement of rage and resentment, with accelerated breathing and the rush of adrenalin, and the explosive consequences that ensue when those forces are manifested in action.

Excessive energy and self-destructive folly

Violent excess brings with it the prospect of divine vengeance: not necessarily for moral or psychological reasons, but because of a more fundamental principle of cosmic order. The gods resent those who rise too high; they bring down and humiliate mortals who try to draw equal with them. In a narrative sequence whose epic affiliations are explicit,[70] Herodotus puts this truth into the mouth of Artabanos, the uncle of the young Persian king Xerxes, warning him not to invade Greece:[71]

> You see that it is against the most prominent creatures that the god hurls his thunderbolts, and that he does not let them indulge their fantasies (*phantazesthai*), but the tiny ones do not vex him at all; and you see that he hurls his missiles at the largest houses and the tallest trees, for the god loves to cut all prominent ones down to size. So a great army may be destroyed by a small one in such a way as this, that the god in his envy throws fear or thunder upon them, and by these they are destroyed in a way unworthy of them. For the god allows no-one to have big thoughts (*mega phroneein*) other than himself. (*Histories* 7.10)

---

[68] This form of words is an attempt to avoid an over-nuanced formulation for the relationship between thought-processes and the body in the Homeric view of man. This issue, which depends largely on one's approach to the relationship between metaphorical and literal language and the cognitive status of embodied imagery for expressing intangible phenomena, has been much debated in Homeric scholarship: see for example Pelliccia 1995; Clarke 1999, ch. 4, with Cairns 2003b, 2014; Long 2015: 15–50.

[69] See below, Ch. 9, n. 16.   [70] Cf. Pelling 2006b.

[71] This passage is well contextualised by Harrison 2000: 31–63, esp. 46 ff.; cf. also De Jong 2013: 273–81.

The teaching is simple: human over-prominence will be beaten down by the jealousy of the gods.[72] Perhaps the formulation in this passage is an echo of old proverbial wisdom, like the story of Polycrates lord of Samos that Herodotus tells earlier in his 'display of investigation' (*Histories* 1.1). Polycrates was warned that his unbroken good fortune would inevitably invite divine jealousy, so he was advised to throw away a beloved ring to reduce his level of good luck – but after he had thrown it into the sea it returned to him a few days later in the belly of the fish he was eating for supper, proving that he would be unable to avoid provoking the coming vengeance (*Histories* 3.40–3). The thought here coincides with the themes we saw first in Mesopotamian wisdom literature, then in the pessimistic philosophy of Hesiod: the gods are unwilling to grant mortals the ease and abundance of life that they enjoy themselves, and so the low and simple life best avoids the risk of disaster (above, pp. 131–132). Later in Herodotus' narrative the same uncle of Xerxes states this again in a still more Hesiodic form:[73] human life is short and wretched and prosperity is unstable, because

> the god gives a taste of sweet vitality (*aiōn*), but it is discovered that he is jealous with this. (*Histories* 7.46)

Here again the cosmic principle is close to the teaching of Hesiod, or of Shiduri in the Old Babylonian *Gilgamesh*: because the gods have been unwilling to grant the fullness of life or of livelihood to mortals, a span of existence spent within modest limits is in harmony with their will. One who refuses to follow this principle, or whose fortunes in life runs against it, will arouse their anger.

In a cosmological sense, then, the universal fact of divine jealousy is prior to any of its manifestations in specific narratives, where it may be shaped into individual resentments, each with a logic of its own – Apollo vindictive against Achilles, Aphrodite against Diomedes, Ishtar against Gilgamesh and Enkidu. The same principle underlies and motivates any discourse that explores human pride or folly or *hubris*, bullying violence driven by one's refusal to remain within the limits of one's own power.[74] To continue with the traditions around Xerxes, Aeschylus in his tragedy

---

[72] Cf. Herodotus on the wisdom that Solon gives to Croesus of Lydia, with the divine resentment (*nemesis*) that comes to Croesus 'because he considered himself to be the most securely-prosperous' (*olbiōtatos*) of all men (*Histories* 1.34). Cf. Pelling 2006a.

[73] See Harrison 2000: 172.

[74] For a nuanced and subtle essay in defining *hubris*, see Cairns 1996, with Van Wees 1992: 109–25; on *hubris* in social and legal practice in the Classical period, see also Cohen 1996: 119–42.

Persians makes the ghost of the king's father, Darius, envision the disastrous failure of his expedition as follows:

> The heaps of corpses, even to the third-sown generation,
> will signal without voice to the eyes of men
> that no mortal should have excess in his thoughts
> > (*huperpheu phronein*),
>
> forviolence (*hubris*) bursts out into a fruitful crop
> of self-destructive folly, when it reaps a harvest full of weeping.
> > (*Persians* 818–22)

My clumsy phrase 'self-destructive folly' translates the elusive Greek term *ātē*, of fundamental importance in psychology and ethics.[75] At the simplest level, it names that which is harmful or destructive: hence in legal language it can refer simply to a fine imposed as a punishment.[76] In loftier contexts, however, it can refer either to the damage done by human folly, or (by an easy shift of meaning) to the damaged or diminished state of mind that engenders such folly – above all, the phenomenon of someone acting in a way that will bring about their own ruin. So arise moral and psychological explanations for processes that could also be seen in purely mechanical terms of action and reaction: the gods are jealous, lightning strikes the highest trees and a man who pushes violence or even self-certainty beyond proper limits will come to disaster.[77] It is because of a similar, if immensely more complex, working-out of that principle that Achilles' rushing vitality will lead him to his untimely death, a death for which no glory can be adequate compensation.

---

[75] The word *ātē* is often translated 'blindness' or similar, but nothing said about *ātē* in the ancient sources suggests such an image, and it seems to have crept in as an overtranslation of German *Verblendung*, which is sometimes used for *ātē* in nineteenth-century dictionaries and commentaries. My account of *ātē* here draws on the recent analysis by Cairns 2012; see also Sommerstein 2013.

[76] The principal evidence is from the Law Code of Gortyn in Crete, where *ata* is translatable throughout as 'damage' or 'fine' according to context. See Gagarin and Perlman 2016: 334–428 *passim*, and see further Cairns 2012: 1 n. 2.

[77] For this analysis of *hubris* and *phthonos* in the speech of Darius' ghost, compare Garvie 2009, pp. xxii–xxiii and pp. 314–15, note at lines 820–31.

9 | The strife of the *Iliad*

In the last part of the previous chapter we saw a series of reflections on the consequences of ignoring the truth about human limitations. Although the story of Achilles in the *Iliad* is variegated by so many other themes, the same principle is at its centre: the excessive energy of the protagonist, and the proximity of his nature to the divine level, is at the root of the passions and disasters that will lead eventually to his fall. What is unique to the *Iliad* is the psychological depth with which these forces are depicted and explored: hence it will be our next task to trace the plot-sequence of the poem through a close analysis of the mental and emotional life of Achilles.

The first word of the *Iliad* is at the centre of this thematic cluster. *Mēnis* has no adequate English translation, but 'Wrath' with a capital *W* will serve as a placeholder for this word, which later poets recognised as the specially marked term for Achilles' passionate anger:[1]

> Wrath – sing, goddess, the Wrath of Peleus' son Achilles,
> ruinous, which threw countless pains on the Greeks
> and cast down to Hades many mighty ghosts
> of heroes, and left the men themselves for dogs to seize
> and for vultures to divide – and Zeus' plan was coming to fulfilment.
>
> (*Il.* 1.1–5)

This rage will be something terrible, something to make men shudder:[2] and it is above all among Achilles' own comrades that the slaughter will be inflicted, providing the proof that they were fools to insult him.

---

[1] Alcaeus, in a passage apparently referring directly to the Iliadic tradition, uses the formulation *tekeos mānis*, 'the anger of [Thetis'] child' (Alcaeus fr. 44.8: Campbell, *GL* 1, pp. 251–61); similarly Bacchylides' evocation of the rage is confidently restored as 'the rough *mānis* in Achilles' breast' (*Odes* 13.111–12), a phrase that associates *mēnis* with the language of human emotion more closely than in any Homeric example (cf. Cairns 2010: 307, note at lines 111–12).

[2] Here I try to evoke the associations of the adjective *oulomenos*, which I have translated as 'ruinous' at *Il.* 1.2. The word is clearly linked to the verb *ollumi* 'destroy, ruin, kill', but its uses suggest that it refers indeterminately to what is *destructive* and what *deserves destruction* – at the latter end of the range, roughly, it marks out its referent as provoking the exclamation *oloio* – 'May you go to ruin!', 'May you be destroyed!'. See *LfgrE* s.v., with Pulleyn 2000: 118, note at line 2.

The significance of the word *mēnis*

How can it make sense to say that the best and brightest of the Greeks brought about such destruction? It seems a paradox, but the word *mēnis* itself encodes the explanation. Elsewhere this word is normally used of the gods: it is the vengeful anger of a god who has been slighted, who has been denied due respect and offerings from mortals.[3] Later in the *Iliad*, when Achilles is about to go out against the Trojans in search of vengeance, a simile sets the Wrath in parallel with just this kind of divine rage:[4]

> As when smoke rises up to the broad sky
> from a burning city, and the *mēnis* of the gods has driven it on,
> and laid trouble upon them all, and brought suffering for many,
> so Achilles set trouble and suffering upon the Trojans.   (*Il.* 21.522–5)

In the opening movement of the *Iliad*, it is because Achilles' energy and vitality are so close to those of a god that his need for respect, and his anger against those who withhold it, are extreme in the same proportion.[5] Paradoxically, perhaps, this explains why such destructive rage is set in motion by strife (*eris, Il.* 1.6) over something that might seem trivial in the scheme of things: a dispute over the assignment among the war-leaders of booty from a minor raid, booty that happens in this case to take the form of

[3] The long scholarly debate on *mēnis* can only be touched upon here. The fundamental question in terms of its lexical meaning is whether it is an emotional or a religious concept – in other words, whether it belongs in the semantic field of anger or that of divine responses to human behaviour. Related to this is the lexical and etymological question – whether it is a cousin of *menos* 'force, movement, onrush', or of words built on the root **mneH2-* 'remember', with the development **mnānis > mānis > mēnis*. A version of the latter argument is powerfully developed by Muellner 1996, who sees the concept of *mēnis* in cosmic terms – a response to a violation of fundamental rules of order. Against this, Cairns has argued for including the word firmly among straightforward (and implicitly non-sacral) vocabulary for anger as an emotion or cluster of emotions (see esp. Cairns 2003a: 31–4). An intermediate view might be that the word represents solemn and insistent anger triggered by an insult or threat to status, and that such anger is particularly closely associated with (but not exclusively defined by) the response of a god to an insult. The issues are summed up succinctly by Latacz et al. 2009: 12–13; cf. Kim 2000: 153–70.
[4] For the parallelism between the *mēnis* of Achilles and of the gods in this simile, cf. Muellner 1996: 47–8, 167–8; Ready 2011: 47–8. For the religious associations of the wording of this simile compare especially 'the *mēnis* of a god, wrathful over the sacrifices' (*Il.* 5.177–8).
[5] Standard studies of the 'Wrath of Achilles' are Latacz 1998: 71–133; Redfield 1994, esp. 3–29; Zanker 1994: 73–113; cf. Schein 1984: 89–167; well-nuanced recent summings-up by Burgess 2014: 44–47, Graziosi 2016: 59–71. Heiden's analysis of the plot-structure, while perhaps over-schematic, is very useful for clarifying the causal linkages (Heiden 2008, esp. diagram on p. 40). There is a good overview of the social issues involved in heroic anger by Harris 2001: 131–56; cf. Van Wees 1992: 126–65.

two sex-slaves. How are we to make sense of that grotesque dispute in terms of the overall destiny of the heroic race?

As we have seen (pp. 160–162), the same words 'the plan of Zeus was being fulfilled' appear also in the *Cypria*, where they refer to the plan to relieve the goddess Earth of her burden. In the opening lines of the *Iliad*, they can be read in the same terms: the ongoing fulfilment of Zeus' plan involves the countless warriors who are driven to death as a result of the quarrel. Regardless of how one models the *intertextual* dynamics between these two occurrences of a single verbal formula, in terms of theology and mythical history they are precisely aligned with each other.[6] We saw also the less clearly attested idea that this sense of a physical burden was linked to the offence caused by the impiety and overweening violence of the heroes – *asebeia, hubrisma*. Guided by this connection, should we conclude that the violent destructiveness of the quarrel was itself a manifestation of the *hubris* of the heroic race? Homer, as usual, never points this moral, and it has seldom been broached in modern readings of the *Iliad*. But to some at least in ancient times it seemed natural to interpret the *Iliad* in a similar way. Here is Plutarch in his treatise *On Listening to Poets*:[7]

> One must understand that when [poets] use the name of Zeus, they are referring sometimes to the god, sometimes to chance, and often to what is fated. For when they say
>
> 'Father Zeus, ruling from Ida … '
>
> and
>
> 'O Zeus, who can declare themselves wiser than you?'
>
> they mean the god himself; but when they speak of Zeus as for the causes of all that happens, and say
>
> 'it cast many strong wraiths down to Hades
> …. and the plan of Zeus was coming to fulfilment',
>
> they [are referring to] what is fated. For the poet does not believe that the god plans evil against humans, but he rightly shows forth the necessary

---

[6] This point is subtly articulated by Clay 1999, and in different but complementary terms by Marks 2002. Allan 2008b argues instead that in a performance context the reference to the 'plan of Zeus' in the proem would have been understood on a generalised cosmic level rather than in terms of the narrower plot-line of the Trojan War itself.

[7] The text is edited with introduction and commentary by Hunter and Russell 2011; text and translation at Babbitt 1927: 74–197. On the educational milieu of the text compare Schenkeveld 1982, emphasising its elementary level, with Hunter's sketch of the text's use of Homeric and other poetry as the foundation for a philosophical education (Hunter 2009: 169–201).

state of things – that it is ordained (*peprōtai*) for cities and armed camps and leaders, if they practise wisdom, to meet success and overcome their enemies, but that if like these men they fall into passion and error, quarrelling with each other and forming factions against each other, they will behave disgracefully and be thrown into disarray, and will come to an evil end. (Plutarch, *De audiendis poetis* = *Moralia* 1.6, 23C–E)

Here the *Iliad* is seen as a story of the just punishment visited on those who fall into pride and violence against each other: their destructive behaviour brings disaster upon themselves, as the outcome of the Iliadic quarrel will demonstrate.[8] This is a simple strategy for interpreting 'the plan of Zeus' in terms that make it a vindication of the moral order. Perhaps this line of interpretation was deliberately intended for those studying Homer as young boys, perhaps it is unduly unfluenced by Plutarch's desire to find sound moral teachings in poetry; certainly, to many modern readers it will seem not merely simple but simplistic. Nonetheless, it is an authentic ancient response, and it will remain with us as we trace the story of the Wrath.

Women as tokens of men's status

As noted above (p. 119), one Homeric name for a poem or its sequence of ideas is *oimē*, literally a route or path.[9] In the world where these poems were composed, roads followed winding and circuitous lines over the contours of the land – unlike the simple straight line of a modern (or imperial Roman) road, or the plot-sequence of a conventional novel with beginning, middle and end. Hence the *Iliad*'s opening movement first plunges into the midst of the story and then moves back and forth to draw out its themes. How the quarrel began is stated clearly only in retrospect, when Achilles explains it to his mother Thetis:

> We went to Thēbē, the sacred city of Ēetion,
>   and we sacked it and brought everything back here:
>   the sons of the Greeks divided it all well among themselves,
>   and for Atreus' son they chose Chryses' fair-cheeked daughter.[10]
>
>   (*Il.* 1.366–9)

---

[8] For this interpretation of the passage, see further Hunter and Russell 2011: 132–33, note at 23D.
[9] See *Od.* 22.347, *Homeric Hymn to Hermes* 451, with Thalmann 1984: 123–5; Ford 1992: 40–8.
[10] Here and everywhere I translate *Chryseïs* and *Briseïs* as 'Chryses' daughter' and 'Brises' daughter': see Ch. 16, n. 25.

The starting-point, then, was one of the minor brutalities of the war: a raid up the coast from Troy, in which the Greeks had sacked a smaller city.[11] Just as the prize in an athletic contest could as much be a woman as a piece of expensive metalwork (see e.g. *Il.* 22.164), so a man's reward for bravery in combat can take either form, as Agamemnon later puts it when he is encouraging one of his peers:

> either a three-legged vessel or a pair of horses with chariot attached
> or a woman, who would climb into the same bed with you.   (*Il.* 8.290–1)

Maybe this is the special savagery of men on a long military campaign, men who have lived under canvas for years with lice gnawing at them – the grotesque image that Aeschylus would evoke in the speech of a messenger announcing the Greek victory at the end of the war (*Agamemnon* 600–2); or maybe this is the permanent brutality of a world where slavery and war and the oppression of women are taken for granted as casualties of the trade in symbols of men's status.[12] Whichever of these is closer to the truth, it cannot be unproblematic that freeborn human beings are being treated as chattels.[13]

The girl's father, Chryses, comes asking for her release: he is a priest of Apollo, and before the whole Greek army (*Il.* 1.15) he begs for her in the name of the god, but Agamemnon threatens him:

> Her I will not release: sooner old age will come upon her
> in my own home, in Argos, far from her father's country,
> going back and forth along the loom and coming to share my bed.
> Go now, do not provoke me, so you will reach your home unharmed.
>
> (*Il.* 1.29–32)

---

[11] Thēbē was not the girl's home city; this city was called Chrysē, as Homer makes clear (*Il.* 1.37, etc.). Later sources record that the *Cypria* explained that the girl was visiting a friend in Thēbē and sacrificing to Artemis (*Cypria*, fr. 24 in West, *GEF*, pp. 100–3). It is economical to guess that a version of this story is in the background for the composer of the *Iliad* too, since otherwise the anomaly would be pointless as well as puzzling. Cf. Davies 1989: 47 Burgess 2001: 151–2.

[12] This question – how to define the theme of the physical realisation of honour (*timē*) in prizes or awards (*geras*) encoding social status – is a standard issue for debate in Homeric scholarship. It has usually been pursued in ethnographic terms, tracing norms rather than deviations (see esp. Donlan 1982; Van Wees 1992, esp. 69–125, and cf. Seaford 1994: 1–73), and has even been addressed through systematic comparison with social life among apes (Gottschall 2008). Earlier accounts applying a strictly competition-based approach to the politics of status, with 'honour' effectively treated as a quantifiable commodity (e.g. Adkins 1960), can still be useful but tend towards an unnecessarily reductive reading of the psychological and social complexity of the issues in question. Zanker 1994: 1–72 remains a sensitive overview of the Iliadic poet's response to the implied value-structures; for more recent studies that explore the quarrel of the *Iliad* in terms of violation or problematisation of the social system, see esp. Wilson 2002a, esp. 13–70, with Cairns 2011a, 2011b.

[13] On gender politics in the use of women as tokens of status in the quarrel between Achilles and Agamemnon, see Dué 2002.

The king has defied a great god, and he has done so in front of an assembly of soldiers who have been separated for years from their own loved ones, precisely in order to win back a stolen woman – the wife of this man's brother.

This moment points towards the uneasy problem at the centre of the Greeks' war. Here again a sidelight can be thrown on this theme by looking at how the idea would be recalled in Aeschylus' *Agamemnon*, a play full of reflections on the epic inheritance as well as of speculative thought about the order of the world. The old men of Mycenae sing of how people mourned over the urns that came home from Troy full of ashes:[14]

> They groan in grief, praising one
> man as an expert in war,
> another for having died a beautiful death in the slaughter,
> for the sake of another man's wife:
> this is what is muttered quietly,
> and resentful pain creeps against
> the sons of Atreus, agents of justice.   (*Agamemnon* 445–51)

Throughout the traditions of the Trojan War, this theme recurs: for example, in Plato's *Laws* the Athenian Stranger recalls as a familiar story the rancour and bitterness with which the victors were received when they returned to Greece (*Laws* 682 d–e).[15] The start of the *Iliad* thus revolves around the central problem: why are so many men to die for the sake of this woman, 'another man's wife'?

This bitterness will now manifest itself in a conflict of a kind familiar throughout the history of warfare, between the brilliance of a young officer and his commander's demand for the respect owed to seniority. The development is worth tracing in detail. In answer to Chryses' prayers, the god comes down to punish the Greeks with the arrows of plague (*Il.* 1.43–52); after ten days of sickness and death, an assembly is called to seek the explanation – but it is called not by the commander but by Achilles on his own initiative. The prophet fears Agamemnon's reaction if he is to reveal the truth: so Achilles undertakes to protect him, *even if you name Agamemnon himself* (*Il.* 1.90–1) – he is already provoking a confrontation.

---

[14] At *Il.* 7.333–5 Nestor prescribes the practice of cremating the dead at Troy so that the remains can be brought back home after the war. The lines describing the repatriation of the remains have been regarded since ancient times as a post-Homeric addition to the text. Given that the custom was instituted for Athens shortly before the *Agamemnon* was composed, it is likely that Aeschylus' lines refer to a contemporary reality, presumably alluding to Athenian involvement in multiple foreign conflicts at the time the play was composed.

[15] Cited by Thomson 1966: 2.45, note on *Agamemnon* 450–1.

When Calchas explains that the god is avenging the insult to his priest, and that the plague can only be ended by giving the girl back, Agamemnon's breast swells with rage[16] against the prophet:

> for I far prefer her to Clytaimestra
> my wedded wife, for she is no worse than her
> in form or in making, in what she thinks or what she does.
>
> (*Il.* 1.113–15)

All the clearer now is his trivialisation of the whole campaign – this slave matters more to him than his own wife, who indeed is also Helen's first cousin. In the course of his speech he suddenly climbs down, undertaking to return the girl in order to save his people (*Il.* 1.116–17), but this is conditional:

> Get ready another prize for me, so that I alone
> of the Greeks will not be prizeless, for that would not be fitting:
> you all see it, how my prize is lost to me.   (*Il.* 1.118–20)

Geras, translated here as 'prize', is a neuter noun: it means a sign of respect, an acknowledgement of social status through a gift or a gesture or a bestowal of privilege.[17] Here of course it is the label for the captive woman, dehumanised and objectified. Achilles responds that redistribution is impossible, the prizes have been assigned and cannot be recalled: Agamemnon should 'give up the girl to the god' (*Il.* 1.127) and wait till Troy falls, when they will compensate him (1.128). Agamemnon rises to a new level of hostility, accusing Achilles of deceit and greed (1.131–2): if the army refuses his demand he will go himself and take the 'prize' that has been assigned to one of his peers – perhaps Achilles' own girl, the daughter of Brises (1.145–7).

This makes the conflict irreparable. Achilles responds with open insults (*Il.* 1.149–51), and the problem of fighting for Helen looms again:

> It was not for the sake of the Trojan spearmen that I came
> to fight here, for I have no cause to blame them;
> they have never stolen my cattle or my horses
> nor ever in Phthia of the rich soil, the land that nourishes men,
> have they destroyed my crops, for there lie between
> many shadowy mountains and resounding sea:

---

[16] On the physical manifestation and psychological essence of Agamemnon's rage here, see for example Cairns 2003a: 41–5; Clarke 1999: 105–7, with Cairns 2003b: 68–70; Pulleyn 2000: 154–5, note at 1.103.

[17] On the meaning of *geras*, see Van Wees 1992: esp. 299–310, with Von Reden 1995: 22–3.

> you we followed, shameless one, so that you would win joy,
> gaining reward for Menelaus and for you, hound-faced,
> from the Trojans …   (*Il.* 1.152–60)

According to a story preserved in the *Catalogue of Women*, Helen's (legal) father had made all those who sought to marry her swear that they would help her husband if trouble came because of her; but Achilles was not there, kept away by his guardian Cheiron the centaur.[18] Perhaps Achilles here implies that difference between himself and his peers; perhaps he simply expresses any man's frustration at toiling in war for such a cause. As he goes on, his complaint becomes still more down-to-earth: throughout the fighting Achilles has worked harder than any other man, yet Agamemnon always ends up with a greater portion for himself (*Il.* 1.163–8). He will give up the war and go home to Phthia, rather than stay here unrewarded (*atimos*), 'dragging up wealth and treasure' for Agamemnon (*Il.* 1.170–1). The response in turn subjects him to a more intense degradation:

> I will bring out Brises' daughter of the lovely cheeks
> going myself to your hut – your own prize, so that you will know well
> how much better a man I am than you, and any other man will fear
> to speak as my equal or set himself on a level against me.   (*Il.* 1.184–7)

What was earlier a vague threat becomes here an emphatic declaration, and it will be impossible from now on for either man to step back without humiliation. Achilles is on the point of drawing his sword to kill Agamemnon, when he draws back from violence and instead makes an oath-bound declaration of defiance, in which his earlier threat to go home is transformed into an outright refusal to fight:

> The longing for Achilles will come to the ships of the Greeks,
> all of them: and despite your pain you will be unable
> to protect them, when many under man-slaughtering Hector
> will fall in death: and you will rend your thought's breath within,
> miserable because you gave no repayment to the best of the Greeks.
>   (*Il.*1.240–4)

The consequence of the insult will be the deaths of Agamemnon's followers and, by implication, the failure of the war effort. All this depends on Achilles' sense that his self-respect depends on the esteem that others show him:

> I would indeed be called a coward and a man of nothing
> if I yielded to you in all things, in whatever you might say:

---

[18] Hes. *Cat.* fr. 155.78–92 Most = fr. 204.78–92 M–W. See Cingano 2005: 127–9.

> give these commands to other men, to me issue no
> orders: I undertake to obey you no more.   (*Il.* 1.293–6)

Such is the logic that makes it impossible for Achilles to yield without
inflicting death on his comrades: an ethic that equates the value of life and
death with the payment of respect and status in the warband.

But in the midst of it all something else has happened, something that
no-one sees except Achilles himself (*Il.* 1.198). At the moment when he is
about to draw his sword on Agamemnon, Athene appears to him:

> While he was drawing his great sword from the scabbard, Athene came
> from the sky: for white-armed Hera had sent her down,
> loving and caring for them both in the breath of her thought.
> She stood behind him, and seized Peleus' son by his yellow hair,
> appearing to him alone, for none of the others saw her:
> Achilles felt awe, and he turned around, and at once he recognised
> Pallas Athene, and his eyes[19] gleamed, terrifying …   (*Il.* 1.194–200)

Here suddenly we move from the earthbound rivalries of men to a higher
and more remote plane, the mingling between gods and demigods that
defines the strangeness and significance of the heroic race. Athene begins
with what sounds like practical advice, urging him to restrict the conflict to
words not actions, but what emerges becomes more like prophecy:

> I will tell you this, and it will come to fulfilment:
> one day there will be beside you three times as many bright gifts
> because of this outrage (*hubris*): restrain yourself, take our advice.
> > (*Il.* 1.212–14)

Ostensibly she says that if Achilles plays a long game he will eventually be
offered still greater respect and praise and *geras*: and indeed Agamemnon
will do so twice – once through the emissaries sent to his hut, and again
when he is about to return to the battle in pursuit of Hector. But by then, as
we will see, the payment will have become meaningless to Achilles, because
he will already be headed towards certain death and all such rewards will
have become contemptible to him. Any ancient audience, even one for
whom the *Iliad* constituted a new version of the story, must have known
that Achilles would die at Troy soon after the events described here: so
Athene's words set up dark hints of their own. If the goddess is not lying,

---

[19] Turkeltaub 2005, drawing on the arguments marshalled by Nörenberg 1972, argues forcibly
that the eyes of *Il.* 1.200 are better understood as those of Achilles rather than of Athene.
Grammatically, either is possible.

what are these 'gifts' that will come to Achilles? The only real gifts he will receive are those of fame and glory when he is in the grave.[20]

Thetis and the plan

After Agamemnon's men have taken Brises' daughter away, Achilles goes down alone to the shore and calls on his mother Thetis, who long ago returned from Peleus' house to her father's home in the depths of the sea (*Il.* 1.358).[21] From his first words, the foreboding of death is coming into clarity:

> Mother, since you gave me birth, short-lived (*minunthadios*) as I am,
> the Olympian one ought to have pledged me payment,
> high-thundering Zeus; but instead he has paid me nothing ...
>
> (*Il.* 1.352–4)

Thetis emerges like a mist, yet takes him by the hand to comfort him as any mother might do (*Il.* 1.359–61). He recalls that he has often heard her boasting of the time when she saved Zeus from peril: three of the other gods had tied him up and made him powerless, but Thetis called up Briareos, a monstrous being from the deep past, and when the rebels withdrew in fear of him she released Zeus from his bonds. This story, virtually unknown from any other ancient source,[22] seems to heighten the disjuncture between mortality and divinity in Achilles' life – his childhood was shaped against the bizarre and lofty background of divine politics, but now he is *minunthadios*, literally 'one who lives only a little while' (*Il.* 1.352). He asks Thetis to remind Zeus that he owes her a return for this old favour – among gods as among men, service is the payment of a debt (cf. *Il.* 1.503–4) – and this is to take the form of inflicting disastrous defeat on his own side in battle:

[20] For this way of interpreting the promise of future gifts, compare the paradigm of Meleager: to say that 'they did not give him the gifts after all' (*Il.* 9.594) is to imply that he died before he had a chance to receive them (as argued below, Ch. 10, n. 46). However, it remains possible to say that Athene's prediction is literally fulfilled by the extravagant recompense that Agamemnon offers in Book 19: for this line see for example Morrison 1992: 17, 122. My own view, argued later in more detail, is that the vital point is that Achilles is indifferent to the gifts by the time they come to him (see esp. *Il.* 19.146–8).

[21] Powerful evocation of Thetis as mother and goddess by Slatkin 1991, esp. 21–52.

[22] I assume here that the episode of Briareos (also known as Aigaion) and Thetis is distinct from and (in terms of the sequence of mythical time) later than the help given by Briareos to Zeus in the conflict between Zeus and the Titans, familiar from Hesiod (*Theogony* 617–719). Apart from scholarly guesses at the interpretation of the present passage of the *Iliad*, the only other early source for Thetis' summoning of Briareos is Ion of Chios (fr. 741 at Campbell, *GL* 4, pp. 354–5). See Gantz 1993: 58–9; Pulleyn 2000: 222, note at *Il.* 1.399–406.

> When you have reminded him of this, sit by him and seize his knees,
> [asking him] if he is willing to give aid to the Trojans
> so that down to the ships' prows along the sea they will drive the Greeks
> as they kill them, so that they will feel the benefit of the king's deeds[23]
> and Atreus' son wide-ruling Agamemnon will know
> his own ruinous folly (*ātē*), that he gave no payment to the best of the
>   Greeks.   (*Il.* 1.407–12)

This, then, is how the *mēnis* will work: the Trojans' success in slaughtering the Greeks will be a device to show how helpless they are without the man whom they have insulted. As we saw above, the plan is so vindictive that we can only make sense of it in terms of the god-like excess of energy and vitality that drives Achilles' nature: his vengeance is as extreme as that of a god belittled by mortals. But Thetis' response is full of the thought of his coming death:[24]

> O my child, why did I rear you, bringing miseries to birth?
> I wish that beside the ships without tears or suffering
> you had remained – for your portion is for a little while (*minuntha*), it is
>   not much.
> Now both swift-fated and wretched beyond all men
> you have been: for I bore you for an evil portion in the palace.
>   (*Il.* 1.414–18)

This is his portion, his share, *aisa*: why is he destined to die so soon? No answer is given, and Thetis seems to accept the plan as if there were no other choice, just as when Achilles will later recall her prophecy that he would be shot by Apollo 'below the wall of the armour-wearing Trojans' (*Il.* 21.277–8). There is no hint that his death could be delayed or avoided, as in so many stories of his childhood and the ruses that were used to keep him from the war.[25] In some mysterious way, shortness of life and great payment of glory are intertwined in Achilles' destiny, as Thetis puts it when she asks Zeus to carry out the plan:

> Repay my son, for more swift-fated than any other man
> he was born; but now the king of men, Agamemnon,

---

[23] This is an attempt to translate the difficult word *epaurōntai*. The verb *epaurisko* most simply means to touch something, hence in its reflexive ('middle') form it has a less tangible meaning: to have contact with something, to feel the results of experiencing it. This is not the only place where it is used ironically: Helen declares her contemptible husband Paris 'to be about to experience the effects' *epaurēsesthai*, of his follies (*Il.* 6.353).

[24] On Thetis' laments in anticipation of Achilles' death see further below, pp. 180–181.

[25] See above, pp. 180–181.

has dishonoured him:[26] he has seized and holds his prize, he stole it
  himself.
But you, repay (*tīson*) him, Olympian Zeus of cunning:
  therefore establish supremacy for the Trojans, so that the Greeks
  will repay my son and magnify him with payment (*timē*).   (*Il.* 1.505–10)

This can be seen as implying the same contract that drove Gilgamesh or
Sarpedon to great deeds of courage and strength: respect and reward and
fame are a recompense or a counterbalance to mortality, and the hero feels
compelled to seek them precisely because he knows that death is coming.
But if this idea is present it remains latent, and the practical basis of the
transaction is simply that Achilles' sufferings and rewards have become a
bargaining chip in the personal disputes of the gods.

The entertainment of the gods

It is on this same level – this bizarrely petty and trivial level, one is tempted
to say – that the next stage of the action unfolds.[27] Zeus at first seems
unwilling, but Thetis coaxes him and threatens to sulk; he explains that he
is afraid of the reaction of Hera, his jealous wife; finally he agrees to Thetis'
request and swears an oath on it, with his great nod that shakes Olympus
(*Il.* 1.528–30) – a moment of cosmic solemnity in stark contrast to this talk
of the tricky relationships between a husband and a wife and his former
lover. Yet afterwards the gods' whimsical comedy continues. Hera accuses
Zeus of secretly plotting with Thetis, and he threatens to beat her (*Il.* 1.560–
7); the other gods are alarmed, and Hephaestus leads them in complaining
of the trouble his parents will cause by stirring up conflict, which he calls by
the ugly name *kolōios*, literally the tumult of crows.[28] Presumably he knows
what is being planned, as Hera does (*Il.* 1.558–9), yet what worries him is
merely the disruption of the gods' easy life:

and in the noble
feast there will be no pleasure, since evil things prevail instead.
(*Il.* 1.575–6, cf. 579)

---

[26] Or 'has refused him his payment' (from *a-timao*).

[27] On the much-discussed problem of the capricious and trivial behaviour of the Iliadic gods, a
thoughtful overview of scholarly responses has been assembled by Van Erp Taalman Kip 2000.

[28] In Homer the word appears nowhere else, but the related verb *koloiao* is used for the complaints
of the ugly Thersites (*Il.* 2.212). On *koloios* as a bird of the crow or jackdaw type, see Aristotle,
History of Animals 617 b.

So he offers her a cup, warning her that if she provokes Zeus to violence she can expect no help from Hephaestus – already, he says, when he tried to help her Zeus flung him from Olympus and he landed on the island of Lemnos below (*Il.* 1.590–4). This, it seems, was when Zeus hung her up in the sky with anvils tied to her feet, to punish her for her hatred of his love-child Heracles (cf. *Il.* 15.18–30)[29] – another strange old story that seems to invite a cosmological reading, with Hera identified as the middle air between the sky-god and the earth.[30] Hephaestus, being lame, is a comical sight for the others as he tries to smooth over the discord:

> Moving rightwards, for all the other gods
> he acted as wine-waiter, drawing sweet nectar from the jar;
> and unquenchable laughter rose among the blessed gods
> when they saw Hephaestus busy at his work.   (*Il.* 1.597–600)

The gods drink not wine but nectar, symbolic of their immortality; and the feast in which they take their pleasure is identifiable with the sacrifices offered by mortals, like those that the Greeks themselves have just offered to Apollo (*Il.* 1.458–74) in ignorance of the disasters that are about to come upon them.

The lightness of the gods' feast is in jarring contrast with the foreshadowings of death that now hang over Achilles, and the suffering about to be inflicted on his countrymen on the battlefield. This scene would be one of those picked out by Plato in the *Republic* to justify banishing the poets from his ideal state, because of the absurd behaviour that Homer attributed to the gods (*Republic* 389a); but it is fair to say that the seeming absurdity is the key to its theological significance. To bring this out, we need to widen our sense of the context. When the Greek army made the sacrifice to Apollo they propitiated him with a song of praise (*paiēōn*), 'and he took pleasure in his thought as he listened' (*Il.* 1.473–4); now the feasting gods listen to the music he makes with his attendant goddesses:

> So then all the day long into the setting sun
> they feasted, and no thought-breath lacked its portion of the equal feast,
> nor of the full-beautiful lyre which Apollo held,
> nor of the Muses, who sang in response to him with beautiful voices.
> (*Il.* 1.601–4)

---

[29] See also Apollodorus, *Library* 1.3.5. Distinguish the story that Hera herself threw Hephaestus down from Olympus at birth, disgusted at his lameness (*Il.* 18.395–405, *Homeric Hymn to Apollo* 316–21). On the relationship between these falls of Hephaestus, see Gantz 1993: 74–6; Pulleyn 2000: 270–1, note at *Il.* 1.590–4.

[30] See Janko 1992: 229–31 for sources and analogues, with the possibility that the anvils (*akmones*) were originally understood as meteorites; and cf. Lamberton 1986: 113.

What did they sing about? That is not an idle question, and a parallel passage in the *Homeric Hymn to Apollo* suggests an answer. Apollo arrives at the home of Zeus on Olympus to make music:

> At once lyre-playing and song become the deathless ones' concern.
> All the Muses together, answering with beautiful voice,
> make a song of the gods' immortal gifts and of humans'
> sufferings, which they hold under the immortal gods
> as they live without wits or resource, nor are they able
> to find a cure for death or a defence against old age.
> > (*Homeric Hymn to Apollo* 188–93)

Our woe and toil (*tlēmosunai*) are the stuff of the gods' entertainment. Later in the *Iliad*, when it begins to move towards its climax in Achilles' battle-rush to slaughter the Trojans and avenge his dead friend, the gods meet to discuss how they should respond. Zeus lets them go down to help their favourites as they wish, while he himself will 'give pleasure to his mind' by watching the combat (*Il.* 20.23).[31] When the supreme god looks on in this way he is a spectator, above the strife and fighting and deaths of mortals. As such, the divine audience is parallel to the human audience of the poem itself, something that Helen herself will suggest later in the *Iliad* when she grieves over the troubles that have been caused by herself and her disastrous husband,

> for whom Zeus set down an evil portion (*moros*), so that in the future
> we can be the subject of song for people who are yet to be.   (*Il.* 6.357–8)

If there is a theological truth in the feast of the gods, it is in the contrast with the universal pain of mortals – a contrast that Achilles himself will express in the long discourse of wisdom that he shares with Priam when they weep together for the loss of loved ones and the brevity of life (see further below, pp. 296–297):

> So the gods have woven it for wretched mortals,
> to live in pain, but they themselves are without care.   (*Il.* 24.525–6)

It is again Aeschylus in the *Agamemnon*, through the choral songs of the old men, who makes explicit the idea that such wretchedness is in some way the means to wisdom:[32]

---

[31] In a thoughtful note, Edwards (1991: 289, at *Il.* 20.20–30) argues that Zeus here is 'taking pleasure' not in the human suffering but in the antics of the interfering gods. But the Greek words admit of either interpretation indeterminately.

[32] For a recent analysis of the theology of this hymn, see Furley and Bremer 2001: 1.286–8.

> Zeus, who has set men on a path towards understanding,
> who has established that learning through suffering (*pathei mathos*) has
>   the mastery.   (*Agamemnon* 176–8)

A fundamental truth about the meaning of life is represented in the dissonance between the feast of the gods and the spilling of blood that is about to ensue in the world below.

Achilles and Patroclus, Gilgamesh and Enkidu

When the sun sets on this feast, Achilles has withdrawn into the isolation of his *mēnis*:

> But that one was raging (*emēnie*) as he sat by the swift-journeying ships,
> the Zeus-born son of Peleus, swift-footed Achilles:
> he did not go back and forth to the assembly that glorifies men,
> nor to the war, and he wore away his own dear heart
> remaining there; but he was longing for the battle-cry and the war.
>   (*Il.* 1.488–92)

The words that I have translated 'he wore away his own dear heart' are difficult. They seem to refer to the gradual diminution of mental energy or bodily health, vitality ebbing away like the waning of the moon or even, potentially, in a movement towards death itself.[33]

Yet he is not quite alone. Beside him is his friend Patroclus. Notice the wording at the moment when Achilles withdraws from the assembly:

> Peleus' son went to the huts and the poised ships
> with Menoitios' son and his own companions.   (*Il.* 1.306–7)

This is the first mention of Patroclus in the poem, yet he is referred to obliquely by the name of his (relatively obscure) father. This suggests strongly that he was already familiar to the first audience of the poem, and that the pairing between the two warriors was an established motif in the tales of the war.[34] This theme deserves careful consideration at this point, because it will become vital both for understanding Achilles' story on its own terms and for pinning down its parallels with that of Gilgamesh.

---

[33] The verb *phthinutho* and its close cognates are used in comparable contexts at *Il.* 16.540, 18.446, *Od.* 10.485–6. For an attempt to trace the semantics of this group of words, see Clarke 1999: 160.

[34] This seems to me an inevitable inference: cf. however the sceptical approach by Scodel 2002: 109–10, opposing the conventional view that I follow here.

In the myths of the heroic race, there is a recurring pattern of companionship between a great warrior and his lesser companion – Heracles and Iolaos, Theseus and Peirithoos, Orestes and Pylades and so on. Within the *Iliad* there seem to be such pairings between Diomedes and Sthenelus (see esp. *Il.* 9.48–9) and between Sarpedon and Glaucus. In the wider tradition another such companionship was between Heracles and Telamon, the father of Ajax who figures so prominently in the *Iliad* itself – in the generation before that of the present war, Heracles sacked Troy with Telamon beside him. But Patroclus is more than a foil or a subordinate. He is older than Achilles, and his father sent him to the war with the instruction to advise and guide his friend, as Nestor reminds him later in the *Iliad*:

> The old man Peleus commanded his son Achilles
> always to do great deeds (*aristeuein*) and to be pre-eminent over others,
> but to you Menoitios, son of Actor, gave this command:
> 'My child, Achilles is higher than you by birth,
> but you are older: and he is far greater in strength (*biē*).
> You are to speak to him with subtle words, and to advise him
> and command him: he will obey you for the good.'   (*Il.* 11.783–9)

Later, after Patroclus' death, his ghost will recall that he became Achilles' friend in childhood, when he was taken in by Peleus as a fugitive after killing another child in a quarrel (*Il.* 23.84–92); it is presumably for this reason that Patroclus much of the time acts as Achilles' squire or helper (*therapōn*, *Il.* 17.164, 271, etc.), almost as his servant (e.g. at *Il.* 1.337–8, 345–7; 9.199–205).

The dynamic between them was a matter of controversy among Athenians in later times, when such a friendship was liable to be interpreted in sexual terms with one partner older and dominant and the other younger and more submissive. Aeschylus, famously, in his play *Myrmidons* made Patroclus take the passive role in their love, and this was considered a serious departure from the Homeric model.[35] In the *Iliad*, however, the relationship seems consistent with the roles described by Nestor.

---

[35] On the relationship depicted in the *Myrmidons*, see Michelakis 2002: 41–53, and on this play see also below, p. 219. For Achilles as the younger partner, the decisive testimony is in the speech of Phaedrus in Plato's *Symposium*. Phaedrus complains that Aeschylus gave Patroclus the role of passive partner (*erōmenos*) despite the fact that the Homeric Achilles is younger, more beautiful and beardless (Plato, *Symposium* 180 a–b). The question over the sexualisation of the relationship looms large in modern debate over Greek homosexuality, starting with J. A. Symonds' brilliant essay 'A problem in Greek ethics' of 1883; see Halperin 1990 and Davidson 2008, esp. 255–84.

Fig. 16 Cup by Sosias: (a) Achilles and Patroclus.

There is an eloquent commentary on this theme in the image on a cup by Sosias of *c.* 500 BCE (Fig. 16).[36] Patroclus, marked as older by his beard, has been wounded by the arrow that lies at his feet; Achilles carefully binds the wound, and it may or may not be significant that the painter (using the then newly invented technique of depicting the eye in profile) has made it look as if he is gazing at the other's genitals. This scene finds no clear model in the surviving textual evidence about Achilles and Patroclus, but it may well be based on an ancient tale-type in which the binding of a wound symbolises the intimate friendship between the hero and his companion.[37] It is thought-provoking that around the edge of this picture runs the triumphal entry into Olympus of Heracles, son of Zeus, the only demigod who achieved the fulness of immortality and entered the society of the high gods. The opposite future awaits Achilles and Patroclus: Patroclus will die before Achilles, having tried recklessly to attack the wall of Troy on his own, and Achilles in turn will move to certain death when he seeks vengeance. This is a case in

---

[36] There are subtle discussions of this vase by Junker 2012 [2005]: 1–18; Lowenstam 2008: 62–5.

[37] As Junker points out, Sthenelus is shown binding a wound on Diomedes' finger on the lost Hope vase of *c.* 550 BCE, at the side of a scene of the battle over the dead Achilles (see below, pp. 304–307 with Fig. 27). Homer, intriguingly, describes something similar: Diomedes is wounded in battle by an arrow, and Sthenelus pulls it out of the wound (*Il.* 5.106–13). In this set of linked images we possibly have fragments of a motif whose full significance is now lost – or the artistic reflection of a series of intertextually linked passages from the Epic Cycle.

Fig. 16 (b) Heracles entering Olympus.

which the *contrast* between the two scenes on the vase may be the key to the iconographic meaning of the ensemble as a whole.

The problem of the heroic race is that superhuman energy tends towards bullying violence, and this problem can be made manifest in the power-politics of sexual access to females. In bare outline, that statement is true of the opening movements both of the *Iliad* and of *Gilgamesh*. There are of course enormous differences too. One story belongs in an armed camp, the other in a city; the tension in one is between a general and a junior commander, in the other it is between the king and his subjects; and in the *Iliad* the aggression over females is that of Agamemnon rather than of the protagonist of the ensuing story. Up to this point we are dealing with broad cultural similarities rather than an objectively tight connection between texts. But with the mention of the son of Menoitios, the lines draw closer together, and the configuration between Achilles and Patroclus begins to mirror that between Gilgamesh and Enkidu. Patroclus like Enkidu is somewhere between the protagonist's servant and his intimate friend, and his role is to moderate the extremity of his energies.

A further point of nuanced similarity may be noted here. In both traditions there are indications that the friendship could be seen in sexual terms, but this theme is not brought into prominence in the canonical version of either narrative. Aeschylus, as we saw above, went beyond anything in Homer when he depicted the relationship explicitly as a physical one, and in his *Myrmidons* the graphic phrase 'I honoured the friendship [or 'company', *homilia*] of your thighs'[38] almost certainly comes from Achilles' address to the dead Patroclus at or after his funeral, picking up on the Iliadic account considered below (Ch. 13, 14).[39] In *Gilgamesh*, the main narrative in Tablets I–XI resembles the *Iliad* in that the friendship, despite its obvious intimacy, is not overtly described as sexual. It is in the Twelfth Tablet – which, as we saw, is a late adjunct to the series – that sexual imagery becomes explicit. The phantom of Enkidu is describing the decay of his body in the Underworld:

> '[*My friend, the*] *penis* that you touched so that your heart rejoiced,
> a grub devours [(it …) like an] old *garment.*'
>   (*SBV* XII 96–7, George 2003: 1.733)

As George argues, the source lines in the Sumerian original refer to the genitals of a female partner, but in the Akkadian they have become those of Enkidu himself.[40] This suggests that the relationship between the two became more explicitly sexualised in the last stages of the development of the epic. Although the parallel is inexact – after all, Aeschylus is potentially opposing himself to the Homeric inheritance – the traditions resemble each other in that the theme of homosexual intimacy emerges only belatedly in the literary development of the story.[41] This, I suggest, may be an example not of borrowing from Mesopotamian to Greek epic but of a shared aesthetic between the two literatures. In both cases the possibility of physical intimacy between the protagonist and his companion is latent, hinted at only at the moment of most agonised loss.

As the plot of the *Iliad* unfolds, we will see how closely the narration of the death of Patroclus and the ensuing suffering of Achilles recalls the story of Enkidu and Gilgamesh, right down to the level of verbal detail, and that in both cases the protagonist's response is to turn towards his own death. In *Gilgamesh*, as we saw, this turning is quite sudden and is worked out through his movement away from society and his journey to the edge of the world, where a different kind of truth awaits him. In the Greek epic, by contrast, the turn is explored at much greater length, and on a more variegated range of levels: after Brises' daughter has been taken away, the next stage of Achilles' story will reveal him as a man who has isolated himself and has turned inside, to probe and undermine the fundamental values of his world.

---

[38] *Myrmidons* fr. 136, sim. fr. 135.   [39] See Sommerstein 2008, notes on pp. 145–7.
[40] George 2003: 2.902–3, note at lines 96–9.   [41] Cf. Halperin 1990.

10 | Achilles looks inward

When Zeus begins to fulfil his promise to Thetis, he does it by auspicious signs to encourage the Trojans, thundering on the right-hand side (*Il.* 8.170–83) to give false hope to their leader Hector, who now surges out to destroy the Greeks (see esp. *Il.* 8.496–541). Agamemnon despairs: he admits to the other leaders that he was a fool to insult Achilles, and they arrange to send three men to plead with him to return to combat.[1] Looking along the plot at the simplest level, one might expect that the plan would now be fulfilled, that they would win Achilles back with the 'three times as many bright gifts' ostensibly predicted by Athene. Instead, there is a shift no less startling than that in *Gilgamesh* when the hero went out into the desert. Achilles in this Book will cease to be an embodiment of warlike energy, and will become one who rejects the norms and assumptions of that way of life.

In terms of traditional expectations about European heroic literature, this might seem like an innovative departure from older norms of battle-narrative towards newly sophisticated and even anti-traditional themes. As we have seen, however, in the cuneiform world the earliest literature of heroic kings is less concerned with battle-narrative than with inner experience: Lugalbanda's story centres on what happened when he was sick and alone in a cave,[2] just as that of Gilgamesh turns on his response to the horror of Enkidu's death. The introversion in the present episode of the *Iliad* may in fact be closer to the pre-existing norms of heroic literature than is apparent from a modern viewpoint.

---

[1] The episode known as the 'Embassy to Achilles' has been the subject of countless studies and monographs. Representative key readings include Schein 1984: 104–16; Zanker 1994: esp. 79–92; Redfield 1994, esp. 3–17; Muellner 1996: 133–43; Kim 2000: 78–103; Wilson 2002a: 71–108. Rinon 2008 is a sensitive reading of the Embassy episode using an ahistorical schema based on analogies with tragedy.

[2] See above, pp. 57–58. This point does not apply with such force to the later periods of the literature, from which there survives an extensive corpus of texts in which Assyrian kings, represented as speaking in their own voices, celebrate their successes in military exploits: see Foster 2007: 19–26. Kitts has a thought-provoking study comparing the imagery of these texts with that of the Iliadic battle-narrative (Kitts 2005: 188–215). For a more sceptical view of posited connections between Homeric and Near Eastern battle-narratives, including the Assyrian royal inscriptions, see Kelly 2014.

The appeal to Achilles

At the point where the chosen three – Ajax, Odysseus and Phoenix – begin their journey towards Achilles' encampment, the transmitted text shows signs of revision and adjustment, at times seeming to imply a scene of just two emissaries walking along the strand.[3] Whatever has really happened here (perhaps a revision just before or after 'Homer' proper?), the oddity encourages the suspicion that something creatively significant will be conveyed by the configuration of personalities. Ajax is the strongest of the Greek warriors after Achilles himself, as well as the most obstinate; Odysseus is the most deft and skilled with words and cleverness. After Achilles' death these two men will dominate the struggle to save his corpse from the Trojans, and the subsequent contest for the award of Achilles' armour (and thereby, it might be guessed, for the title 'best of the Greeks')[4] will pit them against each other and lead to the suicide of Ajax and the shame of Odysseus.[5] The battle over the body of Achilles was narrated in the Cyclic *Aethiopis*, and the contest for the arms loomed large in the *Little Iliad*;[6] it is so well attested in early art, and is so clearly evoked in the *Odyssey*,[7] that it is an attractive guess that this triangular configuration is already foreshadowed when these two men walk along the sea-shore towards Achilles' hut. The third man leading them is the venerable Phoenix, a relatively marginal figure elsewhere: he was a fugitive, cursed to childlessness, who took refuge in the house of Achilles' father Peleus and played an uncle or tutor's role in his childhood.[8] In the upshot, as we will see, Phoenix will turn out to be the crucial participant in the meeting.

---

[3] On the dual verbs at *Il.* 9.182–5, see the summary of possibilities presented by Hainsworth 1993: 85–7. It is clearly a related problem that the vase-paintings of the scene vary the identities of the three emissaries: for example, on vase Paris, Louvre 264 one of the three figures sitting with Achilles is the god Hermes.

[4] The theory developed in successive publications by Gregory Nagy: see for example Nagy 1979: 26–41 and *passim*.

[5] For a recent survey of the evidence for the Judgment of the Arms, see Finglass 2011: 26–36.

[6] Proclus' summary, para. 1 at West, *GEF*, pp. 124–5; fr. 2–3, pp. 126–7; West, *EC* 174–5, cf. Kelly 2015a: 331–3. See also below, pp. 308–311.

[7] See esp. *Od.* 11.543–51.

[8] The D-scholia on *Iliad* 19.326 (= *Cypria* fr. 19: West, *GEF*, pp. 96–9) record from the *Cypria* that when Achilles was being held in disguise as a girl on Scyros in order to keep him away from the war, Phoenix was sent with Nestor and Odysseus to find him and take him; and it is also attested that Phoenix was sent to summon Achilles' son Neoptolemus to the war after his father's death (e.g. Apollodorus, *Epitome* 5.11). Unless these are secondary developments inspired by the *Iliad* itself, they suggest that Phoenix's role as a persuader of Achilles was pervasive throughout the shaping of the Trojan War tradition. The surviving records of tragedies concerning Phoenix raise the same possibility, with the same caveat – some or all of their lore may be expansions

The first sign that things will not go to plan comes when they reach Achilles' hut:

> Him they found bringing pleasure to his thoughts with the shrill lyre,
> beautiful, cunningly wrought, with a bridge of silver upon it,
> which he took from the spoils when he sacked Ēëtion's city;
> with it he was delighting his heart (*thumos*), and he was singing the fames
> of men.
>
> (*Il.* 9.186–9)

The words translated 'fames of men', *klea andrōn*, implicitly refer to the epic tradition itself:[9] Achilles will now be less a participant than a commentator, situating himself outside the world of action in the same way as a poet might do.[10]

This idea of his separation from the ways of his fellow warriors was later to be taken to extremes by Aeschylus, whose play *Myrmidons* was set in Achilles' hut during the time of his refusal to fight.[11] In its opening scene Achilles sat silent and veiled, unresponsive to the pleadings of the other Greeks, as if absorbed in his own thoughts. The eccentricity of Aeschylus' staging was mocked by Aristophanes (*Frogs* 911–12), but Aeschylus' image is paralleled or imitated in several vase-paintings dated to the 490s–470s BCE, within a few years either side of the tragedy's performance.[12] In the example illustrated here (Fig. 17), Achilles sits swathed in his cloak as Brises' daughter is led away: Patroclus, one guesses, is the bearded figure leaning on the tent-pole, and is Phoenix the older man behind Achilles to the right?[13] On another vase of similar date,[14] he sits with his cloak wrapped around his head while Odysseus and Phoenix seem to wait for the meeting to begin: Patroclus stands behind his friend, leaning on a rod that perhaps symbolises his role as guide and mentor. The veiling can be read as an acting-out of mourning or anger or both,[15] but also of separation from warrior society: rejection of the collective values and identities that sparked off the quarrel with Agamemnon. At this

---

from the account he gives of himself at *Il.* 9.438–95. See further Gantz 1993: 618, 640, with Apollodorus, *Library* 3.13.8.

[9] Cf. below, p. 227.

[10] On *klea andrōn* and its resonances here see for example Ford 1992: 59–67; Louden 2006: 165–6, and cf. Heath 2005: 123–30.

[11] See Sommerstein 2008: 134–49 for the fragments; discussion by Michelakis 2002: 22–57.

[12] See Shapiro 1994: 16–21; Giuliani 2013 [2003]: 195–205. Muellner 2012 argues that the image is traditional and need not be due to cross-influence between the tragedian and the artistic tradition as such.

[13] Cf. Shapiro 1994: 13–14.

[14] The vase is attributed to the Kleophrades Painter: Munich, Staatliche Antikensammlung 8770. For a third example see below, p. 245, Fig. 21.

[15] See esp. Muellner 2012, with Cairns 2001b.

Fig. 17 Vase showing the seizing of Brises' daughter.

moment of the *Iliad*, correspondingly, his role will be to interpret, to question and perhaps to subvert the value-system of the 'sacker of cities'.[16]

That is why the appeal to Achilles fails. When the time comes for the visitors to speak, there is a moment of uncertainty: Ajax nods to Phoenix, presumably prompting him to begin, but Odysseus notices (*Il.* 9.222–4) and cuts in with his own speech (9.225–306), crafted with the cleverness that he embodies.[17] The Greeks, he says, are in mortal danger and *only you can save them* – and so, by implication, you can prove your supremacy among them. Your father told you to curb your passions, there is greater *honour* to be gained by goodwill. Agamemnon offers you great *gifts*, including seven women of Lesbos as well as Brises' daughter, with an oath to confirm that she has been left inviolate for you (*Il.* 9.276–8);[18] he offers marriage with his own daughter and lordship in the homeland, where the people will *honour* you as much as they would Agamemnon's own son or a god (*Il.* 9.284, 297). Again, says Odysseus, even if you do not care for what Agamemnon says, the other Greeks will *honour* you like a god

---

[16] Compare Aeschylus' *Agamemnon*, where the Chorus, after describing the troubles that follow upon victory in war, voice the wish not to be either 'a sacker of cities' (*ptoliporthēs*) or the victim of a sacking: secure happiness without envy (*aphthonos olbos*) is best (*Agamemnon* 471–4).

[17] *Mētis*, conventionally rendered 'cunning'. For a recent overview of the semantics of this word see Bracke (forthcoming).

[18] This oath is best understood as guaranteeing that the woman continues to embody Achilles' prestige, rather than as a literal assertion that Agamemnon has not slept with her.

if you save them (302–3); now you can win great *glory*, because Hector is fighting at the forefront of the host and there is a chance to get close enough to kill him (304–6). Though so various on the surface, all his points cluster upon the need for respect and prestige that drives the warrior society throughout the Homeric world.

But Achilles' answer shows that his thoughts now have no place for the things Odysseus spoke of:[19]

> It would be no thing of joy
> to fight ceaselessly forever against enemy men.   (*Il.* 9.316–17)

The mention of 'joy' (*kharis*) strikes a note of sudden contrast: he is thinking not about the warrior lifestyle that has defined him up to now, but about simpler and perhaps less masculine values.[20]

Introversion and poetry

As he expands upon these ideas, the lines that follow are full of verbal subtlety:

> There is an equal *moira* for him who stands in battle,[21] however much he
>   fights:
> the coward and the noble one are in equal honour (*timē*),
> both die alike, the idler and the one whose work is greatest.
>   (*Il.* 9.318–20)

The polysemy of the key word *moira* motivates the whole sequence of thought in these lines. As we saw earlier (p. 155), *moira* in a concrete sense is a share or portion of anything, land or wealth or the food and drink at a feast. When a man or a god is appropriately repaid or respected, he 'has received his portion of honour', *emmore timēs*.[22] But *moira* in a more

---

[19] On the introspective discourse of Achilles and its elaboration of thought, see esp. Martin on the 'expansion aesthetic' (1989: 146–230).

[20] It is a curiosity of Homeric semantics that *charmē* 'battle' is transparently related to *charis* 'joy': the link seems to be made by the phenomenon of 'joy in battle', a cross-cultural topos which it is inviting to attribute to early Greek heroic tradition. The semantic field study by Latacz 1966, esp. 121–6, bears comparison with the sensitive literary treatment by Schein 2016: 149–70.

[21] The participle *menonti* here, literally 'for him who remains', is often taken to refer to hanging back or malingering, in contrast with 'the one who fights most'. However, in the context of battle the simple verb *menō* refers overwhelmingly to disciplined behaviour – 'remain in line, stand in battle' – and this seems to me to fit the syntax better too.

[22] See for example *Il.* 1.278, 15.189; *Od.* 5.335, 11.338. In this turn of phrase the verb *emmore*, perfect (stative) of the verb whose present form is *meiromai* 'deserve, earn, merit', is obviously

solemn sense is the 'portion' assigned to humans as what we might call destiny or fate, and the fundamental *moira* of human beings is death. Here, then, the first line states the overall principle: apportionment comes indiscriminately, regardless of what a man deserves. The next line applies this to the kind of *moira* that passes between men: honour and the signs of status, made meaningless by treatment like that Achilles has suffered from Agamemnon. In the third line this is trumped by the thought of the *moira* that is death, which comes to all men equally, whether the coward or the best of warriors. Achilles is thinking along the semantic range of this complex word, moving beneath the surface of heroic language and probing the dark centre of its ethics. So, as he says next, it follows that there is no gain for him in offering up his life to the chances of war, 'putting the breath of his life at risk' like a gambler's stake.[23]

That these are the thoughts of a man of reflection, not a man of action, becomes still clearer as Achilles elaborates on why he will not go on with the struggle:

> As a bird brings to her flightless chicks
> a mouthful, whenever she can find it, yet suffering comes to herself,
> so I have stayed awake for many sleepless nights
> and I have spent many bloody days in warring,
> fighting on men's behalf for the sake of their wives.[24]   (*Il.* 9.323–7)

For the sake of their wives: this goes to the heart of the problem – the war has been fought to win back Menelaus' woman, yet other women are being traded back and forth among the warriors as if love and affection were irrelevant.

> Why did he gather the people and bring them here,
> Atreus' son? Was it not for the sake of lovely-haired Helen?
> Are they the only ones among living men who love their wives,[25]
> Atreus' sons?   (*Il.* 9.338–41)

This is the problem that has underlain the crudeness of Agamemnon's reckless behaviour in the crisis over the plague, and it is what Thersites the

---

linked to *moira* in terms of sound and meaning as well as derivation, and it is reasonable to assume that this contributed to the ancients' sense of the semantics of this group of words.

[23] This is a tentative explanation of *Il.* 9.321–2, following Martin 1989: 192–3; see also Cairns 2003b: 46–7, modifying my own earlier formulation (Clarke 1999: 45–7). My translation now tries to follow what seems to have been the understanding of the author of the tragedy *Rhesus* in a reworking of the present passage: *psuchēn proballont' en kuboisi daimonos* 'casting forward the soul in the dice-game of the divinity' (Euripides (?), *Rhesus* 183).

[24] The word translated 'wives' here is *oares* (singular *oar*), rare in attested Greek and perhaps rather prosaic – 'spouses', 'wedded wives'. Cf. West 2001: 207.

[25] The old adjective *merops* is here rendered by the vapid 'living', because even among the ancients there was no good knowledge as to its meaning.

begrudger railed against when he tried to subvert the assembly of the whole army (*Il.* 2.225–42). But now it takes a deeper form, because in Achilles' thinking Brises' daughter is no longer a mere token of her man's prestige:

> Just as anyone who is good and sound-minded
> loves and cares for his own woman, so also I
> loved her from my thought's breath (*thumos*), spear-won though she
> was.   (*Il.* 9.341–3)

Here is the sensitivity of one who looks not to the laws of war but the simpler and gentler norms of home and family. Achilles' thoughts find their closest kin not in epic but in the sensual poetry of Sappho:

> Some an army of horsemen, some of foot-soldiers,
> some say a fleet of ships is on the black earth
> the most beautiful thing that exists: but I say it is
> the one that you love.   (Sappho, fr. 16.1–4: Campbell, *GL* 1.66–7)

To the modern reader, Achilles' declaration of love for this prisoner might seem unexpected, even 'anti-heroic'. It is harder to say whether it would have seemed that way to the earliest audiences: but this much is clear in dramatic terms, that in rejecting the world-view that binds the army together he has become ungovernable, he can no longer be drawn into fighting and risking death for the ideals that drive other warriors to valour.

Achilles rejects eternal glory

Achilles goes on to tell of his extraordinary decision. He will fight no more for the sons of Atreus; he will set sail for Phthia in the morning and return to his father's halls; Agamemnon's gifts mean nothing to him, 'I repay him in the portion of a splinter (?)' (*Il.* 9.378) – an image of contempt whose literal meaning is obscure, perhaps because Homer is evoking incoherent anger in confusion of words.[26] All the wealth of the greatest treasury in the world is not worth the value of his own life (*Il.* 9.401); it is not simply because of his anger that no compensation will satisfy him,[27] but because of the realisation that these things are relative while death is absolute:

---

[26] This is of course only a tentative suggestion: the phrase is unparalleled, and ancient and modern interpretations are very doubtful. It is, however, virtually certain that we should reject the suggestion that the word is a form *kērós*, 'of death/of the death-demon'.

[27] The sense is difficult when Achilles says that Agamemnon will not persuade him 'before he pays back to me all the heart-paining disgrace (*lōbēn*)' (9.387). This seems to mean that Achilles will be satisfied only if Agamemnon suffers inner or emotional anguish equal to his own – hence

> Cattle and sinewy flocks can be taken as booty,
> tripods and the tawny heads of horses can be won,
> but a man's last breath (*psuchē*) cannot be taken as booty or seized
> to make it return, once it has passed over the barrier of the teeth.
>
> (*Il.* 9.406–9)

The full implications become plain when he reveals a prophecy from his mother:

> My mother, silver-footed goddess Thetis, says
> that there are two different demons bringing me to death's fulfilment:
> if I stand fast here and fight around the Trojans' city,
> my homecoming is lost, but imperishable fame will be mine.
> But if I make the journey home to the dear country of my fathers,
> noble fame is lost for me, yet for a long time life
> will be in me, and death's fulfilment will not be quick to meet me.
>
> (*Il.* 9.410–16)

As we have seen (pp. 3–6), these words are laden with the weight of traditional language, but they convey a unique revelation. Within and beyond the *Iliad* Thetis gives Achilles many insights into the future, including the shortness of his life and later the prospect of death at Apollo's hands; but only here does she present a choice *between* two kinds of death.[28] The motif itself is not unique to Achilles, and can be seen as traditional,[29] but what makes it extraordinary here is that he *rejects* the choice of short life with eternal glory:

> Tomorrow, on performing the sacred rites for Zeus and the other gods,
> I will rig the ships well, and when I drag them down to the sea
> you will see, if you wish it and it matters to you,
> sailing early over the fish-filled Hellespont
> my ships, and men in them eager to row:
> and if he grants us good sailing, the famous Earthshaker,
> on the third day I could reach Phthia of the rich soil.   (*Il.* 9.357–63)

---

material compensation is insufficient. Later, after the death of Patroclus when Achilles has decided to return to the war, he uses a similar phrase for the prospect of killing Hector in vengeance for it: *epēn teisaimetha lōbēn* (*Il.* 19.208), 'when we win recompense for the disgrace'.

[28] As Burgess shows (2009: 51–3), only here is a prophecy involving a *choice* between two fates evoked for Achilles: Nestor's later reference (*Il.* 11.794–5) is best understood as based on the Embassy's report of the present speech of Achilles.

[29] On the prophecy given to the sons of Euchēnor, which may or may not function as a foreshadowing of the prophecy given to Achilles, see below, p. 262. Similar images in other poetry – for example Mimnermus on the choice between early death and miserable old age (fr. 2.5–10 at Gerber, *GEP*, pp. 82–3) and Pindar on the choice given to Polydeuces by Zeus (*Nemean* 10.80–88) – can be seen either as examples of the same traditional motif, or as reworkings of the present passage inviting an intertextual reading.

It is the enduring strangeness of the *Iliad* that the greatest of the warriors defies what seems to be the essence of heroic ideology. The one who is 'manbreaker, lionspirited', in Hesiod's phrase (*Th.* 1007), the one who was to be canonised as national hero of the Greek nation in the Persian War[30] – here he sets himself up as the antithesis of everything that image represents.

Exile and introspection: Achilles and Gilgamesh

As the scene goes on and Achilles listens to Phoenix's appeal, which we will consider in a moment, Achilles shifts – uneasily or manipulatively? – between his threat to go home and his insistence on fighting only when his own ships are threatened with fire (compare *Il.* 9.618–19 with 650–5). Either would be a rejection of his comrades and their values; and although Ajax has none of Odysseus' manipulative subtlety, when he finally speaks he expresses the disjuncture between Achilles' mood and the world-view of the warrior society. When a murder has been committed, says Ajax, the family of the victim accepts penalty-money, *poinē*, from the murderer, and their anger ends; yet Achilles is persisting in his rage over a single girl, even when he has been offered seven more as part of his compensation (*Il.* 9.632–9). In their reductive simplicity, Ajax's words show how far Achilles' thought has moved from that of his peers – his point throughout has been precisely that his feelings towards Brises' daughter forbid him to dehumanise her like this by treating her as a token with quantifiable value.[31] Achilles respects the straightness of Ajax's words, but his reality now is in his emotional experience:

> Ajax, Zeus-born son of Telamon, leader of the peoples,
> everything that you have said seems to me well fitted to the thought:[32]
> but my heart swells with bile (*cholos*), when those things
> I remember, how he treated me disgracefully among the Greeks,
> Atreus' son, as if I were a refugee to be dishonoured.[33]   (9.644–8)

---

[30] See below, pp. 263–267.

[31] On Ajax's discourse of 'recompense' (*poinē*) in this passage see Wilson 2002a: 104–8, with Cairns 2011a: 92–6. The language of this passage translates irresistibly into the imagery of money and trade, a pattern characteristic of the Homeric representation of social thought. See the ideologically nuanced analyses by Seaford, esp. 1994: 1–29 and 2004: 34–39; but cf. Van Wees 1992, esp. 223–7.

[32] I adhere to the word-by-word sense of the Greek, which is ambiguous and perhaps deliberately so. It is not clear whether the 'thought', *thumos*, here is that of Ajax or of Achilles himself, so it could plausibly be taken either as 'You have spoken in accordance with *your* thinking,' or 'You have spoken in accordance with *my* thinking.' Either way the words make a compliment.

[33] *atimētos* 'fit to be dishonoured': the word also admits the translation 'fit to be left unpaid, unrewarded'.

The word for 'refugee', *metanastēs*, is revealing: such a man is denied honour in the sense that he is cut off from the flow of mutual service and reward that binds the society together.[34] During the original quarrel he said he would be called 'a man of nothing', *outidanos*, if he were to let himself be belittled by Agamemnon (*Il.* 1.293–4); now he has been forced – or has he forced himself? – into the state of mind of a homeless wanderer: his is the misery of the outcast, and perhaps also the outcast's wisdom.

When Achilles' discourse is read in terms of this movement away from the socially driven ethics of the man of action and the seeker of glory, towards the anxiety of the isolated self, we are coming closer to convergence with the themes of the pivotal turn in the *Epic of Gilgamesh*. The Homeric articulation is of course full of a very different kind of dramatic realism, both in the subtlety of Achilles' self-expression and in the intricate unfolding of the plot; and, crucially, it comes in response to a collective insult rather than to the death of his friend, which has yet to emerge in the narrative. But the key similarity remains that the narrative shifts suddenly from the outward world of action and the pursuit of prestige to an inner world of reflection, questioning and preoccupation with the universality of death.

Meleager: a narrative of mortality

I have delayed consideration of the speech of Phoenix, as it is the hardest to analyse, and the themes that are explicit in the words of the other men are here more deeply embedded. Phoenix begins with the language of pure emotion and the appeal to pity.[35] He bursts into tears and asks how Achilles could leave for home and abandon him (*Il.* 9.433–46), then recounts the tangled story of his own life – caught in a triangle of jealousy and violence between his mother and his father's mistress, cursed and alone and wandering through Greece until he found shelter with Achilles' father (9.447–95).[36] But this is only a prelude to what follows. In the slow unfolding of his speech, from personal reminiscence to the truths of older legends, his tone resembles Nestor in the *Iliad* or Alcinous, king of the Phaeacians in the *Odyssey*, or indeed Hesiod himself in the *Works and Days*.

---

[34] On this simile, see Ready 2011: 34–9; Alden 2012.   [35] See esp. Crotty 1994: 51–4.

[36] Cf. Avery 1998; Pratt 2009. On Phoenix's role in relation to that of Cheiron, Achilles' original 'tutor' in the wider tradition, see Mackie 1997; Currie 2016: 74–5.

Phoenix begins with an account of divine beings that he calls the *Litai* or 'Beggings' – personifications, in effect, of the sacred practice of supplication, the act of begging for mercy or help irrespective of one's ability to repay the favour, for which the principal verb is *lissomai*, built on the same root.[37] First there comes among men *Ātē*, the swift-running being who embodies the ruinous and self-destructive behaviour named by that word: it was *ātē*, he implies, that was embodied in the original quarrel between Achilles and Agamemnon. Then the female *Litai* appear, when men beg for forgiveness and reconciliation: we infer that Achilles is now in their presence. If the one who has been offered the supplication yields and respects them, they ensure that he is rewarded; but if he refuses them they go back to Zeus and ask for further *ātē* to come upon him. The *Litai* appear nowhere else in early Greek literature,[38] and presumably they are the creation of Phoenix's own rhetoric. Structurally, however, the pattern of image-making is widely paralleled – for example, we see it in the way Hesiod talks about the countless 'immortal guardians' in the air who flit over the earth on Zeus' behalf, watching out for good and evil behaviour, and among them is the best-known such daughter of Zeus, *Dikē* or Justice (*WD* 252–66).

But something here is less straightforward. What does Phoenix mean when he speaks of the future *ātē* that will be sent to the one who refuses to yield? What is he suggesting will happen to Achilles if he persists? At the moment where one might look for an explanation, Phoenix turns to a different kind of wisdom, that is taught by the deeds of an earlier time:

> So have we heard from earlier times the fames of men,
> heroes (*hērōes*), when swelling bile would seize a man:
> they could be given gifts, they could be advised with words.   (9.524–6)

The fames of men, *klea andrōn*, were the subject of the song that Achilles himself was singing when the three visitors found him. Phoenix has adopted the same long perspective on the lore of the heroic race, to develop what was only hinted at in the image of the *Litai*. The story that he now deploys is complex;[39] although it is impossible to tell whether there is an

---

[37] On *Ātē* and the *Litai* in this passage, reliable recent treatments include Wilson 2002a: 99–101; Yamagata 2005; Cairns 2012: 26–31; see also Crotty 1994, esp. 91–2, and cf. Rinon 2008. On the term *ātē* see also pp. 195–197.

[38] Quintus of Smyrna (*Posthomerica* 10.300–5) is derivative, drawing directly on the present passage. The *Litai* do not appear in art: Shapiro 1993: 20.

[39] The bibliography on the paradigm of Meleager is enormous and cannot be fully treated here. The most influential analyses are well surveyed and developed into a cautious synthesis by Alden 2000: 179–290 *passim*; see also esp. Burgess 2006: 175–6, and Heiden 2008, esp. 132–9,

allusion to a pre-existing poetic narrative, it is a safe guess that its plot-sequence was already well established in the lore of the heroic race,[40] and that its themes were central to the way their psychology was conceptualised. Phoenix begins by recalling elements of the tale out of sequence – a likely indication that the original audience knew its outlines already.[41] By the same token, our interpretation will turn on the episode of failed supplication at its centre (lines 575–96, see below), which is told sequentially and in more explicit language than what precedes and follows it. The change of pace suggests that this part would have been unfamiliar when originally heard, and that it has been reshaped to enmesh it more closely with Achilles' situation.

Oineus, king of Calydon, had insulted Artemis through his own folly (*aāsato*, 9.537), and in vengeance she sent a great boar to ravage his lands; his son Meleager gathered a host of men to hunt it down. The hunt has a prominent place in early vase-painting, and some examples are worth a moment's contemplation.[42] On the François Vase (Fig. 18) and still more clearly in a second black-figure vase of slightly later date (Fig. 19),[43] the focus is on the moment of the killing of the boar. In each case there are assailants gathered on both sides, and several have pierced it, as if in the same assault. The question is prompted: who was responsible for the fatal blow, and who deserves credit for the victory? In Phoenix's version, correspondingly, Artemis roused up a feud over the boar's head and skin – that is, the trophies due to the one who achieved the kill – between the Aetolian men of the city and their allies the Kourētes, the kinsmen of Meleager's mother. Meleager led the men of the city against the Kourētes, but something went wrong:

> . . . . bile (*cholos*) went down into Meleager, bile that in others too
> swells the thought in the breast, even in those of wise thinking.
>
> (*Il.* 9.553–4)

152–60. Here I offer a tentative proposal of my own, close to the standard consensus except for its emphasis on the implication that Meleager *died* before being able to benefit from his return to the war, and that Achilles will suffer an analogous fate. This means, for example, that my analysis differs significantly from that advanced by Morrison 1992: 119–24.

[40] For example, the genealogy of Meleager's family is referred to again at *Il.* 14.115–18; compare 2.638–44, where he is named in the account of the Aetolian contingent in the Catalogue of Ships.

[41] Cf. above, p. 201.

[42] On the Calydonian Boar Hunt in vase-painting, see Schefold 1966: 60–1; Schefold 1992 [1978]: 195–8; Stewart 1983: 63–4; Barringer 2013.

[43] Vase Munich, Antikensammlungen 2243 is discussed by Schefold 1992 [1978]: 197.

Fig. 18 Killing of the Calydonian boar, from the upper rim of the François Vase.

Fig. 19 Cup of *c.* 540 BCE, showing the killing of the Calydonian boar.

In the struggle he had killed his mother's brother (567),[44] and she had called on the gods of the Underworld to send him death:[45]

> . . . and she who flits through the mist, the Fury,
> heard her from the gloom, the one whose heart is unappeasable.
>
> (*Il.* 9.571–2)

So Meleager turned to rage against his mother, withdrew from the defence of his city and stayed in his bedroom beside his wife Cleopatra.

Without him the Aetolians began to fail, and the city was under siege. Its elders came offering great gifts if he would fight again; his friends and his family begged him (*litaneue*, 581: compare the *Litai* above); still he would not yield until finally, with the enemy at the doors of his own quarters, his

---

[44] Nothing in Homer's words sheds light on whether the killing was accidental or deliberate, or at which stage of the sequence it took place.

[45] On her ritual actions, see Ogden 2001: 177–8.

wife pleaded in the name of pity, reminding him of the horrors that come when a city is sacked. This at last persuaded him:

> So from the Aetolians he warded off the evil day,
> yielding to his thought's breath; but after all they did not give him the gifts
> many and beautiful, though he did ward off the evil.   (*Il.* 9.597–9)

The story was first launched as a positive example, of men who accepted appeasement (9.526, above), yet it has now become a warning. Meleager refused conciliation too long, and the gifts never came to him: why? There is a sinister implication when it is said that 'after all they did not give him the gifts', although he had at last returned to the war.[46] The Fury, *Erinys*, is relentless in pursuit of the punishments assigned to her,[47] so to say that she heard his mother's curse is to imply that he indeed died, before the promised gifts could be put in his hands.[48]

With Meleager's story set in parallel with that of Achilles, motifs and events echo each other across the two sequences. First there is an insult to a god, Apollo in one case and his sister Artemis in the other. The vengeance of the god, plague or the boar, is overcome; but a dispute arises between men who should be allies, over ownership of the signs of victorious honour – the captive women, the trophies of the boar. The foremost warrior becomes enraged at his treatment by his own people: the insult to Achilles in the assembly, the curse imposed by Meleager's mother. He withdraws to be alone with his closest companion, the beloved friend Patroclus or the wife Cleopatra; he spurns the entreaties of those who come to beg him to fight. At this point the linkage is clinched by the consonance between names: *Kleopatra*, 'Fame-father', is transparently formed from the same two elements as *Patro-klos*, 'Father-fame'.[49] From here, the story of Meleager becomes a shadowy prophecy for what is before Achilles. He yields at last to the

---

[46] The nuance of these words is easily missed because of the subtlety of the word *ouketi*, conventionally translated 'no longer'. Alden, for example, paraphrases the key words of *Il.* 9.598 as 'his fellow-citizens no longer *cared to* award him gifts' (Alden 2000: 234–5, my emphasis). This strains the sense of the Greek, which says nothing about the wishes of those who had offered the gifts: taken literally, the words are simply 'they *ouketi* fulfilled the gifts'. Wilson 1987 has shown that *ouketi* often does not correspond in meaning to 'no longer', referring instead to the idea that an expected outcome did not happen: hence my 'after all they did not' (Wilson 1987 is cited for this line by *LfgrE*, s.v. *ou* III 3).

[47] On the Erinyes, see for example Sewell-Rutter 2007: 78–109.

[48] See Gager 1992: 183, citing Pausanias' description of a painting depicting Meleager, in which he says that in Homer's version Meleager died because the Fury heard his mother's curse (Pausanias 10.31.3).

[49] On this remarkable correspondence between names, already discussed by Eustathius in the twelfth century CE, see for example Alden 2000: 239, 248, 251–2; Currie 2016: 74–5 with references in n. 220; cf. Tatum 2003: 109–10.

loved one's pleas, but it is too late: he fights but death comes to him, and he can never enjoy the gifts he was offered. Like the forebodings of Enkidu's death that came in dreams, the story of the rage and death of Meleager represents the intrusion of mortality into the passionate certainties of the fighting demigod.

Phoenix's rhetorical strategy was based on seeing Meleager and Achilles as embodiments of the same narrative skeleton, setting down the structure of two heroic biographies in parallel with each other. Although the prediction of his death here is shadowy and indirect, later sources preserve a strange and probably archaic articulation, of the kind associated in old-fashioned scholarship with 'folktales',[50] which throws up the possibility of a further potential interweaving with Achilles' life. When Meleager was a baby, the Moirai told his mother that he would live until a piece of wood, then burning in the fire, would be consumed; she took out the wood and hid it, and when she turned against him in anger at the killing of her brother, she threw it in the fire again and Meleager died. In the Homeric version, the equivalent moment is where she calls up a curse from the gods of the Underworld. It could be claimed that Homer deliberately avoids this overtly magical and fantastic version, or that it is a later invention, or simply that it belongs in a different branch of the traditions of myth-making.[51]

Bacchylides, in a victory ode of *c.* 476 BCE, puts vivid shape on this moment when the dead Meleager, now a wraith in Hades, recalls the moment when his mother let the log burn:

> My sweet soul became diminished:
> I realised that my strength was growing less,
> alas – and breathing my last I wept in my suffering,
> leaving gleaming youth behind me.   (Bacchylides, *Odes* 5.151–4)

The words of the last line are a reworking of the Homeric description of the departure of Patroclus or Hector's last breath at death, flying to Hades:

[50] On the relationships between the varying ancient traditions about Meleager see Gantz 1993: 328–32. Burgess's recent analysis (2017) bears comparison with the still useful observations in Swain 1988.

[51] As far as can be seen from the relevant fragment, the story was absent from the Hesiodic *Catalogue of Women*, which blames Apollo for Meleager' death (fr. 22.9–13 Most = fr. 25.9–14 M–W). The story of the log is attested in Aeschylus, the Chorus of whose *Libation-Bearers* cites Althaea as an example of the viciousness of woman (603–12), while Pausanias (10.31.3–4) says that the story of the log was used by Phrynichus in a tragedy, the *Women of Pleuron*. Bacchylides' version is consistent with these as far as our knowledge goes. Apollodorus synthesises various versions from lost sources, alongside the Homeric account (*Library* 1.8.2–3). The evidence for Stesichorus' version is too slight to shed light on the present discussion. These and other sources are compared in detail by Cairns 2010: 96–9.

wailing for its own death, leaving manliness and youth behind (*Il.* 16.857 = 22.363; see p. 252). Here the shade itself, the breath-like wraith that survives in Hades, is describing its own departure from the dying man.[52]

The link here with the traditions around Achilles is the motif of the mother using fire to achieve magical control over the life of her baby. In the case of Achilles, the nowadays famous story that Thetis dipped him in the river Styx to make him invulnerable, leaving unprotected only the heel by which she held him, is close to the (probably) more ancient idea that she placed the baby in the fire, either to test his mortality or to purify it away; she was interrupted and he remained mortal.[53] The same magic is used by Demeter on Dēmophoōn in the *Homeric Hymn to Demeter* (231–49), and it seems certain that the image is a very ancient one. It may be coincidental that variants upon it appear in the traditions surrounding the deaths of both of the heroes whose coming disasters are paralleled in Phoenix's narration; but it may also be another clue to the way their fates are intertwined.

Achilles and Patroclus isolated

On the surface of Phoenix's discourse, of course, the foreboding of death is no more than a shadowy hint; and for Achilles in his response, the dominant certainty is his own anger and resentment. Just as Phoenix spoke of the bile that swelled the mental apparatus of Meleager (*Il.* 9.553–4), so he now describes the state of his feelings in the same terms:

> My heart becomes swollen with bile, whenever those things
> I remember . . .   (*Il.* 9.646–7)

As the emissaries describe it on their return, this bile still 'holds' him, he refuses to quell or extinguish it, he is filled all the more with its violent force, *menos* (*Il.* 9.675, 678–9).[54] This imagery is part of a consistent descriptive pattern, in which the exuberance of heroic energy and passion – bravery, anger or madness as the case may be – is conceptualised as a swelling and expansion of the vital essence that fills the lungs and the organs of the breast. The kind of man that later Greek would call 'great-

---

[52] I discuss this at Clarke 1999: 302–3. For modifications of that proposal and further parallels see Cairns 2010: 240.

[53] See above, p. 181.

[54] On the twin images of the swelling and the quelling or 'extinguishing' of the anger that is *cholos*, see for example Gill 1996: 190–204; Clarke 1999: 94–5, with Cairns 2003b: 72–5.

souled', *megalopsuchos*,[55] is characterised by a heightening, even an exaggeration, of violent liveliness in these centres of mental and emotional life. So it is that Achilles or Meleager is here living out the essential problem of the race of heroes, the abundance of vitality that leads to strength and bravery and brilliance but also, through its excessive and reckless expansion, to the self-destructive ruin that is *ātē*.

Prospect

When Achilles and Meleager are read as intertwined stories, the suggestion of a parallel with Gilgamesh is effective only at the most generalised level of theme and psychology. It would be an exaggeration to suggest that what we have seen in this chapter gives evidence of tangible influence from text to text, or that it suggests more than a shared conception of the passion and mortality of the demigods of the past. In the next chapter we will begin to get a stronger sense of confluence. What will draw the two narratives together from this point onwards is the relationship between the protagonist and his companion and helpmeet. Patroclus has been alongside Achilles throughout his meeting with the emissaries, and he is glimpsed in the last moments after the negotiation has failed:

> So he spoke. Each of them took the double-handled cup
> and poured an offering, and they went back by the ships: Odysseus led them.
> But Patroclus ordered the companions and the slave-women
> to spread out a thick bed for Phoenix as soon as they could.   (*Il.* 9.656–9)

So alongside Phoenix, Achilles and Patroclus go to bed for the night, each with a captive woman beside him. In the following days, it is through Patroclus that Achilles' plan will come undone: Patroclus will die a pathetic death in Achilles' place, and he himself will rise up in rage and self-loathing to hasten and welcome his own death. It is in this sense that Phoenix's foreboding of death will come to fulfilment:

> but after all they did not give him the gifts
> many and beautiful, though he did ward off the evil.   (*Il.* 9.598–9)

---

[55] See esp. Aristotle, *Nicomachean Ethics* 1123 b 1–4, 15–16, with for example Isocrates, *Evagoras* 3.2. On *megalopsuchos* in Aristotle see the useful survey by Howland 2002. Zanker's essay on the word in relation to Aristotle's response to the Homeric depiction of Achilles (Zanker 1994: 127–54) confuses the issue, in my view, by assimilating the ancient term to the connotations of its modern derivatives ('magnanimous', 'great-hearted', etc.), in a way that takes his reading away from Aristotle and even further away from Homer.

11 | The death of the friend

With Meleager in the last chapter, we saw Homer exploring and exploiting a sense of parallelism between two otherwise separate story-patterns from the deeds of the heroic race. A more covert example of the strategy is suggested by the narration of the next day's sunrise:

> Dawn from her bed beside loud-voiced[1] Tithonus
> rose up to bring light to the deathless ones and to mortals.
>
> (*Il.* 11.1–2 = *Od.* 5.1–2)

The scene is intensely personified (see Fig. 20): this is Dawn the goddess, who took for her husband Tithonus, prince of Troy in the previous generation (*Il.* 20.237). According to a story recalled in the *Homeric Hymn to Aphrodite*, she asked Zeus to make him immortal but forgot to ask for eternal youth, so that he withered and shrivelled and was left with no strength but that of his voice (*Homeric Hymn to Aphrodite* 218–38).[2] Only in later sources is it specified that the shrunken and desiccated Tithonus became a cicada,[3] but there are suggestions that his fate was known in some form to the original audience of the poem.[4] In the *Odyssey*, exactly the same lines open the narrative section in which Odysseus is a captive of the sinister goddess Calypso, who has been trying to make him immortal; he escapes to avoid an eternity as her husband and perhaps, like Tithonus, her victim.[5] It is possible, at least, that this Iliadic image of daybreak foreshadows the plot

---

[1] For this translation of *agauos*, a word which is traditionally rendered more vaguely as 'noble' or similar, see the etymological analysis of the word as a compound originally meaning 'great-voiced' by Blanc 2002: 174–6.

[2] The other early sources are in Mimnermus fr. 4 (Gerber, *GEP*, pp. 84–5) and Sappho (West 2005a: 5–8). On the mythical background to Sappho's account see further Brown 2011.

[3] The earliest unambiguous source Hellanicus, fr. 140 (Fowler 2000–13: 1.206–7, 2.526–7). See Gantz 1993: 36–7, with Faulkner 2008: 270–1, note on *Homeric Hymn to Aphrodite* 218–38.

[4] It is remarkable that in the *Iliad* the nephews and other relatives of Tithonus, now themselves grown old, are compared to cicadas because of their voices (*Il.* 3.145–52). Ancient scholars certainly connected this simile with the Tithonus story: this is explicit in the scholiasts' notes to *Il.* 3.151, discussed by Danek 2006: 66–8. If it is credible that *agauos* at 5.1 retains the active meaning 'loud, great-voiced' (see n. 1 above), we have added grounds for suspecting an allusion to the chirping insect.

[5] Among the many studies of the Calypso episode and its hints at deeper and darker mythical patterns, Crane 1988 remains especially thought-provoking.

Fig. 20 Cup showing Eos (Dawn) and Tithonus.

that will now be set in motion: men's aspirations will be cheated, and the gods will allow them to suffer inexplicable horrors.

Patroclus and Nestor: the beginning of evil

The battle that now begins is further marked by the vivid presence of divine personifications. To rouse up the Greeks to a surge of combat, Zeus sends the goddess Eris – Strife, the deity who has lurked behind the whole war – and she stands on the prow of Odysseus' beached ship, driving the Greeks to valour (*Il.* 11.3–12) and delighting in the slaughter that follows (*Il.* 11.73–4).[6] Zeus drops bloody liquid from above:

> Zeus roused up
> evil tumult in them, and from above he sent down dews[7]
> dripping with blood, because he was about
> to send down to Hades many strong heads. (*Il.* 11.52–5)

The wording of the last line recalls the prologue of the *Iliad*, where the anger of Achilles 'thrust down to Hades many strong ghosts/ of heroes' (*Il.* 1.3–4). This sign presaging the slaughter also looks forward to the gesture of Zeus

---

[6] On this image of *Eris* and related vase-paintings see Shapiro 1993: 51–3.
[7] The word *eersai* could also mean 'raindrops', but the scholia here are clear that the reference is to dew.

when his beloved son Sarpedon is about to die, honouring him with dewy drops that fall as tears would fall (*Il.* 16.459–61).[8] The heightened imagery signifies that the battle now beginning will be a climactic moment in the plot.

Zeus will now orchestrate the action so that the Trojans gain overwhelming success. He sends down Iris, the messenger-goddess associated or identified with the rainbow, to instruct Hector to let Agamemnon advance until he takes a wound, and Zeus pledges that when this happens Hector will win success in counter-attack (*Il.* 11.185–209). All this is then fulfilled: Agamemnon is wounded, Hector leads an attack against the Greeks, and they are beaten back in disarray. It begins to look as if the action is moving towards what Achilles himself has been planning all along, that the Greeks in their disastrous defeat will realise what folly it was to humiliate him.

Instead, however, there is a new turn in the path of the song. As the Trojan onslaught redoubles, one by one the Greek leaders are wounded; among them Nestor rides back from the battle-line in his chariot with Machaon the healer (*Il.* 11.502–20, 596–8). Suddenly we realise that the crisis is being observed from along the strand:

> So they struggled, in the likeness of blazing fire;
> Nestor was borne by the mares of Neleus from the war,
> sweating, and they brought also Machaon, shepherd of the people.
> He saw him and recognised him, did swift-footed bright Achilles:
> for he was standing on the prow of the great-swelling ship,
> looking out at the steep toil and the tear-bringing rout.   (*Il.* 11.596–601)

Achilles calls down to Patroclus:

> He heard, and from the hut
> he came out, equal to Ares, and for him this was the beginning of evil.
> 													(*Il.* 11.603–4)

The beginning of evil: these words are laden with meaning. Centuries later they would be evoked by Herodotus, describing the small thing that would lead by stages to the great war of his age: the Athenians sent twenty ships to support the Ionian Greeks in their rebellion against their Persian overlords, 'and these ships became the beginning of evil for both Greeks and barbarians' (*Histories* 5.97).[9] Up to now, Patroclus has been a silent presence by Achilles' side: here suddenly he comes out like Ares himself, the god who personifies the fury of reckless warfare.

---

[8] I use this nuanced form of words because the association of the gesture with tears of grief seems irresistible, but Homer specifies instead that the drops are a sign of *honour* for Sarpedon (*Il.* 16.460).

[9] See Pelling 2006b: 97–8.

But Achilles, it seems, knows nothing of this. He remarks that the Greeks will soon be seizing his knees to beg him for help (*lissomenous*, *Il.* 11.609–10). As he looks to the expected fulfilment of his plan, everything is going smoothly and he has summoned Patroclus for a simple and casual purpose – his view of the wounded man was blocked by the horses, so Patroclus is to go to Nestor's hut and find out whether it was Machaon (11.611–15). All that has happened is that human curiosity has intervened for a moment in Achilles' grand scheme of revenge.

What follows hinges on Nestor. Elsewhere Nestor's role is to voice the memory of earlier times. In the *Iliad* he marshals his host with chariots to the front and infantry behind, 'in the way that earlier men [did when they] sacked cities and fortifications' (*Il.* 4.308), and in the *Cypria* he narrated other stories from previous generations,[10] just as in the *Odyssey* he recounts the story of the Trojan War itself to the young in later years (*Od.* 3.102 ff.). When Patroclus enters his hut, the old man is drinking from his huge cup, decorated with golden doves, the cup that Nestor alone among men could lift with ease (*Il.* 11.624–37).[11] The long description of the ancient cup signals the tone of what will follow: Nestor has the wisdom of experience that stretches back to earlier and perhaps more mysterious times.

He holds Patroclus there with many words (*Il.* 11.656–803). In his youth, he says, his father tried to dissuade him from taking up arms against an attacking force, but Nestor defied him and went to fight anyway; led by Athene, he did great deeds and might have killed two formidable (even monstrous) sons of the sea-god Poseidon, the Moliōne, had their father not rescued them from the combat.[12] From this Nestor earned great praise:

Everyone spoke exultantly of Zeus among gods, of Nestor among men.

(*Il.* 11.761)

The story may seem rambling, but woven into it is something to appeal directly to Patroclus. Nestor won this glory by fighting *despite* a command not to do so, and his achievement was for the common good, not for

---

[10] *Cypria*, Proclus' summary, para. 4: West, *GEF*, pp.70–1. See Sammons 2017: 55–61.

[11] See also above, pp. 121–123.

[12] Here and in another of Nestor's reminiscences (*Il.* 23.638–42) the Moliōne are a pair who fight as one, and from the Hesiodic *Catalogue* onwards they are described as conjoined twins (Hes. *Cat.* fr. 13–15 Most = fr. 17–18 M–W, including Homeric scholia on the present *Iliad* passages; see also Ibycus, fr. 285 at Campbell, *GL* 3, pp. 254–5). (It is remarkable that what looks like a double-bodied being fights on foot or rides a chariot in several painted vases from the eighth century BCE; this could be the Moliōne, but it may alternatively be a pair of charioteers seen from the side. See Giuliani 2013 [2003]: 35–7 for the latter argument; cf. also Snodgrass 1998: 28–31; Hainsworth 1993: 304, note on *Il.* 11.750.)

individual prestige or advantage.[13] The relevance of the first point to Patroclus is left only as an implication, but the second becomes an open complaint against Achilles:

> Such I was among men – if indeed I was;[14] but Achilles
> alone will benefit from his prowess (*aretē*), and I think he will
> weep greatly for it, when the host has been slaughtered.   (*Il.* 11.762–4)

With these first suggestions established, Nestor launches into open persuasion. Patroclus' father told him to help the younger man with sound advice, so now he must try to make him return to the combat (*Il.* 11.785–93). Then comes the fatal turn. If Achilles is refusing to fight because of a prophecy he has heard – meaning perhaps the one that he revealed to the emissaries? – then at least he could let Patroclus help the Greeks by fighting in his place:

> Let him give you his beautiful armour to wear to the war,
> so that maybe they will mistake you for him and hold back from combat,
> the Trojans, and the warlike sons of the Greeks will find rest
> in their weariness . . .   (*Il.* 11.798–801)

The ruse seems strange from a practical point of view: one would not expect a helmet in this warfare to cover the whole face like a late-medieval knight in tournament gear, so it is hard to see why the Trojans will believe so easily that its wearer must be Achilles (once close combat has begun, at least). The key is the armour itself, the gods' wedding gift to Peleus:[15] the sight of this famous panoply will be enough to turn the Trojans to terror at the return of Achilles.

---

[13] For this interpretation see Alden 2000: 88–101, esp. 96.

[14] The parenthesis seems to be a wistful thought – he is now so feeble that his remembered youth no longer seems real (cf. Hainsworth 1993: 306, note at *Il.* 11.762).

[15] For the armour as a wedding gift to Peleus see *Il.* 17.194–7, 18.84–5; schol. A on *Il.* 16.140; further references collected by Lowenstam 1993: 140 n. 43. However, the evidence of non-Homeric sources is less consistent. One of the songs of the Chorus in Euripides' *Electra* describes the Nereids bringing armour made by Hephaestus to Achilles when he first goes to the war, decorated with images which partially recall those of the shield made by Hephaestus in *Iliad* 18, but with more baroque mythological depictions of monsters and the like (*Electra* 432–86). This seems to imply that his armour was *not* that given to Peleus at his wedding, and the same assumption seems to implicit in a briefer reference to Achilles' armour in the song given to the centaurs at the wedding itself, reimagined by another Euripidean chorus at *Iphigeneia at Aulis* 1067–75 (cf. Torrance 2013: 76–82). Similarly, Lowenstam discusses the problem of vase-paintings depicting Achilles taking up arms: do such scenes depict his arming before he went to the war, or do they depict the more famous gift of arms from Thetis after Patroclus' death in the *Iliad*? The vase-painters may, of course, be evoking a more generalised traditional association between Achilles and the giving of wondrous armour, not tied to a specific moment in the story.

As Patroclus runs back, he meets a wounded warrior, dripping with sweat and blood, and rails against the sufferings his leaders are inflicting on their followers:

> Ah you wretched ones, you who lead and take counsel for the Greeks,
> far from our dear ones and our fatherland you intended
> to glut the nimble dogs in Troy with our gleaming fat.   (*Il.* 11.816–18)

He helps the man to his hut and tends his wounds, a moment of pity and tenderness in the midst of the savagery of the battle. Pity, as we will see, drives the next movement: Patroclus' anguish at the thought of the suffering Greeks will force his friend to relent enough to lend him the armour as Nestor proposed.

The Trojan onslaught continues, and they storm the stockade around the Greek camp. During the battle the gods hold one of their periodic meetings, and Zeus explains what will happen when Hector is close to setting fire to Achilles' ships:

> [Achilles] will rouse up his friend
> Patroclus; him glorious Hector will kill with his spear
> in front of Troy, the killer of many of the other
> allies, among them my own son bright Sarpedon.
> In anger at this bright Achilles will kill Hector;
> from then on I will bring it about ever continuously
> that they will be driven back from the ships, until the Greeks
> will seize steep Troy through the plans of Athene.   (*Il.* 15.64–71)

Patroclus will die in Achilles' armour. The question 'Why?' is never posed and never answered, yet somehow everything that will happen from now on is part of this plan. The unanswered question is the same as hangs over the divine council that led the gods to condemn Enkidu but not Gilgamesh to destruction (above, pp. 77–80). There, as we saw, the slender evidence of the Hittite paraphrase suggests that it was argued out on the level of the favouritisms and enmities of individual deities, especially Enlil, elsewhere named as 'father who begot the great gods'.[16] What Zeus, 'father of gods and men' in the Homeric formula, says at the present council does not seem to allow for any loftier or more profound level of explanation; the two texts reflect the same set of basic assumptions about the unknowability of the gods' motivations when they manipulate human lives and human suffering.

---

[16] For this and other titles of Enlil, see for example the hymn to Enlil 'Spoken by a person in authority': Foster, *BTM*, pp. 652–3.

Patroclus appeals to Achilles' pity

When Patroclus appears at Achilles' hut, they communicate in an emotional language far removed from the calculated assertion of status that drove Achilles to his anger. First Patroclus says nothing, but weeps,

> pouring out warm tears like a black-water spring,
> which down from a steep[17] crag pours its murky water.   (*Il.* 16.3–4)

Achilles in turn feels sympathy for him (*ōiktire*, 16.5) yet seems to sneer, telling him he is like a little girl who runs in tears to her mother and plucks at her dress, begging to be lifted up. Is this contempt a mask for the pity that he also feels? Both men's fathers are still alive, says Achilles, so bad news from home cannot be the cause of his trouble: he asks whether Patroclus is weeping for the plight of the Greeks,

> that they are being slaughtered
> beside the hollowed ships because of their own arrogance?
>
> (*Il.* 16.17–18)

The harsh word that I translate as 'arrogance' – *huperbasiē*, literally 'the act of overstepping' one's proper limits – implies that he blames them for their own suffering, just as vindictively as before; but Patroclus responds by speaking out against his anger:

> I hope it will never seize me, this bile that you are guarding in yourself,
> woe in valour:[18] who apart from you will benefit, even if born in the
>   future,
> if you will not ward off wretched destruction from the Greeks?
>
> (*Il.* 16.30–2)

These words closely follow Nestor's (*Il.* 11.762–3), but he continues with an image whose like has not been heard before:

---

[17] The adjective *aigilips*, only ever found with *petra* (cf. *Il.* 9.15, also Aeschylus, *Suppliants* 794–6), was interpreted by ancient scholars as 'goat-abandoned', too steep for even goats to climb. I cannot make 'goat-deserted' fit sensibly into a translation of the passage, hence the vaguer rendering used here.

[18] The difficult word *ainaretēs* was explained in antiquity as 'holding virtue along with evil'. Janko (1992: 319, note at 28–31) compares *dusaristotokeia* 'wretched for having given birth to the best one' (*Il.* 18.54). Homeric passages of heightened emotional tone seem often to include hard words that were mysterious even to learned native speakers, in the Alexandrian period and perhaps earlier.

> Pitiless one, your father was not the horseman Peleus,
> nor was Thetis your mother: the grey sea gave you birth
> and the crags no-one can climb,[19] for your thought is unyielding.
>
> (*Il.* 16.33–5)

To be born of the sea and the crags is an image of harshness and barren-ness. This is invective, akin to that developed by Semonides in his mis-ogynistic poem where different kinds of women are characterised as fashioned or brought to birth by Zeus from different creatures – pig, fox, dog, ass, weasel, mare, monkey, bee – or from elemental substances: the lazy and inert woman from earth, the unstable and irascible woman from the sea (Semonides, fr. 7: Gerber, *GIP* 304–13).[20] Yet alongside satirical mockery Patroclus' word-picture moves among the shapes of Achilles' own identity. Indeed his mother is in and of the sea, though not identified directly with it in the way that Ocean, for example, is an actual body of water as well as a personal being; when he turns to speak to her he stretches out his arms towards the waters (*Il.* 1.350–1, etc.).[21] To say that 'the grey sea gave you birth' is especially vicious because it moves so close to the strange truth about Achilles' parentage.[22]

The death of the substitute

Patroclus goes on following Nestor's advice almost word for word. He suggests that Achilles may be holding back because of a prophecy revealed to him by his mother (*Il.* 16.37, cf. 11.794–5), hinting perhaps that he could be accused of cowardice – it is striking that in answer Achilles seems to be evasive at best (*Il.* 16.49–51), denying that he has learnt of any such thing from his mother when in fact he has already spoken in Patroclus' presence of exactly this kind of prophecy (*Il.* 9.410–16: see above, pp. 223–225). This is the cue for Patroclus to introduce Nestor's suggestion that he should go

---

[19] *ēlibatos* is another obscure adjective. My tentative translation 'that none can climb' corresponds to one of the suggestions in the scholia on *Il.* 15.273; cf. also *Il.* 15.619.

[20] On this poem see Morgan 2005.

[21] Similarly, when Peleus tried to seize Thetis and she slipped from shape to shape, her ever-changing form was based on the ways of water: see above, p. 178.

[22] Cf. Most 1993. The ancient scholia on the passage (cited by Most, n. 6) anticipate this point and match it to the less direct idea that the 'crags' allude to the association between Peleus and the mountain Pelion. Note also that when the lyric poet Alcaeus speaks of the 'child of the rock and the grey sea' he means the limpet (Alcaeus, fr. 359 at Campbell, *GL* 1.390–3, cited by Janko on the present passage of *Iliad* 16). Although there is not necessarily an allusion to the present passage of the *Iliad*, the parallel confirms that in Patroclus' image Achilles is accused of being or resembling a *creature* of the sea.

into battle disguised as Achilles, leading their fresh and unwearied followers, the Myrmidons, to relieve their exhausted comrades (16.38–45).
This is stated as a matter of practical tactics, just as when Nestor first raised
it, yet Homer's words now invest it with deeper significance:

> So he spoke, begging him, great fool: for in truth he was about
> to ask for an evil death and doom for himself.   (*Il.* 16.46–7)

The words translated *begging* and *to beg*, *lissomenos* and *litesthai*, correspond
exactly to the forces that Phoenix spoke of: the *Litai*, spirits that preside over
and personify the act of begging for an end to anger and vindictiveness (above,
p. 227).[23] Achilles rejected them then: why does he yield this time?

Thinking of his motivation in terms of real-life human behaviour, we
might guess that the difference is that the request comes from the one to
whom he is bound by tender affection, not merely by the mixture of
fellowship and rivalry that he shared with Odysseus and Ajax and the
other leaders of the Greek army. But even if this is right, the reciprocal
logic of honour and status remains prominent in Achilles' language:

> But this terrible pain comes to my heart and my thought's breath,
> since he was willing to rob a man who was his own equal
> and take away my prize, because he surpassed me in power:
> this is a terrible pain to me, since I suffered woe in my thought's breath.
> The girl whom the sons of the Greeks took away, my prize (*geras*),
> whom I won with my spear, when I sacked that city with its fine walls –
> he took her back out of my hands, ruling Agamemnon,
> Atreus' son, as if I were a refugee to be dishonoured (*atimētos*).
>   (*Il.* 16.52–9)

Although some of the wording looks back to what he said to the emissaries
(see esp. 9.648), there is a difference: at this point he does not speak of the
girl's humanity, and she matters as *geras*, a chattel, a sign of the success in
combat by which she was won. Similar ideas are foremost when he tells
Patroclus how to fight in the disguise of his armour:

> But obey, as I place the fullness of this word in your thoughts,
> so that you will win great honour (*timē*) and glory for me
> from all the Greeks, and to me the very beautiful girl
> they will give back, and present me with the bright gifts:
> when you have driven them from the ships, turn back, and if to you
> he grants that you win glory, Hera's loud-thundering husband,

---

[23] I assume here that these words form a single family in communicative practice as well as in
etymology.

> you must have no desire to make war without me
> against the war-loving Trojans, for you would place me in less honour
> (*atimoteros*).   (*Il.* 16.83–90)

The thought here is entirely driven by Achilles' continuing need for respect: if Patroclus were to win so much success as to outshine him, this would work against his hope of vindicating himself through his comrades' humiliation. In this mood, Achilles is still rooted in the painfully reductive value-system of the Greek army.

But Achilles' words also show that he is more aware than the other Greeks of the gods' involvement in what is going on. He warns that if Patroclus goes too far, he may provoke the Trojans' divine protector:

> . . . Do not revel in war and the press of battle,
> slaughtering the Trojans, to lead the way towards Troy,
> lest from Olympus one of the gods, of the everlasting race,
> might come down – for much does farshooter Apollo love the Trojans –
> but turn backward again, when light to the ships
> you have brought, and let them struggle along the plain.   (*Il.* 16.91–6)

This foreboding approaches the level of prophecy, because Patroclus will indeed go too far and be beaten down by Apollo.

The question of destiny and human folly raises itself again here. We saw that when Patroclus first voices the plan to go out and fight in Achilles' armour, Homer can call him a 'fool' (*nēpios, Il.* 16.46), for wishing his own death on himself. *Nēpios* is a harsh word, normally used of infantile recklessness, the folly of those who cannot foresee the consequences of their actions. Yet on the surface the stratagem seems reasonable, however desperate: where is the folly of it? Why will the plan bring about Patroclus' death? In due course this will be worked out along the familiar pattern of the warrior who goes too far at the point of success: Patroclus will again be called *nēpios* when he disregards Achilles' warnings and tries to storm Troy himself (*Il.* 16.684–6). In the present context, however, it is less clear how the plan in itself could be seen as bringing about his self-destruction. To explore this question fully, we need to move away from the ostensible motivations of the characters and into a deeper mythical background.

Mesopotamian and Hittite parallels

Even on a superficial reading, the suggestion arises here that in some sense Patroclus is taking on the identity of Achilles when he is clothed in his armour, and that when he dies he will be given up in his place. In terms of the comparative reading that we have been developing, a further parallel with Enkidu now suggests itself. We have observed (above, pp. 82–84) that royal substitution rituals, involving the death of the substitute in place of the king, were significant in Babylonian state ideology, and that this schema is alluded to explicitly on at least one occasion with reference to Enkidu: Tablet II of the Standard Babylonian Version of the *Epic of Gilgamesh* includes a line in which he is named as the substitute, *pūḫu*, of Gilgamesh (*SBV* II 110), indicating that for the author or redactor of this tablet his role was associated with that of the 'substitute victim' in the royal rituals.

To contextualise this theme we must begin by looking across the wider horizons of Greek and Near Eastern lore. The concept of the human substitute is an extension or variation of that of the scapegoat, by which an animal is invested with the evil that hangs over the king or the people as a whole and is expelled into another territory, bringing the evil with it. Versions of the scapegoat concept recur throughout the ancient Near East and the Mediterranean world,[24] as in the mythical schema by which a human victim is about to be sacrificed but an animal or other substitute is put in his or her place just before the moment of death. The most famous example, the sacrifice of Isaac in the Hebrew Book of Genesis (Gn 22: 2–13), is closely matched in the Cyclic *Cypria* by the story of Iphigeneia:[25] the girl, about to be sacrificed to Artemis by her father Agamemnon, is replaced at the last moment by a deer according to the will of the goddess herself.[26]

Intriguingly, a related myth-pattern seems to underlie the iconographic scheme of a painted vase of *c.* 470 BCE (Fig. 21).[27] On one side is the Embassy to Achilles, a scene akin to those examined in the previous chapter; on the other are two warriors, one identified as Hector and the

---

[24] See the collection of evidence by Bremmer 2008: 169–214. For the Hittite evidence, the concept of scapegoat 'carrier' of evil (*nakkušši*) merges with that of substitute victim (*tarpalli* etc.) even within individual texts, as noted by Gurney 1977: 52–3.

[25] On this version of the Iphigeneia myth as an allomorph of the sacrifice of Isaac cf. Bremmer 2002.

[26] See Proclus' summary, *Cypria* Arg. 8, at West, *GEF*, pp. 74–5; this is discussed further by West, *EC*, p. 110, and Currie 2015: 291–2. The *Cypria* version corresponds to that picked up by Euripides as the background to *Iphigeneia among the Tauri*: this and other sources are discussed by Gantz 1993: 466–8. See also above, p. 184.

[27] Stamnos by the Triptolemos Painter, Basel, Antikenmuseum BS 477. See Griffiths 1985, and cf. Griffiths 1989, adducing a possible related image in a fragmentary vase of *c.* 430 BCE (Malibu, J. Paul Getty Museum, 86.AE.213) where a warrior slaughters a ram while two others duel. The argument is reviewed by Tarenzi 2005: 36–38 and Kitts 2005: 106–10.

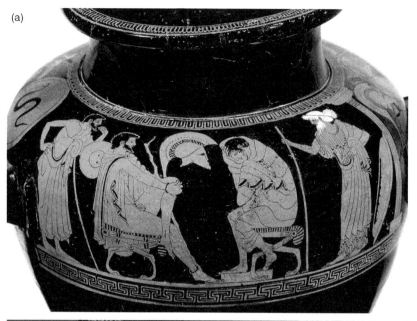

Fig. 21 Vase of *c.* 500–450 BCE: (a) Achilles and the Embassy, (b) combat over a dead ram.

other as Ajax, preparing to fight over a corpse while an old man pleads with each of them – Phoenix at one end, Hector's father Priam at the other. As Alan Griffiths has shown, the scene suggests a variant account of the battle over the dead Patroclus that dominates Book 17 of the *Iliad*, but the corpse over which they fight, labelled with a name whose opening letters are legible as *PAT* . . ., is not a man but a ram with its throat cut. The vase-painter seems to be articulating a version in which Patroclus' death was associated with the use of a ram as a scapegoat victim. If something akin to this is a reality (however shadowy) in the background to the Iliadic version, it suggests that the Patroclus narrative could have been developed along lines parallel to that of Iphigeneia and the other analogues.

In one strand of Homeric scholarship it has long been argued that there is a link between Patroclus and rituals prescribed in Hittite tablets of the mid-second millennium BCE.[28] These texts give detailed prescriptions for a procedure whereby, in response to a threat posed by sickness or plague or an evil omen, a living substitute would be installed to draw the evil down on itself and divert the threat.[29] The prescribed substitute may for example be a ram, who takes the pestilence upon itself to draw it away from the people,[30] but in other examples humans are used. In one,[31] the king has been threatened by an evil omen in the stars, and the evil is transferred to a prisoner, who is anointed with oil and dressed in royal robes before being expelled into his own country, bringing the evil with him and (it seems to be implied) going to his own death in the process.[32] A variant ritual employed both a male and a female prisoner as well as animals.[33]

The most striking example of this group is the 'Great Substitution Ritual',[34] whose colophon states clearly that the ritual is to be used 'if

---

[28] The argument is best known in the version developed in many publications by Gregory Nagy (the best-known is Nagy 1979, esp. 292–5; for a recent reformulation see Nagy 2013: 146–68), which depends on Van Brock 1959 for the claim of a semantic and cultural mapping between *therapōn* and the Hittite *tarpalli* group, but in fact goes far beyond Van Brock's original suggestion, according to which the original meaning of the Hittite term has been lost in the use and meaning of the attested Greek word, with the story of Patroclus preserving only hints of a schema that was no longer understood (Van Brock 1959: 125–6). The motif of substitution is further used by Sinos 1980: 29–38 and Lowenstam 1981: 126–31, in reconstructions that can be best appreciated as variant articulations of that proposed by Nagy (or vice versa). It is worth noting that Van Brock subsumed the reconstruction into the archetypal pattern of the 'sacrifice of the divine king' from Frazer's *Golden Bough* (Van Brock 1959: 125) – a paradigm that few scholars in the field nowadays would consider objectively valid.

[29] The texts are edited and translated by Kümmel 1967; for a new edition of *CTH* 419 see García Trabazo 2010. The standard study is Haas 1994: 216–19; cf. Gurney 1977: 52–8; Goedegebuuro 2002; Bryce 2002: 206–8.

[30] *CTH* 757: text translated by Goetze, *ANET* 347–8.

[31] *CTH* 419, Kümmel 1967: 7–37; older translation by Goetze, *ANET* 355–6; cf. Haas 1994: 207–8.

[32] For the prospect of the substitute's death, see the text at Kummel 1967: p. 11, verse 22' (sim. García Trabazo 2010: 39) for the image that the evil will being 'short years and short days' of life.

[33] *CTH* 584, Kümmel 1967: 111–25; Bryce 2002: 206.

[34] *CTH* 421, Kümmel 1967: 50–110; the vital sections are also presented by Gurney 1977: 57–8, following Kümmel; cf. Haas 1994: 208–10.

death is predicted for the king, whether he sees it in a dream or it is made known to him by divination from the entrails or by augury, or if some omen of death occurs in front of him'.[35] After the robing of the living prisoner, a wooden effigy of the king is made; it is offered in case the gods of the Underworld are the source of the ill-will, while the living substitute is temporarily accorded royal honours and the real king retreats into a pretence of obscurity. The ritual continues:

> Then they bring the prisoner in . . . He says to the king: 'Leave the palace!' The king answers: 'I will go' . . . When he has uttered these words, he goes down from the palace and no one speaks his name any more . . . If anyone comes up into the city, people do not say 'The city in which the real king is' – not so (but) 'The city in which the new king is, that is where the king is.' And the king kneels daily before the Sun-god of heaven in the early morning and prays: 'Sun-god of heaven, my lord, what have I done? You have taken the throne away from me and given it to another . . . You have summoned me to the shades. But I have appeared before you, Sun-god of heaven. Release me from the realm of the shades.' Then they perform the royal ritual for the new king. They serve him with food and drink, his bed is placed in the bedroom, the chamberlains watch over him at night, . . . he sits down in the place where the true king sits.[36]

The next sentence is the crux: 'He dies on the seventh day'. The verb translated 'dies' is incompletely preserved, but this restoration follows from the comparative evidence and the fact that in the subsequent stages of the ritual the original king, now back in the open, is the only one referred to.[37]

In this connection a remarkable lexical correspondence has been proposed. One of the key Hittite terms for the 'ritual substitute' is *tarpalli*, with the closely related forms *tarpanalli, tarpaššaš*; and the similarity of sound makes it possible to argue that the Greek word *therapōn* – 'companion, squire' – is a borrowing built on one of the *tarp*–[38] words from what was, at least in the Bronze Age, the dominant neighbouring power on the east of the proto-Greek world. Although a warrior who stands by and serves another can be referred to as *therapōn* without a hint of any deeper theme,[39] it is

---

[35] Gurney's (1977: 57) translation, following Kümmel's text.   [36] Gurney 1977: 57–8.

[37] Kümmel 1967: pp. 62–3, at B Rs. 29'; discussion, pp. 93–4.

[38] Or possibly via Luwian, in which the same word-group is also attested.

[39] The sense is perhaps more profound when the poet himself is *therapōn* of the Muses (Hes. *Th.* 100), or a warrior is *therapōn* of Ares, the god who personifies the wildness of battle (*Il.* 2.110, etc.). In such cases, arguably, there is a sense in which the god enters into or possesses his follower – but it would be another matter entirely to say that poet or warrior is a 'ritual substitute' for the god, as Nagy's essays on the subject seem to imply.

striking that Patroclus is referred to as '*therapōn* of Achilles' three times when he is fighting in his friend's armour, and again four times when he is lying dead after the failure of his attack.[40]

The proposed Hittite parallel remains problematic in detail. It is difficult from a purely historical perspective to posit direct influence on the Patroclus narrative from such a source, because the rituals functioned as part of the official apparatus of the Hittite state and would have disappeared with its extinction, many generations before the *Iliad* came together.[41] None of the attested instances of *therapōn* actually refers in context to the idea of substitution – in fact nothing in the usage of the word *anywhere* points explicitly to this idea – and there are yawning differences between the Hittite ritual and the Iliadic narrative. Patroclus is a friend, not a prisoner, and there is no indication that he is meant to be seen as a surrogate Achilles by the gods, but only by the Trojans.

However, the picture changes when we treat the Hittite rituals in the way they are regarded by specialists, not as an indigenous creation of Anatolian (let alone Indo-European) culture but as an example of the adoption and naturalisation of Mesopotamian practices. Indeed, the Hittite texts sometimes use the term *puḫišu*, borrowed from the Akkadian word for 'royal substitute', *pūḫu*, discussed above in the context of Enkidu.[42] The lore of evil omens in the stars, which is central to the Hittite material, is directly derived from Mesopotamian celestial science, and it is a fair inference that the concept of royal substitution was absorbed as part of the same complex of ideas.[43]

This leads to a fundamental reassessment of the status of the Hittite rituals: they begin to look less like a formative influence on the *Iliad*, and more like a different and independent manifestation of a Mesopotamian theme that influenced the Homeric creation by a much more direct route, within the nexus of cross-influence from Akkadian to Greek epic narrative. The parallelism between Patroclus and Enkidu as substitute victims is between analogous characters in epic poems that are already comparable in generic and thematic terms. The *manner* of articulation is comparable as well. The *pūḫu* idea was most likely introduced into *Gilgamesh* as an allusive interpretation comparatively late, when the Standard Babylonian

---

[40] *Il.* 16.165, 243, 653; *Il.* 17.164, 271, 388; cf. 18.152, 23.90. Tarenzi 2005 argues that this cluster of instances refers specifically to the concept of Patroclus as ritual substitute, and that other uses of *therapōn* do not carry the same allusive charge: this seems to me to be special pleading, though the observation remains thought-provoking.

[41] Broodbank 2013: 458–9; Cline 2014: 124–6.

[42] Gurney 1977: 58; discussion by Kümmel 1967: 81.   [43] Haas 1994: 214.

Version was taking shape or already framed, and we have seen that the direct evidence is limited to a single line in one surviving tablet.[44] Similarly, in the *Iliad* the idea is almost entirely submerged, and the Patroclus narrative only hints sidelong at the concept of the secondary warrior as a scapegoat-type victim. Just as we argued with the example of the rhetoric of Poseidon in *Iliad* 15 and of Enlil in *Atrahasis* (above, pp. 27–31), *Gilgamesh* and the *Iliad* meet here both in their basic narrative materials and in the compositional techniques applied to them by the poets. Similar allusive techniques have been applied in two narrative sequences that were already analogous to each other in outline.[45]

The wraith flies to Hades

From this point onwards, Achilles will be defined more and more closely by his pairing with Patroclus, and the dynamic between them will recall Gilgamesh and Enkidu with increasing intensity. Each pair of heroes stands at the summit of heroic intensity, and the vengeance – or justice, or jealousy, or incomprehensible destiny – of the gods causes the lesser of the two to be sent to his death.

At the end of his advice to Patroclus not to try to storm Troy, Achilles wishes for something that he knows will never happen:

> I wish, O father Zeus and Athene and Apollo,
> that none of the Trojans would escape death, as many as they are,
> nor any of the Greeks, but that we two would emerge from the destruction,
> so that we alone would unloose the holy head-veils of Troy.   (*Il.* 16.97–100)

A pair of champions, battling together and without help from others: the notion that such a pair might sack a city on their own has already emerged when Diomedes, angry at Agamemnon's despair, threatens that he and Sthenelus will remain on their own until they storm Troy (*Il.* 9.48–9). Both images perhaps looks back to the patterning of earlier exploits, for example that of Heracles and Iolaos, the nephew and companion who accompanies him (see e.g. Hesiod, *Shield* 77–121). Closer still is the story of how Heracles stormed Troy himself in the time of Priam's father: his companion was Telamon, father of the Ajax of the Iliadic war. According to an

---

[44] See above, Ch. 3, n. 105.
[45] For the methodological issues here, compare Currie's contributions discussed in the Introduction (nn. 109–11) and Conclusion (pp. 330–332).

account preserved in late mythographic sources,[46] Telamon was first of the two to break through the wall; fearing that Heracles would kill him for having usurped the primacy, Telamon immediately gathered stones from the broken wall and said that he was building an altar in Heracles' honour. This story seems almost comical, but it is underlain by the same archetypal concept, a pair of heroes breaching the city wall together.

Patroclus puts on the armour of Achilles, the Myrmidons gather for the onslaught, and Achilles prays to Zeus that his *therapōn* (*Il.* 16.244) will win glory and return unharmed (*Il.* 16.238–48); but the god's response is unrelenting:

> So he spoke in prayer, and Zeus of cunning (*mētieta*) heard him.
> To him one of these things the Father granted, the other he denied;
> that he would thrust back from the ships the war and the fighting
> he granted, but with upward nod he refused his safe return from the
>   battle.   (*Il.* 16.249–52)

In the way that we have seen so many times in this study, Homer puts no gloss of reason or meaning on the upward nod of refusal (*aneneuse*, *Il.* 16.250) with which Zeus determines that Patroclus will die.

That said, however, in Patroclus' onslaught on the Trojans we have another case of the pattern that we first saw clearly with Diomedes (above, pp. 188–197). The further the warrior goes towards the height of success, the closer he moves towards forgetting his human limitations. As the Trojans retreat in disarray and more and more of them are slain, including Zeus' son Sarpedon, Patroclus begins to abandon restraint:

> Patroclus gave the command to the horses and Automedon
> and pursued the Trojans and Lycians, and he fell into ruin (*aasthē*),
> the witless one (*nēpios*); if he had guarded the word of Peleus' son,
> he would have escaped from the dark demon of black death . . .
>   (*Il.* 16.684–7)

The verb translated as 'he fell into ruin' is *aasthē*, from the same root as *ātē*, the force of self-destructive recklessness that we saw explored by Phoenix in his warnings to Achilles. Maybe there is a psychological inevitability in what is happening here, but Homer sees it as the will of Zeus:

> . . . But always the thought of Zeus is stronger than that of men:
> he routs the man of valour, and he takes away victory

---

[46] Apollodorus, *Library* 2.6.4; Hellanicus, fr. 109 at Fowler 2000–13: 1.194. Hellanicus possibly took it from an epic source such as the lost epic *Herakleia* of Peisandros (thus Fowler 2000–13: 2.313). On Heracles' sack of Troy see also Gantz 1993: 442–4.

easily, when he himself urges one on to fight:
he it was who roused up the thought in his breast.   (*Il.* 16.688–91)[47]

Human success is unstable, triumph entails disaster: this is Zeus, 'who has
loosened the heads of many cities and will loosen more, for his power is the
greatest' (*Il.* 2.118–9 = 9.24–5). On this theological level we continue to
wonder why such things are happening to Patroclus, why 'the gods were
calling [him] to death' (*Il.* 16.693), but the force of *ātē* remains as
a psychological explanation – the warrior's excessive energy drives him
to the folly that destroys him.

   Patroclus surges forward as if to storm the wall of Troy, defying Achilles'
exact instructions (*Il.* 16.92–3); the Greeks would have taken the city, had
Apollo not confronted him (16.698–701). Three times Patroclus tries to
breach the corner-angle of the wall, three times Apollo repels him with
a push to his shield. The fourth time, he makes him hear the warning:

   'Yield, Zeus-born Patroclus: it is not your portion (*aisa*)
   for the city of the haughty Trojans to be sacked under your spear
   nor even that of Achilles, who is a much greater man than you.'
                                                   (*Il.* 16.707–9)

For the moment Patroclus draws back, but from this point onwards he is
rushing towards his death, and Apollo disguises himself as a mortal to
encourage Hector to stand and face him. Patroclus mocks a man as he kills
him, laughing at the way he falls from his chariot in death –

   ' . . . Light is the man, how easily he somersaults!
   if he were in the fish-filled sea, this man would satisfy many, diving for
       shellfish . . . '   (*Il.* 16.745–6)

– and his next attack is accompanied by an ominous simile:

   So speaking he went against Cebriones the hero
   with the surge of a lion, who when ravaging the farmyards
   is struck on the breast, and his own valour destroys him.   (*Il.* 16.751–3)

His own valour destroys him: as we will see more fully later, this is the
essence of what it means to be a lion in battle.[48] Hector and Patroclus
struggle over the fallen man, and again three times Patroclus leads
a charge before the wall. The fourth time Apollo, unseen, strikes him

[47] Lines 16.689–90 are formulaic, appearing elsewhere in the *Iliad* (*Il.* 17.177–8), and it is possible
that in the present passage they are a late insertion; whether or not that is the case, they
accurately represent the themes underlying the plight of Patroclus.
[48] See Ch. 14.

with a body-blow of the flat of his hand and makes him stumble, his helmet falling from his head, and *ātē* fills his thought;[49] a minor Trojan warrior, Euphorbus, takes this moment to strike him, then Hector delivers the final thrust (16.828), calling him again *nēpie* 'witless' (16.833) for daring to boast that he would storm the city. If there is a sense in which Patroclus has been brought low because he took on the doom of the 'ritual substitute' by putting on the armour and identity of Achilles, this is not stated in Homer's words, which look to something simpler and more bitter: the nod of Zeus, which brought about this death for no reason that words ever state.

Did Patroclus give in to blind arrogance in his hour of triumph, so making himself something like the familiar 'tragic hero' of conventional literary history? Did he anger the gods by presuming that he could sack the city unaided? Or was it his crime or sin or error (there is no adequate term in English) to try to usurp the privilege that was proper to Achilles himself, the privilege of being the first to burst through the walls of the city? Along any such line of thought, it is possible – albeit speculatively – to align the force that drives Patroclus to self-destruction with the heroic *hubrisma* that motivated the distress of mother Earth in the *Cypria*. The crime is to move beyond one's proper limitations and attempt a level of self-assertion, even self-glorification, that invites the retribution of the gods.

It is possible, I believe, that a hint of Enkidu is heard one more time in the story of Patroclus' end. When Hector stands over him, the climactic moment attracts heightened imagery:

> When he had spoken, the fulfilment of death covered him over,
> and his breath-soul (*psuchē*), flying from his lips,[50] went to Hades,
> wailing for its own death, leaving manliness and youth behind.
>
> (*Il.* 16.855–7)

Within the *Iliad*, these lines look forward to the coming death of Hector in vengeance for Patroclus, when the same words will be used (*Il.* 22.361–3), and as a result these lines tend to be considered most often in terms of the deictic patterns of Homeric composition by formulae.[51] However, the image of flying is also suggestive of parallels further afield. It has often

---

[49] I take it that *ātē* in this instance is the 'taking-away of his wits' in the most direct sense – he is dazed and stumbling under the blow.

[50] For this translation of *rhethea*, more traditionally rendered 'limbs', see Clarke 1999: 133–4.

[51] See for example Clarke 1999: 148–51. The passage in *Odyssey* 24 in which the *psuchai* of the suitors are described as 'gibbering like bats' while being led to Hades by Hermes is best seen as a (later) development on the basis of this Iliadic image (*Od.* 24.5–10: see Clarke 1999: 227–8).

been observed that the depiction of the wraiths of the dead as winged beings is paralleled in Aegean art of the mid-second millennium BCE,[52] and Greek vases of the Classical period also show figures in bird-form in funerary contexts, evidently representing the shades of the dead.[53] But the affinities of this motif are ultimately Mesopotamian, and in Akkadian literature the dead in the Underworld are several times described as feathered.[54] We have already observed a version of this passage in *Gilgamesh* (see above, p. 81), one of a group in various texts employing similar formulae. I cite the reconstructed text from *Nergal and Ereshkigal*:[55]

> [To the road whose journey] has no return,
> [to the house whose entrants] are bereft of light,
> [where dust is their sustenance and] clay their food.
> [They are clothed like bi]rds in wings for garments,
> [they see no light] but dwell in darkness,
> [   ] moaning,
>   they moan] like [do]ves.
>   (*Nergal and Ereshkigal*, Late Version, ii 1'–7', *BTM*, p. 516)

It has been observed many times that this imagery resembles that of the flying *psuchē* – the wraith is in bird-form and making sounds of misery.[56] On its own, however, this is only a partial parallel: Patroclus' *psuchē* is *travelling* to Hades, but the dead in the passage just cited are already dwellers in the Underworld. Remarkably, however, there is an image in *Gilgamesh* that deploys the bird-image in the context of the journey to death. As we saw, it was in a sinister dream, presaging his own death, that Enkidu saw himself being first transformed into a bird and captured in a cage, then sent to the Underworld where the dead dwell, again in bird-form:

> [*He struck*] *me*, he turned me into a dove.
> [He bound] my arms like (the wings of) a bird,
> to lead me into the house of darkness, the seat of Irkalla:
> to the house which those who enter cannot leave,
> on the journey whose way cannot be retraced;

---

[52] Immerwahr 1995.   [53] Vermeule 1979: 8, 17–19, 65.

[54] Good overview of this area of Mesopotamian imagery by Lapinkivi 2004: 37–41.

[55] For the parallel passages in *Gilgamesh* and *The Descent of Ishtar*, on which the supplements for the lacunae have been based, see above, p. 81, nn. 93–4; for the textual data on all the variants of the passage see the diplomatic score edition at Lapinkivi 2004: 15.

[56] For suggestions of a parallel with the flying *psuchai* of Patroclus and Hector see West 1997: 162–3; Clarke 1999: 5–6. On more general parallels between Greek and Mesopotamian Underworld lore cf. Röllig 2001.

> to the house whose residents are deprived of light,
> where dust is their sustenance, their food clay.
> They are clad like birds in coats of feathers,
> and they cannot see light but dwell in darkness.   (*SBV* VII 182–90)

The bird-image continues from the moment of death to the inner land-scape of the Underworld itself, albeit in a much more complex sequence than that enacted in the Homeric passage. This parallel must remain tentative, as it relies on matching a dream in the first work to straight narration in the second, and it cannot take account of the parallel description of Hector's death later in the *Iliad*. Potentially, however, it stands as the first member of a group of close verbal parallels between the two epics that will punctuate the following chapters, when we will observe how the response of Achilles to the death of Patroclus converges repeatedly with Gilgamesh's response to the death of Enkidu.

12 | Achilles responds

When Achilles spoke to the three emissaries, revealing so much of his inner life – his loneliness, his loathing of war, his knowledge that the price of glory would be an early death – his thoughts were also full of affection, a young man's longing for his father and a lover's bond with a woman who has become like a wife to him. Now with Patroclus dead, and dead because Achilles sent him out to fight, all his passion and energy will settle on that one love alone. In the coming chapters, we will see him moving gradually towards a state like that of a wild beast, driven by a need for vengeance that refuses to be curbed by humane self-restraint. Behind it all the time will be his increasingly urgent awareness that he will soon be killed. Despite the obvious differences in the articulation, this can be seen as parallel to the movement that drove Gilgamesh to try to escape from his own mortality and ultimately to achieve unlooked-for wisdom. If *learning through suffering*, in Aeschylus' phrase, is fundamental to the narrative patterning of the heroic past, Gilgamesh encourages us to ask whether there is also a sense in which Achilles eventually moves towards a new level of self-understanding, even of acceptance.

Intimations of mortality

As the two hosts fight for possession of Patroclus' corpse, the struggle is full of ominous foreshadowings. The Trojans eventually succeed in stripping the armour that Patroclus wore, the armour that the gods gave to Peleus on his wedding day, so that Hector can put it on himself:

> [Hector] put on the immortal armour
> of Peleus' son Achilles, which the sky-born gods had given
> to his dear father, and which he himself gave to his child
> when he grew old: but his son did not grow old in his father's harness.
>
> (*Il.* 17.194–7)

The son did not grow old: again the poet looks to the prospect of Achilles' death, as his mother did when she greeted him on the seashore after the strife with Agamemnon had begun. Somehow – Homer never specifies how – the armour itself is bound up with that death, as when Hector took Achilles' helmet from the dying Patroclus (*Il.* 16.799–800), and as Zeus himself announces when Hector has arrayed himself in Achilles' panoply:

> But now I will pledge you great mastery (*kratos*),
> in recompense (*poinē*) for this, that from you returning home from the battle
> Andromache will never receive the famous weapons of Peleus' son.
>
> (*Il.* 17.206–8)

But Zeus says these things inwardly to himself (*Il.* 17.200), and the mortals below struggle on for honour, status, prestige – and bring forward the same 'beautiful death' that has already left Patroclus bloodied in the dust.[1] The focus shifts for a moment to the horses that had drawn Patroclus to battle in Achilles' chariot – another of the wedding gifts of Peleus and Thetis, this time that of Poseidon (*Il.* 16.866–7, 23.277–9, etc.).[2] Automedon tries to urge them into action, but they have stopped to mourn:[3]

> The two horses' of Aeacus' grandson, being far apart from the battle,
> wept when first they heard that the charioteer
> had been thrown in the dust by manslaying Hector.   (*Il.* 17.426–8)

He tries to make them move, but they remain motionless:

> As a grave-marker remains unmoving, which on the tomb
> stands, of a man or a woman who has died:
> so they remained unharmed, holding the beautiful chariot,
> bending down their heads to the ground, and from them hot tears
> flowed earthward from their eyes as they mourned
> in longing for the charioteer.   (*Il.* 17.434–9)

Purely as a visual image, this would be a reminder of the disjuncture between the horrors of the battlefield and the high glamour of the world where Achilles' parents were united: but Homer allows it to speak more eloquently, focalising the word-picture through Zeus' personal response. He sees the horses and speaks with pity of the contrast between their immortality and the striving of the death-bound men who fight around them:

---

[1] On the concept of the 'beautiful death' the classic study remains Vernant 2001a [1982], with Loraux 1995: 63–139 *passim*.

[2] That the horses were among the wedding-gifts is explicit in line 867a, cited in the scholia and probably a post-Homeric addition: 'on the day when he married Thetis in her shining head-veil'. See also Janko 1992: 333–4, note on *Il.* 16.130–54, and cf. Harrison 1991.

[3] On the horses of Achilles in this scene see further Schein 2016: 11–26.

> there is nothing at all more wretched than man
>> of all things that breathe and creep across the Earth.   (*Il.* 17.446–7)

This is gnomic wisdom, the truth of human weakness and instability. Close to it in the *Odyssey* are the words Odysseus uses when he moves disguised as a beggar among the arrogant 'suitors' who are trying to bully his wife into marriage, and stops to speak to the only one among them who has offered him kindness:[4]

> Now I will say this to you, so understand it and listen to me:
> Earth nourishes nothing more insubstantial[5] than humanity[6]
> of all things that breathe and creep across the Earth.   (*Od.* 18.129–31)

The suitors will disregard such warnings, whether because the arrogant are reckless by nature or because the gods are drawing them towards their deserved destruction. The moral edge of the Iliadic scene is less easily reduced to simple right and wrong, but the sense of human futility is no less bitter.

Chains of prophecy

Achilles had warned Patroclus not to pursue the fight too far because this would detract from his own prestige (*atimoteron de me thēseis*, 16.90) and might provoke a god to rise up against him (*Il.* 16.91–6); but he did not mention a fear that his friend might be killed. When the battle rages over the corpse, Homer shifts for a moment to explain why he had not foreseen it:

> This [Achilles] never expected in his thought,
> that he would die; rather that alive, after drawing near to the gates,
> he would come home: since indeed he never expected at all
> to sack the citadel, whether without him or with him.   (*Il.* 17.404–7)

Like all Achilles' foreknowledge, this was from Thetis:

---

[4] On the resonances of this passage see Rutherford 1986.

[5] This is only a guess at the meaning of the remarkable word *akidnoteron*. The adjective **akidnos* is found only in the comparative, and the early attestations are all in the *Odyssey*: contextual glosses that work well in translating the various instances might include *feeble, weak* or *ugly* as well as *insubstantial*.

[6] The word here is *anthrōpos*, gender-neutral meaning 'human being', while in the corresponding *Iliad* line (17.446) Zeus speaks of 'man' using a gendered term (*anēr*, virtually 'warrior'). This reflects the difference of context: Zeus is looking at a battlefield, Odysseus is talking about human life in general.

> Often he had learned this from his mother, hearing her far off,[7]
> for she used to reveal to him the thought (*noēma*) of great Zeus.
>
>   (17.408–9)

Later, mourning over Patroclus, Achilles will explain that he had believed that his own death would come first, and that Patroclus would return to Phthia to welcome Achilles' son into his inheritance (*Il.* 19.328–33). Fitting this together with the prophecy that neither of them would sack the city, it follows that Achilles pictured Patroclus leaving the war after his own death and returning home while the war was still in progress. This in turn is consistent with his earlier words, when he wished *in vain* that he and Patroclus would be able to sack Troy on their own (*Il.* 16.97–100).[8]

Prophecies, however, are always shadowy and ill-understood, as Achilles says elsewhere in his lamentations when he recalls telling Patroclus' father that he would return home laden with the spoils of the sack of the city:

> But Zeus does not bring to fulfilment all thoughts (*noēmata*) for mortals:
> for both of us it has been assigned (*peprōtai*)[9] that we should redden the same earth
> here in Troy. . .   (*Il.* 18.328–30)

Whatever Achilles heard from his mother, it was doubtful and ambiguous and perhaps self-contradictory. Now, hearing the increased tumult of the battle, his thoughts turn to another prophecy:

> May the gods not bring to completion my thoughts' evil cares,
> as once my mother revealed to me, when she told me
> that the best of the Myrmidons while I was still living
> would under the Trojans' hands depart from the light of the sun.
>
>   (*Il.* 18.8–11)

Once these thoughts have become words, he guesses that Patroclus has disobeyed his warnings, pursued the onslaught too far, and met his death (*Il.* 18.12–14).

---

[7] Presumably meaning 'in isolation from others'.

[8] Cf. Edwards's valuable note (1991: 101–2, note at 17.404–11), which suggests the interpretations that I try to unravel here.

[9] The verb *peprōtai* is a perfect (stative) form, built on the root seen in the aorist *e-poron*, used of granting, bestowing, giving gifts or favours. *Peprōtai* is often translated 'it is fated', 'it is ordained', 'it is destined', but this is perhaps too precise in specifying the terminology of divinely ordained causation. Although *peprōtai* is indeed associated with such forces (see e.g. *Il.* 15.209, 16.401 = 22.179), it is not clear that there is any clearly defined divine agency here. Only in later Greek does the derived participle *to peprōmenon* take on such a meaning: see e.g. the passage from Herodotus discussed above, p. 155.

Choosing death over life

When Antilochus arrives to confirm what has happened, Achilles flings himself on the ground:

> With both hands he took the tawny[10] dust
> and poured it down from his head, and ravaged his lovely face,
> and the black ashes settled on his fragrant tunic.   (*Il.* 18.23–5)

Dust poured on the head is a symbol of being buried, and the bystanders fear that he will cut his own throat (18.34): like Gilgamesh mourning Enkidu in the Standard Version, his grief and lamentation represent a turning towards his own death.[11] For Achilles, however, this is much more than an aspect of ritual: it will also involve self-loathing, and the threat of suicide is real.

The voice that articulates this next movement is not that of a warrior but of a sorrowing mother. Just as Ninsun grieved for the 'restless spirit' of her son (see above, p. 69), so Thetis' forebodings of death have loomed over the *Iliad* from the start.[12] When Achilles first raged against Agamemnon, she was already speaking of the sorrow of raising him for an untimely death (p. 208). Now again she hears the voice of his misery and emerges from her father's home under the sea, responding as if to the news that Achilles has already died, with herself as the chief mourner surrounded by the Nereids who dwell with her. The effect is the same whether we interpret this as an expression of her prophetic awareness of his coming end, or as an inter-textual allusion to the narration of his funeral later in the sequence of the Trojan War, as told in the Cyclic *Aethiopis*.[13] To her companions she names herself as *dusaristotokeia*, 'wretched for having given birth to the best one':[14] he sprang up like a young tree in the corner of the garden (*Il.* 18.56–7), and now

> I will never welcome him again
> returning homeward to the house of Peleus.   (*Il.* 18.59–60)

She emerges from the sea to Achilles, and when he picks up the words of her grief he brings them to a place still darker:

---

[10] I can make no better sense of *aithaloeis*, which seems indeterminately poised between a colour term ('yellow, flamelike') and an image of something burnt and ashen. See *LfgrE* s.v.

[11] Cf. Rendu 2008: 206–7.

[12] On Thetis and prophetic lamentation a key reading is Slatkin 1991, esp. 21–52.

[13] For a powerful recent articulation of this line of interpretation see Tsagalis 2004, with Currie 2016: 119–26; but compare also the counter-argument by Kelly 2012.

[14] On the force of this compound in the context of lamentation see Tsagalis 2004: 17–20.

> Now there will be ten-thousandfold grief in your thoughts
> on the death of your son, whom you will never welcome again
> returning homeward, for my thought's breath does not urge me
> to live and remain among men, unless Hector
> first is struck by my spear and loses his life,
> and pays recompense for Patroclus, Menoitios' son.   (*Il.* 18.88–93)

Thetis grieves for the sorrow and inevitability of his death, as any mother might speak when her son faces a battle from which he cannot return alive. But Achilles speaks of a more terrible state of mind, the fury – or perhaps even madness – of the warrior whose desire for revenge is so overwhelming that he would rather pursue it than preserve his own life. In a world whose ethics are driven by the compulsive need for balance and repayment, this follows with savage literalism from having loved Patroclus 'equal to my own head' (*Il.* 18.82), as much as life itself. But Thetis answers it with another revelation:

> Swift to your portion (*ōku-moros*) you will be, my child, with what
>   you say:
> for death is ready for you straight after Hector.   (*Il.* 18.95–6)

This prophecy is absolute and unconditional, with no sense of a choice between alternatives, and Achilles' response is equally decisive:

> Let me die at once, since to my friend I could not
> be a defence . . .   (*Il.* 18.98–9)

With this willing acceptance of the price of vengeance, Achilles now knows how and why he will never return home to his fatherland: instead of being a light of hope to Patroclus and his other companions he has been sitting idle, 'a useless burden on the ploughland' (*Il.* 18.104) – the image, as we saw (above, p. 169) that perhaps makes a sweeping linkage between his fate and the plan to remove the burden of the scandalous heroic race from Earth's back. As Achilles continues, he rages against the forces that led to the disaster:

> If only strife (*eris*) could be destroyed from among gods and men,
> and bile, which drives even a deep-thinking man to resentment,
> and which is much sweeter than dripping honey
> as it rises up in the breasts of men like smoke:
> so now he drove me to bile, the king of men, Agamemnon.
>   (*Il.* 18.107–11)

Strife among gods and men: it is tempting to speculate that this alludes to another fraught moment in the origins of the war, the meddling of the goddess Strife at the wedding of Achilles' parents. The turning-point of the epic, and the fate of the heroic race as a whole, is bound up with their ungovernable passions.

Patroclus has died because of Achilles' *cholos*. I have translated the word very literally as 'bile', because when it refers to bitter resentful anger it remains tied to its literal and tangible meaning, the ebbing and flowing substance in the body that embodies and propels that emotion.[15] Earlier, when his Myrmidons were about to go to battle behind Patroclus, Achilles imagined how his followers would have spoken against him in resentment of his anger:

> And each of you accused me:
> 'Wild son of Peleus, your mother nourished you with bile,
> pitiless, for you are holding back your companions unwilling by the
> ships.'
> (*Il.* 16.202–4)

A later Greek poet refers to the custom that weaning mothers would smear bile (*cholē*) on their nipples to discourage the infant from sucking:[16] the reversal in the Myrmidons' words evokes the perversity of Achilles' disposition when he refused to fight. Now when he calls bile 'sweeter than honey', the irony expresses a psychological insight: the hatred he felt for Agamemnon and the Greeks was perversely pleasant to taste, and this has worked his ruin and brought on the early death that he tried to spurn when he spoke to the emissaries.

Nonetheless Thetis, as the emissaries heard, had also said that with that choice of early death would come fame that would last for ever. Achilles turns at once to the task ahead: he will go now and find Hector, and he will accept his meeting with the demon of death when the time comes. Even Heracles could not escape death, so Achilles will submit when he is slain (*Il.* 18.115–26) – but first he will give the Trojan women cause to weep, and so he will win noble fame, *kleos esthlon* (Il. 18.121). This last phrase comes close to the words of Thetis' earlier prophecy, *kleos aphthiton* 'imperishable fame': this partial match seems more than accidental, and it closes the circle between the inner turmoil of the Iliadic Achilles and the tradition of simpler and more straightforward articulations of the

---

[15] On *cholos* as a bodily substance and an emotional force, see e.g. Padel 1992, ch. 2; Clarke 1999, ch. 4, esp. 92–7, on which cf. Cairns 2003b; Cairns 2003a, esp. 26–7. On *cholos* in the discourse of the *Iliad* see for example Gill 1996: 191–204; Walsh 2005: 109–213 *passim*.

[16] Padel 1992: 23–4 adduces a fragment of the New Comedy poet Diphilus (at Athenaeus 6.247c) as evidence for this practice, which she uses to elucidate *Il.* 16.202–4. In post-Homeric Greek the usual form is *cholē* (*a*-stem feminine) rather than *cholos* (*o*-stem masculine), but the difference seems to be purely formal.

heroic ideal, potentially stretching back to the 'name that is eternal' (*šuma ša darû*, *OB III* 148) sought by Gilgamesh when he went against Humbaba.[17] Achilles will indeed win his glory, but not by following the simple social contract described by Sarpedon (see pp. 143–146): instead he will throw away his life in anger and hatred, before which fame slips into insignificance.

Here and there earlier in the *Iliad*, Homer has given glimpses of men who faced choices similar to that of Achilles, holding privileged knowledge because their fathers were prophets. Euchēnor had been told that he could either die of a slow sickness at home, or could go to Troy and be brought down by the enemy: he chose the latter, 'avoided both the sickness and the fine for refusing to serve', and he died at Paris' hands (*Il.* 13.663–72). The notion that he went to war to avoid a financial penalty seems almost comically down-to-earth,[18] but there is no room for anything less than horror when Homer says that the two sons of the prophet Merops disregarded his warnings and went to Troy 'because the demons of death (*kēres*) were drawing them on' (*Il.* 2.830–4, 11.328–32).[19] Perhaps such images function as foreshadowings of what will happen to Achilles, or perhaps (also) they look back to a darker instantiation of the same story-pattern earlier in the history of the heroic race: the fate of the prophet Amphiaraus in the Theban war. By his foresight Amphiaraus knew the attack of the Seven against Thebes would fail, and that he and all but one of the other leaders would die, but he had long ago sworn an oath to obey his wife's will in any quarrel between himself and her brother, Adrastus, who was now the leader of the expedition. Bribed by Adrastus, she forced Amphiaraus to go to war, and so he went under sentence of death. When he tried at the end to flee from the battlefield, Zeus struck him in the back with a thunderbolt and the earth swallowed him up so that he was removed directly to Hades. It is not known whether the story was narrated in the epic *Thebaid*, but its themes if not its substance may well have been known in the tradition behind

---

[17] Cf. above, Ch. 1, n. 20.

[18] If the reference to the 'fine' that he avoided is comical or ironic, it is similar in spirit to Homer's better-known aside when Glaucus exchanges his own golden armour for Diomedes' bronze armour, and the poet says that Zeus must have 'taken away his wits', giving 'the value of twenty cows in return for the value of nine' (*Il.* 6.234–6). To the modern reader at least, the mention of mercenary calculations at such a moment seems incongruous or bathetic, but it is hard to tell whether such a response should be projected back onto the ancients – perhaps the sense of incongruity has less to do with Homer than with our own bourgeois sensibilities. On Diomedes and the armour cf. Scodel 1992, with Seaford 1994: 15–16; Postlethwaite 1998: 94–6; Alden 2000: 305–8.

[19] For another, briefer example, see *Il.* 5.148–51.

Homer.[20] However baroque the form taken by each of these stories, they are all based on the fundamental truth that *every* warrior, every human being, knows he will die: hence, potentially, Achilles' defiance can serve as an image of the courage of any man who is put to the test in war and stands unflinchingly.

The defiance of death in Homeric reception

As suggested at the outset of this book, a reading of Achilles in terms of frenzy and death-wish sits uneasily with the traditional assumption that the epic portrays its hero in an uncomplicatedly positive light. In view of this disjuncture, it is worth pausing here to consider some key responses from the early centuries of Homeric reception. The earliest extended examples of Homeric heroism redeployed as a matter for praise and celebration are in the verses of Tyrtaeus, said to have been composed to urge the Spartans to redouble their efforts in war,[21] where familiar Homeric words and images are reshaped into pictures of glamorous self-sacrifice:

> He falls in the first rank and loses his breath of life,
> glorifying (*eukleïsas*) his city and his people and his father,
> pierced many times through his breast and his bossed shield
> and through his body-armour from the front:
> him they mourn, alike young men and old men,
> and all the city grieves in wretched grief at his loss,
> and his tomb and his children are conspicuous among the people,
> and likewise his children's children, and his descendants thereafter,
> and his noble fame is never destroyed, nor his own name,
> and although he is below the earth, he becomes immortal.
> (Tyrtaeus fr. 12.23–32: Gerber, *GEP*, pp. 58–61)

Tyrtaeus' model soldier has gained 'noble fame', *kleos esthlon*, as his reward for accepting death: this is the ideal that makes a man hate life and 'love the black spirits of death as much as the rays of the sun' (fr. 11.5–6). An Acarnanian tomb-inscription of the third century BCE commemorates a young man's death in war: 'he nourished the declaration of Tyrtaeus in

---

[20] For summary versions see Apollodorus, *Library* 3.6.2, 3.6.8, with full review of artistic and textual sources by Gantz 1993: 506–10, 518–19. Eriphyle is mentioned in the *Odyssey* (11.326) and the scholia expand upon the present story as the background. On the question whether these details correspond to the lost *Thebaid* see Davies 1989: 22–8; Davies 2014: 123–8.

[21] Fragments are cited from Gerber, *GEP*, pp. 36–71.

his breast, he chose valour in preference to life'.[22] But although Tyrtaeus'
poetry has such close affinities to the Homeric inheritance, perhaps alluding directly to the epics as we know them, it has lost the subtleties and
ironies of the Homeric text proper: neither Homer nor his characters ever
invoke the idea that patriotic virtue involves a wish to die for its own sake.[23]

Evidence in a similar direction is provided by Simonides' elegiac poem
celebrating the recent victory of the Greeks over the Persians at Plataea in
479 BCE.[24] The poem begins with an invocation of Achilles, giving him the
status of one venerated in hero-cult: the address *chaire* . . ., 'Be glad . . .' can
be heard as signifying that he is one of the blessed or immortalised dead of
old, to whom the dead of the battle will be assimilated.[25] The concrete
reality of the heroic presence in this war should not be underestimated: in
the same campaign, according to Herodotus, Achilles' father Peleus and his
brothers were brought (in the form of statues) from their home in Aegina
to be present at the great sea-battle at Salamis.[26] Fundamental in Simonides
is the fact that the heroic race was short-lived, 'swift to doom' (*ōkumoros*:
fr. 11.18 in West, *IEG2*), an adjective that Thetis applies to Achilles in the
climactic scene discussed earlier in this chapter (*Il.* 18.95). In the invocation of Achilles, to judge by the surviving fragments, the focus was on his
glorious death:

> It was not another mortal, a creature of a day, who overmastered you,
>   but you were mastered when you were struck by the hands of Apollo.
>   (Simonides, fr. 11.7–8 in West, *IEG2*, with restorations)[27]

When the heroes went on to sack 'the city much sung of' (fr. 11.13), says
Simonides, they were made famous by Homer's poetry: revealingly, however, the events of the war that he specifies are not those of the *Iliad* – they
are the death of Achilles, the sack of the city, the homecomings of the heroes
(fr. 11.6–19).[28] The standardised image of Achilles was not dependent on the

[22] Tyrtaeus, *Testimonia* 9: Gerber, *GEP*, pp. 32–33.   [23] See below on Hector, p. 322 with n. 20.
[24] I cite the fragments with the standard numeration as at West, *IEG2* 2.114–22. The fundamental
   collection of studies is Boedeker and Sider 2001, with a further edition of the fragments and
   accompanying translation. For the discussion in this chapter see esp. West 1993; Boedeker
   2001a and 2001b; Bremmer 2006; Grethlein 2010: 47–73.
[25] Boedeker 2001a: 156–7, building on Sourvinou-Inwood's (1995: 180–216) analysis of *chaire*
   'hail!' as implying blessedness in the afterlife. However, Bremmer 2006: 25 argues against this
   interpretation and holds that the address *chaire* merely signals a turning-point in the discourse
   of the poem. Cf. Van Wees 2005.
[26] Herodotus, *Histories* 8.83–4, with 8.64.
[27] This is a conjectural rendering, using the supplements proposed by M. L. West.
[28] Interestingly, ancient scholarship preserved the tradition that Simonides, like Ibycus, had told
   the story that Achilles was married to Medea in his afterlife on the Elysian plain (scholiast on

text of the *Iliad* at all. He became a symbol of the 'beautiful death' and an idealised image of heroic glamour, but Homer's exploration of the Wrath and its aftermath does not govern that image: rather, it should be seen as a meditation upon the image's inherent problems.

For a more fine-grained response we must look later in time, to the Athens of the (so-called) Classical period.[29] Plato's *Apology* is one of many works imagining or re-creating the speech that Socrates made at his trial on a capital charge – directed at a jury of several hundred male Athenians, randomly chosen from all strata of the society of the free-born, and perhaps dominated by those poor enough to be attracted to jury service by the daily wage. Socrates is explaining why he has followed his life's mission: specifically, why he has obeyed the god's command that he should spend his time 'seeking wisdom and investigating myself and other men' (*Apology* 28 e), inviting envy and resentment by asking them awkward questions and undermining their security and self-satisfaction (*Apology* 29 c–30 b, etc.). He imagines someone asking him if he is not ashamed to have practised the way of life that is now leading him towards a death sentence. The answer is that the demigods who died at Troy would seem absurd (*phauloi*) if judged by that principle (*Apology* 28 b–c). Among them he enlarges upon the case of Achilles,

> who despised danger in comparison with enduring disgrace to such an extent that when he told her that he would kill Hector, his mother (who was a goddess) spoke, I believe, such words as these: 'O my child, if you avenge the murder of your friend Patroclus and kill Hector,' she said, 'doom is ready for you straight after Hector': and on hearing this he belittled death and danger, but feared much more to live as a coward (*kakos*) and not to take vengeance for his friends, and he said 'Let me die at once, setting justice on one who did injustice, so that I will not remain here to be laughed at by the beaked ships, a burden on the ploughland.' You do not think that he considered death and danger, do you? (*Apology* 28 c 1–28 d 5)

As if recalling the scene in the poem from memory, Socrates maps it onto the situation of a soldier whose sense of values forces him to undergo mortal danger. As he goes on, he makes this still clearer:

Apollonius of Rhodes, *Argonautica* 4.814–15a; see Simonides fr. 558 at Campbell, *GL* 3.448–9). This is evidently an antecedent or variant of the story of his revitalisation on the Isles of the Blest, as alluded to in Phaedrus in the *Symposium*. Even assuming that the tradition on Simonides is accurate, however, there is no guarantee that the Plataea poem was the place where he mentioned this version of Achilles' afterlife.

[29] Useful treatments of the image of Achilles in the *Apology* are Metcalf 2009; Kohen 2013: 81–102. On Plato's reception of Homeric material in general see Yamagata 2012.

> I believe that wherever a man takes his stand (*heauton taxēi*), either after
> deciding this is the best thing to do or because he has been set there by his
> leader, there he must remain and face the danger, and must not make the
> slightest reckoning of death or of anything else except disgrace. (*Apology*
> 28 d 6–10)

The verb that I have translated 'takes his stand' refers specifically to mar-
shalling men for battle – the phrase could equally be translated 'occupies his
place in the battle-line'. Socrates goes on to name the battles in which he, like
other citizen-soldiers, duly obeyed his commanders and risked death by
remaining where he was stationed: Potidaea, Amphipolis, Delium (28
d 10–29 a 1). That this is a man's duty is taken as the shared belief of the
Athenian community, and he extends the same principle to his own obedi-
ence to the god's command that he risk death by his search for wisdom.

   Elsewhere in Plato's reimagining of Socrates' response to his condemnation, the image of Achilles appears again. In the *Crito*, a dramatic dialogue
set after the conclusion of the trial in the prison where Socrates awaits
execution, he tells Crito that he has had a dream in which a woman
appeared to him and said, '*On the third day from now you would reach
Phthia of the rich soil*' (*Crito* 44 b 1–2). These are Achilles' words when he
tells the Embassy that he is going to abandon the war and go home (*Il.*
9.363). In the immediate context the dream-figure seems to be predicting
the day on which he will depart in death, but as the dialogue develops and
Crito tries to persuade Socrates to escape from the unguarded prison, the
words take on a new meaning: just as Socrates will refuse this chance and
will undergo death for the sake of his ideals, so Achilles did not return to
Phthia as he had threatened, but remained at Troy and died for the sake of
his need for revenge.

   On this reading, then, the virtue that Socrates sees in Achilles is bound
up with devotion to duty, which means vindicating the honour of the man
he loved. The same theme is taken up again in Plato's *Symposium*, in
Phaedrus' speech in extravagant praise of the god Love. Phaedrus says
that one of a pair of lovers will go to any length to avoid disgrace in the eyes
of the other, and will even accept death for love's sake (*Symposium* 178
d 1ff.). Achilles is his climactic example:

> [T]he gods honoured Achilles son of Thetis and sent him to the Isles of
> the Blest, because when he heard from his mother that he would die after
> killing Hector, but that if he went home he would die in old age, he was so
> brave that he chose to bring help to his lover Patroclus, and in avenging
> him he did not merely die for his sake, but died after him, for Patroclus

had already been killed; and on that account the gods in their admiration
gave him this special honour, because he set such value on his beloved.
(*Symposium* 179 e 1–180 a 3)

Phaedrus' speech has become famous because it assumes that the relationship between the two heroes is sexual, a belief for which there is no clear
support in the Homeric text; but this is not the only way that it reflects
a skewed and indirect reception. He has merged two quite separate episodes into one, Achilles' choice between life and glory in Book 9 and his
response to Hector's death in Book 18; and he connects this in turn to the
legend that Achilles was granted eternal life on the Isles of the Blest, which
looks not to the *Iliad* but to Hesiod and perhaps the *Aethiopis*. In other
words, even if Phaedrus (or Plato through Phaedrus) is thinking about
a text of Homer much the same as ours, he is filtering and reshaping it
through the wider traditions of the Trojan War – including, presumably,
the oral traditions of the time, but also later literary creations like the
Achillean tragedies of Aeschylus, to which he refers elsewhere in the same
passage. This is Homer's Achilles reimagined and distorted, perhaps also
sanitised and made conventional. The Spartan ideal tells men to choose
'noble fame' in preference to life, but the *Iliad* turns on Achilles' failed
attempt to reject the life that will lead to 'imperishable fame'. In Homer's
depiction, when his plan turns awry and he is forced to accept death and
glory as the price of taking vengeance on Hector, his unbending defiance is
much more than an image of what is expected of all young men who go to
fight: this is a man whose intensity of suffering, as well as his divine blood
and unmatchable valour, place him outside the limits of mortal experience.

Achilles rises up transformed

In his separation from social values the Iliadic Achilles will move, as
Aristotle says of the man who rejects community, towards the state of
a god or of a wild beast (*Politics* 1253 a 28–9). The former comes to
prominence first. Achilles' return to combat has been delayed while new
armour is being made for him by Hephaestus, and without him the Greeks
are about to lose the struggle over the dead Patroclus (*Il.* 18.161–5); at the
suggestion of Hera's messenger Iris he suddenly takes a stand unclothed on
the rampart overlooking the battlefield:

> But Achilles rose up, dear to Zeus, and Athene around
> his strong shoulders cast the tasselled goatskin;

> his head she encircled with a cloud, bright one among goddesses,
> a golden cloud, and from it she made burn a flame that appeared to all.
>
> (*Il.* 18.203–6)

The 'goatskin', the *aigis*, is the divine garment that warlike Athene has from her father Zeus: with the divine light that is cast around Achilles, it makes him seem superhuman. In a complex simile Homer compares the light rising up from his head to the fires sent up by the people in a besieged city, signalling to their allies to come to their aid:

> As when smoke, coming from a city, reaches the high air,
> from a distant island around which enemies are fighting,
> who all day long are struggling in hateful war
> from their own city, and at the sinking of the sun
> watchfires blaze out in succession, and high up a gleam
> arises darting up for those who dwell nearby to see,
> in hope that they will come in ships to defend them from harm:
> so from Achilles' head the brightness reached the high air.
>
> (*Il.* 18.207–14)

Like many significant Homeric similes, this works by reversal:[30] the fire on Achilles' head is the opposite of a beacon appealing for hope, being a sign of his hostility and also of his separation from the ways of other men (cf. *Il.* 18.215–16). Naked and isolated, he cries out three times and Athene's voice mingles with his own: this trumpet-like voice and the preternatural light set blazing on his forehead seem to raise him above the human level. The Trojan forces are flung into disarray in their terror, chariots are driven into confusion and men are trampled to death (*Il.* 18.229–31).[31] But although the image of movement towards the state of a god, or virtual god, dominates this first revelation of his new mood on the battlefield, in the scenes that follow it is the image of the beast – lion or wolf or leopard – that will emerge with growing clarity in the depiction of the doomed man.

---

[30] For 'reverse similes' see esp. *Il.* 24.480–4, where Achilles reacts to seeing Priam as men react to seeing a murderer in their midst; *Od.* 8.523–31, where Odysseus, hearing of his own exploits as a sacker of cities, weeps as a woman weeps during the fall of her city; *Od.* 5.432–5, where Odysseus' skin ripped off on the rocks is like an octopus dragged from the seabed with pebbles adhering to its feet. On the concept of the 'reverse simile' in general see H. P. Foley 2009; Ready 2011: 265–6 with n. 12; and see further below, pp. 296–297.

[31] The suggestion that the underlying image is one of the *magical* destructive power of the hero's cry is thought-provoking but seems to me to go beyond the sense of the passage (cf. Griffin 1980: 39).

13 | From lamentation to vengeance

Gilgamesh turns from the life of action and achievement to a quest that moves first towards escape from mortality, and then towards wisdom, but Achilles' awareness of his coming death is inextricably bound up with his urge to revenge, and he will be impelled not to inward reflection but to outward violence. Though both are moving towards confrontation with their own deaths, they are doing so along utterly different paths; nonetheless, we will see that at the moment of the initial response to the companion's death their depictions coalesce, right down to the details of the imagery that expresses their grief and turmoil.

A lioness deprived of her cubs

When Achilles' display on the rampart has driven back the Trojans, the Greeks bring back the dead Patroclus and the mourning begins (*Il.* 18.231–42).[1] He leads them in their wailing through the night:

> Among them Achilles began the close-packed lamentation,
> setting his man-slaying hands on the breast of his companion,
> moaning in close succession, like a lion (*lis*) fine-bearded
> whose cubs a deer-hunting man has snatched away
> from the dense wood. It is in anguish coming after,
> and goes through many hollows searching after the man's traces,
> in hope to find him, for bitter bile grips it:
> so, groaning deeply, he spoke to the Myrmidons . . .   (*Il.* 18.316–23)

There are remarkably close correspondences here with *Gilgamesh* (above, pp. 89–91). When Gilgamesh embraced the dead Enkidu in the midst of his lamentation, he 'felt his heart, but it was not beating any more' (*SBV* VIII.58), just as Achilles here places his hands on the breast of the dead Patroclus.[2] The lion-simile that follows matches the central image of Gilgamesh in his agony:

---

[1] The narrative sequence is interrupted here by a move to the Trojan host and Hector's deliberations (*Il.* 18.243–314), but continues seamlessly once the focus returns to the Greeks.
[2] West (1997: 342) points out that whereas Gilgamesh touches the corpse to find that the heart is not beating, in Achilles' case the gesture 'has lost its rationale' – which can be restated as saying

> He covered (his) friend, (veiling) his face like a bride,
> circling around him like an eagle.
> Like a lioness who is deprived of her cubs,
> he kept turning about, this way and that.   (*SBV* VIII 59–62)

A lioness deprived of her cubs: the same word-picture at the same point in the narrative, the hero's mourning over the corpse after the untimely and senseless death of his friend.

Two striking identities of detail emerge from a closer look at the variant readings of the two manuscript witnesses, respectively a tablet from the Ashurbanipal archive at Nineveh and an Assyrian exercise tablet from Sultantepe with instances of unusual variant wording as well as errors and oddities of transcription. The Nineveh text uses the Akkadian feminine noun *nēštu*, gendered as 'lioness', while the other manuscript uses a Sumerian logogram without specifying that the beast is female. Given the overall character of the Sultantepe manuscript, the latter is probably error or vagueness on the scribe's part.[3] Following the Nineveh tablet, then, Gilgamesh's beast is female; similarly in the Greek, the noun *lis* 'lion' could grammatically be either gender, but the accompanying adjective 'fine-bearded' (*ēugeneios*) was taken by ancient scholars to indicate a lioness, on the grounds that the female is distinguished by her beard and the male by his mane.[4]

The second point is contextual: why would this beast have lost her cubs in the first place? For the Iliadic simile, it has been suggested (without any reference to *Gilgamesh*) that a possible background may lie in the Mesopotamian – and specifically Assyrian – practice of trapping animals from the wild in order to rear them in captivity for use as stock in royal gardens or victims in ritualised hunting.[5] This time it is the Sultantepe manuscript that throws up the parallel: here the key line (*SBV* VIII 61) has a variant wording which makes perfect sense, translated 'whose cubs (are)

that its purpose is unspecified and could just as well be interpreted as a gesture of love in an extreme state of emotional turmoil (cf. Gazis 2018: 49–51).

[3] On the oddities and inaccuracies in the Sultantepe manuscript (George's MS *e*) see George 2003: 1.369–71, 1.408–9, with Gurney's suggestion that the scribe 'was working from dictation, without understanding what he was writing' (Gurney 1954: 90). George's transliteration of the passage (George 2003: 1.656, at line 61) shows that the relevant sign here in this manuscript is the Sumerogram UR.MAH, 'lion': Gurney had represented this as *nēšu*, Akkadian for a (male) lion, in his original publication (Gurney 1954: 93, at line rev. 14), and this is repeated by West 1997: 342.

[4] Schol. AT on *Il.* 18.318 (see Edwards 1991: 184, note on *Il.* 18.318).

[5] See Alden 2005, citing royal inscriptions from the Neo-Assyrian period. On royal lion-hunts in artistic iconography see also Ataç 2010, esp. 16–18, 70–4.

in pits' – clearly referring to the use of hidden pitfalls to trap the cubs.[6] The scribe or his exemplar understood the simile scene in just the same way as has been proposed for the Iliadic lines.

These correlations on three levels – the details of the image, the scene to which it is applied, and its location in the sequence of the narrative – are so precise that they go beyond anything that could be attributed to general stylistic similarities between the two narrative traditions, or to what might be described as 'floating motifs'. Everything points to the conclusion that at this point the composer of the *Iliad* is somehow involved with *Gilgamesh*.[7] This intertextual configuration demands an explanation, however tentative it must remain at this stage of our discussion. To return to the terminology suggested in the Introduction (above, pp. 31–34), what we have seen meets the formal criteria for an *implicit quotation*: the Greek poet seems to be recognising and exploiting the parallel between Achilles' grief and that of Gilgamesh.

However, to say that the simile originated in *Gilgamesh* is not to suggest that it is in any way alien to the discourse of the *Iliad*.[8] As we will shortly see, it is quintessentially Homeric – without *Gilgamesh* before us, we would never have guessed at its Mesopotamian affinities. This might be seen as an example of 'art that hides art', a technique of assimilation where the source text is completely obscured in what is produced: or we could speculate (if no more) that there may once have been an audience or readership ready to recognise the resonance for what it is, so that it would serve as an active *allusion* to the mourning for Enkidu.[9] Alternatively, one could guess that the simile originated in a pre-Homeric narrative in which the relationship with *Gilgamesh* was openly and even persuasively exploited, but that when it passed to the *Iliad* poet its original intertextual network was forgotten. Either way, at this stage in the narrative the details of the texts are pointing towards something increasingly resembling an intertextual unity, at least from our own viewpoint across the millennia.

Let us now explore the further resonances of the simile within the *Iliad*. Across the whole poem or even across the epic genre as a whole, it forms part of a chain of imagery in which individual lion-scenes reverberate with each other.[10] Several such similes match the warrior's mood to that of a lion

[6] George (2003: 2.857) describes this variant as the result of corruption. However, unlike many of the other variant readings in the manuscript (on which see above), it makes perfectly good sense in context, perhaps as a contextual gloss replacing the original phrasing.
[7] The correlation between these two similes has been noticed many times. See West 1997: 341–3, with references to earlier scholarship in n. 19.
[8] See Introduction, p. 33 with 112, for Burkert's 'argument from isolation' as a criterion for identifying 'eastern motifs' in Homer.
[9] See also below, p. 333.   [10] For bibliography see below, Ch. 14, n. 6.

protecting its young. So, for example, our simile looks back to one in the preceding episode of the combat over the dead Patroclus:

> Ajax, covering Menoitios' son with his broad shield,
> stood like some lion over its own cubs,
> when, as the lion leads those helpless ones, hunting men
> meet them in the wood ...   (*Il.* 17.132–5)

In turn this looks back to another at the start of the combat over Patroclus, when Menelaus stood over the corpse like a cow over her calf (*Il.* 17.4–5): in terms of the visual themes of the *Iliad*, all three similes are part of a mutually reinforcing sequence.[11] Looking more widely, the association of the lion with frantic despair is also paralleled in the *Odyssey*, when Penelope is troubled over how to resist the men who are trying to pressurise her into marriage:

> Just as a lion ponders among the crowd of men
> in fear, when they have drawn a guileful circle around him,
> so was she considering when unhappy sleep came upon her ...
>   (*Od.* 4.791–3)

Here the *psychological* state of the lion is remarkably close to that of Achilles in his simile – the verb *mermērixe*, rendered above as 'ponders', suggests a state of troubled anxiety more sharply than I can suggest with any one English word.[12]

In its more immediate context in the *Iliad*, the simile of the trapped cubs is the first in a long sequence of co-ordinated beast-images exploring the inner state of Achilles as he moves from mourning to fury, which will be traced in full in the next chapter of this book. The essence is in the word *cholos*, the force that 'seizes' their mother when she turns to go after the hunter. As we saw earlier, *cholos* is literally identified with bile, and in Homeric psychology it is one of the liquid essences that fill the breast with emotions and passions.[13] Throughout the *Iliad*, the swelling of bile has been the force driving Achilles to resentment, anger and violence: from now on, it will propel the lion-like rage that sends him towards his final vengeance on Hector.

---

[11] In broader terms, the simile's imagery has strong affinities elsewhere in Homer. For example Edwards (1991: 63, note at *Il.* 17.3–6) adduces as parallels the Greek host compared to wasps or other insects defending their children (*Il.* 12.167–72, 16.259–66), and even Odysseus in his frustrated endurance growling like a bitch over her puppies (*Od.* 20.14–16).
[12] See Pache 2016 for the simile of Penelope compared with Iliadic lion-images.
[13] See above, esp. pp. 232–233, 261.

After the simile of the trapped cubs, Achilles' groans develop into words addressed to all his Myrmidon followers, in which he looks back on his former hope that Patroclus would return home with the spoils from Troy, and foresees that he will now join him in death:

> But Zeus does not bring all men's thoughts to fulfilment for them:
> for it is ordained (*peprōtai*) for us to make red the same earth
> here at Troy . . .   (*Il.* 18.328–30)

At first hearing those words might suggest resignation, even stoicism, at the realisation that the end is inevitable; but Achilles now shifts to a sinister and unexpected vow:

> Now therefore, Patroclus, since after you I will go down below the earth,
> I will not perform your funeral rites, until I have brought here Hector's
> armour and his head, the one who murdered you of the great heart:
> and before the pyre I will cut the throats of twelve
> gleaming children of the Trojans, filled with rage (*cholōtheis*) at your
>   death.   (*Il.* 18.333–7, sim. 23.23–4)

Achilles has announced that he will offer human sacrifice, and that he will mutilate and abuse the corpse of his enemy. This desire belongs ultimately in the culture of reciprocal payment that structures all the social interactions of Homeric warriors: its positive enactment is in the flow of honour and reward, but it also encompasses revenge as the exacting of penalties for harm done. *Poinē* 'recompense, punishment' is another reflex of the same lexical root as *timē* 'honour', and they each look to the same verb *apotinemen* 'to exact payment, to recompense', in positive and negative aspects.[14] But to sacrifice captives and mutilate the dead is to go beyond any conceivable version of such a norm. In Greek thought (at least as attested in later writings), such behaviour would entail pollution or uncleanness, marking out the inhuman savagery that puts the beast or the barbarian apart from civilised humanity.[15] Although dire extravagances are often threatened in the rhetoric of verbal duelling before combat,[16] his vow cannot be explained away as mere bombastic language:

[14] On *poinē* as a transaction that rectifies an imbalance in status by effecting a transfer from the offending party to the aggrieved, see Wilson 2002a, esp. 13–39. Wilson's analysis is open to the objection that it is overly schematic, and that the meanings she attributes to *poinē* and *apoina* do not coincide with the evidence for the uses of those words in other Greek literature: see the important criticisms and modifications by Cairns 2011a.

[15] On prohibitions and sacral practices concerned with the corpse, see Parker 1983, esp. 34–48, 66–73 and cf. Bendlin 2007.

[16] On the (potential or threatened) mutilation of the corpse as a recurrent *Iliad* motif, see esp. Vernant 2001a [1982].

in due course he will indeed cut the throats of twelve noble Trojan youths and throw them into the funeral pyre to burn (*Il.* 23.174–83). If anywhere in the Homeric depiction of the heroic past there is an unmistakeable example of *hubris*, the outrageous behaviour that (according to the *Cypria* story) justifies Zeus in wiping out their entire race, it is here.

Maggots in the corpse

As we saw, Tablet VIII of the Standard Babylonian *Gilgamesh* is occupied by the protracted funeral rites of Enkidu – the grief of Gilgamesh, his long poem of lamentation, the making of the statue and the grave-goods. Similarly, the entire sequence of the *Iliad* in Books 18–23 is structured by the funeral of Patroclus, extended by shifts of narrative direction centred on the killing of Hector, which is essential for providing the dead man with due honour. Nor is this digressive pattern solely a narrative device: within the action it takes tangible form when Achilles fears the corpse is rotting, as he tells his mother,

> But most terribly
> I fear that now Menoitios' mighty son will be
> entered by flies through his wounds pierced by bronze,
> and that they will breed maggots there, and defile the dead man –
> for the force of life has been put to death[17] – and all his flesh will rot.
>
> (*Il.* 19.23–7)

Here another motif from *Gilgamesh* has surfaced at the same moment of the event-sequence, because the defilement that Achilles fears is what actually happened, according to Gilgamesh, because of the delay with Enkidu's funeral:

> [I did not give him up for burial,]
> [until a maggot fell from his nostril.]   (*SBV* X 59–60)[18]

This sits alongside the simile of the lioness and cubs as another indication that at this point the intertextual relationship between the *Iliad* and

---

[17] The difficult phrase *ek d' aiōn pephatai* must be read as a parenthesis or interjection here, and I tentatively take it to mean that the essence of vitality has been 'killed' and destroyed in death. Much depends on the translation of *aiōn*, which normally and etymologically means 'time [of life], span of time', but in the language of early Greek poetry it sometimes refers to vitality as manifested in bodily substances such as tears or bone-marrow. See Clarke (forthcoming (b)).

[18] On the restoration of these lines see above, Ch. 4, n. 3.

Gilgamesh is an objective reality;[19] like the lion-simile, however, it too has been seamlessly integrated, and it surfaces only as a fear, which is answered by his mother's assurance that the corpse will be divinely protected from decay (*Il.* 19.29–33).

Prominent in the long sequence that follows is the description of the new armour that Hephaestus makes for Achilles. The shield is a foundational example of *ekphrasis*, the description of a work of art whose inner narrative takes on poetic life of its own.[20] The scenes on it go beyond the turmoil of the war to become a representation of the totality of the world, but among them there is one that speaks clearly to Achilles' bile and rage. Two cities are shown, one at peace and one at war; paradoxically, perhaps, it is the city at peace that evokes the state of mind of Achilles, being the setting for a legal dispute:[21]

> The people were gathered in the meeting-place; there a quarrel
> had arisen, and two men were quarrelling over the penalty-money (*poinē*)
> for a man who had been killed: one man said he would give over everything,
> declaring it to the community, but the other refused to accept anything.
>
> (*Il.* 18.497–500)

Homicide has been committed, and the killer – or perhaps the head of his family – wants to pay compensation or 'blood-money', *poinē*, to the family of the dead man. The implication is that by refusing to take this money, 'the other' – that is, the injured party – insists on continuing the pursuit of violent vengeance. In the Embassy scene, Ajax described Achilles' obstinacy in an almost identical word-picture:

---

[19] West 1997: 343.

[20] On the thematics of the Shield of Achilles see (e.g.) the classic treatment by Taplin 2001 [1980], with the rigorous (but potentially over-schematic) interpretation of the dynamics of *ekphrasis* by Becker 1995.

[21] In my translation I adopt the interpretation proposed by Westbrook 1992 and followed (e.g.) by Edwards (1991, at the end of his note on the passage), and by Wilson 2002a: 159–60. The question hinges on the force of the infinitives *apodounai* 'to give over' and *helesthai* 'to take'. In each case the aorist stem-form means that the infinitive may be interpreted either (a) in terms of *aspect*, referring to the completion of the action without specifying whether it is in the past or the future, or (b) in terms of *tense*, making it refer to past time relative to the main verb. The tense-based interpretation would lead to the translations 'declared that he had given over', and 'denied that he had accepted'. This would be consistent with the normal patterns of later Greek syntax (which explains why the bT scholia take it this way), but would yield a relatively trivial meaning – the dispute would be over a mere question of fact, whether the money has or has not been paid. In Homeric Greek, however, the aspect-based interpretation would be just as normal grammatically, and it also yields far stronger sense in context. For these reasons I adopt it here.

> ... a man accepts *poinē* from the murderer
> of his brother, or of his son who has been killed;
> this one remains there in the community after making the big payment,
> and the other's heart and over-manly thought-breath are curbed
> when he has received the *poinē* ...   (*Il.* 9.632–6)

By the time Hephaestus fashions the Shield, Patroclus' death has been the consequence of Achilles' refusal to turn away from bitterness and 'tame his great *thumos*' (*Il.* 9.496).[22] When the time comes to accept the arms, his followers do not dare to look on them in their terror (*Il.* 19.12–15), but the anger grows further in him at the sight:

> But when Achilles
> saw the arms, then bile (*cholos*) went into him the more, and his eyes
> beneath his eyebrows flashed terribly like a gleam of light.   (*Il.* 19.15–17)

The force filling his breast is the same force that made him unable to yield to pity and mercy, and his shield will now carry a visible sign that he rejects the very possibility of extinguishing this bile.

Achilles returns to war

When Achilles prepares for combat by making peace with Agamemnon, his words have a brutal clarity of purpose. He wishes Brises' daughter had died as soon as she was captured, so as never to bring about the quarrel between them (*Il.* 19.59–62); he sets aside his wrath and resentment against the commander, because all that matters now is that the men rally for his surge against the Trojans (67–73). Agamemnon's long theological speech of apology or self-defence, and his renewed offer of women and treasure and princely honour, are met with impatient dismissal: Achilles does not care whether he gets these gifts or not, because his only concern is to end the delay and begin the onslaught (146–53).[23] When Agamemnon and the other leaders prudently advise a proper meal, Achilles refuses to eat with his fellow men, and Zeus arranges that he is fed in secret with the gods' own food of nectar and ambrosia (*Il.* 19.340–354). Ostensibly the refusal to eat together expresses the urgency of Achilles' urge for vengeance: but it means something more sinister as well, because in this as in any closely bonded

---

[22] The image implied by the verb *damazo* is best visualised as taming or breaking a horse.

[23] Achilles describes what has been happening with the infinitive verb *klotopeuein* (19.149), paired with *diatribein* 'to waste [time]'. Coincidentally or not, the verb *klotopeuō* is attested nowhere else in early Greek literature.

group of fighting men the feast is an enactment of unity and comradeship –
the social values that Achilles has abandoned.

The prophecy of the horse

Achilles clothes himself in the divine armour (*Il.* 19.351–98), and the
solemn – even cosmic – significance of this moment is marked by
a sequence of similes as the warriors gather. The earth shines or laughs
with the light that flashes from the bronze (*Il.* 19.362–3) – perhaps
a mere figure of speech, or perhaps a hinting allusion to the goddess
Gaia, whose burden is about to be lightened all the more by the coming
battle.[24] Then comes one of those rare moments when the *Iliad* seems
to move onto a more extreme level of fantastic imagination: Achilles
speaks with his horses, which we have already seen as symbols of his
parentage and his destined death.[25] He tells them to keep him safe, not
to abandon him as they abandoned Patroclus (*Il.* 19.400–403), and
through the power of Hera one of them, Xanthus, is given the power
to speak: this strange motif is perhaps drawn from the traditions of the
Theban war in the previous generation of the heroic race.[26] The horse
renews the prophecy of death:

> We two would run as fast as the breath of Zephyrus,
> who they say is the swiftest one of all; but for you now
> it is apportioned (*morsimon*) to be brought down in force by a god and
>   a man.   (*Il.* 19.415–17)

Achilles responds in almost the same words that he used to Thetis
(*Il.* 18.120–5):

---

[24] This should not be pressed too far, since the earth is named non-mythologically here as *chthōn*.

[25] On the horses in connection with Achilles' death see above, pp. 256–257, with Heath 1992: 396–9.

[26] Homer refers in passing to Arion, the horse of Adrastus 'of divine parentage' (*Il.* 23.346), and the D-scholion on this passage (combined with a mention in Pausanias) provides the information that in the Cyclic *Thebaid* Adrastus escaped from the siege on his wondrous horse Arion, child of Poseidon by a Fury (*Erinys*). In Roman sources this horse is said to have spoken words of prophecy: note esp. Statius' phrase 'Arion warning of death' (*Thebaid* 11.442–43), and cf. Propertius' 'Arion of the voice' (*Elegies* 2.34.37). This encourages the guess that the same prophecy was in the Cyclic *Thebaid*, and thus that there may be an intertextual link with the present prophecy by Achilles' horse. See West, *GEF*, pp. 52–5, Cyclic *Thebaid*, fr. 11–12, with West's n. 11 there; Davies (2014: 84–8) examines this and other evidence more sceptically.

> Well I know it myself, that it is my portion (*moros*) to die here,
> far from my dear father and mother; but nonetheless
> I will not stop before I have driven the Trojans far enough through war.
>
> (*Il.* 19.421–3)

But there is a difference now, the picture is becoming clearer: the horse has specified that his death will be at the hands of 'a god and a man'. The god is Apollo, who has already taken the lead in the killing of Patroclus, and the man (as will become clear) is Paris, the one whose lust and dishonesty began the war.

Achilles goes to battle now as one marked as the target for Apollo's arrow. Apollo's association with Achilles' mortality runs deep, but its ultimate motivation is never stated: in our discussion above (pp. 184–188) we had to turn to non-Homeric evidence, largely vase-painting, to find clear signs that the god's anger could be explained by the vicious killing of Troilus at the beginning of the war. As ever, we are left to speculate about the causes of the gods' friendships and hatreds. Just as *Gilgamesh* leaves us guessing as to how Enlil's hatred, or 'destiny' itself, might be the unseen hand behind all the disasters, so here Homer offers no ordered explanation for the workings of the divine will, nothing to give a happier answer to the problem of human misery than the words Shakespeare in *Lear* puts in Gloucester's mouth when he has been blinded and tormented:

> As flies to wanton boys are we to the gods:
> They kill us for their sport.   (*King Lear*, Act 4 Sc. 1)

14 | Achilles like a lion

With the narrative approaching its murderous climax, the next scene is marked by the personal involvement of many gods. At Zeus' command the Olympians have been gathered to council by Themis, the personification of eternal law; Zeus, taking pleasure in the spectacle (*Il.* 20.23–4),[1] sends them down to stir up the conflict and prevent Achilles from storming the Trojan wall 'beyond the proper portion' or 'beyond his destiny', *huper moron* (*Il.* 20.29–30). Athene cries out against the Trojans in union with Strife in person, *Eris* (*Il.* 20.48): it is suggestive that Eris is named here, especially since she emerges from a meeting planned by Zeus and Themis.[2] Here stands the goddess who personifies the crisis that began the anger of Achilles[3] – and who, in the *Cypria*, acted out the plans of Zeus and Themis to spark off the entire war. This configuration of deities points to the cosmic scale of what is happening. Likewise Zeus thunders, Poseidon shakes the earth, and Hades fears that his subterranean realm will be broken open (*Il.* 20.61–65)[4] – an image that perhaps looks back to lost narratives of the battle between Olympian gods and Titans in the depths of time.[5]

As the action unfolds, Homer evokes Achilles' state of mind through a series of variations on the lion-imagery that we saw first evoked in the mourning for Patroclus. Coming as they do in the context of battle, the conceptual associations of this series of similes are vital to our theme. In the symbolic world of early Greek poetry, the meaning of the lion is

---

[1] On the notion that the gods take *pleasure* in the spectacle of war and human suffering, cf. Clay 2011, esp. 3–6; Golden 1989: 9–11, responding to Griffin 1980: 184–204.

[2] On the significance of the pairing of Zeus and Themis here, there are thought-provoking observations by Janko in his note on *Il.* 15.87–8 (Janko 1992: 237–8). See further above, pp. 157–162.

[3] Compare Achilles' complaint against strife, *eris* (*Il.* 18.107), a passage without explicit personification (above, pp. 260–263).

[4] See further Gazis 2018: 41–5.

[5] On possible resonances with the Titanomachy in such passages see Mondi 1986: 42–4, and compare the evidence for the Cyclic *Titanomachy* (D'Alessio 2015: 202–12).

fraught and ambivalent: the epithet 'lion-spirited' (*thumoleonta*, *Il.* 5.639, 7.228) for Achilles or Heracles is potentially problematic where modern-language terms like *lionhearted* are merely conventional and glibly positive.[6] It is fundamental that the lion seizes on the raw flesh of its victims, and is thus potentially an image of barbarity. Its energy and courage, the very qualities that make it admirable, are uncontrolled and unbounded and hasten its own death, as in the lion-simile of Patroclus in his fatal surge to the walls of Troy: 'its own valour (*alkē*) destroys it' (*Il.* 16.754).[7] The wild beast's fury can represent the savage joy of the warrior about to sate his desire for slaughter (see e.g. *Il.* 3.23–28), but it also implies his willing embrace of the prospect of death (see e.g. *Il.* 12.41–46, 12.299–308, 21.573–82). The dark resonances with Achilles' situation and state of mind are obvious.

Achilles' first single combat, with Aeneas, is marked by the most closely delineated of all these lion-similes:

> Achilles from the other side rose against him like a lion,
> marauding, whom men rush forward to kill,
> all the people gathered: the lion first, unheeding,
> goes in, but when one of those battle-swift youths
> strikes it with his spear, it crouches gaping-jawed, foam around its teeth
> appears, and in its heart its valiant spirit roars,
> with its tail its ribs and flanks on both sides
> it lashes, and urges itself on to fight,
> and flashing-eyed it is borne forward in strength, in hope to kill
> one of the men, or to be destroyed itself at the front of the throng:
> so Achilles was driven by his force and his over-manly thought (*thumos*)
> to go against great-hearted Aeneas.   (*Il.* 20.164–75)

The lion hurls itself towards the slaughter of its enemies but also, in an even balance of possibilities, towards the prospect of its own death. The gleam of its glare[8] resonates throughout the *Iliad* with a series of images of flashing

---

[6]   On the symbolic value of the lion in similes throughout the *Iliad*, and applied to Achilles in particular, see Lonsdale 1990; Clarke 1995a; Wilson 2002b; Heath 2005: 119–69; Gottschall 2008, esp. 160–5; Scott 2009: 65–77. On interpretative strategies for Homeric similes in general, a useful study is Danek 2006, treating the poet of *Iliad* and *Odyssey* as an individual whose similes represent an allusive and multivalent manipulation of (*ex hypothesi* oral) tradition.

[7]   For this formulation compare Andromache's warning to Hector, 'Your own valour (*menos*) will kill you' (*Il.* 6.407), and likewise 'its own bravery destroys it' in a simile-image of a boar to which Hector is compared (*Il.* 12.46). See further Clarke 1995a: 151–2; Graziosi and Haubold 2003.

[8]   The image recurs with the same unusual participle *glaukioōn* 'gleaming' in the Hesiodic *Shield of Heracles* (426–35), describing Heracles facing Ares in combat.

eyes,[9] starting with the first disastrous quarrel (*Il.* 1.104) and picked up, as we
have seen, in the eyes of Achilles when he sees the armour and is filled with
cholos (*Il.* 19.17). Now the image is focussed on the beast whose need to
throw itself on its enemies will push it towards the risk of self-destruction.

In the main narrative, too, Achilles' savagery has become bestial. He
selects the twelve Trojan youths, 'terrified like young deer' (*Il.* 21.29), to be
put to death as reciprocal payment (*poinē*, 21.28) for Patroclus, and the
same spirit drives him when he encounters Lycaon, a Trojan prince whom
he had previously captured but spared and sold back (*Il.* 21.34–48).[10]
Lycaon begs again for the mercy he received the last time, but Achilles'
answer shows how Patroclus' death has brought forward the prospect of
his own:

> But you, friend, die also: why do you wail like this?
> Patroclus also died, and he was a much better man than you.
> Do you not see me, how tall and beautiful I am?
> I am the son of a noble father, the mother who bore me is a goddess:
> but death and strong Portion (*Moira*) stand over me too.
> There will be a dawn or an evening or a noonday
> when someone in war will take my life-breath from me,
> striking me with a spear or with an arrow from a bowstring.
>
> (*Il.* 21.106–13)

It is difficult to tell whether such refusal of mercy would have been
condemned out of hand in the moral codes of those among whom the
poem was composed,[11] but it is impossible not to feel revulsion at the
grotesque mockery that Achilles hurls at Lycaon after he is vanquished:
Lycaon's mother will not mourn over him, he says, but the corpse will roll

---

[9] See Turkeltaub 2005, discussing these and other images of flashing eyes as a sign of warrior fury
in the *Iliad*.

[10] On the *Cypria* version of this episode, of which only the outline is known, see West, *EC* 122.

[11] The classic case of this question is posed when Adrestos, on his knees, begs Menelaus to spare
him for a ransom, but Agamemnon persuades his brother to put him to death (*Il.* 6.45–66).
Homer describes Agamemnon as *aisima pareipōn* (6.62): this invites the translation 'advising
appropriate things', which is the only possible meaning for the sole other instance of this phrase
in the *Iliad* (7.121). However, on the basis that the parent noun *aisa* is ambiguous between 'due
portion, share' and 'death, mortality', Goldhill (1990) has argued that the *aisima* of 6.62 are
'fatal things' rather than 'appropriate things', aligned in meaning with the formulaic phrase
aisimon ēmar 'fatal day, day of death'. If this is right, nothing like approval of killing a suppliant
is implied. However, it seems to me unlikely that the two instances of *aisima pareipōn* would
refer respectively to completely different parts of the semantic range of the parent noun. If we
discount Goldhill's argument, Agamemnon's viciousness (as we today might see it) is being
judged morally reasonable, perhaps especially in the circumstance of the broken truce. Cf.
Yamagata 1994: 118; Wilson 2002a: 166; Stoevesandt in Latacz et al. 2009: 152–5.

out to sea in the river-waters, and the fishes will leap in the waves after feeding on his flesh (*Il.* 21.122–7). In the *Odyssey* Odysseus, with the wisdom that comes of victory after a *return* from death, says that it is an unholy thing to speak words of triumph over the corpses of dead enemies (*Od.* 22.412): if this is a fixed and abiding rule of moral wisdom, Achilles by renouncing it has passed beyond the limits of human restraint and decency.

Achilles' words to Lycaon, cited above, also show that the shape of his own approaching death is growing clearer. Of its twin images of spear and arrow, the latter looks towards the narrative of Achilles' death in the Cyclic *Aethiopis* – shot by Paris before the walls of Troy with an arrow guided by Apollo (below, pp. 303–307).[12] This is again echoed in Achilles' words a little later, when the enraged river Scamander – himself a god, like any river – hurls his waters at him in anger, and Achilles fears that the torrent will batter him to death:

> No other of the immortals is so much to blame for this
> as my dear mother, who lulled me with lies:
> she said that below the wall of the armour-clad Trojans
> I would be destroyed by Apollo's swift missiles.   (*Il.* 21.275–8)

Again the clarity of the scene is increasing: it will be beside the walls, the arrow will be that of Apollo – the wording allows the possibility that the one who actually shoots it is a mortal, so this is precisely consistent with the *Aethiopis* version. Achilles begs to be saved from an undignified death by drowning, but when Poseidon reassures him his words are subtly ominous:

> Let your hands not cease from equal-matched battle,
> until you have driven the host to below Troy's famous walls,
> the Trojan host in flight, and after taking Hector's life-breath
> you will return to the ships: we grant that you will earn your boast.
>   (*Il.* 21.294–7)

Until . . . : Achilles will fight long enough to achieve his revenge and win his glory, but after that it will be time to cease, to make an end.

As he continues, these foreshadowings run alongside the increasing strangeness of his state of mind, which now attracts a significant name:

---

[12] For the pattern where two futures are foreseen and the second corresponds to that attested in the Cyclic tradition, compare Andromache's prediction, in her lament over Hector, that the child will *either* accompany her into slavery *or* be flung from the tower of Troy to the ground (*Il.* 24.732–8). The latter is what was narrated in the *Little Iliad* (West, *GEF*, pp. 134–41, *Little Iliad* fr. 18, 29; see also *EC* 216, 219–20).

> He pursued relentlessly with his spear, and forceful *lussa*
> ever held his heart, as he raged to win glory for himself.   (*Il.* 21.542–3)

This word *lussa* is built on the root *luk-* (< *wl̥kʷ-*), 'wolf', and it names what in our own language might be called rabid or berserk fury.[13] The concept represented by this etymology is still active when Greek thought links it to bestial aggression – for example, its close derivative appears in the collocation *kuna lussētēra* 'hound behaving like a wolf' (*Il.* 8.299).[14] This in turn draws in an association with the idea of delusion, of misguidedness: *lussa* is ascribed to Hector too in his surge against the Greeks, gripped by his false hope in Zeus' help (*Il.* 9.238–9), and he is called *lussōdēs* 'full of *lussa*'[15] when, as Poseidon alleges, he has formed the belief that he is himself a son of Zeus (13.53–4).[16]

Delusion and wolfishness: how do these ideas combine? The scattered Homeric examples can be usefully supplemented with a look forward in time to the richer evidence from Athenian tragedy, where the personified Lussa repeatedly figures as a character on stage. Aeschylus' *Xantriai* had her inspiring the followers of Dionysus to tear apart the god's enemy: in a surviving fragment the goddess speaks of 'the goad of *lussa*, the dart of the scorpion'.[17] When Euripides portrays the infanticide committed by Heracles, Lussa compares herself to hounds following a huntsman (*Heracles* 860–1), and even describes how she will take possession of Heracles:

> ... the sea, roaring with waves, will not be so wild,
> nor earth's quaking and the thunderbolt's sting, which breathes out
>   agonies,
> as I will be when I leap the distance across into Heracles' breast ...
>
>   (*Heracles* 861–3)

---

[13] On *lussa* and related forces in the *Iliad* see esp. Heath 2005: 135–43, with Redfield 1994: 201–2; cf. Seaford 1993: 142–6. For the current state of scholarship on the lore of the Northern *berserkr*, with which this Greek theme invites comparison, see O'Connor 2016.

[14] This is the heightened metaphorical language of insults, though it is remarkable that here too the reference is to Hector. The image of 'wolf' as an insult recurs in later Greek in the metaphorical language of political polemic (see Kunstler 1991).

[15] The formation in *–ōdēs* suggests that the meaning was originally something like 'smelling of *lussa*', but it is unlikely that this meaning is active in the second element of the compound: compare for example *psamathōdēs* (*Homeric Hymn to Hermes* 75, etc.), which seems to mean no more than 'sandy'.

[16] See below, pp. 322–323.

[17] Aeschylus, *Xantriai*, fr. 169 Sommerstein. Shapiro suggests (1993: 169–70) that this personification may even have been invented by the tragedians, starting with Aeschylus in this play.

This is a personal being, 'Night's Gorgon daughter, gleaming-faced with the hundred-headed gapings of serpents' (*Heracles* 883), but she is equally an intangible essence:[18] Lussa even describes Heracles' future suffering as *emas lussas*, 'my madnesses', letting the gap open up between the two senses of the word.[19]

The *Bacchae* presents a still more startling evocation, with *lussa* ascribed both to the fool who is led to destruction and the avengers who kill him like wild beasts.[20] Dionysus describes how the young king will be induced by 'giddy madness', *elaphrē lussa* (*Bacchae* 851), to spy on his followers disguised as a woman, so that he can be overpowered; when the time comes for them to attack and dismember him, the Chorus shape this into an image of the goddess:

> Go, swift hounds of Fury (*Lussa*), go to the mountain,
> where the daughters of Cadmus gather their band:
> goad them into frenzy
> against the man in woman's garb,
> the maddened one (*lussōdēs*) who spies upon the wild women.
>
> (*Bacchae* 977–81)

The wolfish associations are articulated in a distinct way here when Lussa is accompanied by a pack of hounds: they personify her destructive power and link her implicitly to the Erinyes, the Furies, but above all they associate this madness with the devouring of raw flesh, the rending (*sparagmos*) of Pentheus' body.[21] Similarly, a rare artistic depiction of Lussa from about the same period places her in a scene of savage violence by hounds: Actaeon is being torn apart by his own hunting-dogs after insulting Artemis, and the figure who gazes on the attack with hands outstretched is labelled *LUSA*, her head shown with the partial form (*protomē*) of a wolf or hound emerging from it (Fig. 22).[22] The extraordinarily heightened level of personification seen in these tragedies is characteristic of Euripides' generation,[23] but the correspondences between

---

[18] Franzino 1995 defends the sequence of lines found here in the manuscripts, and clarifies how Lussa accompanies Hera and Iris like hounds with a hunter. On the personified Lussa in this play in relation to the depiction of Heracles' madness as a bodily and potentially a medical phenomenon, cf. Holmes 2008, with Padel 1995: 17–20.

[19] Cf. above, p. 163 n. 53, and compare Teiresias' evocation of Dionysus in Euripides' *Bacchae*: since Dionysus *is* wine, in the offering of ritual libations 'one who was born a god is poured out for the gods' (*Bacchae* 284).

[20] See Segal 1997: 302, and cf. Dodds 1951: 64–101, 270–82.

[21] See Dodds 1960: 199, note at lines 977–8; cf. Padel 1995: 134–6.

[22] The vase is discussed by Shapiro 1993: 169–70.

[23] Cf. Papadopoulou 2005: 58–128, esp. 60–61, with Smith 2011: 36.

Fig. 22 Vase of *c.* 440 BCE, showing the death of Actaeon.

imagery and etymology are unlikely to have been invented out of nothing. Here and in Homer the association of *lussa* with hounds and wolves is tied to the psychological force of compulsive delusion.

No oaths between lions and men

These themes are heard most clearly when Achilles has finally encountered his enemy. Hector tries to set up a formal duel, with each man swearing that if he gains the victory he will return the other's body respectfully to his people (*Il.* 22.254–59),[24] but Achilles answers:

> Hector, *alaste*,[25] do not speak to me of sworn agreements:
> just as between lions and men there are no oaths to be trusted,

---

[24] Compare a more formal version of the same configuration in a set duel, *Il.* 7.76–91.

[25] The meaning of this word has always been disputed. Etymologically it seems to be associated with words meaning 'forget': thus 'doer of unforgettable deeds', or 'a man who cannot be ignored'. Many translators use contextual glosses here like 'wretch' or 'accursed', words that sound suitable in context but have no independent support.

> nor do wolves and sheep have the same thought in their breasts,
> but they think evil endlessly against each other,
> so for you and me there will be no friendship, nor will there be
> oaths between us, until one of us has fallen
> and with his blood gluts Ares, the warrior of the ox-hide shield.
>
> (*Il.* 22.261–7)

Achilles, as we have seen, uses the arts of language more subtly than other Iliadic warriors – singing of the heroes of the past like a poet, or explaining the bitterness of his feelings in rich imagery and even similes (above, pp. 221–223). Here that introspection is full of darkness when he compares *himself* to a wild beast, and does so in order to refuse to engage with the laws of human decency.[26] With the wild energy (*menos agrion*, 22.312–13) in whose grip he finally subdues Hector, he says that he will let the dogs and vultures defile him when Patroclus receives his burial rites (22.335–6); Hector with his last breath begs that his corpse be respected 'for the sake of your breath of death (*psuchē*), your knees[27] and your parents', and Achilles' reply fulfils the darkest implications of being like a lion or a wolf:

> Do not beg me, dog, in the name of my knees or my parents:
> I wish my fury (*menos*) and my thought-breath (*thumos*) would drive me
> to cut off your flesh and eat it raw, for the things you have done to me.
>
> (*Il.* 22.345–7)

It might have been possible to suppose that his earlier words of 'no oaths between lions and men' were mere hyperbole, but this latest threat confirms that their meaning revolves around the devouring of human flesh.

With his last words – and, one guesses, with the foresight granted to one on the point of death[28] – Hector reveals the consequences that will follow from Achilles' savagery:

---

[26] Clarke 1995a, 144–7; cf. Gottschall 2008, esp. 160–5, and compare the reformulation by Wilson 2002b, esp. at 240–1.

[27] In early Greek sources, both within and beyond Homer, the gesture of supplication – that is, of begging unconditionally for mercy – is regularly centred on seizing the knees of the assailant while invoking things symbolic of mortality (Gould 1973; Naiden 2006). It is doubtful whether this reflects the concept that the knees are in some sense the seat of vitality, as has sometimes been claimed (cf. Onians 1951: 174–86).

[28] For prophecy at the point of death, the other Homeric example is Patroclus (*Il.* 16.844–54), in a scene full of thematic and verbal resonances with the death of Hector. Independent Greek testimony to this idea is, however, limited. De Jong cites the words given by Plato to Socrates at the time of his condemnation to death: 'I am now at the point where men are most wont to prophesy, when they are about to die' (*Apology* 39 c: De Jong 2012: 149, note on lines 356–60).

> Take thought now, lest I become the cause of divine wrath (*mēnima*)
>   against you,
> on that day when Paris and Phoebus Apollo will destroy you,
> noble though you be, in front of the Scaean gates.   (*Il.* 22.358–60)

The prophecy is taking ever clearer form, naming even the point in the
circuit of the walls at which he will be shot. Whether or not there is room
here for deeper causes of vengeance, as suggested speculatively above (pp.
186–187), the immediate cause of Apollo's anger (*mēnima*) will be the
slaughter of Hector and the further insult of defiling the corpse and
refusing proper burial. The obvious implication is that this will fulfil
Thetis' prophecy, 'Death is waiting for you straight after Hector'. But as
soon as Hector has completed this causal chain, Achilles' answer sums up
his defiance:

> Die: but I will meet the death-demon (*kēr*), whenever
> Zeus wishes to bring fulfilment, and the other immortal gods.
>   (*Il.* 22.365–6)

There is an uncanny single-mindedness here: all Achilles' thought is driven
by the need to avenge Patroclus through the death and degradation of those
who killed him.

The mutilation of Hector

Is this the admirable steadfastness of one who puts duty and love above all
other things, or is it grief and anger pushing beyond the bounds of sanity?
Although, as we have seen (above, pp. 263–267), Plato's Socrates or
Phaedrus would encourage the former kind of reading, there is an unmistakeable sense of the sinister when Achilles is driven by the need to inflict
such terrible things on a man who is already dead. He begins to talk tactics,
planning to move his men closer towards the walls (*Il.* 22.381–4), but
suddenly he turns aside, using the same words as warriors do when moving
between cowardice and courage in battlefield soliloquy,[29] and remembers
a more pressing need:

> But why has my dear thought-breath spoken these things to me?
> He lies beside the ships, a corpse, unwept, unburied,
> Patroclus: him I will not forget, as long as
> I remain among the living and my dear knees are in motion.
>   (*Il.* 22.385–88)

---

[29] *Il.* 22.385 = 11.407, 17.97, 21.562, 22.122. On such speeches see Gaskin 2001 [1990].

This need will not be met by the due rite of burial alone: Achilles must go further.[30] He drills holes in the feet of Hector's corpse in order to lash him behind his chariot, and drags him away to where Patroclus awaits burial with the human sacrifice (*Il.* 22.395–404, with 23.1–11, 22–3).

These acts are described in Homer's own voice as *aeikea … erga* (*Il.* 22.395, 23.24), a phrase somewhere between 'unseemly deeds' or 'disfiguring deeds'.[31] If the former translation is accepted, we have here an example of something very rare in the *Iliad*: explicit condemnation of a person's actions in the unmediated voice of the poet rather than that of a character.[32] With the latter, what he is inflicting on the corpse is *aeikes* in the sense that he is making it ugly or degraded by the mutilation:[33] but even with this reading there is no doubt that such actions are seen as vicious. In Classical Athenian law *aikia* – lexically equivalent to 'doing *aeikea* things' to someone – is defined as a crime, a manifestation of bullying violence that shades into *hubris*.[34] This confirms that Achilles' behaviour should be understood in terms of the darkest themes of the heroic race, alongside such extremes of violence as the cannibalism of Tydeus: the *hubris* of the heroic race is exemplified in their violence towards the helpless and the dead. A variant tradition, alluded to by Sophocles in his *Ajax*, even had Achilles mutilating Hector while still alive (*Ajax* 1030–1).[35]

Through all this, despite the pleadings of others, Achilles is refusing to wash the blood of his victims from his own body, even when the time comes to eat a meal together:

---

[30] On possible wider resonances of this episode cf. Redfield 1994: 160–223.

[31] The adjective refers essentially to ugliness, 'what does not seem good' or 'what does not seem beautiful', enabling three distinct interpretations: 'deeds that are disgraceful [to Achilles]', 'deeds that are disgraceful [to Hector]', or 'deeds that mar the appearance [of the corpse]'. The first has the advantage that it harmonises with the complaints made by Apollo about the next stage of Achilles' mistreatment of the corpse (see below); the second, however, can be defended by comparison with Achilles' use of the adverbial form of the same word when he crows over Hector that the dogs and vultures will ravage him *aikōs* 'in disgraceful fashion' (*Il.* 22.356, cited by Richardson 1993: 147, note at *Il.* 22.395). The problem of *aeikea erga* is carefully discussed by De Jong (2012: 162–3, note at *Il.* 22.395); however, De Jong's conclusion that the image of *aeikea erga* represents 'pathos' rather than 'moral criticism' (aligned implicitly with the third of the alternatives listed above) seems to me to invoke a false dichotomy, as if excessive rage were unconnected to the qualities that define the nature of Achilles and his race. See further Redfield 1994: 160–4.

[32] See above, n. 11.   [33] See Vernant 2001 [1982].

[34] See for example Demosthenes, *Against Meidias* (*Private Speeches* 21) 35, with Yunis 2005: 206–7. Similarly, in Demosthenes' speech against Conon (*Private Speeches* 54) the charge is one of *aikeia*, effectively 'battery', but Demosthenes' discourse is full of the language associated with *hubris*.

[35] Cited by De Jong on 22.395 (see above). Finglass considers it possible that the image may be an invention by Sophocles (Finglass 2011: 431, note at *Ajax* 1029–31).

> It is not right for the bath to come near to my head
> before Patroclus is laid in the fire and a mound is raised
> and his hair is shorn, for there will be no second time when such
> grief will enter my heart, while I remain among the living.   (*Il.* 23.44–7)

The gore on his body is a physical manifestation of the state of mind that sets a bar against any opportunity for Achilles to reintegrate in human society.

Echoes of the ghost of Enkidu

We have noted that the long sequence from the news of Patroclus' death to the end of book 23 invites a structural comparison with the extended funeral of Enkidu in Tablet VIII of *Gilgamesh*, and that this is confirmed by the echo of the lion-and-cubs simile and the image of the maggot in the festering corpse. We will now see this pattern extended in the next episode, following the feast for which Achilles refused to wash himself.

Withdrawing again from human company, he goes down to the strand, 'the clean place, where the waves washed against the land' (*Il.* 23.61),[36] and falls asleep in exhaustion. The shade[37] of Patroclus appears to him while the actual corpse is lying nearby:[38]

> Then came the shade (*psuchē*) of Patroclus the wretched,
> all resembling the man himself in shape and in beautiful face
> and in voice, and wearing similar clothes on his flesh,
> and stood over his head and spoke these words to him,
> 'Are you sleeping, have you forgotten me, Achilles? . . . '   (*Il.* 23.65–9)

---

[36] *En katharōi* 'at the clean place, at the pure place': there is perhaps a hint here of the image of water washing away blood from his hands, as in a cleansing ritual after pollution.

[37] I use *shade* here to translate Greek *psuchē* in the context of the afterlife. *Psuchē* is the regular name for the insubstantial, flitting remnant of the dead person in Hades, but the word is also used of the last breath gasped out by the dying man, and also functions as a sign or summation of life itself: hence my use of translations like 'breath of life' or 'breath of death' according to context. The relationship between these senses is difficult and undoubtedly shifts over time in the history of the Greek language, leading to the reification of *psuchē* in dualistic terms, 'soul, spirit, self', in the Classical period and perhaps earlier as well. Among recent publications on the question see Long 2015: 15–88, Edmunds 2015. My own early attempt to keep the two senses sharply separate in Homeric interpretation (Clarke 1999: 129–55) involved serious difficulties and is countered at length by Cairns 2003b. A positive revision of the argument would, I suggest, involve the hypothesis that Homeric discourse partially (but not completely) *avoids* articulating a dualistic concept of body and *psuchē* that was current at the time of composition.

[38] For a recent analysis of the dream scene see Gazis 2018: 62–76.

The line *and stood over his head . . .* is standard for Homeric dreams,[39] and the scene can be understood as a dream in the literal sense – though the same form of words can also be used for a visit from a god in the waking world, and the two narrative patterns are very close to each other.[40] Patroclus urges Achilles to bury him immediately, so that he can 'pass through the gates of Hades' and join the main throng of the dead in the Underworld; he reaches out for one last embrace and repeats the prophecy of Achilles' death, asking that their bones should be mingled in the same urn, in memory of their friendship shared since childhood (*Il.* 23.83–92, recalled at *Od.* 24.71–9).[41] When Achilles reaches out to hold him, the shade slips away under the earth 'like smoke', wailing as it goes (*Il.* 23.100–1); Achilles wakes up with a start and speaks of the insubstantial nothingness of the dead in the afterlife,

> *O popoi*,[42] there is even in the houses of Hades
> a shade and an image, but there are no thinking innards (*phrenes*) at all in it;
> for all night the shade of wretched Patroclus
> stood beside me mourning and wailing,
> and made many requests to me, and it resembled him wondrously.
>
> (*Il.* 23.103–7)

This prompts him and his companions to resume their lamentations, even before the sun rises and the funeral can be brought to completion. So described, this episode is seamlessly integrated into the themes and narrative sequence of its context in the *Iliad*; but it also finds an exact correlate in *Gilgamesh*. This is one of the best-known and most compelling equations between Greek and Mesopotamian narrative poetry,[43] and it will repay close examination.

As we have seen (pp. 108–110), at a relatively late stage in the development of the Standard Babylonian Epic a prose translation of the latter part of the Sumerian text *Gilgamesh, Enkidu and the Netherworld* was appended as the Twelfth Tablet. At Gilgamesh's request it is arranged that the sun god Shamash will bring up the ghost of Enkidu when he rises at dawn; the two heroes embrace, and a long dialogue ensues among them about the

---

[39] See e.g. *Il.* 2.20, 2.59, 24.682.

[40] For example, the same line is used for a god coming to speak at night to one who is specifically said *not* to be asleep (*Od.* 20.32).

[41] On the urn in question see above, pp. 176–177.

[42] These words typically begin a speech of surprise and sudden realisation. I cannot translate them sensibly into English.

[43] See West 1997: 344–6.

fortunes of different kinds of people in the land of the dead. Here are the lines in which Shamash raises him from the Underworld:

> The young hero Shamash, [. . .] son of Ningal,
> opened a chink in the Netherworld,
> He brought the shade of Enkidu up from the Netherworld like
>   a phantom.
> They hugged each other, kissing one another,
> sharing thoughts and exchanging questions.   (*SBV* XII 85–9)

In each case the man is visited by his friend's shade or ghost, Greek *psuchē*, Akkadian *utukku*;[44] Achilles at the end of the scene tries to embrace Patroclus, Gilgamesh at the beginning embraces Enkidu; Patroclus' ghost is 'like smoke' when it slips away from the embrace (*Il.* 23.100), and Enkidu's comes to the meeting 'like a phantom'. 'Phantom' here translates Akkadian *zāqīqu*, a word whose range of meaning 'ghost, nothingness, phantom'[45] suggests the idea of insubstantial nothingness in a similar way to 'like smoke'. Even the timing is the same: it is the sun-god who raises Enkidu's ghost at his rising in the morning (*SBV* XII.81–7),[46] while it is just before the breaking of dawn (23.109–10) that Achilles awakes to tell that he has met the shade of Patroclus.[47]

Vitally, there is also a correlation in the things the two ghosts speak about. Patroclus' urgent wish is for the burial to be completed, so that he can become a full member of the community of the dead:

> Bury me as quickly as you can, so I may pass[48] through the gates of Hades.
> The shades are keeping me outside, images of the outworn,
> and they will not let me mingle with them beyond the river,
> but instead I am wandering along by the broad-gated house of Hades.
>   (*Il.* 23.71–4)

The point here is that there is a precise equivalence between the treatment of the dead by the living and the experience of the survivor on the other side, and that the committal of the body to the earth will bring about or

---

[44] On *utukku*, the word translated as 'shade' here, see above, p. 109 with n. 45.

[45] *CAD* s.v. *zaqīqu*.

[46] Ritual texts show that Shamash was the key god in Mesopotamian necromancy: see Finkel 1983/4, with George 2003: 1.529.

[47] Cf. Steele 2002, showing that the imagery applied to Helios in the proem to the philosophical poem of Parmenides corresponds closely to that associated with Shamash.

[48] I take the verb *perēsō* here as an aorist subjunctive, but it could equally be translated as a future indicative: 'I will pass through'.

correspond to the passage of the dead into the fulness of the afterlife.[49]
Enkidu's ghost, as we saw, lists a much broader range of such correspondences: the more surviving sons the dead man has to mourn him the better
his consolations in the land of the dead, the one who has no heirs to mourn
him is left miserable, the warrior who has died bravely in battle is honoured
(*SBV* XII 102–53). Among this series, however, is the man who has been
left unburied:

> 'Did you see the one whose corpse is left lying in the open countryside?' 'I
> saw (him).
> His ghost does not lie at rest in the Netherworld.'   (*SBV* XII 150–1)

Although the location is significantly different – *ṣēru* 'countryside' is the
uncultivated plain – nonetheless this could almost be a description of how
Patroclus himself is suffering, lying unburied on the ground while the
funeral is delayed. Arguably that is coincidental, being just one item of
an enumerated list; alternatively, perhaps, we have here another clue to the
influence of *Gilgamesh* on the shaping of the *Iliad*.

In *Gilgamesh* the addition of the episode of the ghost serves, through its
images of the consolations and sufferings of different kinds of people in the
Underworld, to reinforce the message that after death human life is
validated by continued commemoration by family and community. Can
a similar model somehow be applied to Achilles? Is there a sense in which
Achilles finds new wisdom after his confrontation with the world beyond
the grave, or is the concluding movement one of unrelieved savagery? This
question will hover over the final movement of the *Iliad*.

The problem of the corpse

The funeral of Patroclus concludes, according to custom, with competitive
games, in which Achilles seems again to be socially integrated among the
Greeks – there is no hint of the violent anger that has possessed him up to
now, and even when he speaks of Patroclus it is with gentle restraint
(*Il.* 23.280–4, 618–23). But when the rituals are completed, he seems to
return to darkness: restless and sleepless, he laments through the night, and
at dawn he again ties Hector behind his chariot and drags him around
Patroclus' grave-marker (*Il.* 24.14–18),[50] as if unwilling to move on from

---

[49] See Clarke 1999: 211–13, 283; Gazis 2018: 65–8.

[50] In point of fact the tomb is still empty, as Achilles' instruction (*Il.* 23.243–4) was that the bones
should be kept until the time comes to mingle them with his own.

the transitional moment of the funeral. Where Gilgamesh sang a song of lost love, and made a statue of precious substances, Achilles can express himself only through hatred.

Up to now, Aphrodite and Apollo together have protected Hector's corpse – Aphrodite kept the dogs and vultures from mauling him as Achilles wished, and Apollo saved the corpse from decomposition (*Il.* 23.184–91, 24.19–21) – but as the outrage continues it becomes a crisis for the gods, and Apollo speaks out against their ingratitude.[51] Despite Hector's pieties they have not allowed his family to bury him,

> . . . but instead, gods, you prefer to help accursed (*oloos*) Achilles,
> whose thoughts (*phrenes*) are not held in due measure, nor is the
>   intention
> curbed in his breast, but his will is savage, like a lion
> who to his great force and his over-manly thought-breath (*thumos*)
> yields when he goes against the flocks of mortals, to seize his feast:
> so Achilles has abandoned all pity, and there is him no
> abashment, the thing that brings great help and harm to men.
>
> (*Il.* 24.39–45)

The word clumsily translated here as 'abashment' is *aidōs* – the fear of loss of reputation, the fear that induces men to behave with respectful restraint and proper courage.[52] Instead there is a swelling, an expansion of fury and passion beyond due limits. Apollo goes on to complain that all men suffer the loss of loved ones, of brothers and sons, and after due grief and lamentation they put an end to it (*Il.* 24.46–9); in his relentless continuation of savagery even against the corpse, Achilles 'is abusing dumb earth' (24.54), humiliating the helpless and defenceless flesh of the dead man.[53]

With the *Iliad* in the background, Aeschylus in the tragedy known as *The Ransoming of Hector*[54] explored the theological dimension of this behaviour, in a speech in which Hermes described the evil of Achilles' violence

---

[51] See e.g. Redfield 1994: 210–18, and above, pp. 152–154.
[52] On *aidōs* the definitive treatment remains Cairns 1993.
[53] This is one of two possible interpretations of *kōphē gaia* 'dumb earth' (*Il.* 24.54). With the other, the 'earth' referred to would be the goddess Gaia herself, who as a guardian of fundamental pieties would be appalled by Achilles' behaviour. Although this would fit well with other allusions to the role of Gaia as an unheard presence in the *Iliad*, it remains on balance less likely. Words closely related to *aeikizei*, the verb translated here as 'abuses', are used elsewhere to refer precisely to the defilement of the corpse (*Il.* 22.336, 22.395=23.24, 24.19), and there is a parallel in Homeric rhetoric for *gaia* referring to a human body reduced to mere 'earth' (*Il.* 7.99). It can of course be argued that even with this sense uppermost there is still a hinted allusion to the goddess' personal outrage at Achilles.
[54] Also known as *Phrygians*, after the identity of its Chorus: see Sommerstein on Aesch. fr. 263–4, Sommerstein 2008: 262–9.

against the dead Trojan. The corpse itself feels nothing, he says, but the gods turn against the abuser:

> The resentment (*nemesis*) that we feel is more powerful,
> and Justice works her bitterness on behalf of the dead man.[55]
>
> (Aesch. fr. 266)

Here the language is that of divine law, the gods' guardianship of cosmic order: Achilles is defying the most basic moral laws, and there will be vengeance. In Apollo's words in the *Iliad*, the gravity of the same transgression is explained only on the level of his psychological state: his lack of human restraint, his refusal to keep his thoughts 'curbed', is identified with the marauding lion in the simile. The final outcome, in narrative sequence and (one infers) in the implementation of justice, will be his death.

The meeting between Priam and Achilles

Zeus finally commands that Thetis must persuade Achilles to release Hector for burial (*Il.* 24.74–6). When she has done so, the gods work through a plan which, as so often in Homer, is indirect and depends on the manipulation of human will. A further divine visit is made to Priam, to prompt him to give effect to the wish that he already expressed in vain to his family, to cross the enemy lines and ask for his son's corpse:

> I will beg this man, this reckless one, this doer of terrible deeds,
> in hope that he will be abashed (*aidessetai*) before my years and will take pity
> on my old age: and indeed his father is such a one as I am,
> Peleus, who brought him forth and reared him to be a trouble
> to the Trojans . . .   (*Il.* 22.418–22)

So the scene is set for this last extraordinary encounter, between Priam and the man who has destroyed his family. Nothing in the narrative of Achilles' rage against Hector up to this point suggests that there is any hope in such an appeal to his humanity, but Iris the messenger-goddess repeats Zeus' assurance that he will restrain himself:

> When [sc. Hermes] leads you into the hut of Achilles,
> he will not kill you, and he will hold back the other men:
> he is not mindless or heedless or vicious,
> but in goodwill (?)[56] he will spare the one who comes as a suppliant.
>
> (*Il.* 24.184–7)

---

[55] Or possibly 'the bitterness *of* the dead man', as if he is the ultimate agent of the anger.
[56] The meaning of this word *endukeōs* is doubtful.

She can say this because the gods know that Achilles has been given the command to spare him (24.133–40), but Priam is ignorant of this, and Hecuba fears that Achilles' rage will erupt:

> If he sees you with his eyes and seizes you,[57]
> this savage man, not fit to be trusted, will not take pity on you,
> nor will he be abashed (*aidesetai*) before you.   (*Il.* 24.206–8)

The word translated 'savage' is *ōmēstēs*, eater of raw flesh: Hecuba is describing the lion-like Achilles, the one who has abandoned oaths and compacts and divinely ordained restraint. This in turn leads into a grotesque image: since Achilles has left Hector to be devoured by the dogs, she says, she wishes that she could take her recompense (*tita erga* or *antita erga*) by seizing on his liver herself and devouring his flesh (*Il.* 24.212–15). Here in the rhetoric of high emotion[58] she is imagining an impossibility, much more so than when Achilles originally threatened to eat Hector's flesh raw after killing him.[59] As Priam prepares for the confrontation with Achilles, he voices the fear that he will murder him, a defenceless old man (*Il.* 24.224–7, cf. 328) – the very crime, indeed, that Achilles' son Neoptolemus would go on to commit in the fall of the city, when (according to the Cyclic *Sack of Troy*) he violated the same divine law of the protection of suppliants, putting Priam to death when he had sought sanctuary at the altar of Zeus (see above, pp. 187–188 with Fig. 15 (b)).[60]

But something different happens. Under Hermes' guidance Priam enters the encampment unnoticed, so that he and Achilles suddenly find

---

[57] Literally 'If he seizes you and sees you with his eyes'. Unless the verb translated *seizes* (*haireō*) is being used in a metaphorical sense, the sequence is idiomatically reversed.

[58] Apart from Achilles' threat against Hector, this strange hyperbolic image is also paralleled in a conversation among the gods, Zeus mocking Hera's hatred of the Trojans (*Il.* 4.34–6). The imagery of this speech, as often in conversations among the gods, seems to replicate the rhetorical strategies of mortals on a deliberately trivialised, almost satirical level.

[59] In later Greek sources, beginning with the *Hecuba* of Euripides, we find the tradition that Hecuba in her mourning for Hector underwent a metamorphosis into a dog (see Gantz 1993: 660–1; Forbes Irving 1990: 207–10). There is no evidence for any vestige of this grotesque story before Euripides, but it is remarkable that in the Iliadic speech cited here Hecuba aspires to the characteristic behaviour of the Homeric dog. Perhaps there was a text which took this thread of imagery from the *Iliad* and reworked it as her physical transformation.

[60] For this episode of the *Sack of Troy* see Proclus' summary, para. 2 at West, *GEF*, pp. 144–5, with West *EC* 234; a version of the same episode is also attested in a variant form for the *Little Iliad* (fr. 25: West, *GEF*, pp. 136–8), without the motif of the altar of Zeus. See further M. Anderson 1997: 28–38.

themselves alongside each other. Priam seizes his knees in supplication and 'kisses the manslaying hands that had killed many of his sons' (*Il.* 24.478–9). There follows a complex simile:[61]

> As when dense ruin (*átē*) seizes a man, who in his fatherland
> has killed another man, and he arrives in the settlement of others,
> at a wealthy man's house, and amazement seizes those who gaze upon him,
> so Achilles was amazed when he saw the godlike Priam.   (*Il.* 24.480–3)

Achilles' wonder at seeing the old man is like what people feel when a murderer, with the pollution of bloodshed on his hands, arrives in the midst of their community: but on the plane of the main narrative it is Achilles who fills the role of the killer, and Priam that of the non-combatants looking on with horror and fear. This is one of many Homeric similes that work by reversal of imagery – we have already seen a classic example, in which the divine fire burning on Achilles' head when he threatened the Trojans was like a beacon sent up from a besieged city appealing for help[62] – but the present example is more than just a twist of associative imagination. These two men necessarily hate and fear one another; but despite the depth of alienation, despite the terrifying imbalance between the man of war and the old king on the threshold of death (*Il.* 24.487, *sim.* 22.60), they both experience the same sense of the uncanny when face to face with each other.

As a stylistic phenomenon, the expression of a *psychological* insight through a reverse simile is remarkably subtle, and it is worth pausing to contextualise it more clearly. There is a close (and, so far as I know, unique) parallel in the *Odyssey* when Odysseus, lost and nameless, hears a poet singing of his own past deeds when his cunning achieved the sack of Troy:

> As a woman weeps, falling upon her dear husband,
> who before his city and its people has been killed,
> from his city and his children fending off the pitiless day:
> when he is dying and groaning she sees him
> and pours herself over him with shrill lament – and they
> beat with their spears on her back and her shoulders
> and drag her off into slavery, to toil and suffering,
> and with most pitiful pain her cheeks are ravaged:
> so Odysseus poured a pitiful tear from under his brows.   (*Od.* 8.523–31)

---

[61] Key treatments of the encounter between Achilles and Priam are Crotty 1994: 70–80, Redfield 1994: 203–18; Zanker 1998 with Zanker 1994: 115–25; Kim 2000: 9–14 and *passim*; Wilson 2002a: 126–33.

[62] See p. 268.

Odysseus' sorrow, at the gulf between the glamour of his fame and the depth of his current abandonment, has converged with the feelings of the people whose sufferings he inflicted at the highest point of his glory.[63] Whether or not one believes that the *Iliad* and *Odyssey* are products of a single creative intelligence, the comparison clarifies the insight in the simile of the exiled murderer: the encounter between Priam and Achilles will turn on the universality of sorrow, irrespective of the rights and wrongs and opposed allegiances of war.

In the moment framed by this simile, Priam – just as he had originally planned (*Il.* 22.420–2) – speaks first not of justice or even pity, but of Peleus:

> Call to mind your own father, Achilles who resemble the gods,
> a man of my own years, on the wretched threshold of old age . . .
> (*Il.* 24.487–8)

Maybe Peleus is being harried by enemies, without his son to protect him, but he can rejoice in the news of his son's deeds and look forward to seeing him return home – so Priam speaks of a father's consolations, not realising that Achilles already knows that day will never come. But for Priam himself there is only grief at the deaths of his sons, above all that of Hector:

> But be abashed (*aideo*) before the gods, Achilles, and take pity on me,
> remembering your father. (*Il.* 24.503–4)

So they weep together, Priam remembering Hector and Achilles thinking both of his father and of Patroclus: 'and their groan rose up through the house' (*Il.* 24.512). Then Achilles seats the old man before him, pitying his old age (*Il.* 24.516), and begins a long discourse of wisdom. Though he is very young, this is a speech of the kind generally associated with voices of experience and authority – Nestor and Phoenix and Agamemnon in the *Iliad*,[64] or indeed the overall poetic persona of Hesiod in the *Works and*

---

[63] For a careful analysis of this as a 'reverse simile', see De Jong 2001: 216–17, note at lines 521–31; cf. Pucci 1987: 222, and Garvie 1994: 339. For the idea that the simile represents Odysseus' understanding, through his own sufferings, of the pain he inflicted on the Trojans in the sack of Troy, De Jong compares *Od.* 23.306–7, where he is described as telling Penelope of 'all the cares he inflicted on other men'.

[64] The classic Iliadic examples of this kind of discourse are Phoenix's exposition of the *Litai* in Book 9, and Agamemnon's account of Ate the daughter of Zeus in his 'apology' speech (*Il.* 19.92–139). In the *Works and Days* I would especially compare the sequence of *logoi* serving to explain the current state of human wretchedness (esp. *WD* 42–285). It is characteristic of such discourse that it constructs new doctrines and narratives within forms that claim traditional authority. See further Heath 2005: 143–5.

Days. The gods have so woven it[65] for mortals, says Achilles, that we live in pain when they are free of care (*Il.* 24.525–6). Before Zeus' doorway there is a jar of good things and another (or another two: the Greek is ambiguous[66]) full of evil things: sometimes the god gives a man a mixture of both kinds, or he may give to him only from the jar of evils, so that he wanders as an outcast over the earth. So it was for Peleus and Priam: each began with wealth and kingship, but it has been Peleus' misfortune to father only one child, who will never take care of him in his old age, and Priam's to suffer the ravages of war and now the death of his son. Here there is a bleak but humane message. Endless grief will be fruitless, and the only response to the human condition is to endure it: 'there is no profit to be had from baleful lamentation' (*Il.* 24.547–51).

All this might be seen as a kind of inner calming, the cancellation of the savagery that drove Achilles against Agamemnon and then against Hector: after all that rage and bile, he now resigns himself to accepting the truth about the human condition. On such a reading, the scene could be fitted smoothly onto the template provided by Tablets X and XI of *Gilgamesh*, where Uta-napishti expounded the necessity of accepting the inevitability of death – allowing, of course, for the obvious difference that this time the message is mediated through the voice of the grieving demigod himself.[67] So described, the vocalisation would match that of Achilles' speeches in the ninth Book, when he took on a poet's persona to sing of *klea andrōn* and expound the truths of his inner experience.

This may well be part of the truth about the meaning of the meeting with Priam, but it is not the whole truth. The teaching about the jars of good and evil is followed by an episode of subtly nuanced tension, enough to show that these moments of humanity were only a pause on Achilles' descent into darkness. He ends with counsel of simple resignation – 'you cannot bring him back to life' (551) – but Priam seems to become hasty: he asks

[65] 'It' here is a dummy: the verb *epeklōsanto* has no object in the Greek.
[66] This is difficult. Verbally, the straightforward interpretation is that there are two (*doioi*) jars of evils and another one (*heteros*) of good things. *Heteros* would normally indicate a contrast between two individuals, or in the plural between two groups; here, on this reading, a single jar is being set in opposition to a pair. Alternatively, one can understand the entire image as referring to the contrast between two jars in total, in which case the phrase *kakōn heteros d' eaōn* must be reckoned as elliptical – '[one jar] of evils, [and] another of good things'. As Richardson points out (1993: 330–1, note at 527–33), the ancient evidence is equivocal. Pindar assumes two-plus-one jars if he is recalling the passage when he says that 'earlier men' teach that 'the gods distribute two troubles to mortals alongside one good thing' (*Pythian* 3.80–1), but Plato on the other hand cites the text as if with two contrasted jars (*Republic* 379 d), albeit giving slightly different wording to the Homeric passage when he recalls it. Cf. Alden 2000: 33 n. 60.
[67] Compare the study of this parallel by Haubold 2013: 44–51.

Achilles 'do not make me sit down yet' (*Il.* 24.553), as if he has been asked to delay, and suggests that Hector be released at once so that he can hand over the payment (*Il.* 24.555–6). At this Achilles seems suddenly to become confrontational again, and there is an ominous edge to the warning 'Do not provoke me'.[68] He reveals that the command to yield up the corpse has come to him in advance from the gods, and that Priam has obviously had their aid (*Il.* 24.560–7), but he nonetheless threatens open violence:

> So now do not rend my thought-breath any more in my miseries,
> old man, or I might not let you alone in my hut
> though you are a suppliant, and I might break Zeus' commands (*alitōmai*
>   *ephetmas*).   (*Il.* 24.568–70)

The sacredness of the suppliant who comes begging for mercy (the *hiketēs*) is a fundamental precept of Greek ethics, and this barely veiled threat is hardly less brutal than the declaration of a wish to feast on Hector's flesh. The next lines reinforce this feeling, conjuring up the last in the sequence of lion-similes:[69]

> So he spoke, and the old man became afraid and obeyed what he had said,
> and Achilles leapt like a lion out of the house to the door.   (*Il.* 24.571–2)

Achilles is still beast-like, still gripped by the sinister mood in which he has been approaching his end.[70] Although the exchange of the corpse for the ransom is carried out with care and ceremony, the danger remains that fury will erupt on both sides, and the slaves are told to wash Hector out of sight in order to avoid this:

> in case Priam might not hold back his anger (*cholos*) in his grieving heart
> on seeing his son, and Achilles' heart would be rent apart
> and he would kill him, and would defy Zeus' commands.   (*Il.* 24.584–6)

After these signals that rage is barely being contained, the surface calm of the last part of the meeting is broken by further moments of tension.

---

[68] The formulation here (*mēketi nun m' erethize*) is difficult because of the nuances of *mēketi*. I take it that here the word is being used in a way similar to that posited above for *ouketi* at *Il.* 9.598, referring to the contrast between what has happened and what might have happened (see above, p. 230 n. 46). If this is right, the present phrase would effectively mean 'do not provoke me [instead of placating me]'. Compare Agamemnon against Chryses: 'Go, do not provoke me, so you will reach your home unharmed' (*Il.* 1.32).

[69] On this lion-simile see esp. Wilson 2002b: 130–31; Heath 2005: 152–5, with the articles cited in n. 71 below.

[70] On the ambiguities in the portrayal of Achilles in this scene, see further Daix 2014.

Achilles invites Priam to stay the night and shares a meal with him, discoursing of myth again when he recalls how even Niobe took food in her grief after her children had been killed through the jealousy of gods (24.603–15). After eating the two men sit and gaze at each other (24.628–32), and with what seems like perfect courtesy Achilles questions Priam on the Trojans' funeral customs, so that he can arrange a truce to last until the burial is complete (24.656–70); but when Achilles tells Priam he must sleep outside, in case one of the other Greek leaders might come in and see him, Homer describes him as *epikertomeōn*, something like 'confusing him, startling him, putting his thoughts in disarray' – as if it is Achilles' purpose to destroy the peacefulness that has arisen between them.[71] But even here there is a counterbalance, and as their meeting ends Achilles takes Priam's hand in his to calm his fears (*Il.* 24.671–2). All this makes best sense, I suggest, as the portrayal of a man in a state of turmoil. There is no lasting resolution here, and (to look beyond the *Iliad* again for a moment) Achilles is moving all along towards the time when his ashes will lie in the urn that Dionysus brought to his parents' wedding.

Closure in the *Iliad*

Achilles' mortality has loomed over the entire action since the death of Patroclus: in the encounter with his mother on the sea-shore, in the prophecy by his horse, in the Lycaon scene, and in Hector's warning at the point of death. Patroclus' ghost predicts that it is his portion (*moira*) to die 'under the walls of the Trojans of great wealth' (*Il.* 23.80–1), and Achilles alludes to this himself in the course of the ritual (23.150); since their bones will one day be mingled together, by burning Patroclus he is already preparing for his own funeral (*Il.* 23.243–4, cf. 23.126). When Iris goes to seek Thetis she finds her weeping with the other sea-goddesses, for her son 'who was about to die in Troy of the rich soil, far from his fatherland' (24.85–6), and when she in turn sees him brooding over Hector's corpse she reminds him that 'Death and powerful Portion (*Moira*) stand beside you' (24.131–2). Speaking to Priam, Achilles says that the only son of

---

[71] This is the most reasonable consensus explanation that I can frame for *epikertomeōn* (*Il.* 24.649). For the debate on the word see Clarke 2001b; Lloyd 2004; Gottesman 2008. Richardson 1993: 344 notes that its meaning is already a matter of debate in Eustathius' commentary.

Peleus is *panaōrios*, 'all untimely', 'all deprived of his time' (24.540)[72] –
a word whose bitterness is heightened by the fact that Priam seems not
to understand it, since a few moments later he will offer his good
wishes for Achilles' future in his homeland (24.556–7).[73]

All this is leading towards the final bowshot below the city walls: but the
path of the song swerves yet again. When the meeting with Priam has
ended with that last ominous lion-simile, Achilles turns to sleep, with
Priam near him and Brises' daughter at his side (24.676); and the *Iliad*
continues to its end without ever turning to his later thoughts and deeds. In
the following chapter we will glean what knowledge we can of the death of
Achilles as told elsewhere in the early epic corpus, before returning to the
very different discourse with which the *Iliad* concludes: the voices of
lamenting women in the funeral of his greatest enemy, Hector of Troy.

---

[72] The difficult adjective *panaōrios* is transparently built from *pan-* 'all' with the negative prefix *a-*
on the noun *hōrē* 'season, time, best time', but its exact sense has invited doubt since ancient
times. Depending on which part of the semantic range of *hōrē* is prominent, it refers either to
Achilles' death depriving him of the 'best time' of his life, or to the more mundane notion that
the events of his life have not come at their proper times or are more vaguely 'miserable' (see
LfgrE s.v., with James 1986). Either way, Priam's response seems jarring.
[73] On these prophecies cf. Burgess 2009: 43–55.

15 | Mortality and wisdom

Our closest guide to how Homer and his audience might have visualised the death of Achilles is the surviving summary of the *Aethiopis*, which was the next epic in the sequence of the Cycle and is usually dated as early as late seventh century BCE.[1] In outline, at least, its account dovetails with the prophecies and foreshadowings in the *Iliad*.

Within the inevitable limits of our knowledge, the following sequence can be reconstructed. Memnon the *aithiops* – 'burnt-face' – son of the goddess Dawn from the remote edge of the world, came as the Trojans' latest ally; Thetis prophesied to Achilles about his coming struggle with Memnon; when Memnon had killed Antilochus, second only to Patroclus among Achilles' people, they fought a duel resonating intertextually with that with Hector in the *Iliad*.[2] Dawn, and perhaps Thetis too, made a speech in support of her son's claim to Zeus' favour, and Memnon was assigned to defeat but was granted either a gentle death or immortal resurrection (or both).[3] On the vase illustrated here (Fig. 23) each mother stands behind her son, while they face each other over a corpse. If this is indeed the duel of Achilles and Memnon (and the identification seems irresistible), then the corpse must be Antilochus. Clues from Athenian tragedy as usual enhance the details. Aeschylus reprised the episode in his *Psychostasia*,[4] in which the scales of Zeus were set up between the combatants and each mother pleaded for her son until the scales fell, determining

---

[1] For the *Aethiopis* the most convenient presentation of the evidence is West's edition of the summary by Proclus (*GEF*, pp. 110–13). As usual, however, this must be used with caution, because West adds (within angle brackets) supplementary information from the related account in Apollodorus, not all of whose details necessarily go back to the *Aethiopis* itself. There is an excellent survey of the evidence by Burgess (2009: 27–42). See also Rengakos 2015; West, *EC* 129–62.

[2] The evidence is too slight to judge whether the *Aethiopis* alluded to the *Iliad*, or the *Iliad* to a forerunner of the *Aethiopis* (or, indeed, some other variant of either configuration). The issue is reviewed by Currie 2016: 55–72; see also Rengakos 2015: 315–17; Sammons 2017: 133–8. Burgess 1997 (partly reprised in Burgess 2009) argues that it is impossible to substantiate the theory that the Iliadic narrative of Hector killed in vengeance for Patroclus resonated closely with that of Memnon killed in vengeance for Antilochus.

[3] Proclus' summary of the *Aethiopis* is the only unambiguous textual source for the granting of immortality. See Burgess 2009: 35–8; West, *EC* 148–9.

[4] Sommerstein 2008, pp. 274–5; see further West *EC* 148–9, with West 2000; Burgess 2004b; Burgess 2009: 33–4.

Fig. 23 Vase of *c.* 510 BCE, probably showing Achilles and Memnon.

which would die. There are kindred scenes on several vases dated to roughly the same period as the tragedy, exhibiting a significant variation of detail. Some show tiny winged beings in the scales (see Fig. 24), while others show miniature humans – armoured in one case (Fig. 25), featureless and shadowy in another (Fig. 26). The *Iliad* itself includes episodes in which Zeus decides the outcome of a battle by weighing death-demons (*kēres*),[5] and the beings in Fig. 24 are likewise being weighed by Hermes. Ancient commentators on the *Iliad* record that in the *Psychostasia* Aeschylus departed from the Homeric model, replacing the demons with the heroes' shades or wraiths (*psuchai*):[6] the shifting imagery of the vases seems to correspond closely to this ambiguity, with the miniature humans representing *psuchai*. For us, the most significant point here will be that in the *Aethiopis*, as in the play of Aeschylus, the bitterness of mortality was expressed in the eloquence of grief-stricken women.

Achilles pursued Memnon's host as far as the walls of Troy, when at the point of bursting through into the city[7] he was shot dead with an arrow by

---

[5] Compare *Il.* 22.209–13, where Zeus weighs the *kēr* of Achilles against that of Hector. As usual, it is possible *either* that the *Aethiopis* poet took these lines of the *Iliad* as a starting-point, *or* that our *Iliad* recalls or alludes to a version of the narrative that later took shape as the *Aethiopis* proper, *or* that both draw independently on the same traditional motif.

[6] Schol. A on *Il.* 8.70, schol. bT on *Il.* 22.209: see Clarke 1999: 5.

[7] This detail is doubtful. Already in the *Iliad* it is prophesied that Paris and Apollo will kill Achilles 'in the Scaean gates' (*Il.* 22.360): but what is meant by 'in'? The claim that Achilles had already penetrated the entrance when he was struck depends on Proclus' summary of the *Aethiopis*, where the words are that Achilles was killed *eis tēn polin suneispesōn*: the final word here, an aorist participle, is most naturally taken as 'after bursting in' to the city. See Burgess 2009: 39, adducing Horace's detail of Achilles 'shaking the towers of Troy' (*Odes* 4.6.7) – but is this wording merely figurative?

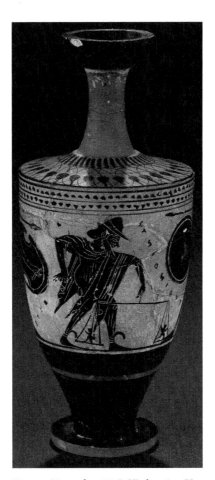

Fig. 24 Vase of *c*. 490 BCE showing Hermes with the scales of battle.

Paris, helped by Apollo[8] in accordance with the prophecies. Greeks and Trojans battled over the corpse, an episode that was the subject of an extraordinary vase-painting (now lost), dated by its style to the mid-500s BCE (Fig. 27).[9] For the first time in a surviving source, the positioning of

---

[8] As Burgess points out (2009: 39), the artistic evidence suggests overwhelmingly that the agent was Paris: artistic survivals vary as to whether Apollo is depicted with him. A fragment of Pindar (*Paean* 6.79–80) has been convincingly reconstructed to read that Achilles was shot by Apollo disguised as Paris, as also in the late mythographer Hyginus (*Fabulae* 107). At a guess, the characteristic Homeric/Cyclic articulation would be that the god collaborated with the mortal, directing his aim or shooting on his behalf.

[9] *LIMC*, Achilleus no. 850, finely discussed by Lowenstam 2008: 37–8. The vase was in the Hope Collection at the Deepdene, Dorking, Surrey, England, but had disappeared before the collection was sold off in a bankruptcy sale in 1917 (the auctioneer's catalogue includes several later Greek vases, but not this one). All pictures of the vase known to me are from the reproduction of Hope's drawing printed as Rumpf 1927, plate 12: I have been unable to locate the original drawing.

Fig. 25 Vase of *c.* 460 BCE, showing the scales of battle.

Fig. 26 Vase of *c.* 490–480 BCE showing Eos (Dawn) and Thetis pleading for their sons.

the arrows matches the tradition (nowadays so familiar) that he was killed by an arrow in the ankle, or more vaguely in the heel.[10] There is no early evidence to link this to the story of Thetis' failed attempt to render him invulnerable by dipping him in the Styx, with the ankle by which she gripped him remaining unprotected; irrespective of that question, however, it is a fair guess that part of the horror of his end was the very indignity of death from an arrow-wound, delivered by the contemptible dandy Paris with the weapon that Homeric spearmen mock and belittle

---

[10] This detail is not mentioned in Proclus' summary of the *Aethiopis*, but it is found in the corresponding passage of Apollodorus, *Epitome* 5.3: see West, *GEF*, pp. 112–13, with *EC* 150.

Fig. 27 Battle over the dead Achilles, from an illustration of an amphora attributed to the Inscription Painter, now lost.

(see e.g. *Il.* 11.385–90)[11] – but of course this cannot be put to the test as long as the evidence for the *Aethiopis* remains so slight.

In the *Aethiopis*, the woman's voice came into clarity again when Thetis and the other daughters of Nereus emerged from the sea to mourn for the dead Achilles. Although for the details we have only Proclus' meagre summary, the event is recalled in the account of the Underworld in the last book of the *Odyssey*, most likely added to it by a post-Homeric poet. Agamemnon's shade is speaking to that of Achilles:

> Your mother came from the sea with the immortal sea-women
> on hearing the news: and a cry rose up over the waters,
> astonishing, and fear went in among the Greeks …

[11] In the passage referenced here from *Iliad* 11, Paris has just shot Diomedes in the heel. It is a fascinating possibility that this episode, with its motif of an arrow-wound to the heel, is actually alluding to an *Aethiopis*-like account of the death of Achilles, already current before the *Iliad* was composed: cf. Fenno 2008.

Fig. 27 (cont.)

and around you stood the daughters of the old man of the sea,
mourning pitifully, and they clad you in immortal garments.

(*Od.* 24.47–9, 58–9)

All the evidence suggests that this version of the funeral of Achilles
matches that of the *Aethiopis*. There is an obvious resonance with the
earlier scene of the two goddesses pleading by the scales of battle: together,
these wisps of evidence suggest that the theme of grieving motherhood was
prominent in various parts of this epic.

However that may be, it is also certain that the *Aethiopis* articulated a
theme that has no place in the *Iliad* when Thetis and her sea-women took
the dead Achilles from the pyre and brought him for reburial or immortality on the White Island, said to have been in the Black Sea.[12] The myth is
later alluded to by Pindar (see esp. *Olympian* 2.79, *Nemean* 4.49–50),[13] and
is recreated in Euripides' *Andromache* in a prophecy by Thetis to Peleus,
whose fate will be to remain forever in the sea with her and her father:

[12] For sources see Burgess 2009: 40–42.   [13] Currie 2005: 41–6, 362, 398.

From there, when you lift your dry foot from the sea,
you will see your dearest child and mine,
Achilles, living in his island home
on the strand of Leuke, in the sea no stranger enters.

(Euripides, *Andromache* 1259–62)

This promise for Achilles corresponds closely with the tradition which we observed in Hesiod's *Works and Days*, that the dead heroes were given new life in the Isles of the Blest (*WD* 168–73), and it played a part in the shaping of later Greek myths of personal immortality, as well as apparently inspiring a real-life cult of Achilles on an island near the mouth of the Danube.[14] Thus the *Iliad* differed from the *Aethiopis* – and, indeed, from much else in early Greek literature – in depicting death as an absolute finality for Achilles as for the other half-gods of the heroic race. It may of course be the case that the Iliadic version is the more ancient one, and that the story of Achilles' immortalisation is a later development in myth and cult (cf. above, pp. 137–144), but it is equally plausible that the poet of the *Iliad* is bypassing an already well-established tradition.

The fight for the dead Achilles

Deep problems of ethics and psychology were held up for exploration in the tale of the aftermath of Achilles' death, centred on the dispute over who should take his place as the supreme Greek warrior. To pick up the story as told in the *Aethiopis*, with an eye also on the vase by the Inscription Painter: in the fighting over the corpse great deeds were done by Ajax and Odysseus, with Ajax carrying the huge body on his back to safety while Odysseus fought off the Trojans behind him.[15] Ajax's achievement was an enduring subject for the vase-painters, seen already on each of the handles of the François Vase; but it was also the occasion for a new episode of strife, described both in the *Aethiopis* and (probably more fully) in the *Little Iliad*.[16] At Thetis' prompting,

[14] See West, *EC* 155–6; Burgess 2009: 98–131.
[15] See Proclus, summary of the *Aethiopis*, para. 4, at West, *GEF*, pp. 112–13; *Aethiopis*, fr. 3, at pp. 114–15; compare the consistent though briefer account at *Od.* 24.37–42, and allusion at *Od.* 5.308–20. Discussion of the evidence for the *Aethiopis* by Rengakos 2015: 311–12; West, *EC* 151–2; Burgess 2009: 39–40.
[16] The account that follows here of the award of the arms to Odysseus, and the madness of Ajax, inevitably depends on a synthesis between various sources, many of them slight. See Proclus' summary of the *Aethiopis*, para. 4 at West, *GEF*, pp. 112–13, with *Aethiopis*, fr. 6; also Proclus' summary of the *Little Iliad*, para. 1 at pp. 120–1, with *Little Iliad*, fr. 2 and Apollodorus, *Epitome* 5.6, possibly influenced by later sources; discussion by Rengakos 2015: 308–9; West, *EC* 159–62, 174–7.

there was a contest to decide which of the two champions would be awarded Achilles' arms and armour. Seeking evidence to decide, Nestor sent spies to eavesdrop on Trojan girls,[17] one of whom was heard arguing that to carry the corpse was a lesser feat than to fight off the enemy behind.[18] The source for this episode records that the woman who argued in this way did so 'through the foresight (*pronoia*) of Athene',[19] probably referring to manipulative interference by the goddess;[20] so, fairly or otherwise, Odysseus was awarded the victory. Ajax in a frenzy of rage, which again was due in some way to Athene's prompting, went slaughtering cattle under the delusion that they were the comrades who had so insulted him. According to a tradition that probably goes back to the epic, when he slaughtered the animals he 'laughed in mockery at them' in his madness (*kategelā mainomenos*), and the phrase *Aianteios gelōs* 'laughter like that of Ajax' became proverbial.[21] But when his mind cleared and he realised what he had done, he threw himself on his sword.

The conflict between Ajax and Odysseus seems to have revolved around the elemental contrast between the two men's personalities or excellences – a contrast that is articulated even within the *Iliad*, above all in the different ways that the two men speak to Achilles as emissaries in Book 9. Ajax is obstinate in strength and defiance, but lacking in the arts of speech and subtlety. Odysseus, in contrast, is smaller and wiry and his greatest excellence is with 'cunning intelligence' (*mētis*), the verbal and rhetorical art that shades into deceitful manipulation. It is because of Ajax's extreme simplicity that suicide is the only way he can respond to the disgrace. His final self-defeat is eloquently represented on the famous vase believed to be by Exekias, whose stark lines seem to speak of the mental inflexibility that has driven him to despair (Fig. 28).[22]

The same moment is central to the *Ajax* of Sophocles, the one surviving tragedy that explores the suicide of Odysseus' opponent. When his delusion clears, and he realises what he has done and how he has been humiliated, Ajax begins to consider what must come next. Now that all his comrades

---

[17] In Odysseus' brief reference to the judgment of the arms, the line 'the children of the Trojans and Pallas Athene judged [it]' (*Od.* 11.547) is consistent with this account of the *Little Iliad* version, if 'the children of the Trojans' is taken as referring to the Trojan people as a whole, like 'the sons of the Achaeans' for the Greek warriors as a group.

[18] *Little Iliad*, fr. 2 in West, *GEF*; discussion by Rengakos 2015: 331–2; West, *EC* 175–6.

[19] The source for *Little Iliad*, fr. 2 is a scholion on Aristophanes, *Knights* 1056a. The wording resembles that of Proclus, 'according to the wish (*boulēsis*) of Athene' (Proclus' summary of the *Little Iliad*, para. 1).

[20] Odysseus in the *Odyssey* says only that both Athene and the Trojans made the judgment (*Od.* 11.547), which is more ambiguous.

[21] See West, *EC* 177; also Sophocles, *Ajax* 303, with Finglass's note at lines 302–4 (Finglass 2011: 228–9).

[22] The iconography of the vase and its Homeric background are discussed eloquently by Moignard 2015: 17–31.

Fig. 28 Vase attributed to Exekias showing the suicide of Ajax.

hate and despise him, he cannot stay among them; he cannot go home and face his father empty-handed; and if he deliberately throws away his life in a futile assault on Troy, it will only please his enemies among the Greeks. Only one course remains open:

> Some test must be sought
> which will show the old man, my father,
> that I was not born from him a gutless coward.
> It is disgraceful for a man to yearn for long life
> when he has no turning-away from evils:
> what pleasure is there in day that follows day,
> carrying forward and backward from death?
> I would buy for any price a mortal
> who can be made warm by mere empty hopes.
> But either a beautiful life or a beautiful death
> is right for the nobly born: you have heard my every word.

(*Ajax* 470–80)

The final option for a beautiful death is deep in the epic tradition, and reduced to the most stark simplicity by the filtering voices of propagandist poets like Tyrtaeus (see above, pp. 263–265). Perhaps Ajax here represents an aristocratic ideal that was becoming outmoded in the Athens of Sophocles' time; perhaps he simply expresses the extremes to which men of war are liable to push themselves in every age.[23] Either way, these are the words of a man whose values have become so constricting that he has no outlet but to destroy himself.

Surprisingly, perhaps, it was possible in later Greek thought to represent Ajax's suicide as an act of heroic excellence, and it is cited in this spirit by Aristotle, for example, alongside Achilles and Socrates among examples of 'great-spirited' men (*megalopsuchoi*) who chose to die rather than submit to insult.[24] Within the action of the Cyclic poems, however, it was treated with contempt: in the *Little Iliad* Agamemnon ordered that Ajax should be buried by inhumation in a coffin, not 'appeased by fire' (*Il.* 7.410, etc.) in the customary ritual of cremation. As well as vengeance for his crazed attempt to slaughter Agamemnon and the others, this extreme dishonour seems to have marked the evil of the act of suicide itself.[25]

But once the controversy over the contest is included, the victory of Odysseus becomes overlain by doubt: did he deserve to win the prize over Ajax, 'bulwark of the Achaeans'? Is his cunning a legitimate aspect of heroic excellence, or the trait of a liar and a cheat? This exact question is raised, for example, by Pindar in odes in honour of victors from Aegina, whose people claimed kinship with Ajax.[26] From the very start, perhaps, the notion of Odysseus as a supreme example of heroic excellence – familiar from the surface narrative of both *Iliad* and *Odyssey* – was never to be left immune to doubt and challenge.

---

[23] The most influential version of the view that the Ajax of Sophocles' play represents an archaising heroic ethic, outdated in the era of the democratic *polis*, is that advanced by Bernard Knox (e.g. Knox 1961, esp. 20–2; cf. Zanker 1994: 64–71). For a brief but well-articulated critique of this theory, with a review of subsequent scholarship, see Finglass 2011: 44–6, and cf. Kelly 2015c.

[24] Aristotle, *Posterior Analytics* 97 b 16–25, well discussed by Howland 2002.

[25] See *Little Iliad*, fr. 3 in West, *GEF*, with Apollodorus, *Epitome* 5.7; discussion by West, *EC* 178–9. Admittedly, the only direct evidence for the notion that the inhumation was occasioned by condemnation of the act of suicide is from a late and often extravagantly revisionist source, the *Heroicus* of Philostratus. Holt 1992, cited by West, suggests that the tradition of the inhumation of Ajax looks back to the prevalence of inhumation in Mycenaean burials, and that this was originally one of a group of archaising traditions associated with Ajax: on this view, the explanations concerned with humiliation and condemnation of suicide would be later impositions. This, however, seems to me very doubtful, in the absence of a supporting example of an epic poet linking archaic practices to conservative attitudes.

[26] See esp. *Nemean* 7.20–27, 8.23–34. The origins of the Aeginetans' claim to descent from Aeacus are explored by Burnett 2005, esp. 17–23. For a recent close reading of *Nemeans* 7 and 8, two much-discussed odes, see Burnett 2005: 179–202, with Currie 2005: 296–343. For other and different Pindaric perspectives on the judgment and on the suicide of Ajax see *Isthmian* 4.35–39, and compare the eulogy of Ajax at 6.35–56; see further Finglass 2011: 31–2.

The shades of the dead

In this way, the aftermath of the death of Achilles became an occasion for reflection and debate on the moral and ethical basis of heroic excellence and heroic death, played out through the contrasted personalities of Ajax and Odysseus. Against this background, it makes sense to look onwards to Odysseus' account of his own subsequent wanderings in the *Odyssey*. Once the possibility of an allegorical interpretation is admitted, the wanderings can be read as an inner journey, through disorientation and loss of identity to new wisdom gained from suffering and a series of encounters with death and the dead.[27] On the broadest typological level, as has often been observed, this invites comparison with the journey of Gilgamesh;[28] but for the themes of our present enquiry the pivotal episode is in the midst of his visit to the Underworld.[29]

Odysseus, now a nameless and isolated beggar, has been recounting his adventures to Alcinous the king of the Phaeacians and his courtiers, culminating in his journey through the mists 'to the houses of Hades and dreaded Persephone' (*Od.* 10.491–95). First he carries out a ritual of necromancy,[30] calling forth the shades from the Underworld and making the offerings that will enable them to speak to him; but as he continues, he seems progressively to move inwards into the landscape of Hades.[31] He suddenly interrupts himself to tell Alcinous that he needs sleep (*Od.* 11.330–32), but the king encourages him with praise, saying that he has told his tale 'with knowledge, like a poet' (*Od.* 11.368), and asks him to continue and tell whether he met any of his fellow warriors from the Trojan War (*Od.* 11.370–2). This interlude imposes a double distancing on what follows, inviting the suspicion that the discourse is moving to a less literal and perhaps more profound level. At this stage he meets a group of wraiths of the foremost warriors of the Trojan War:

[27] A classic statement of this strategy for reading the wanderings of Odysseus is Segal 1994: 3–109 *passim*; cf. also Cook 1995: 49–92. The theory that *nostos* is fundamentally a 'return to light and life', as advanced in a celebrated essay by Frame (1978), drastically needs to be taken back down to earth: cf. Bonifazi 2009.

[28] Cf. e.g. Burgess 1999; Louden 2011: 205–11.

[29] On the *Nekuia* of *Odyssey* 11, important recent studies are Gazis 2018: 95–206 *passim*, and Martin 2014, each with accounts of the voluminous earlier bibliography.

[30] Cf. Sourvinou-Inwood 1995: 10–107 *passim*. On the relationship between the *Odyssey* scene and the realities of Greek *nekuomanteia* see Ogden 2001: 43–65.

[31] On this shift see Clarke 1999: 215–25; Dova 2012: 1–18; and cf. the insightful comparative study by Louden 2011: 197–221.

> There came the wraiths of Peleus' son Achilles
> and of Patroclus, and blameless Antilochus,
> and Ajax, who was the greatest in appearance and form
> above all the other Greeks, after Peleus' blameless[32] son.
>
> (*Od.* 11.467–70)

The configuration evokes the final episodes of Achilles' life: here with him are the two companions whose deaths drove him to his fiercest deeds – Patroclus for whose sake he killed Hector, Antilochus whom he avenged by killing Memnon – and alongside them is Ajax, who carried Achilles' own corpse from the Trojan onslaught. Odysseus tries to speak of Achilles' high status in the world below, imagining that he now 'rules over the dead men' just as the Greeks in his life 'honoured him as much as the gods' (*Od.* 11.484–6), but the shade replies with the dead weight of pessimism:

> Do not speak to me of death, glorious Odysseus.
> I would rather be on the land,[33] as a hired man for another,
> for a man of no allotment (*aklēros*), one with no great livelihood,
> than be king over all these dead corpses. (*Od.* 11.488–91)

These often-cited lines have sometimes been taken as a riposte to the ideals represented by the Achilles of the *Iliad*. I do not believe that this question can be proved either way, and I will not pursue it here,[34] but clearly this talk of the emptiness of the men's aspirations runs directly against the pursuit of status and prestige that drove all those who fought at Troy. For this reason above all, Achilles' next words take on heightened significance. He

[32] In both cases in this passage, 'blameless' is the traditional placeholder translation for the doubtful word *amumōn*.

[33] *Eparouros*, literally 'on the ploughland'. It is difficult to say whether this refers to the state of serfdom – 'a land-labourer' – or simply to the physical plane of life in the upper world as opposed to below in Hades. The latter is certainly the sense of the similarly formed adjective *epichthonios* 'upon the earth'. Compare Achilles' description of himself as a 'burden of the ploughland' at *Iliad* 18.104, discussed above at pp. 169, 260.

[34] On the much-debated question of whether these lines can be seen as a rejection of the Iliadic 'heroic ideal', earlier contributions are reviewed by Schmiel 1987, while an excellent survey of more recent scholarship, with a nuanced conclusion emphasising the futility of Achilles 'ruling' the dead, is offered by Dova 2012: 18–69. The question of the relationship between the discourse of this speech and the depiction of Achilles in the *Iliad* is made particularly difficult by two questions: (i) Do the words 'you rule (*krateeis*) over the dead' (11.484) and 'to be king (*anassein*) over the corpses of the dead' (11.491) refer to kingship in something like the political sense, or more vaguely to supreme prestige and respect? (ii) Is Odysseus' assertion that 'we honoured you in life as much as the gods' (11.484) a general reference to the respect in which Achilles was held by all, or a specific and even ironic allusion to the disrespect with which he was treated in the Iliadic quarrel with Agamemnon? I suggest that in both cases the former option is more straightforward semantically, and argues against the supposition that the present scene alludes specifically to the *Iliad*.

asks about his son Neoptolemus, who was reared on the island of Scyros before he went to the war:

> But come, tell me the story (*muthos*) of my great-voiced[35] child,
> whether he followed as a champion in the war, or did not.
>
> (*Od.* 11.492–3)

Achilles continues at length, asking about his father Peleus, whether he is suffering from rivals and enemies in his old age without his son to protect him (*Od.* 11.494–503). The pairing of these two questions recalls the one place in the *Iliad* when Achilles spoke of Neoptolemus. Mourning over Patroclus, he said that he would be suffering less pain if he had heard that his father were dead,

> or the dear son who is being reared for me on Scyros,
> if indeed he is still alive, godlike Neoptolemus.   (*Il.* 19.326–7)

In that Iliadic speech Achilles described how he had planned for Patroclus to fetch the boy after his own death and bring him back to his inheritance in Phthia (*Il.* 19.328–33); now in Hades his pre-occupations are different. The chain of ideas behind his questions is easy to reconstruct: the life of the seeker after glory leads to futility, but the hopes and worries of a father for his son endure forever. In answer, Odysseus recounts the boy's successes when he was brought to Troy following his father's death:[36]

> When we were devising our plans around the city of Troy,
> he always spoke first, and never missed the mark in what he said,
> though Nestor the godlike and I alone had the victory.
> But when we Achaeans fought in the plain of the Trojans,
> he never hung back in the throng of men, or the crowd,
> but always he ran forth, yielding to no-one in his force,
> and he slew many men in the bitter combat.   (*Od.* 11.510–16)

He goes on to name many whom Neoptolemus killed in battle, and then gives a still more certain proof of his excellence – the test of courage that the boy underwent while hidden in the Wooden Horse, waiting for the time to emerge and attack:

> There the Greeks' other leaders and counsellors
> were wiping away tears, and their legs were trembling under each of
>   them,

---

[35] On this interpretation of *agauos* see Ch. 11, n. 1.

[36] For this event see Proclus' summary of the *Little Iliad*, para 3: West, *GEF*, pp. 122–3.

but him did I never at all see with my eyes
growing pale in his beautiful face, or wiping
a tear from his cheeks; he continually begged me
to let him out from the horse, he reached for his sword-hilt
and his spear heavy with bronze, and willed evil upon the Trojans.

(*Od.* 11.526–32)

He goes on to say that at the end of the war Neoptolemus set sail for home unharmed, carrying a 'noble award' (*geras esthlon*) of plunder from the sack (*Od.*11.533–7);[37] and without a word the wraith of Achilles walks away across the asphodel meadow,

rejoicing because I had told him that his son was outstanding.

(*Od.* 11.540)

Achilles' words and feelings in this scene fly in the face of his old image. In spirit, indeed, they resonate precisely with the thoughts and hopes for his son's future that Hector, his antithesis in the *Iliad*, speaks of when he stands by the battlements with his wife, looking forward to the day when people will call the boy a better man than his father (*Il.* 6.474–81: see below in the next chapter).

But while he spoke to Achilles and the other dead, says Odysseus, one of them stood apart: the shade of Ajax, 'in rage (*kecholōmenē*)' against Odysseus because of his defeat in the contest for the arms (*Od.* 11.533–6). So the scene completes the taut triangular structure – Achilles as the apogee of the heroic race, Odysseus the supple survivor, Ajax the inflexible and unyielding one who drove himself to suicide. Odysseus cries out to him, railing against his own victory in the contest and its terrible consequences:

Ajax, son of blameless[38] Telamon, could you not
even in death forget your anger (*cholos*) against me, because of those

---

[37] Odysseus says nothing of the atrocities that Neoptolemus was said to have committed in the sack of Troy, especially the murder of Priam when he was a suppliant at the altar of Zeus (see Proclus' summary of the *Sack of Troy*, para. 2: West, *GEF*, pp. 144–5). It is impossible to tell whether he could be said to be suppressing this part of the story for Achilles' sake, or whether it is simply the case that this story is absent from the tradition known to the author and original audience of the *Odyssey*. The same applies to the dark account given in later sources of Neoptolemus' death. Pindar, for example, says that in recompense for the sacrilegious killing of Priam Apollo killed Neoptolemus at Delphi, during a dispute with the attendants at the god's sanctuary (Pindar, *Paean* 6.105–122). A scholiast claims that *Nemean 7*, with its praises of Neoptolemus alongside Ajax among the descendants of Aeacus, was composed as a corrective to the negative account of him given in the *Paeans*, but this is probably no more than a guess (see Race 1987: 2.261; Rutherford 2001: 313–15; Currie 2005: 321–30).

[38] Again *amumōn* (see above, n. 32).

accursed arms? The gods set these things as an affliction for the Greeks:
such a champion was destroyed when you died.   (*Od.* 11.553–6)

Odysseus blames what has happened upon Zeus' anger, a hatred (the verb
is *echthaire*, 11.560) that he does not explain or specify – like the anger of
Athene, who imposed a 'terrible journey home' (*Od.* 1.327) on the Greeks,
this is part of the mysterious background role of the gods. He ends with a
plea to Ajax:

> But come here, king, so that you can hear a word and a discourse
>   (*muthos*)
> from me: but conquer your force and over-manly thought-breath (*thu-*
>   *mos*).   (*Od.* 11.561–2)

Ajax answers nothing, and passes with the other wraiths into the inner
gloom of Hades (11.563–4). His silence and his obstinacy stand in bitter
contrast both to the suppleness of Odysseus and to the new humanity that
the wraith of Achilles has been seen embracing with his thoughts of his son.
Most revealing of all, the phrasing of Odysseus' plea includes a further
echo: *cholos*, the present rage of Ajax, is the same force that drove the wrath
of Achilles, and Odysseus' last words here recall the plea that Phoenix made
in vain to Achilles when he begged him to give up his rage and return to the
war – 'Achilles, conquer your mighty thought-breath (*thumos*): it is not
right for you to have a pitiless heart (*ētor*)' (*Il.* 9.495–6).

Anti-heroic wisdom?

When Ajax plants his sword in the sand and dies, he becomes an image of
the futility of the ideals that drove the half-gods of the Trojan War.
Odysseus' survival in the *Odyssey* represents an escape from that futility;
and behind them both is Achilles' movement from supreme excellence
through rage and defiance to the emptiness of his eternal glory. If what
Odysseus has seen and heard can be interpreted in this way, we are
immediately encouraged to remember Gilgamesh – not just by the overall
thematic configuration but also, more closely, by the moment when the
shade of Achilles, recognising the futility of the heroic way of life, finds
consolation in the news of the praise now being won by his son. Here,
however, the precise point of parallel is *not* with the Standard Babylonian
Version but with the Old Babylonian version of the epic, in one of the
passages which – for reasons no longer recoverable – did not become part

of the canonical edition assembled by Sîn-lēqi-unninni (above, pp. 110–113). Here Shiduri warns Gilgamesh of the futility of his quest for immortality:[39]

> You, Gilgamesh, let your belly be full,
> keep enjoying yourself, day and night!
> Every day make merry,
> dance and play day and night!
> Let your clothes be clean!
> Let your head be washed, may you be bathed in water!
> Gaze on the little one who holds your hand!
> Let a wife enjoy your repeated embrace!
> Such is the destiny (*šīmtu*) [*of mortal men*] …   (OB VA+BM, iii 6–14)

The next line is broken, but there is enough here to show the essence of the teaching: because death is inescapable, it is better to take solace in family and everyday pleasures than in endless striving – whether that striving is Gilgamesh's current search for immortality, or any hero's yearning for a name that will live forever. Looking between the two traditions across nearly a thousand years, the Old Babylonian command *Gaze on the little one who holds your hand* is answered in Achilles' joy when he strides away knowing that his son has grown into a man to be proud of.

An irony is coming into focus. In the literary traditions represented by the Gilgamesh epic and the Homeric poems, we find signs of the same awareness that the demigod's passion for self-validation is barren beside the goodness of everyday things. For all the brilliance of these men of the remote past, the forces that propel them fall short as guiding principles for life: what is truly ordained, *šīmtu*, is the absolute validity of loving one's wife and children. If epic encodes ideals for men of war to follow, it also subverts those ideals and exposes their emptiness: to be Gilgamesh or Achilles is to end in self-defeat, by descending into the darkness of the Underworld or by coming home weary to the walls of Uruk.

---

[39] The parallel is well evoked by Graziosi 2016: 66–7.

16 | The truths of lamentation

Any authentic account of the *Iliad* must include the Trojan champion Hector, whose life and death run in counterpoint with those of Achilles. If we have barely considered Hector up to now, this has been an inevitable consequence of the comparative method: his story does not obviously recall that of Gilgamesh, and indeed it is much harder to find close parallels for him anywhere in the corpus of Mesopotamian literature.[1] His parents and grandparents are mortal, and the divine element in his lineage is remote: this is a man less high and less full of supernatural vitality than Achilles, but also less remote and incalculable.[2] Throughout the *Iliad* and (so far as we know) the poems of the Epic Cycle, his story revolves around practical things: the protection of his city and family and the realities of tactics and leadership on the battlefield. As such he is much closer to the world of the Homeric audience, in terms of ethics and personality as well as action; but he is still a member of the heroic race, even if his descent from divine ancestors is distant by seven generations,[3] and his life and above all his death are part of the same web of ideas that we have traced up to now.

The warrior and the city

The Greeks of the *Iliad* live in the brutally masculine world of an armed camp, but Hector in contrast is prince of a city, a place of order and stability, where the presence of normal social life tempers the ferocity of war.[4] Troy's bane has been Paris' reckless passion[5] and his father's refusal

---

[1] So far as I know, the only close Mesopotamian parallel that has been proposed for Hector is Bachvarova's study comparing the Iliadic Hector with the traditions of Sargon and the *Cuthean Legend of Naram-Sin* (Bachvarova 2016: 166–98). The points of correspondence pointed out by Bachvarova, while striking, seem to me to reflect either typological similarity or (as Bachvarova herself prefers) indirect transmission through a lost intermediary tradition, probably Hittite.

[2] The classic study of Hector in contrast to Achilles remains Redfield 1994: 99–223 *passim*. See the thoughtful reconsideration by Graziosi and Haubold 2005, 98–103; cf. Burgess 2014: 48–50, and my own sketch of the contrast between Hector and Achilles in Clarke 2004, on which I draw closely here.

[3] This is explicit in the genealogy recounted by Aeneas at *Il.* 20.215–40 (see pp. 1–2 above).

[4] Scully 1990.   [5] See esp. *Il.* 3.337–57, 6.280–5, 6.326–30, 6.521–5.

318

to surrender Helen to her people – a refusal that is challenged without success in the public assembly of the Trojans (*Il.* 7.345–79) by Priam's kinsman Antenor, who even at the war's beginning had urged fair treatment for the Greeks.[6] Hector knows the shabby motives of those who insist on persisting with the war, and like any soldier he knows fear. When he faces Ajax in single combat, his heart first palpitates with terror before he masters himself and stands his ground (*Il.* 7.216–18), and likewise he runs from Achilles before controlling himself and facing the combat, deceived into hope by Athene (*Il.* 22.136–44, 248–59). The force that compels him has none of the loftiness of Achilles' passions: it is *aidōs*, the fear of loss of reputation, one of the fundamental ethical forces of ancient Greek society.[7] Twice when advised to avoid a hopeless confrontation he replies with the need to avoid disgrace:

> Terribly
> I feel *aidōs* before Troy's men and its women with their trailing gowns,
> if like a coward I were to linger away from the war:
> my thought-breath does not allow me, because I have learnt to be valorous (*esthlos*)
> always, and to fight among the foremost Trojans,
> defending my father's great fame and my own.
>
> (*Il.* 6.441–6; cf. 22.99–110)

Any everyday soldier might feel such a force acting upon him: its imperatives are those of community, not the intense and self-directed compulsion that drives Achilles or Gilgamesh.

Above all, what associates Hector with ordinary lives and feelings is the fact that he is a loving husband and father.[8] Returning from the battle to order the women to beseech Athene to spare the city – a prayer which she will refuse (*Il.* 6.311) – he goes first to the house of his brother Paris. Paris, already saved from death at Menelaus' hands by his mother Aphrodite, is lurking away from the fighting in which men are dying for his sake, taking this chance to spend the afternoon in bed with Helen (*Il.* 6.326–41).[9] She joins Hector in his bitterness against Paris, wishing that she had died at birth, or that she were the wife of a better man like her first husband (*Il.* 6.349–53, cf. 3.429). From this seedy scene Hector goes to find his wife and child, Andromache and Astyanax – 'king of the city' people call the boy,

---

[6] Apollodorus' account of this episode (*Epitome* 3.28–9) is as usual inserted by West in his edition of Proclus' summary of the *Cypria* (*GEF*, pp. 78–9).

[7] On Hector and *aidōs* see Cairns 1993: 78–83; Redfield 1994: 113–19.

[8] Cf. Burgess 2014: 120–3.   [9] For the beginning of the bedroom scene see *Il.* 3.424–46.

because his father is Troy's saviour (6.403). Andromache has gone to the Scaean gate – 'like a woman in frenzy', he is told (6.389) – and there they greet each other as any wife and husband might do in the midst of war. She begs him to avoid exposing himself to a fatal attack, but *aidōs* prevents him.[10] Yet even as this intensely public sense of moral compulsion is worked out, the thought of the family is uppermost. For Andromache, who has lost all her birth-family in the war, Hector is everything – 'you are my father and mother and brother, and you are my flourishing bedmate' (*Il.* 6.429–30) – and for him too the prospect of defeat is less than the thought that she will be led away to slavery in a distant land (6.447–65). So he goes to lift up Astyanax, putting his aside his crested helmet to quieten the baby's fears, and he prays for his future:

> Zeus and you other gods, grant that this boy of mine
> will become, as I have been, outshining[11] among the Trojans,
> and likewise great in strength, so that by strength he will rule Troy:
> and one day may someone say 'This man is much greater than his father'
> as he comes back from the war, and may he carry the bloody spoils
> after killing an enemy man: and may his mother then be glad.
>
> (*Il.* 6.476–81)

For all Hector's need for victory and praise, his wish for his son to surpass him goes beyond the circles of an ethic based on seeking honour, and it is all the more generous for defying the certainty that its hope cannot be fulfilled. Hector knows that Troy will fall,[12] and there is no comfort in his assurance to his wife that 'no man will send me to Hades beyond the due portion' (*huper aisan*, 6.487).[13] In the staging of this scene there is a dark shadow of the future: the tower at which they stand is the one from which the child will be flung when the city falls – an episode in the Cyclic *Sack of*

---

[10] For a careful analysis of this scene and its ethical background see Graziosi and Haubold 2003, with 2010: 44–7; cf. Schadewaldt 1997 [1961].

[11] The root *prep-* on which *ariprepēs* is built seems basically to refer to shining light, and it can be translated either (a) 'outshining', as of a star (*Il.* 8.556), or (b) in a less vivid sense 'conspicuous, outstanding' (*Il.* 9.44, 23.453). The more vivid translation is encouraged here by the simile at the beginning of the scene comparing Astyanax to 'a beautiful star' (6.401).

[12] Hector's line 'There will be a day when holy Troy will be destroyed' (*Il.* 6.448) repeats words of Agamemnon to Menelaus (*Il.* 4.164), and perhaps reflects the idea that the prophecy of the coming fall of Troy is common knowledge on both sides of the conflict, as originally prophesied by Calchas at Aulis (*Il.* 2.308–29; compare e.g. Diomedes at *Il.* 7.401–2, with *Cypria* Arg. 6 at West, *GEF*, pp. 72–3, and cf. *EC* 104–5).

[13] Note, however, that variant traditions existed in which Astyanax survived and founded a new Troy: it is just possible that Homer through Hector's words is alluding sidelong to such lore (references at West, *EC* 240).

Troy[14] that is already prophesied by Andromache in the *Iliad* after Hector's death (*Il.* 24.734–8). In terms of the broadest typological similarity, if nothing more, Hector in this scene *exemplifies in practice* the ethical ideal towards which Shiduri urged Gilgamesh in the Sippar tablet. The difference, of course, is that he does so at the same time as pursuing the compulsion towards heroic action, valuing glory above the preservation of his own life.

Moving towards excess

Hector's career through the *Iliad* can be plotted along the same curve towards excess and recklessness that we first saw with Diomedes and traced under varying forms in the trajectories of Patroclus and Achilles. Unlike Achilles, however, he is cut off from any understanding of his place in the plots of the gods. Unaware that he is an instrument of Zeus in the plot made with Thetis,[15] he is given hope by auspicious portents in the sky (*Il.* 8.75–7, 8.170–183), and leads a great surge to drive the Greeks back to their ships in defeat. Pursuing this success, he spends the night with his host on the plain outside the city, but his words of encouragement to the men end ominously:

> If only I
> could be immortal and ageless all the days,
> I would be honoured as Athene and Apollo are honoured,
> as now this day brings evil to the Argives.   (*Il.* 8.538–41)

Why does success in battle make this man wish he were a god? What does it say about his susceptibility to folly? As he fights his way towards the ships, the suggestion of an aspiration to become divine reappears in different forms,[16] but it is gradually overshadowed by a cluster of images comparing him to a wild beast – less extreme and less emphatic than the sequence that we plotted for Achilles, but drawing on the same symbolic resources. When Odysseus speaks to Achilles of Hector's wildness, he uses the word *lussa* ('wolf-madness')[17] for the force that fills him (*Il.* 9.238–9); and when eventually, after disregarding Poulydamas' warnings, he bursts through the stockade around the Greek camp, a related idea is developed in a beast-simile similar to others that we observed:

---

[14] *Sack of Troy* fr. 3 at West, *GEF*, pp. 148–9, with Proclus' summary, para. 4 on pp. 146–7. See discussion by Burgess 2001: 65–7; West, *EC* 240–1. Morris 1995 points out that the artistic evidence tends to depict the child being killed at an altar, suggesting a variant tradition (with strong Near Eastern analogues) in which Astyanax was the victim of a human sacrifice.

[15] See Zeus' words to Hera at *Il.* 8.469–77.

[16] He repeats his boast aspiring to immortality at *Il.* 13.825–8.   [17] See above, pp. 282–285.

> As when among dogs and hunting men
> a boar or lion twists around, surging in great strength,
> and towerwise they rally each other
> and stand against it and launch the thronging
> spears from their hands, and its glorying heart
> does not fear or draw back, and excessive manhood[18] kills it . . .
>
> (*Il.* 12.41–6)

Here the words *excessive manhood kills it* are another variant on the formulation seen in the lion-simile applied to Patroclus, 'his own valour destroys him', (*Il.* 16.753: see above, pp. 251–252). As the battle draws closer to the ships Poseidon, disguised as the prophet Calchas to encourage the Greeks, combines the images of bestiality and delusions of divinity:

> Indeed the rabid one (*lussōdēs*) like flame is leading them,
> Hector, who boasts that he is the son of Zeus of great strength.
>
> (*Il.* 13.53–4)

Here, albeit in the words of a god trying to manipulate his enemies into action, Hector is portrayed as making a claim that seems calculated to invite disaster.[19] In the struggle that follows, his mood becomes more and more extreme. He urges his men to accept death if it comes to them, 'it is no disgrace to die in defence of the fatherland' (*Il.* 15.497–8),[20] and the wildness is increasing:

> He was raging as when spear-brandishing Ares or destroying fire
> rages in the mountains, in the thickets of the deep wood;
> foam appeared around his mouth, and his two eyes
> blazed under his bristling[21] brows, and his helmet
> shook terrifyingly around his temples as Hector
> fought . . .   (*Il.* 15.605–10)

Zeus, says Homer, is allowing him now to win glory, but already the god is preparing his death at Achilles' hands (*Il.* 15.612–14); yet Hector knows

---

[18] For this translation of *agēnoriē* cf. Graziosi and Haubold 2003.

[19] It may or may not be a clue to the background to this theme that a variant tradition, ascribed in the ancient sources to Stesichorus and Ibycus, made Hector a son of Apollo and thus Zeus' grandson (see Stesichorus fr. 224 at Campbell, *GL* 3.156–7; Ibycus fr. 295 at *GL* 3, pp. 260–1). This tradition is alluded to by Lycophron (*Alexandra* 264), and commentaries on Lycophron are the main source of knowledge about it.

[20] This is the earliest known enunciation in Western tradition of what has come to be known as the Old Lie, 'It is sweet and fitting to die for one's country' in the familiar words of Horace (*Odes* 3.2.13). Horace's formulation is significantly more emphatic than Hector's, and there is no reason to take the words 'it is no disgrace' as a rhetorical understatement. It is a reasonable guess that there was a lost intermediate text (perhaps in Tyrtaeus?) that exaggerated Hector's words into a more extreme command.

[21] Or in a less concrete sense 'terrifying': *blosuros*, a difficult word.

nothing of this, and in the same ignorance he continues the struggle. When he brings Patroclus to his knees, with the foresight of the dying man his victim warns him that his death is near at the hands of Achilles, but Hector replies that no-one can tell which of them will kill the other (*Il.* 16.851–61). Again, when he faces Achilles he clings to the doomed hope that he may be able to overcome him in combat (see esp. *Il.* 22.129–30, 22.250–9, 22.279–88). But when he finally realises that Athene has tricked him and that he has nothing to hope for, he returns to the simple ethical principles that have shaped him:

> May I not die without a struggle, or without winning fame,
> but after doing a great deed that people of the future will hear of.
>
> (*Il.* 22.304–5)

So framed, these words perfectly encapsulate the warlike ideal in its simplest form, the form in which it would become normative for Tyrtaeus and the Spartans. This is how Hector would become a symbol not of the problematic side of heroism but of the virtuous response to the challenge of patriotic courage, up to the point of laying down one's life for that cause.

The voice of a woman

Although Hector is the model of courage, there is also a darker and more problematic issue here. Did his decisions serve the purpose for which he had taken his stand – that of protecting the city from destruction? Above all, did he need to die? In what Andromache says there is a cogent and consistent argument that he did not. In the scene where they meet on the battlements, her first words sum it up:

> Crazed one,[22] your own force will destroy you, and you have no pity
> for this helpless child or for me, bereft of everything.[23]   (*Il.* 6.407–8)

---

[22] *Daimonie*: although the word seems literally to mean 'possessed', 'in the grip of a divinity', it is often used in gentle mockery, so a harsh translation would be misleading even here.

[23] This is an attempt to render *ammoros*, a difficult word to translate well. If the *a*– is the negative prefix, as seems certain, it ought to indicate the *absence* of the thing named in the second element of the compound; the *–moro–* element would then be understood either as 'portion, share' or 'destiny', like the closely-related nouns *moira, moros*. It does not make sense to say that a person has 'no destiny', since everyone dies. It is better to take the word in something like the sense 'with no share, bereft of everything', comparing *ammoros* said by Helen of herself (*Il.* 24.773), and *dusammoroi* (*Il.* 22.485, 24.727), again Andromache on the wretchedness of herself and Hector.

Your own force will destroy you: this formulation will be repeated in
Homer's own words when Hector penetrates the Greek stockade like
a savage boar (*Il.* 12.46, see above), and here it is virtually a prophecy of
what will happen when he comes face to face with Achilles. She advises him
to draw up his men in the battle-line at the place where the city wall is
weakest, and where the Greeks have previously concentrated their assaults
(*Il.* 6.431–9). This is sound advice to prolong the city's survival, but Hector
answers that the need to strike out for glory overrides such considerations –
in effect, that it overrides tactical prudence – and that the city will fall,
whatever is done to delay its end (*Il.* 6.441–9). In the end, his decision to
stand and face Achilles is prompted by fear of the rebuke he would
suffer for ignoring the warnings of his prudent brother Poulydamas
(*Il.* 22.99–103); and the rebuke would be justified, because his onslaught
on the Greeks has exposed him at the forefront and drawn Achilles out
against him.[24] When Hector has been killed and the women are heard
wailing on the ramparts, Andromache guesses what has happened:

> But terribly
> I fear that bright Achilles has cut fierce Hector off
> in isolation, and has pursued him from the city to the plain,
> and has stopped him from that wretched over-manliness (*agēnoriē*)
> that used to seize him, when he would never remain in the throng of men,
> but rushed out far in front of them, yielding to no-one in his force.
>
> (*Il.* 22.454–9)

In recognising the disastrous consequences of Hector's 'over-manliness',
and in seeing the prudence of a course of action that ignores the need to
seek honour, Andromache sets herself against the dominant norms of the
warriors' world. In that sense, this is essentially a woman's wisdom.

The literature of Hellenic antiquity is shaped and transmitted overwhelmingly by men, and very few female voices survive unmediated – the only
substantial exception is the fragmentary poetry of Sappho. Yet
Andromache's is part of a web of feminine voices that runs through the
Iliad, submerged most of the time but offering a consistent set of alternatives to the values that rule the battlefield. Already in the opening
conflict between Achilles and Agamemnon, in which the women are
treated so brutally as tokens of male prestige, there is a hint of that
alternative voice, when Achilles' sex-slave is seized and taken from his hut:

[24] Hector and the Trojans disregard Poulydamas 'because Athene took away their wits (*phrenes*)'
(*Il.* 18.310–11), an unusually overt statement that their action was folly.

> [The heralds] walked back alongside the ships of the Achaeans,
> and the woman, unwilling, was going alongside them.   (*Il.* 1.347–8)

The one word 'unwilling' opens a window for a moment on the feelings and experiences of this wretched woman, Brises' daughter who is given no name of her own;[25] but thousands of lines of verse pass before we learn more of her experience.

When we do, characteristically, it is in lamentation for the dead, the arena that in Greek and other European traditions has always been the special preserve of the woman's voice.[26] When Agamemnon has finally returned her to Achilles' encampment – along with other gifts, gold and treasure and women – she immediately sees the corpse of Patroclus and sings over him (*Il.* 19.282–300). The song dwells on the sufferings of her own life – her husband and brothers were killed before her own city, one misery succeeding another – but she returns to the dead man himself with an unexpected twist of thought:

> But you would not leave me – when my husband was slain
> by Achilles, and he sacked the city of godlike Mynes –
> you would not leave me to weep, but you said that for godlike Achilles
> you would make me a wedded wife, and bring me in the ships
> to Phthia, and enact our marriage among the Myrmidons.
> So I weep helplessly[27] for you at your death, you who were always
>   gentle.   (*Il.* 19.295–300)

In this celebration of gentleness, and this focus on the miseries that women must endure because of the savagery of men's wars, Brises' daughter opens an alternative, feminised vision of the ethical and psychological world of the warrior.[28]

---

[25] *Briseïs* and *Chryseïs* are transparently patronymics, and although the name of the former's father is not preserved it was presumably parallel to that of *Chryseïs*' father, Chryses the priest of Apollo (*Il.* 1.11, etc.). The use of patronymics for the two girls possibly reflects the realities of naming practices in one or other regional or archaic variety of Greek, but the pattern is so unusual in the epic corpus that it is reasonable to guess at a stylistic or thematic significance. In a translation, to call the girls 'Briseis' and 'Chryseis' is no more necessary than rendering *Hērakleïdēs* (*Il.* 5.628, etc.) as 'Heraclid' rather than 'son of Heracles'. On the thematic implications of this use of patronymics to name the girls, see Dué 2002: 49–65.

[26] The classic longitudinal study of ancient and later Greek lament is Alexiou 2002. For cross-cultural perspectives on ancient lament see Suter 2008.

[27] *amoton*, a difficult word. Forssman (1986) showed that *amoton* is ultimately built on the root **men-*, as also in *menos, memona*, etc., and that the collocation *amoton memaōs* (*Il.* 4.440, 13.40, etc.) in its original form included a chiming linkage (*figura etymologica*) between two words embodying this same root, with a meaning something like 'rushing after things that should not to be rushed after'. In the present phrase, if we take *amoton* in the same way as in *amoton memaōs*, we will get a meaning on the lines of 'weeping without force, without effect'.

[28] Cf. Pucci 1998: 97–112.

The same discourse of woman's wisdom is central to the lamentations
that dominate the account of Hector's funeral after the path of the poem
has led away from Achilles for the last time (*Il.* 24.688).[29] This final scene
evokes a social reality, the dialogue of song between the chief mourners and
the chorus of women.[30] Andromache is the first: she sings above all of the
suffering of their child, who will be enslaved or flung from the tower by
a Greek taking vengeance for someone whom Hector slew, 'for your father
was not gentle in grim battle' (*Il.* 24.739). Then his mother Hecuba sings of
the strange things that the gods have done for him in death, for despite
what Achilles did he now seems unblemished:

> Now dewy and newly slain, it seems to me, in the halls
> you lie, like a man whom Apollo of the silver bow
> has slain, coming upon him with his mild darts.   (*Il.* 24.757–9)

The significance of dew in early Greek thought is profound, it is the essence
of moist and flowing life: to say that Hector looks 'dewy', *hersēeis*, is to say
that his body still has the gleaming vitality of living flesh.[31] Poet and
audience know that this preservation is indeed Apollo's work; but to
these women the sense of calmness is mysterious, and it opens up the
theme of which Helen sings next:

> Now indeed for me this is the twentieth year
> since I came from there [i.e. Greece] and departed from my fatherland;
> but never yet did I hear an evil word from you, or insulting,
> and whenever anyone else in the halls would rebuke me
> of my husband's brothers, or his sisters or his brothers' wives in their
>   trailing gowns,
> or my mother-in-law – though my father-in-law was always gentle like
>   a father –
> you always admonished them with words and restrained them,
> with your kindness of thought and your gentle words.
> So I weep both for you and for myself, bereft of everything,[32] miserable in
>   heart:
> for no-one else to me in broad Troy
> is mild or friendly, they all shudder before me.   (*Il.* 24.765–75)

Like any Trojan, Hector had ample cause to hate Helen as his family did,
but he chose instead to be polite and friendly to her – to this bitch, as she

---

[29] Useful studies of the laments for Hector are Pantelia 2002; Perkell 2008; cf. Redfield 1994: 245,
and Tatum 2003: 171–5.

[30] On the social context of the laments cf. Calame 2001: 82–3; Alexiou 2002: 102–3.

[31] See Clarke 1999: 161, with Boedeker 1984.   [32] *ammoros*: see n. 23 earlier in this chapter.

calls herself,[33] on whose account they have suffered and died. Even to put her praises into the words of our own language seems impossible without bathos, without climbing down from the high register that seems proper to epic poetry. The bathos is an artefact of translation, but the sense of an extraordinary change of thought is authentic.

In the last glimpse that Homer gave of Achilles, he was poised between the compulsion of his lion-like fury and the conciliation that seemed briefly to become possible when he wept with Priam. But that ambiguity was not resolved, and we looked in vain for a summing-up like that at the end of the eleventh tablet of *Gilgamesh*, where the hero's reintegration into the city could be seen (albeit only implicitly) as drawing together the competing currents of thought that flow through the narrative. Unexpectedly, perhaps, the lamentation over Hector provides the resolution that is needed, but in a way that sets at nothing the system of values that has propelled the war and driven the anger of Achilles to its disastrous conclusion. The energy of the warrior, his striving for the stability and security of an escape from death or the surrogate immortality offered by honour and fame – here capping it all is the abiding glory of the simple kindness Hector offered to one who could so easily have been denied it. Here, I suggest, in this dissonance between a woman's words of praise and the ethical and psychological norms of men's wars, is Homer's final expression of the limitations of the ideals for which the demigods strove.

---

[33] For Helen as 'bitch', a label applied to her by herself as well as by others (*Il.* 6.344, 6.356, *Od.* 4.145, etc.), see esp. Blondell 2010, emphasising Helen's assertion of agency in appropriating this negative imagery with her own voice.

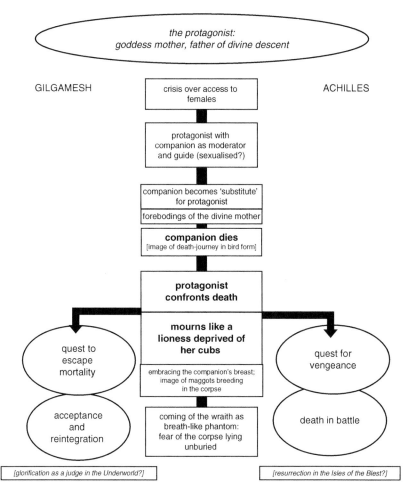

GILGAMESH

ACHILLES

the protagonist:
goddess mother, father of divine descent

crisis over access to
females

protagonist with
companion as moderator
and guide (sexualised?)

companion becomes 'substitute'
for protagonist

forebodings of the divine mother

companion dies
[image of death-journey in bird form]

**protagonist
confronts death**

**mourns like a
lioness deprived of
her cubs**

quest to
escape
mortality

quest for
vengeance

embracing the companion's breast;
image of maggots breeding
in the corpse

acceptance
and
reintegration

coming of the wraith as
breath-like phantom:
fear of the corpse lying
unburied

death in battle

[glorification as a judge in the Underworld?]

[resurrection in the Isles of the Blest?]

Diagram 3 Schematic representation of parallels between Achilles ~ Patroclus and Gilgamesh ~ Enkidu.

Conclusion | The slender-winged fly

The minimal hope behind this book has been that a comparative reading of Greek and Mesopotamian epic would bring us closer to the ancient realities than would a reading of the Homeric poems in isolation. In practice, however, we have been led much further, and the combination of broad thematic similarities with close parallels of wording and imagery asks to be explained in terms of a tighter mode of intertextuality. I will end by proposing a hypothesis, however speculative, to suggest how and why a Greek poet or poets might have allowed elements of the *Epic of Gilgamesh* to become enmeshed in the narrative of Achilles.

Greek and Mesopotamian narrative poetry are fundamentally united by the basic tenets of their theology and cosmology.[1] The presiding divinities of the world are a family of gods, linked by shared structures of kinship and powers over specific areas of the physical universe and of human experience. They can each be identified, to a greater or lesser degree of literalness, with the area of the world in which their power lies; it is their custom to dispute with each other for supremacy, and to make collective decisions in councils or dialogues presided over by the sky-god who acts as their father and leader. When this shared theology includes the principle that the boundaries of each god's powers are ill-defined and debatable, and that this can become the grounds for conflict between them, the parallelism becomes more precise, and it is easy to imagine this providing rich opportunities for the transfer of specific narratives or even chunks of poetic creation from Mesopotamian to Greek literature.

This, or something like it, underpins the multiple correspondences that we observed between the divine politics of *Atrahasis* and Poseidon's complaints about Zeus' usurpation of the rights bestowed in the casting of lots by himself and his brothers (above, pp. 27–34). The point is not merely that the two mythological systems are very similar, or that a particular line or lines have been borrowed from *Atrahasis* and incorporated into the Homeric poem. Rather, the underlying conception of divine

---

[1] On the methodological implications of this principle, see esp. the important exposition by Haubold 2013: 44–72.

power-politics in the two languages was so similar already that it was both easy and natural for this or that specific motif or line of poetry to become re-embedded in the receiving literature.

Gilgamesh and the composition of the *Iliad*

What happens when we try to apply this strategy to the apparent confluence between the narratives of Achilles and Gilgamesh? Here, I suggest, the starting-point should be in the shared conception of the contrast between gods and mortals. Mankind today is weak and feeble, but the poetic tradition looks back to a time closer to our origins when there were men, identifiable as the ancestors or forebears of later kings, who were close to the power and vitality of the gods themselves. Such men, located at the junction between unknowable primeval times and those of familiar human history, are the preoccupation of a genre of serious narrative poetry – epic – whose themes and messages look across towards those of wisdom literature. Added to this is the more precisely focussed concept that a decisive, destructive intervention by the gods ended the time of close mingling between gods and mortals. In early Greek tradition, the Trojan War played a similar role to the Flood in Mesopotamian lore; because of this deep conceptual affinity it became possible for the author of the *Cypria* (or a predecessor) to borrow a narrative akin to or identical with the story of the overpopulated earth in *Atrahasis*, in order to set up an explanation for Zeus' decision to destroy the Race of Heroes in war. Characteristically, that wordsmith left a trace of his source by including the specific motif of destruction by flood as an option that was considered by the god but not implemented (above, p. 161). At this distance one can only speculate whether an original audience might have heard in the *Cypria* an allusion to the Flood narrative proper. A Cypriot might well have been sensitive to resonances and subtleties that were lost when the poem was heard in other areas of the Greek-speaking world.

It is not coincidental, I think, that many of the most convincing examples adduced by scholars for correlations between Greek and Mesopotamian poetry have been concerned with status-relationships among individual gods (as in the 'gods playing dice' discussed above), or between gods and the members of the ambiguous race of heroes, caught just within the limits of mortality. An instructive example here is the remarkable passage of *Iliad* 5 in which Diomedes fights the goddess Aphrodite (see above, pp. 193–195). The correlations between the goddess's behaviour and that of Ishtar in the *Epic of Gilgamesh* are so close, and involve such precisely structured similarities – right down to the naming of Aphrodite's parents as a pair mirroring Anu and Antu – that the argument for direct influence feels overwhelming. As Currie puts it,

> [t]he correspondences seem specific and extensive enough to rule out parallel development in independent but similar poetic traditions. This is not the reception of an isolated motif, but of several motifs structured in a particular narrative sequence.[2]

The vital point here is the alliance between similarity of structure and identity of motifs: the systematic nature of the correspondences encourages the suspicion that we are coming to grips with the creation of poetic meaning by an active agent or agents, rather than mere autonomous drift of ideas and images.

   Diomedes' encounter with Aphrodite is, of course, a short episode in a poem more largely concerned with the struggles of mortals against each other. As we have noted (above, p. 57, cf. 318), in Sumerian and Akkadian there is comparatively little evidence for narrative myth whose central concern is with human interactions in battle, still less for a focus on relationships *between* warriors fighting alongside each other in the battle-line. In international terms, the Trojan War tradition from which the *Iliad* was created may well have been rather unusual. But we can speculate further. It would be reasonable to presume that even *before* the composition of our *Iliad*, the accepted version of the conflict between Achilles and Agamemnon took a form suggestively similar to the internationally established narrative sequence centred on Gilgamesh. It revolves around an archetypally brilliant hero who has a goddess for a mother and a father who is mortal but ultimately of divine ancestry. Conflict is set in motion by strife arising from the abuse of the royal power of privileged sexual access. This leads to a new narrative movement centred on the intimate friendship between the protagonist and his companion, in which the companion meets an inglorious end; the death is followed by the protagonist's inevitable movement towards his own death. So far, these resemblances are partial and imperfect, and do not need to be more than an effect of the general cultural affinities between the two traditions; but they explain why a Greek composer, Homer or a predecessor, *might* have seen that Gilgamesh and Enkidu would serve as a model for shaping or reshaping a narrative of Achilles and Patroclus, and that this would add depth and

----

[2] Currie 2016: 174.

meaning to his new account of the tragic outcome of their friendship. The result is the system of structural parallels and local correspondences summed up in Diagram 3 (p. 328). This should be seen not as an historical reconstruction but as a purely abstract summary of the parallels that we have adduced in the course of this study, with the relative strength of the individual parallels indicated by variations in the prominence of the type.

The crux is the conceptualisation of the friendship itself. The companion has been assigned to guide and moderate the protagonist, whose very brilliance is problematic: this is the reason why Enkidu was created (*SBV* I 97, etc.), and it is the reason (albeit very differently articulated) why Patroclus was sent to the war with Achilles (*Il.* 11.786–9; see above, p. 213). In each case the friendship is intensely bonded, and open to a potentially sexualised reading, but this is not (yet) made explicit in the text. The protagonist's divine mother foresees that he is doomed to die, but cannot stop it. The turning-point comes when the companion is assigned to death in place of the protagonist. The decision to doom the lesser man instead of the greater is sanctioned by the great sky-god, but the motivation or the moral justification for the decision remains mysterious: why did Zeus deny Achilles his prayer that Patroclus should return safe from his attack (*Il.* 16.249–52), and why did Enlil demand the death of Enkidu alone to satisfy him for the injuries they had done to him together (above, pp. 78–79)?[3] In both epics there is a potential allusion to the idea that the companion dies as a substitute victim in place of the protagonist. This is only a doubtful inference in the *Iliad*, but in *Gilgamesh* it is momentarily made explicit when Enkidu stands in Uruk as the 'substitute' (*pūḫu*) for Gilgamesh (see above, pp. 82–84, 241–249). So he dies a death of inglorious failure: despite the obvious differences in the articulation, this theme is seen both when Enkidu slips away from sickness, and when Patroclus is beaten down before the walls of Troy.

The first possible *verbal* correlation comes at this point, the death of the companion. In one of his dreams foretelling his own death, Enkidu describes himself as transformed into a dove and led captive to the Underworld, where the dead dwell in feathered form; the breath-soul of Patroclus, similarly, is described as flying to Hades as if it were in bird-form, crying out in dismay at its own death (*SBV* VII 182–90, *Il.* 16.855–7; above, pp. 81, 252–254). This particular instance is only a tentative suggestion; but the correspondences are unmistakeable when the protagonist

---

[3] As noted (p. 77), there is a gap here in the Standard Babylonian Version, so we depend largely on speculation for this point.

responds to the companion's death. When Achilles places his hands on Patroclus' breast and groans like a lion whose cubs have been stolen by a hunter, we have virtually a word-for-word assimilation into Greek of a sequence from the Akkadian text, placed at precisely the same point in the narrative structure (see above, pp. 269–271). The festering of maggots in the body is the next direct linkage: it is stated in *Gilgamesh*, and feared as a prospect in the *Iliad* (pp. 274–275). Near the very end of each epic, the wraith of the companion appears to the protagonist in a dream, moving like wind or smoke; he discourses to his friend on the fate of the dead in the afterlife, including that of the unburied dead who wander disconsolate – an image which Enkidu includes among a sequence of sufferers in the Underworld, but which Patroclus identifies as his own plight as long as Achilles refuses to commit his corpse to the earth (above, pp. 110, 289–292).

The set of *Gilgamesh* images in the story of Achilles and Patroclus has two remarkable characteristics. First, the images are perfectly integrated: as noted each time in our study, if the Gilgamesh epic did not survive we would never guess that these things were anything but pure Homeric invention. Second, they follow the same *sequence* in the two epics: in other words, they serve to articulate the Achilles ~ Patroclus narrative along the structural template provided by Gilgamesh ~ Enkidu. I argue that the pattern cannot be sufficiently explained simply as independent developments from the common cultural background; nor is this merely a 'cluster' of stray borrowings, to be explained by proposing that this particular section of the *Iliad* originated in a place where Near Eastern influences were unusually strong.[4] In either case it would be an implausible coincidence for the motifs both to serve such similar poetic functions and to occur in the same linear order. The correlations are so tightly woven, and so systematic, that they begin to look like the result of a creative intellect reaching from one story-line to another.

If we are right to see this as the work of a single project of adaptation, and a deliberate one, we can be more precise about the nature and even the date of what has happened. Because the final point of parallel, the ghost of Patroclus in *Iliad* 23, finds its match in the Twelfth Tablet of *Gilgamesh*, it

---

[4] An explanation of this kind is proposed, for example, by Burkert to explain the apparent 'clustering' of images with Near Eastern affinities in the 'Deception of Zeus' section of *Iliad* 14 (Burkert 1992 [1984]: 91–6; Burkert 2004: 29–34). Even without invoking the trenchant critique of this approach by Kelly 2008: 274–92, the vital difference is that the relationship between Gilgamesh ~ Enkidu and Achilles ~ Patroclus is ordered and structured, suggesting a meaningful project of composition rather than the atomistic and unsystematic borrowing process implied by Burkert. See also above, Ch. 1, pp. 31–34.

follows that the process of assimilation was enacted at some time after the Twelfth Tablet had been added to the original eleven-tablet epic that concluded with Gilgamesh's return to Uruk (see Ch. 4, n. 42). This rules out locating the key moment back in the Mycenaean period, and suggests that the contact came relatively late in the development of the Greek epic tradition towards Homer, postdating the editorial work of Sîn-lēqi-unninni and the dissemination of *Gilgamesh* in this form as a standard text.

Beyond that, we can only speculate how this happened. The entire configuration could be seen as the result of transference by singers and storytellers in an oral mode, whose communicative world is lost to us by definition, but (in the absence of any direct evidence) it is no less realistic to imagine a Homer who was somehow aware of the canonical *Epic of Gilgamesh* and mapped it onto Achilles as a conscious creative project. That Homer was certainly open to the compositional strategy of setting one 'heroic biography' in parallel with another is shown (for example) by the subtle and brilliant grafting of the story of Meleager onto that of Achilles in the speech of Phoenix (above, pp. 226–232).[5] The difference here, of course, is that the Gilgamesh material remains submerged, and the parallelism is never explicitly acknowledged, but this too might be part of the poetic art, just as episodes of our *Iliad* can be seen as covertly foreshadowing or alluding to other episodes of the Trojan War as told in the predecessors of the Cyclic epics.[6] Nor is there any reason to draw a sharp divide between oral and text-based transference. It is harmless to wonder what might have happened if a future poet in Archaic Greece had been lulled to sleep in childhood by a slave-woman who had listened, in the days before her abduction, to stories told by a husband who worked as a scribe copying archive tablets of Babylonian narrative literature.[7] Such is the power of invisible cultural networks, in that or any world.

Uta-napishti and Simonides

Even if this tentative reconstruction carries conviction, however, it is only one aspect of an analysis of the *Iliad*. Part of the lesson of this study should be that in essential respects the Homeric creation is utterly different from

---

[5] The list of possible examples of this phenomenon could be extended indefinitely: see for example West 2005b, proposing a pre-Homeric version of the *Argonautica* as an implicit model or template for the wanderings of Odysseus in the *Odyssey* (and, incidentally, proposing that there are *Gilgamesh* elements involved here too).

[6] For this analogy see Currie 2016, esp. 208–28.

[7] On women as mediators between traditions cf. López-Ruiz 2010: 36–8, 199–201, and above, p. 19.

Gilgamesh – as, indeed, from anything known from the literary inheritance of the lands east of the Aegean. Above all, the contrast must inform our assessment of the ways in which the two protagonists turn towards their own deaths. The savagery of Achilles' drive to kill Hector in vengeance, and the defiance of his own coming death that speaks so powerfully to the Socrates of Plato's *Apology*, have no model or counterpart in the journey of Gilgamesh and his meeting with Uta-napishti. To help the two traditions to meet again, we had to fall back on a looser mode of analogy. However intimate the *thematic* resonances between the *Odyssey*'s Achilles in Hades and the Old Babylonian version of the teaching of Shiduri (above, pp. 312–317), they depend on bringing together passages with completely different contexts and dramatic forms. Nonetheless the affinity of mood and message is powerfully clear, showing that the idea of the inadequacy of the heroic ideal was integral to both traditions.

This last point is vital. The central matter is the deeds and deaths of men of war, but the central wisdom relies on stepping outside the arena of action and exploring not its glamour but its futility. Here, as in our discussion of Hector in the last chapter, we need to listen again to voices of lamentation. The Greek poets of choral lyric are best known for their songs in praise of warriors and athletes, associating them with the glamour of the Race of Heroes; but they also worked in the genre of composition called *thrēnos*, lamentations to be sung by girls and women as part of the funerary ritual.[8] From Simonides and Pindar there survives a handful of short quotations from these songs, mostly enunciations of pessimistic wisdom – the brevity of life, the universality of suffering, the powerlessness of man under the gods. Among them is the following:

> Since you are human, never say what will happen tomorrow,
> and when you see a man fortunate you cannot say how long he will
>   remain;
> swift is the passing-away, swifter than that of a slender-winged fly.
> > (Simonides fr. 521.1–4: Campbell, *GL* 3, pp. 416–19)

Without the original context, we cannot reconstruct for certain the discourse of which this formed a part: does *metastasis* 'passing-away' refer to the instability of fortune or the inevitability of death – or both? The question is a fine one,[9] but either way the image of human instability as

---

[8] On the definition of *thrēnos* see Alexiou 2002: 11–13, 102–4.

[9] In detail the question comes down to the syntax implied by the words 'for how long a time he will be (*essetai*)'. In Greek the verb 'to be' can be used in two ways, for predication ('x is y') and for existence ('x exists'). The present instance is ambiguous. If the word *olbios* 'fortunate' is implicit

the passing-away of a fly (*muia*) recalls Uta-napishti's words when he taught Gilgamesh about the universality of death:

> At some time the river rose (and) brought the flood,
> the mayfly floating on the water.
> Its countenance was gazing on the face of the sun,
> then all of a sudden nothing was there!   (*SBV* X 312–15)

The exact parallel in Simonides' image might encourage the suspicion that this is another case of direct reception; but even without such a claim, the similarity is testimony to the kinship between Greek lamentation and the traditions of wisdom literature in which Uta-napishti's whole speech is immersed.

Mortality defeats the striving of demigods and the aspirations of those who follow their path: this insight is bound up with recognising the feebleness and uncertainty of the mortal condition, just as Simonides' dirge and Uta-napishti's teaching urge us to do. Both have much in common with the pessimistic son in *Shima Milka*:

> My father, you built a house,
> you elevated high the door; sixty cubits is the width of your (house).
> But what have you achieved? . . .
> Few are the days in which we eat (our) bread, but many are the days in
>   which our teeth will be idle,
> few are the days in which we look at the Sun, but many will be the days in
>   which we will sit in the shadows.[10]

It is no coincidence, I suggest, that the thought in these lines is so closely shadowed in the words used both by Zeus when he looks down on the struggles of warriors on the battlefield (*Il.* 17.446–7), and by Odysseus after the sufferings of experience have brought him to nothingness and back again:

> Earth nourishes nothing more insubstantial than humanity
> of all things that breathe and creep across the Earth.
> No-one ever says that he will suffer evil in the future,

here after 'will be', suppressed in the clause because it has already appeared earlier in the sentence, then we have an instance of the predicative sense of 'be': 'you cannot say how long he will be [prosperous]'. If on the other hand *essetai* is taken on its own, it signifies existence – 'you cannot say how long he will exist, how long he will live'. Presumably we could choose decisively if we had access to the longer passage of which these lines were once a part. The translation displayed here adopts the 'existence' interpretation, which seems to me more satisfactory because otherwise *essetai* must be read with an awkward ellipsis.

[10] See above, pp. 54–56.

while the gods give him valour (*aretē*) and he can move his knees;
but when the immortal gods bring evil to fulfilment,
this too he must bear in degradation, in his suffering thought;
for earth-dwelling humans have only this to expect,
whatever the father of gods and men will bring from day to day.

(*Od.* 18.130–7)

Gilgamesh and Achilles begin from the compulsion to exalt oneself above smaller and weaker men, to achieve an everlasting name and avoid disgrace above all things; but they are led, and they lead us who contemplate them, towards the truth that the heroic ideal slips away in face of the instabilities of mortal life. This, I suggest, is the fundamental wisdom that brings the Greek and Mesopotamian heroic narratives into alignment with each other.

Bibliography

Abusch, T. (1998), 'Ghost and god: some observations on a Babylonian understanding of human nature', in A. I. Baumgarten, J. Assmann and G. G. Stroumsa (eds.), *Self, Soul and Body in Religious Experience* (Leiden), 363–83.

　(2001), 'The development and meaning of the Epic of Gilgamesh', *Journal of the American Oriental Society* 121, 614–22 [also reprinted in Abusch (2015), 119–26].

　(2015), *Male and Female in the Epic of Gilgamesh: Literary History and Interpretation* (Winona Lake, IN).

Abusch, T., J. Huehnergard and P. Steinkeller (eds.) (1990), *Lingering over Words: Studies in Ancient Near Eastern Literature in Honor of William L. Moran* (Atlanta, GA).

Adkins, A. W. H. (1960), *Merit and Responsibility: A Study in Greek Values* (Oxford).

Adler, W. and P. Tuffin (2002), *The Chronography of George Synkellos: A Byzantine Chronicle of Universal History since the Creation* (Oxford).

Ahrensdorf, P. J. (2014), *Homer on the Gods and Human Virtue: Creating the Foundations of Classical Civilization* (Cambridge).

Alden, M. (2000), *Homer Beside Himself: Para-Narratives in the* Iliad (Oxford).

　(2005), 'Lions in paradise: lion similes in the *Iliad* and the lion cubs of *Il.* 18.318–22', *Classical Quarterly* 55, 335–42.

　(2012), 'The despised migrant (*Il.* 9.468 = 16.59)', in Montanari et al. (2012), 115–39.

Alexander, M. (2001), *Beowulf: A Verse Translation*, rev. edn. (Harmondsworth).

Alexiou, M. (2002), *The Ritual Lament in Greek Tradition*, 2nd edn. (Lanham, MD).

Allan, W. (2006), 'Divine justice and cosmic order in early Greek epic', *Journal of Hellenic Studies* 126, 1–35.

　(ed.) (2008a), Euripides, *Helen*, Cambridge Greek and Latin Classics (Cambridge).

　(2008b), 'Performing the will of Zeus: the *Dios boulē* and the scope of early Greek epic', in M. Revermann and P. Wilson (eds.), *Performance, Iconography, Reception: Studies in Honour of Oliver Taplin* (Oxford), 204–16.

Al-Rawi, F. N. H. and A. R. George (2014), 'Back to the Cedar Forest: the beginning and end of Tablet V of the Standard Babylonian *Epic of Gilgamesh*', *Journal of Cuneiform Studies* 66, 69–86.

Alster, B. (1990), 'Lugalbanda and the early epic tradition in Mesopotamia', in Abusch et al. (1990), 59–72.

(1997), *Proverbs of Ancient Sumer* (Bethesda, MD).

(2005a), *The Wisdom of Ancient Sumer* (Bethesda, MD).

(2005b), 'Demons in the Conclusion of *Lugalbanda in Hurrumkurra*', *Iraq* 67, 61–71.

Anderson, M. (1997), *The Fall of Troy in Early Greek Poetry and Art* (Oxford).

Anderson, O. (1997), 'Diomedes, Aphrodite and Dione: background and function of a scene in Homer's *Iliad*', *Classica et Mediaevalia* 48, 25–36.

Anthony, D. W. (2007), *The Horse, the Wheel, and Language: How Bronze-Age Riders from the Eurasian Steppes Shaped the Modern World* (Princeton).

Antonaccio, C. M. (1995), *An Archaeology of Ancestors: Tomb Cult and Hero Cult in Early Greece* (Langham, MD).

(2006), 'Religion, *basileis* and heroes', in Deger-Jalkotzy and Lemos (2006), 381–95.

Aruz, J. (2013), 'Seals and the imagery of interaction', in Aruz et al. (2013), 216–25.

Aruz, J., K. Benzel and J. M. Evans (eds.) (2008), *Beyond Babylon: Art, Trade and Diplomacy in the Second Millennium BC*, exhibition catalogue (New York).

Aruz, J., S. B. Graff and Y. Rakic (eds.) (2013), *Cultures in Contact: From Mesopotamia to the Mediterranean in the Second Millennium BC* (New York).

Aruz, J., S. B. Graff and Y. Rakic (eds.) (2014), *Assyria to Iberia: Art and Culture in the Iron Age*, exhibition catalogue (New York).

Aruz, J. and R. Wallenfels (eds.) (2003), *The Art of the First Cities: The Third Millennium BC from the Mediterranean to the Indus*, exhibition catalogue (New York).

Asheri, D., A. Lloyd, and A. Corcella (2007), *A Commentary on Herodotus Books I–IV* (Oxford).

Ataç, M.-A. (2010), *The Mythology of Kingship in Neo-Assyrian Art* (Cambridge).

Austin, N. (1994), *Helen of Troy and Her Shameless Phantom* (Ithaca, NY).

Avery, H. A. (1998), 'Achilles' third father', *Hermes* 126, 389–97.

Babbitt, F. C. (ed.) (1927), Plutarch, *Moralia*, vol. 1 (Loeb Classical Library) (Cambridge, MA).

Bachhuber, C. (2006), 'Aegean interest on the Uluburun ship', *American Journal of Archaeology* 110, 345–63.

Bachvarova, M. R. (2008), 'The poet's point of view and the prehistory of the *Iliad*', in B. J. Collins, M. R. Bachvarova and I. C. Rutherford (eds.), *Anatolian Interfaces: Hittites, Greeks and Their Neighbours* (Oxford), 93–106.

(2016), *From Hittite to Homer: The Anatolian Background of Homeric Epic* (Cambridge).

Bader, F. (1989), *La Langue des dieux, ou l'hermétisme des poètes indo-européens* (Paris).

Baker, H. D., E. Robson and G. Zólyomi (eds.) (2010), *Your Praise Is Sweet: A Memorial Volume for Jeremy Black* (London).

Barker, E. (2008), '*Momos advises Zeus:* changing representations of *Cypria* Fragment 1', in E. Cingano and L. Milano (eds.), *Papers on Ancient Literatures: Greece, Rome and the Near East* (Padua), 33–74.

Barré, M. (2001), '"Wandering about" as a topos of depression in ancient Near Eastern literature and the Bible', *Journal of Near Eastern Studies* 60, 177–87.

Barringer, J. M. (2013), 'Hunters and hunting on the François vase', in Shapiro et al. (2013), 153–67.

Baumbach, M., A. Petrovic, and I. Petrovic (eds.) (2010), *Archaic and Classical Greek Epigram: Contextualization and Literarization* (Cambridge).

Becker, A. S. (1995), *The Shield of Achilles and the Poetics of Ekphrasis* (Maldon, MD).

Beckman, G. (2001), 'The Hittite Gilgamesh', in Foster (2001), 157–65.

(2003), 'Gilgamesh in Hatti', in G. Beckman, R. Beal and G. McMahon (eds.), *Hittite Studies in Honor of Harry A. Hoffner Jr.* (Winona Lake, IN), 37–57.

(2013), 'Under the spell of Babylon: Mesopotamian influence on the religion of the Hittites', in Aruz et al. (2013), 284–97.

Beckman, G., T. R. Bryce and E. H. Cline (2011), *The Ahhiyawa Texts* (Atlanta, GA)

Beecroft, A. (2006), '"This Is Not a True Story": Stesichorus's *Palinode* and the revenge of the epichoric', *Transactions of the American Philological Association* 136, 47–69.

(2010), *Authorship and Cultural Identity in Early Greece and China: Patterns of Literary Circulation* (Cambridge).

(2011), 'Blindness and literacy in the Lives of Homer', *Classical Quarterly* 61, 1–18.

Bendlin, A. (2007), 'Purity and pollution', in Ogden (2007), 178–89.

Black, J. (1998), *Reading Sumerian Poetry* (Ithaca, NY).

Black, J. and A. Green (1992), *Gods, Demons and Symbols of Ancient Mesopotamia* (London).

Black, J., G. Cunningham, E. Robson, and G. Zólyomi (2004), *The Literature of Ancient Sumer* (Oxford).

Black, J., A. George, and N. Postgate (eds.) (2000), *A Concise Dictionary of Akkadian*, 2nd edn. (Wiesbaden).

Blanc, A. (2002), 'Disguised compounds in Greek: Homeric *ablēchros, agauos, akmēnos, tēlugetos* and *chuliphrōn*', *Transactions of the Philological Society* 100, 169–84.

Blondell, R. (2010), '"Bitch that I am": self-blame and self-assertion in the *Iliad*', *Transactions of the American Philological Association* 140, 1–32.

Boedeker, D. (1984), *Descent from Heaven: Images of Dew in Greek Poetry and Religion* (Chico, CA).

(2001a), 'Paths to heroization at Plataea', in Boedeker and Sider (eds.) (2001), 148–63.

(2001b), 'Heroic historiography: Simonides and Herodotus on Plataea', in Boedeker and Sider (2001), 120–32.

Boedeker, D. and D. Sider (eds.) (2001), *The New Simonides: Contexts of Praise and Desire* (Oxford).

Bonifazi, A. (2009), 'Inquiring into *nostos* and its cognates', *American Journal of Philology* 130, 481–510.

Borg, B. E. (2010), 'Epigrams in archaic art: the 'Chest of Cypselus', in Baumbach et al. (2010), 81–99.

Borger, R. (1974), 'Die Beschwörungsserie *Bīt Mēseri* und die Himmelfahrt Henochs', *Journal of Near Eastern Studies* 33, 183–96.

(1994), 'The incantation series *Bīt Mēseri* and Enoch's ascension to Heaven', in R. S. Hess and D. T. Tsumura (eds.), *I Studied Inscriptions from Before the Flood: Ancient Near Eastern, Literary, and Linguistic Approaches to Genesis 1–11* (Winona Lake, IN), 224–31.

Bottéro, J. (1992), *Mesopotamia: Writing, Reasoning, and the Gods* (Chicago) [translated from *Mésopotamie: L'écriture, la raison et les dieux* (1987)].

Boureau, A. (1998), *The Lord's First Night: The Myth of the* Droit de Cuissage (Chicago).

Bracke, E. (forthcoming), 'Between cunning and chaos: the entry for *mētis*', in Stray et al. (eds.), *Liddell and Scott* (forthcoming).

Bremmer, J. (2002), 'Sacrificing a child in ancient Greece', in E. Noort and E. Tigchelaar (eds.), *The Sacrifice of Isaac: The Aqedah (Genesis 22) and Its Interpretations* (Leiden), 21–43.

(2006), 'The rise of the hero cult and the new Simonides', *Zeitschrift für Papyrologie und Epigraphik* 158, 15–26.

(2008), *Greek Religion and Culture, the Bible and the Ancient Near East* (Leiden).

Brisch, N. (ed.) (2008), *Religion and Power: Divine Kingship in the Ancient World and Beyond* (Chicago).

Broodbank, C. (2013), *The Making of the Middle Sea: A History of the Mediterranean from the Beginning to the Emergence of the Classical World* (London).

Brown, C. G. (2011), 'To the ends of the earth: Sappho on Tithonus', *Zeitschrift für Papyrologie und Epigraphik* 178, 21–5.

(2014), 'Vipers and lost youth: a note on old age in early Greek epic', *Classical Quarterly* 64, 825–7.

Brownlee, A. B. (1995), 'Story lines: observations on the Sophilan narrative', in Carter and Morris (1995), 363–72.

Bryce, T. (2002), *Life and Society in the Hittite World* (Oxford).

(2006), *The Trojans and Their Neighbours* (London).

Budin, S. (2010), 'Aphrodite *Enoplion*', in Smith and Pickup (2010), 79–112.

Burgess, J. S. (1995), 'Achilles' heel: the death of Achilles in ancient myth', *Classical Antiquity* 14, 217–43.

(1997), 'Beyond neo-analysis: problems with the vengeance theory', *American Journal of Philology* 118, 1–19.

(1999), 'Gilgamesh and Odysseus in the Underworld', *Classical Views/Échos du Monde Classique* 43, 171–210.

(2001), *The Tradition of the Trojan War in Homer and the Epic Cycle* (Baltimore).

(2004a), 'Untrustworthy Apollo and the destiny of Achilles: *Iliad* 24.55–63', *Harvard Studies in Classical Philology* 102, 21–40.

(2004b), 'Early images of Achilles and Memnon?', *Quaderni Urbinati di Cultura Classica* 76, 33–51.

(2006), 'Neoanalysis, orality, and intertextuality: an examination of Homeric motif transference', *Oral Tradition* 21, 148–89.

(2009), *The Death and Afterlife of Achilles* (Baltimore).

(2012), 'Intertextuality without text in Greek epic', in Ø. Andersen and D. T. T. Haug (eds.), *Relative Chronology in Early Greek Epic Poetry* (Cambridge), 168–83.

(2014), *Homer* (London).

(2017), 'The tale of Meleager in the *Iliad*', *Oral Tradition* 31, 51–76.

Burkert, W. (1992), *The Orientalising Revolution: Near Eastern Influences on Greek Culture in the Early Archaic Age* (Cambridge, MA). [originally published as *Die Orientalisierende Epoche in der griechischen Religion und Literatur* (Heidelberg, 1984)].

(2004), *Babylon, Memphis, Persepolis: Eastern Contexts of Greek Culture* (Cambridge, MA).

Burnett, A. P. (2005), *Pindar's Songs for Young Athletes of Aigina* (Oxford).

Burrow, J. A. (1986), *The Ages of Man: A Study in Medieval Writing and Thought* (Oxford).

Busco, M. F. (1988), 'The Achilles in Hyde Park', *Burlington Magazine* 130, 920–4.

Cairns, D. L. (1993), *Aidos: The Psychology and Ethics of Honour and Shame in Ancient Greek Literature* (Oxford).

(1996), '*Hybris*, dishonour, and thinking big', *Journal of Hellenic Studies* 113, 1–32.

(ed.) (2001a), *Oxford Readings in Homer's* Iliad (Oxford).

(2001b), 'Anger and the veil in ancient Greek culture', *Greece and Rome* 48, 18–32.

(2003a), 'Ethics, ethology, terminology: Iliadic anger and the cross-cultural study of emotion', in S. Braund and G. Most (eds.), *Ancient Anger: Perspectives from Homer to Galen* (Cambridge), 11–49.

(2003b), 'Myths and metaphors of mind and mortality', *Hermathena* 175, 41–75.

(ed.) (2010), Bacchylides, *Five Epinician Odes* (Cambridge: Francis Cairns Publications).

(2011a), 'Ransom and revenge in the *Iliad*', in S. Lambert (ed.), *Sociable Man: Essays on Ancient Greek Social Behaviour in Honour of N. R. E. Fisher* (Swansea), 87–116.

(2011b), '*Poine* and *apoina* in the *Iliad*', in M. Linder and S. Tausend (eds.), '*Böser Krieg*': *Exzessive Gewalt in der antiken Kriegsführung und Strategien zu deren Vermeidung* (Graz), 35–50.

(2012), '*Atē* in the Homeric poems', *Papers of the Langford Latin Seminar* 15, 1–52.

(2014), '*Psuche, thumos* and metaphor in Homer and Plato', *Études platoniciennes* 11, www.etudesplatoniciennes.revues.org/566.

Cairns, D.L. and R. Scodel (eds.) (2014), *Defining Greek Narrative* (Edinburgh).

Calame, C. (2001), *Choruses of Young Women in Ancient Greece: Their Morphology, Religious Role, and Social Functions*, rev. ed. (Lanham, MD).

Canevaro, L. G. (2015), *Hesiod's* Works and Days: *How to Teach Self-Sufficiency* (Oxford).

Carpenter, T. (2015), 'The Trojan War in early Greek art', in Fantuzzi and Tsagalis (2015a), 178–95.

Carter, E. and S. P. Morris (2014), 'Crisis in the eastern Mediterranean and beyond: survival, revival and the emergence of the Iron Age', in Aruz et al. (2014), 14–23.

Carter, J. B. and S. P. Morris (eds.) (1995), *The Ages of Homer: A Tribute to Emily Townsend Vermeule* (Austin, TX).

Cartledge, P. (1993), *The Greeks: A Portrait of Self and Others* (Oxford).

Cavigneaux, A. and F. N. H. Al-Rawi (1993), 'Gilgameš et le taureau de ciel (Šul-mè-kam) (Textes de Tell Haddad IV)', *Revue d' Assyriologie et d'archéologie orientale* 87, 97–129.

Cavigneaux, A. and F. N. H. Al-Rawi (2000a), 'La fin de *Gilgamesh, Enkidu et l'Enfers* d' après les manuscrits d'Ur et de Meturan (Textes de Tell Haddad VIII)', *Iraq* 62, 1–19.

Cavigneaux, A. and F.N.H. Al-Rawi (2000b), *Gilgameš et la Mort. Textes de Tell Haddad VI* (Winona Lake, IN).

Chadwick, H. M. (1912), *The Heroic Age* (London).

Chadwick, H. M. and N. K. Chadwick (1932–40), *The Growth of Literature*, 3 vols. (Cambridge).

Chen, Y. S. (2013), *The Primeval Flood Catastrophe: Origins and Early Development in Mesopotamian Traditions* (Oxford).

Childs, W. A. P. (2003), 'The human animal: the Near East and Greece', in Padgett (2003), 49–72.

Chiodi, S. M. (1995), 'Il prigioniero e il morto: *Epopea di Gilgameš* Tav. X r. 318–20', *Orientis antiqui miscellanea* 2, 159–71.

Cingano, E. (2005), 'A catalogue within a catalogue: Helen's suitors in the Hesiodic *Catalogue of Women*', in Hunter (2005a), 118–52.

Clackson, J. (2007), *Indo-European Linguistics: An Introduction* (Cambridge).

Clarke, M. (1993), 'Heroic second selves' (review of Van Nortwick (1992)), *Classical Review* 43, 68–70.

(1995a), 'Between lions and men: images of the hero in the *Iliad*', *Greek, Roman and Byzantine Studies* 37, 137–59.

(1995b), 'The wisdom of Thales and the problem of the word *hieros*', *Classical Quarterly* 45, 296–317.

(1999), *Flesh and Spirit in the Songs of Homer: A Study of Words and Myths* (Oxford).

(2001a), 'Thrice-ploughed woe: Sophocles, *Antigone* 859', *Classical Quarterly* 51, 368–73.

(2001b), 'Heart-cutting talk: Homeric *kertomeo* and related words', *Classical Quarterly* 51, 329–38.

(2004), 'Manhood and heroism', in Fowler (2004), 74–90.

(2005), 'Etymology in the semantic reconstruction of Greek words: the case of *anthos*', *Hermathena* 179, 13–37.

(2006), 'Achilles, Byrhtnoth, and Cú Chulainn: continuity and analogy from Homer to the medieval North', in Clarke et al. (2006), 243–71.

(forthcoming (a)), 'The barbarity of the Ulstermen', in E. Boyle (ed.), *Ulidia V: Proceedings of the 5th International Conference on the Ulster Cycle of Tales* (Dublin).

(forthcoming (b)), 'Looking for unity in a dictionary entry: a perspective from cognitive theory', in Stray et al. (eds.), *Liddell and Scott* (forthcoming).

Clarke, M., B. Currie and R. O. A. M. Lyne (eds.) (2006), *Epic Interactions: Perspectives on Homer, Vergil and the Epic Tradition Presented to Jasper Griffin by his Pupils* (Oxford).

Clay, J. S. (1999), 'The whip and will of Zeus', *Literary Imagination* 1, 40–60.

(2003), *Hesiod's Cosmos* (Cambridge).

(2005), 'The beginning and end of the *Catalogue of Women* and its relation to Hesiod', in Hunter (2005a), 25–34.

(2009a), '*Works and Days*: tracing the path to *arete*', in Montanari et al. (2009), 71–90.

(2009b), 'How to be a hero: the case of Sarpedon', in E. Karamalengou and E. Makrygianni (eds.), *Antiphilesis: Studies in Classical, Byzantine and Modern Greek Literature and Culture in Honour of J. T. A. Papademetriou* (Stuttgart), 30–8.

(2011), *Homer's Trojan Theater: Space, Vision and Memory in the* Iliad (Cambridge).

(2014), 'The Hittite *Song of Emergence* and the *Theogony*', *Philologus* 158, 1–9.

(2016), 'Homer's epigraph: *Iliad* 7.87–91', *Philologus* 160, 185–96.

Cline, E. H. (2013), 'Aegean-Near East relations in the second millennium BC', in Aruz et al. (2013), 26–33.

(2014), *1177 BC: The Year Civilization Collapsed* (Princeton).

Cohen, D. (1996), *Law, Violence and Community in Classical Athens* (Cambridge).

Cohen, Y. (2012), '"Where is Bazi? Where is Zizi?" The list of early rulers in the *Ballad* from Emar and Ugarit, and the Mari rulers in the Sumerian King List and other sources', *Iraq* 74, 137–52.

(2013), *Wisdom from the Late Bronze Age* (Atlanta, GA).

Čolaković, Z. (2006), 'The singer above tales: Homer, Mededović and traditional epics', *Seminari Romani* 9, 161–87.

Collon, D. (2005), *First Impressions: Cylinder Seals in the Ancient Near East*, 2nd edn. (London).

    (2007), 'Babylonian seals', in Leick (2007), 95–123.

Cook, E. (1995), *The* Odyssey *in Athens: Myths of Cultural Origins* (Ithaca, NY).

Cooper, J. (2002), 'Buddies in Babylonia: Gilgamesh, Enkidu, and Mesopotamian homosexuality', in T. Abusch (ed.), *Riches Hidden in Secret Places: Ancient Near Eastern Studies in Memory of Thorkild Jacobsen* (Winona Lake, IN), 73–86.

    (2008), 'Divine kingship in Mesopotamia, a fleeting phenomenon', in Brisch (2008), 261–5.

    (2010), '"I have forgotten my burden of former days!" Forgetting the Sumerians in ancient Iraq', *Journal of the American Oriental Society* 130, 327–35.

Cox, J.L. (2017), 'The debate between E. B. Tylor and Andrew Lang', in P.-F. Tremlett, G. Harvey and L. T. Sutherland (eds.), *Edward Burnett Tylor, Language and Culture* (London), 11–28.

Crane, G. (1988), *Calypso: Backgrounds and Conventions of the* Odyssey (Frankfurt).

Crotty, K. (1994), *The Poetics of Supplication: Homer's* Iliad *and* Odyssey (Ithaca, NY).

Currie, B. (2005), *Pindar and the Cult of Heroes* (Oxford).

    (2012a), 'The *Iliad, Gilgamesh* and Neoanalysis', in Montanari et al. (2012), 543–80.

    (2012b), 'Hesiod on human history', in L. Llewellyn-Jones, J. Marincola and C. A. Maciver (eds.), *History without Historians: Greeks and Their Past in the Archaic and Classical Age* (Edinburgh), 37–64.

    (2015), 'Cypria', in Fantuzzi and Tsagalis (2015a), 281–305.

    (2016), *Homer's Allusive Art* (Oxford).

    (forthcoming), 'Etana in Greece', in Kelly and Metcalf (eds.), *Divine Narrative* (forthcoming).

D'Alessio, G. (2015), 'Theogony *and* Titanomachy', in Fantuzzi and Tsagalis (2015a), 199–212.

Daix, D.-A. (2014), 'Achille au chant XXIV de l'*Iliade*: lion exécrable ou héros admirable?', *Revue des Études Grecques* 127, 1–28.

Danek, G. (1994/5), 'Der Nestorbecher von Ischia, epische Zitiertechnik und das Symposion', *Rheinisches Museum* 107/8, 29–44.

    (2006), 'Die Gleichnisse der Ilias und der Dichter Homer', in Montanari and Rengakos (2006), 41–78.

    (2015), 'Nostoi', in Fantuzzi and Tsagalis (2015a), 355–79.

Davidson, J. (2007), *The Greeks and Greek Love: A Radical Reappraisal of Homosexuality in Ancient Greece* (London).

Davies, M. (1989), *The Greek Epic Cycle* (London).

(2003), 'The judgments of Paris and Solomon', *Classical Quarterly* 53, 32–43.

(2014), *The Theban Epics* (Cambridge, MA).

De Jong, I. J. F. (2001), *A Narratological Commentary on the* Odyssey (Cambridge).

(2006), 'The Homeric narrator and his own *kleos*', *Mnemosyne* 59, 188–207.

(ed.) (2012) Homer, *Iliad Book XXII*, Cambridge Greek and Latin Classics (Cambridge).

(2013), 'Narratological aspects of the *Histories* of Herodotus', in Munson (2013), vol. 1, 253–91.

Deger-Jalkotzy, S. and I. Lemos (eds.) (2006), *Ancient Greece: From the Mycenaean Palaces to the Age of Homer* (Edinburgh).

Delattre, C. (2006), 'Entre mortalité et immortalité: l'exemple de Sarpédon dans l' *Iliade*', *Revue de Philologie* 80, 259–71.

Delnero, P. (2010), 'Sumerian extract tablets and scribal education', *Journal of Cuneiform Studies* 62, 53–69.

(2012), 'Memorization and the transmission of Sumerian literary compositions', *Journal of Near Eastern Studies* 71, 189–208.

Dickey, E. (2007), *Ancient Greek Scholarship* (Oxford).

Dillon, J. (2004), 'Euripides and the philosophy of his time', *Classics Ireland* 11, 47–73.

Dodds, E. R. (1951), *The Greeks and the Irrational* (Berkeley).

(ed.) (1960), Euripides, *Bacchae*, 2nd edn. (Oxford).

Doherty, L. E. (ed.) (2009), *Oxford Readings in Classical Studies: Homer's* Odyssey (Oxford).

Donlan, W. (1982), 'Reciprocities in Homer', *Classical World* 75, 37–75.

Dooley, A. (2006), *Playing the Hero: Reading the Irish Saga* Táin Bó Cúailnge (Toronto).

Dova, S. (2012), *Greek Heroes In and Out of Hades* (Lanham, MD).

Du Sablon, V. (2014), *Le Système conceptuel de l'ordre du monde dans la pensée grecque à l'époque archaïque:* timē, moira, kosmos, themis *et* dikē *chez* Homère et Hesiode (Louvain).

Dué, C. (2002), *Homeric Variations on a Lament by Briseis* (Lanham, MD).

(ed.) (2009), *Recapturing a Homeric Legacy: Images and Insights from the Venetus A Manuscript of the* Iliad (Washington, DC).

Duhoux, Y. and A. Morpurgo Davies (eds.) (2008–14), *A Companion to Linear B: Mycenaean Greek Texts and Their World*, 3 vols. (Louvain-la-Neuve).

Edmunds, R., 'Imagining the afterlife' (2015), in Eidinow and Kindt (2015), 551–63.

Edwards, M. W. (1991), *The* Iliad: *A Commentary Volume V: Books 17–20* (Cambridge).

Edzard, D. O. (1993), *'Gilgames und Huwawa.' Zwei Versionen der sumerischen Zedernwaldepisode nebst einer Edition von Version B*, Bayerische Akademie der Wissenschaften Philosophisch-historische Klasse, Sitzungsberichte 1993, IV (Munich).

Eidinow, E. (2011), *Luck, Fate and Fortune: Antiquity and Its Legacy* (London).

Eidinow, E. and J. Kindt (eds.) (2015), *The Oxford Handbook of Ancient Greek Religion* (Oxford).

Fantuzzi, M. (2015), 'The aesthetics of sequentiality and its discontents', in Fantuzzi and Tsagalis (2015a), 405–29.

Fantuzzi, M. and C. Tsagalis (eds.) (2015a), *The Greek Epic Cycle and Its Ancient Reception: A Companion* (Cambridge).

Fantuzzi, M. and C. Tsagalis (2015b), 'Introduction', in Fantuzzi and Tsagalis (2015a), 1–40.

Faraone, C. A. (1996), 'Taking the "Nestor's Cup" inscription seriously', *Classical Antiquity* 15, 77–112.

Faulkner, A. (2008), *The Homeric Hymn to Aphrodite* (Oxford).

Fenno, J. (2008), 'The wrath and vengeance of swift-footed Aeneas in *Iliad* 13', *Phoenix* 62, 145–61.

Fincke, J. C. (2003–4), 'The Babylonian texts of Nineveh: report on the British Museum's Ashurbanipal Library Project', *Archiv für Orientforschung* 50, 111–49.

(2017), 'Assyrian scholarship and scribal culture in Kalḫu and Nineveh', in E. Frahm (ed.), *A Companion to Assyria* (Oxford), 378–97.

Finglass, P. J. (ed.) (2011), Sophocles, *Ajax* (Cambridge).

Finkel, I. L. (1983/4), 'Necromancy in ancient Mesopotamia', *Archiv für Orientforschung* 29/30, 1–17.

Finkelberg, M. (1986), 'Is *kleos aphthiton* a Homeric formula?', *Classical Quarterly* 36, 1–5.

(2005), *Greeks and Pre-Greeks: Aegean Prehistory and Greek Heroic Tradition* (Cambridge).

(2007), 'More on *kleos aphthiton*', *Classical Quarterly* 57, 341–50.

(ed.) (2011), *The Homer Encyclopedia*, 3 vols. (Oxford).

(2015), 'Meta-Cyclic epic and Homeric poetry', in Fantuzzi and Tsagalis (2015a), 126–38.

Fleming, D. E. and S. J. Milstein (2010), *The Buried Foundations of the Gilgamesh Epic: The Akkadian Huwawa Narrative* (Leiden).

Foley, H. P. (2009), '"Reverse similes" and sex roles in the *Odyssey*', in Doherty (2009), 189–207.

Foley, J. M. (1999), *Homer's Traditional Art* (University Park, PA).

(2002), *How to Read an Oral Poem* (Urbana, IL).

(ed.) (2009), *A Companion to Ancient Epic* (Oxford).

Forbes Irving, P. M. C. (1990), *Metamorphosis in Greek Myths* (Oxford).

Ford, A. (1992), *Homer: The Poetry of the Past* (Ann Arbor, MI).

Forssman, B. (1986), 'Homerisches *amoton*', in A. Etter (ed.), *O-o-pe-ro-si. Festschrift für Ernst Risch zum 75. Geburtstag* (Berlin), 329–39.

Fortson, B. W. (2010), *Indo-European Language and Culture: An Introduction*, 2nd edn. (Oxford).

Foster, B. R. (1987), 'Gilgamesh: sex, love, and the ascent of knowledge', in J. H. Marks and R. M. Good (eds.), *Love and Death in the Ancient Near East: Essays in Honour of Marvin H. Pope* (Guildford, CT), 21–42.

(2001), *The Epic of Gilgamesh: A New Translation, Analogues, Criticism*, Norton Critical Editions (New York).

(2005), *Before the Muses: An Anthology of Akkadian Literature*, 3rd edn. (Bethesda, MD).

(2007), *Akkadian Literature of the Late Period* (Münster).

Fowler, R. L. (2000–13), *Early Greek Mythography*, vol. 1, *Text and Introduction;* vol. 2, *Commentary* (Oxford).

(2011), '*Mythos* and *logos*', *Journal of Hellenic Studies* 131, 45–66.

(ed.) (2004), *The Cambridge Companion to Homer* (Cambridge).

Frahm, E. (1999), 'Nabû-zuqup-kēnu, das Gilgameš-Epos und der Tod Sargons II', *Journal of Cuneiform Studies* 51, 73–90.

Frame, D. (1978), *The Myth of Return in Early Greek Epic* (New Haven, CT).

Frame, G. and A. George (2005), 'The royal libraries of Nineveh: new evidence for King Ashurbanipal's tablet collecting', *Iraq* 67, 265–84.

Franzino, E. (1995), 'Euripides' *Heracles* 858–73', *Illinois Classical Studies* 20, 57–63.

Frazer, J. (ed.) (1921), Apollodorus, *The Library* (Loeb Classical Library) (Cambridge, MA).

Furley, W. D. (2011), 'Homeric and un-Homeric hexameter hymns: a question of type', in A. Faulkner (ed.), *The Homeric Hymns: Interpretative Essays* (Oxford), 206–31.

Furley, W. D. and J. M. Bremer (2001), *Greek Hymns: Selected Cult Songs from the Archaic to the Hellenistic Period*, 2 vols. (Tübingen).

Gadotti, A. (2006), 'Gilgamesh, Gudam, and the singer in Sumerian literature', in Michalowski and Veldhuis (2006), 67–83.

(2014), Gilgamesh, Enkidu and the Netherworld *and the Sumerian Gilgamesh Cycle* (Berlin).

Gagarin, M. and P. Perlman (2016), *The Laws of Ancient Crete c. 650–400 BC* (Oxford).

Gager, J. G. (ed.) (1992), *Curse Tablets and Binding Spells from the Ancient World* (Oxford).

Gantz, T. (1993), *Early Greek Myth: A Guide to Literary and Artistic Sources*, 2 vols. (Baltimore).

García Trabazo, J.V. (2010), 'Ritual de sustitución real: edición crítica y traducción', *Historiae* 7, 27–49.

Garvie, A.F. (ed.) (1994), Homer, *Odyssey Books VI–VIII* (Cambridge).

(ed.) (2009), Aeschylus, *Persae* (Oxford).

Gaskin, R. (2001), 'Do Homeric heroes make real decisions?', in Cairns (2001a), 147–69 [first published 1990].

Gazis, G. A. (2018), *Homer and the Poetics of Hades* (Oxford).

George, A. (1999), *The* Epic of Gilgamesh: *The Babylonian Epic Poem and Other Texts in Akkadian and Sumerian* (Harmondsworth).

(2003), *The Babylonian Gilgamesh Epic: Introduction, Critical Edition and Cuneiform Texts*, 2 vols. (Oxford).

(2007a), 'The Gilgamesh epic at Ugarit', *Aula Orientalis* 25, 237–54.

(2007b), 'The civilizing of Ea-Enkidu: an unusual tablet of the Babylonian Gilgamesh Epic', *Revue d' Assyriologie et d' archéologie orientale* 101, 59–80.

(2007c), 'Gilgamesh and the literary traditions of ancient Mesopotamia', in Leick (2007), 447–59.

(2009), *Babylonian Literary Texts in the Schøyen Collection* (Bethesda, MD).

(2010a), 'The Epic of Gilgamesh', in C. Bates (ed.), *The Cambridge Companion to the Epic* (Cambridge), 1–12.

(2010b), '*Bilgames and the Bull of Heaven*: cuneiform texts, collations and textual reconstruction', in Baker et al. (2010), 99–115.

(2012), 'The mayfly on the river: individual and collective destiny in the *Epic of Gilgamesh*', *KASKAL: Rivista di storia, ambienti e cultura del Vicino Oriente Antico* 9, 227–42.

George, A. and F. N. H. Al-Rawi (1996), 'Tablets from the Sippar library VI. *Atra-ḫasīs*,' *Iraq* 58, 147–90.

Gill, C. (1996), *Personality in Greek Epic, Tragedy and Philosophy: The Self in Dialogue* (Oxford).

Gill, C., N. Postlethwaite, and R. Seaford (eds.) (1998), *Reciprocity in Ancient Greece* (Oxford).

Giuliani, L. (2013), *Image and Myth: A History of Pictorial Narration in Greek Art* (Chicago) [translated from *Bild und Mythos: Geschichte der Bilderzählung in der griechischen Kunst* (2003)].

Glassner, J. J. (2004), *Mesopotamian Chronicles* (Atlanta, GA).

Goedegebuuro, P. M. (2002), 'KBo 17.17 +: remarks on an Old Hittite royal substitution ritual', *Journal of Ancient Near Eastern Religions* 2, 61–73.

Golden, L. (1989), '*Dios Apatē* and the unity of *Iliad* 11', *Mnemosyne* 42, 1–11.

Goldhill, S. (1990), 'Supplication and authorial comment in the *Iliad: Iliad* Z 61–2', *Hermes* 118, 373–6.

González, J.M. (2010), 'The *Catalogue of Women* and the end of the Heroic Age (Hesiod fr. 204.94–103)', *Transactions of the American Philological Association* 140, 375–422.

Gottesman, A. (2008), 'The pragmatics of Homeric *kertomia*', *Classical Quarterly* 58, 1–12.

Gottschall, J. (2008), *The Rape of Troy: Evolution, Violence, and the World of Homer* (Cambridge).

Gould, J. (1973), 'Hiketeia', *Journal of Hellenic Studies* 93, 74–103.

(2013), 'Herodotus and religion', in Munson (2013), vol. 2, 183–97 [first published 1994].

Graziosi, B. (2002), *Inventing Homer: The Early Reception of Epic* (Cambridge).

(2016), *Homer* (Oxford).

Graziosi, B., and J. Haubold (2003), 'Homeric masculinity: *ēnoreē* and *agēnoriē*', *Journal of Hellenic Studies* 123, 60–76.

Graziosi, B., and J. Haubold (2005), *Homer: The Resonance of Epic* (London).

Graziosi, B., and J. Haubold (eds.) (2010), Homer, *Iliad Book VI*, Cambridge Greek and Latin Classics (Cambridge).

Grethlein, J. (2006), *Das Geschichtsbild der Ilias: Eine Untersuchung aus phänomenologischer und narratologischer Perspektive*, Hypomnemata 163 (Göttingen).

(2010), *The Greeks and Their Past: Poetry, Oratory and History in the Fifth Century BCE* (Cambridge).

Griffin, J. (1977), 'The Epic Cycle and the uniqueness of Homer', *Journal of Hellenic Studies* 77, 39–53, reprinted in Cairns (2001a), 365–84.

(1980), *Homer on Life and Death* (Oxford).

Griffiths, A. (1985), 'A ram called Patroklos', *Bulletin of the Institute of Classical Studies* 32, 49–50.

(1989), 'Patroklos the ram (again)', *Bulletin of the Institute of Classical Studies* 36, 139.

Gunter, A. C. (2009), *Greek Art and the Orient* (Cambridge).

Gurney, O. R. (1954), 'Two fragments of the *Epic of Gilgamesh* from Sultantepe', *Journal of Cuneiform Studies* 8, 87–95.

(1977), *Some Aspects of Hittite Religion* (Oxford).

Haas, V. (1994), *Geschichte der hethitischen Religion* (Leiden).

(2006), *Die hethitische Literatur. Texte, Stilistik, Motive* (Leiden).

Hadjicosti, I. L. (2006), 'Apollo at the wedding of Thetis and Peleus: four problematic cases', *L'Antiquité Classique* 75, 15–22.

Hainsworth, B. (1993), *The* Iliad*: A Commentary Volume III: Books 9–12* (Cambridge).

Hall, J. (2002), *Hellenicity: Between Ethnicity and Culture* (Chicago).

Halliwell, S. (1998), *Aristotle's Poetics*, 2nd edn. (London).

Hallo, W. M. (1990), 'Proverbs quoted in epic', in Abusch et al. (1990), 203–17.

Halperin, D. (1990), 'Heroes and their pals', in *One Hundred Years of Homosexuality and Other Essays on Greek Love* (London), 55–87.

Hansen, P. A. (1983), *Carmina Epigraphica Graeca Saeculorum VIII–V a. Chr. n.* (Berlin).

Harris, W. V. (2001), *Restraining Rage: The Ideology of Anger Control in Classical Antiquity* (Cambridge, MA).

Harrison, E. L. (1991), 'Homeric wonder-horses', *Hermes* 119, 252–4.

Harrison, T. (2000), *Divinity and History: The Religion of Herodotus* (Oxford).

Haubold, J. (2000), 'Greek epic: a Near Eastern genre?', *Proceedings of the Cambridge Philological Society* 48, 1–19.

(2005), 'Heracles in the Hesiodic *Catalogue of Women*', in Hunter (2005a), 85–98.

(2006), 'Homer between east and west', *Classics@* 3, www.zeus.chsdc.org/chs/ files.

(2010), 'Shepherd, farmer, poet, sophist: Hesiod on his own reception', in G. Boys-Stones and J. Haubold (eds.), *Plato and Hesiod* (Oxford), 11–30.

(2013), *Greece and Mesopotamia: Dialogues in Literature* (Cambridge).

(2014), 'Beyond Auerbach: Homeric narrative and the *Epic of Gilgamesh*', in Cairns and Scodel (2014), 13–28.

(2015), '"Shepherds of the people": Greek and Mesopotamian perspectives', in Rollinger and van Dongen (2015), 245–54.

Haubold, J., G. B. Lanfranchi, R. Rollinger and J. Steele (eds.) (2013), *The World of Berossos* (Wiesbaden).

Haul, M. (2000), *Das Etana-Epos: Ein Mythos von der Himmelfahrt des Königs von Kish* (Göttingen).

Hays, C. B. (2007), 'Chirps from the dust: the affliction of Nebuchadnezzar in Daniel 4: 30 in its Ancient Near Eastern context', *Journal of Biblical Literature* 126, 305–25.

Heath, J. (1992), 'The legacy of Peleus: death and divine gifts in the *Iliad*', *Hermes* 120, 387–400.

(2005), *The Talking Greeks: Speech, Animals, and the Other in Homer, Aeschylus and Plato* (Cambridge).

Heiden, B. (2008), *Homer's Cosmic Fabrication: Choice and Design in the* Iliad (Oxford).

Heimpel, W. (1986), 'The sun at night and the doors of heaven in Babylonian texts', *Journal of Cuneiform Studies* 38, 127–51.

Hermann, V. R. and J. D. Schloen (eds.) (2014), *In Remembrance of Me: Feasting with the Dead in the Ancient Near East*, Oriental Institute Museum Publications 37 (Chicago).

Heslin, P. (2005), *The Transvestite Achilles: Gender and Genre in Statius'* Achilleid (Cambridge).

Hiller, S. (2008–14), 'Religion and cult', in Duhoux and Davies (2008–14), vol. 2, 169–211.

Hodder, I. (2011), *Çatalhöyük: The Leopard's Tale* (London).

Hoffner, H. A. (1990), *Hittite Myths*, 2nd edn. (Atlanta, GA).

(2009), *Letters from the Hittite Kingdom* (Atlanta, GA).

Holmes, B. (2008), 'Euripides' Heracles in the flesh', *Classical Antiquity* 27, 231–81.

Holt, P. (1992), 'Ajax's burial in early Greek epic', *American Journal of Philology* 113, 319–31.

Holton, M. and V. D. Mihailovich (1997), *Songs of the Serbian People from the Collections of Vuk Karadžić* (Pittsburgh, PA).

Hornblower, S. (ed.) (2015), Lykophron, *Alexandra: Greek Text, Translation, Commentary, and Introduction* (Oxford).

Horowitz, W. (1998), *Mesopotamian Cosmic Geography* (Winona Lake, IN).

Howland, J. (2002), 'Aristotle's great-souled man', *Review of Politics* 64, 27–56.

Hunter, R. (ed.) (2005a), *The Hesiodic Catalogue of Women: Constructions and Reconstructions* (Cambridge).

(2005b), 'Introduction', in Hunter (2005a), 1–4.

(2009), *Critical Moments in Classical Literature* (Cambridge).

(2010), 'Language and interpretation in Greek epigram', in Baumbach et al. (2010), 265–88.

(2018), *The Measure of Homer: The Ancient Reception of the* Iliad *and* Odyssey (Cambridge).

Hunter, R. and D. Russell (eds.) (2011), Plutarch, *How to Study Poetry*, Cambridge Greek and Latin Classics (Cambridge).

Hunter, R. and I. Rutherford (eds.) (2009), *Wandering Poets in Ancient Greek Culture* (Cambridge).

Immerwahr, S. (1995), 'Death and the Tanagra larnakes', in Carter and Morris (1995), 109–21.

Irwin, E. (2005), 'Gods among men? The social and political dynamics of the Hesiodic *Catalogue of Women*', in Hunter (2005a), 35–84.

Izre'el, S. (2001), *Adapa and the South Wind: Language Has the Power of Life and Death* (Winona Lake, IN).

Jackson, K. (2010), 'Father-daughter dynamics in the *Iliad*: the role of Aphrodite in defining Zeus' regime', in Smith and Pickup (2010), 151–63.

James, A. W. (1986), 'The meaning of *panaōrios* as applied to Achilles', *Classical Quarterly* 36, 527–9.

Janko, R. (1992), *The* Iliad: *A Commentary Volume IV: Books 13–16* (Cambridge).

Jensen, M. Skafte (2009), 'Performance', in J. M. Foley (2009), 45–54.

Jiménez, E. (2014), 'New fragments of Gilgamesh and other literary texts from Kuyunjik', *Iraq* 76, 99–121.

Judah, T. (2010), *The Serbs: History, Politics and Myth* (New Haven, CT).

Junker, K. (2012), *Interpreting the Images of Greek Myths* (Cambridge) [translated from German edition of 2005].

Jursa, M. (2011), 'Cuneiform writing in Neo-Babylonian temple communities', in Radner and Robson (2011), 184–204.

Karahashi, F. and C. López-Ruiz (2006), 'Love rejected: some notes on the Mesopotamian *Epic of Gilgamesh* and the Greek myth of Hippolytus', *Journal of Cuneiform Studies* 58, 97–107.

Katz, J. T. (2010), 'Inherited poetics', in E. Bakker (ed.), *A Companion to the Ancient Greek Language* (Oxford), 357–69.

Kearns, E. (2004), 'The gods in the Homeric epics', in Fowler (2004), 59–73.

Kelly, A. (2008), 'The Babylonian Captivity of Homer: the case of the *Dios Apatē*', *Rheinisches Museum* 151, 259–304.

(2012), 'The mourning of Thetis: 'allusion' and the future in the *Iliad*', in Montanari et al. (2012), 221–65.

(2014), 'Homeric battle narrative and the ancient Near East', in Cairns and Scodel (2014), 29–54.

(2015a), '*Ilias parva*', in Fantuzzi and Tsagalis (2015a), 318–43.

(2015b), 'Stesichorus' Homer', in P. J. Finglass, and A. Kelly (eds.), *Stesichorus in Context* (Cambridge), 21–44.

(2015c), 'Aias in Athens: the worlds of the play and the audience', *Quaderni Urbinati di Cultura Classica* 111, 61–92.

Kelly, A. and C. Metcalf (eds.) (forthcoming), *Divine Narrative in Greece and the Near East*.

Kilmer, A. F. (1987), 'The symbolism of the flies in the Mesopotamian flood myth and some further implications', in F. Rochberg-Halton (ed.), *Language, Literature and History: Philological Studies Presented to Erica Reiner* (New Haven, CT), 175–80.

Kim, J. (2000), *The Pity of Achilles: Oral Style and the Unity of the* Iliad (Lanham, MD).

Kirk, G.S. (1990), *The* Iliad: *A Commentary Volume II: Books 5–8* (Cambridge).

Kitts, M. (2005), *Sanctified Violence in Homeric Society: Oath-making Rituals and Narratives in the* Iliad (Cambridge).

Klein, J. (1976), 'Shulgi and Gilgamesh: two brother peers (*Shulgi O*)', in B. L. Eichler (ed.), *Kramer Anniversary Volume: Cuneiform Studies in Honor of Samuel Noah Kramer* (Kevelaer).

(1980), *Three Shulgi Hymns: Sumerian Royal Hymns Glorifying King Shulgi of Ur* (Ramat-Gan, Israel).

Klein, J. (1981), 'The Royal Hymns of Shulgi king of Ur: man's quest for immortal fame', *Transactions of the American Philological Society* 71, 1–48.

Knapp, A. B. (2008), *Prehistoric and Protohistoric Cyprus: Insularity, Identity and Connectivity* (Oxford).

Knox, B. (1961), 'The *Ajax* of Sophocles', *Harvard Studies in Classical Philology* 65, 1–37.

Koenen, L. (1994), 'Greece, the Near East, and Egypt: cyclic destruction in Hesiod and the *Catalogue of Women*', *Transactions of the American Philological Association* 124, 1–34.

Kohen, A. (2013), *Untangling Heroism: Classical Philosophy and the Concept of the Hero* (London).

Konstan, D. (2003), '*Nemesis* and *phthonos*', in G. Bakewell and J. Sickinger (eds.), *Gestures: Essays in Greek History, Literature and Philosophy in Honor of Alan Boegehold* (Oakville, CT), 74–87.

(2006), *The Emotions of the Ancient Greeks: Studies in Aristotle and Classical Literature* (Toronto).

Kopanias, K. (2008), 'The late Bronze Age Near Eastern cylinder seals from Thebes (Greece) and their historical implications', *Mitteilungen des Deutschen Archäologischen Instituts, Athenische Abteilung* 123, 39–96.

Kreuzer, B. (2013), 'Reading the François Vase: myth as case study and the hero as *exemplum*', in Shapiro et al. (2013), 105–17.

Kselman, J. S. (2002), '"Wandering about" and depression: more examples', *Journal of Near Eastern Studies* 61, 275–7.

Kuhrt, A. (1995), *The Ancient Near East c. 3000–330 BC*, 2 vols. (London).

Kullmann, W. (2012), 'Neoanalysis between orality and literacy: some remarks on the development of Greek myths including the legend of the capture of Troy', in Montanari et al. (2012), 13–25.

(2015), 'Motif and source research: Neoanalysis, Homer, and Cyclic epic', in Fantuzzi and Tsagalis (2015a), 108–25.

Kümmel, H.M. (1967), *Ersatzrituale für den hethitischen König* (Wiesbaden).

Kunstler, B. (1991), 'The werewolf figure and its adoption into the Greek political vocabulary', *Classical World* 84, 189–205.

Kvanvig, H. (2011), *Primeval History, Babylonian, Biblical and Enochic: An Intertextual Reading* (Leiden).

Lam, J. (2010), 'The invention and development of the alphabet', in Woods (2010), 189–95.

Lambert, W. G. (1957–8), 'A part of the ritual for the substitute king', *Archiv für Orientforschung* 18, 109–12.

(1959–60), 'The ritual for the substitute king: a new fragment', *Archiv für Orientforschung* 19, 119.

(1960), *Babylonian Wisdom Literature* (Oxford).

(1980), 'The theology of death', in B. Alster (ed.), *Death in Mesopotamia* (Copenhagen), 53–66.

(2010), 'Gilgamesh in literature and art: the second and first millennia', in Steymans (2010), 91–112.

(2013), *Babylonian Creation Myths* (Winona Lake, IN).

Lambert, W. G. and A. R. Millard (1969), *Atra-ḫasīs: The Babylonian Story of the Flood* (Oxford).

Lamberton, R. (1986), *Homer the Theologian: Neoplationist Allegorical Reading and the Growth of the Epic Tradition* (Berkeley, CA).

Lang, A. (1893), *Homer and His Age* (London).

Lang, M. (2013), 'Book Two: Mesopotamian early history and the Flood story', in Haubold et al. (2013), 47–60.

Lapinkivi, P. (2004), *The Neo-Assyrian Myth of Ishtar's Descent and Resurrection*, State Archives of Assyria Cuneiform Texts 6 (Helsinki).

Latacz, J. (1966), *Zum Wortfeld 'Freude' in der Sprache Homers* (Heidelberg).

(1998), *Homer: His Art and His World* (Ann Arbor, MI).

Latacz, J., R. Nünlist and M. Stoevesandt (2009), *Homers* Ilias: *Gesamtkommentar 1.2, Erster Gesang* (Berlin).

Leick, G. (2001), *Mesopotamia: The Invention of the City* (London).

(ed.) (2007), *The Babylonian World* (London).

Lesky, A. (2001), 'Divine and human causation in Homeric epic', in Cairns (2001a), 170–202 [abridged from article first published in German, 1961].

Livingstone, A. (1986), *Mystical and Mythological Explanatory Works of Assyrian and Babylonian Scholars* (Oxford).

(1989), *Court Poetry and Literary Miscellanea*, State Archives of Assyria 3 (Helsinki).

Llewellyn-Jones, L. and J. Robson (2010), *Ctesias'* History of Persia: *Tales of the Orient* (London).

Lloyd, M. (2004), 'The politeness of Achilles: off-record conversation strategies in Homer and the meaning of *kertomia*', *Journal of Hellenic Studies* 124, 75–89.

Lloyd, S. (1980), *Foundations in the Dust: The Story of Mesopotamian Exploration*, rev. edn. (London).

Long, A. A. (2015), *Greek Models of the Mind and Self* (Cambridge, MA).

Lonsdale, S. H. (1990), *Creatures of Speech: Lion, Herding, and Hunting Similes in the* Iliad (Stuttgart).

López-Ruiz, C. (2010), *When the Gods Were Born: Greek Cosmogonies and the Near East* (Cambridge, MA).

  (2014), 'Greek and Near Eastern mythologies: a story of Mediterranean encounters', in L. Edmonds (ed.), *Approaches to Greek Myth*, 2nd edn. (Baltimore), 152–99.

  (2015), 'Gods-origins', in Eidinow and Kindt (2015), 369–82.

Loraux, N. (1995), *The Experiences of Tiresias: The Feminine and the Greek Man* (Princeton).

Louden, B. (2006), *The* Iliad: *Structure, Myth and Meaning* (Baltimore).

  (2011), *Homer's* Odyssey *and the Ancient Near East* (Cambridge).

Lowenstam, S. (1981), *The Death of Patroclus: A Study in Typology* (Baltimore).

  (1992), 'The use of vase-depictions in Homeric studies', *Transactions of the American Philological Association* 122, 165–98.

  (1993), 'The arming of Achilles on early Greek vases', *Classical Antiquity* 12, 199–218.

  (2008), *As Witnessed by Images: The Trojan Tradition in Greek and Etruscan Art* (Baltimore).

Mackie, C. J. (1997), 'Achilles' teachers: Chiron and Phoenix in the *Iliad*', *Greece and Rome* 44, 1–10.

  (1998), 'Achilles in fire', *Classical Quarterly* 48, 329–38.

  (2013), '*Iliad* 24 and the judgment of Paris', *Classical Quarterly* 63, 1–16.

Marks, J. (2002), 'The junction between the *Cypria* and the *Iliad*', *Phoenix* 56, 1–24.

Martin, B. (2014), 'Blood, honour and status in *Odyssey* 11', *Classical Quarterly* 64, 1–12.

Martin, R. (1989), *The Language of Heroes: Speech and Performance in the* Iliad (Ithaca, NY).

  (2005), 'Pulp epic: the *Catalogue* and the *Shield*', in Hunter (2005a), 153–75.

Martin, S. R. (2017), *The Art of Contact: Comparative Approaches to Greek and Phoenician Art* (Philadelphia).

Mayer, K. (1996), 'Helen and the *Dios Boulē*', *American Journal of Philology* 117, 1–15.

Meier, C. (2011), *A Culture of Freedom: Ancient Greece and the Origins of Europe* (Oxford) [translated from German original of 2009].

(1941–4), 'Die zweite Tafel der Serie *bīt mēseri*', *Archiv für Orientforschung* 14, 139–52.

Metcalf, C. (2015), *The Gods Rich in Praise: Early Greek and Mesopotamian Religious Poetry* (Oxford).

Metcalf, R. (2009), 'Socrates and Achilles', in P. Fagan and J. Russon (eds.), *Re-examining Socrates in the* Apology (Evanston, IL), 62–84.

Michalowski, P. (2008), 'The mortal kings of Ur: a short century of divine rule in ancient Mesopotamia', in Brisch (2008), 33–46.

Michalowski, P. and N. Veldhuis (eds.) (2006), *Approaches to Sumerian Literature: Studies in Honour of Stip (H. L. J. Vanstiphout)* (Leiden).

Michelakis, P. (2002), *Achilles in Greek Tragedy* (Cambridge).

Miles, B. (2011), *Heroic Saga and Classical Epic in Medieval Ireland* (Cambridge).

Minchin, E. (2001), *Homer and the Resources of Memory: Some Applications of Cognitive Theory to the* Iliad *and the* Odyssey (Oxford).

Moignard, E. (2015), *Master of Attic Black-Figure: The Art and Legacy of Exekias* (London).

Mondi, R. (1986), 'Tradition and Innovation in the Hesiodic Titanomachy', *Transactions of the American Philological Association* 116, 25–48.

Montana, F. (2013), 'Hellenistic scholarship', in Montanari et al. (2013), 60–183.

Montanari, F. (1995), 'The Mythographus Homericus', in J. G. Abbenes, S. R. Slings and I. Sluiter (eds.), *Greek Literary Theory after Aristotle* (Amsterdam), 135–72.

Montanari, F. and A. Rengakos (eds.) (2006), *La Poésie épique grecque* (Vandoeuvres-Genève).

Montanari, F., A. Rengakos and C. Tsagalis (eds.) (2009), *Brill's Companion to Hesiod* (Leiden).

Montanari, F., A. Rengakos and C. Tsagalis (eds.) (2012), *Homeric Contexts: Neoanalysis and the Interpretation of Oral Poetry* (Berlin).

Montanari, F., S. Matthaios and A. Rengakos (eds.) (2013), *Brill's Companion to Ancient Greek Scholarship* (Leiden).

Moran, W. M. (1978), 'An Assyriological gloss on the new Archilochus fragment', *Harvard Studies in Classical Philology* 82, 17–19.

Morgan, T. J. (2005), 'The wisdom of Semonides fr. 7', *Cambridge Classical Journal* 51, 72–85.

Morris, S.P. (1992), *Daidalos and the Origin of Greek Art* (Princeton).

(1995), 'The sacrifice of Astyanax: Near Eastern contributions to the siege of Troy', in Carter and Morris (1995), 221–45.

Morris, S.P. (2006), 'The view from East Greece: Miletus, Samos and Ephesus', in C. Riva and N. C. Vella (eds.), *Debating Orientalization: Multidisciplinary Approaches to Change in the Ancient Mediterranean* (London), 66–84.

Morrison, J.V. (1992), *Homeric Misdirection: False Predictions in the* Iliad (Ann Arbor, MI).

Most, G. (1993), 'Die früheste erhaltene griechische Dichterallegorese', *Rheinisches Museum* 136, 209–12.

(1998), 'Hesiod's myth of the five (or three or four) races', *Proceedings of the Cambridge Philological Society* 43, 104–27.

(1999), 'From *logos* to *mythos*', in R. Buxton (ed.), *From Myth to Reason? Studies in the Development of Greek Thought* (Oxford), 25–47.

(ed.) (2006), Hesiod, *Works*, 2 vols. (Loeb Classical Library) (Cambridge, MA).

Muellner, L. (1996), *The Anger of Achilles:* Mênis *in Greek Epic* (Ithaca, NY).

(2012), 'Grieving Achilles', in Montanari et al. (2012), 197–220.

Mullen, A. and P. James (eds.) (2012), *Multilingualism in the Graeco-Roman Worlds* (Cambridge, 2012).

Munson, R. V. (ed.) (2013), *Oxford Readings in Classical Studies: Herodotus*, 2 vols. (Oxford).

Murphy, G. (1955), *Saga and Myth in Ancient Ireland* (Dublin).

Murray, P. (1997), *Plato on Poetry:* Ion, Republic *376–398b,* Republic *595–608b* (Cambridge).

(2005), 'The Muses: creativity personified?', in Stafford and Herrin (2005), 147–60.

Nagy, G. (1979), *The Best of the Achaeans: Concepts of the Hero in Archaic Greek Poetry* (Baltimore).

(1983), 'On the death of Sarpedon', in C. A. Rubino and A. W. Shelmerdine (eds.), *Approaches to Homer* (Baltimore), 189–217.

(1990), *Greek Mythology and Poetics* (Ithaca, NY).

(2012), *Homer: The Preclassic* (Berkeley).

(2013), *The Ancient Greek Hero in 24 Hours* (Cambridge, MA).

Naiden, F. S. (2003), 'The words of the alewife at line 42 of Hesiod's *Works and Days*', *Journal of Near Eastern Studies* 62, 263–6.

(2006), *Ancient Supplication* (Oxford).

Nelson, S. (1998), *God and the Land: The Metaphysics of Farming in Hesiod and Virgil* (New York).

Nissinen, M. (2010), 'Are there homosexuals in Mesopotamian literature?', *Journal of the American Oriental Society* 130, 73–7.

Noegel, S. B. (2007), 'Greek religion and the ancient Near East', in Ogden (2007), 21–37.

Nörenberg, H. W. (1972), 'Zu Homer *Ilias* A 200', *Hermes* 100, 251–4.

North, R. J. (2006), *The Origins of* Beowulf: *From Vergil to Wiglaf* (Oxford).

Noussia-Fantuzzi, M. (2015), 'The Epic Cycle, Stesichorus, and Ibycus', in Fantuzzi and Tsagalis (2015a), 430–49.

Novokhatko, A. (2013), 'Greek scholarship from its beginnings to Alexandria', in Montanari et al. (2013), 3–59.

O'Connor, R. (2016), 'Monsters of the tribe: berserk fury, shapeshifting and dysfunction in *Táin Bó Cúailnge, Egils saga* and *Hrólfs saga kraka*', in J. E. Rekdal and C. Doherty (eds.), *Kings and Warriors in Early North-West Europe* (Dublin), 180–326.

(ed.) (2014), *Classical Literature and Learning in Medieval Irish Narrative* (Cambridge).

O'Rahilly, C. (ed.) (1976), *Táin Bó Cúailnge Recension I* (Dublin).

O'Sullivan, S. (2018), 'Glossing Vergil and Pagan Learning in the Carolingian Age', *Speculum* 93, 132–65.

Ogden, D. (2001), *Greek and Roman Necromancy* (Princeton).

(ed.) (2007), *A Companion to Greek Religion* (Maldon, MD).

Onians, R. B. (1951), *The Origins of European Thought about the Body, the Mind, the Soul, the World, Time, and Fate* (Cambridge).

Ormand, K. (2014), *The Hesiodic Catalogue of Women and Archaic Greece* (Cambridge).

Ornan, T. (2010), 'Humbaba, the Bull of Heaven and the contribution of images to the reconstruction of the Gilgamesh epic', in Steymans (2010), 229–60.

Osborne, R. (1998), *Archaic and Classical Greek Art* (Oxford).

(2009), *Greece in the Making 1200–479 BC*, 2nd edn. (London).

Pache, C. (2016), 'Mourning lions and Penelope's revenge', *Arethusa* 49, 1–24.

Padel, R. (1992), *In and Out of the Mind: Greek Images of the Tragic Self* (Princeton).

(1995), *Whom Gods Destroy: Elements of Greek and Tragic Madness* (Princeton).

Padgett, J. M. (ed.) (2003), *The Centaur's Smile: The Human Animal in Early Greek Art* (Princeton).

Pantelia, M. C. (2002), 'Helen and the last song for Hector', *Transactions of the American Philological Association* 132, 21–7.

Papadopoulou, T. (2005), *Heracles and Euripidean Tragedy* (Cambridge).

Parker, R. (1983), *Miasma: Pollution and Purification in Early Greek Religion* (Oxford).

(2008), 'Aeschylus' gods', in J. Jouanna and F. Montanari (eds.), *Eschyle à l'aube du théâtre occidental* (Vandoeuvres–Genève), 127–64.

Parker, S. B. (1997), *Ugaritic Narrative Poetry* (Atlanta, GA).

Parks, W. (1990), *Verbal Dueling in Heroic Narrative: The Homeric and Old English Traditions* (Princeton).

Parpola, S. (1970), *Letters from Assyrian Scholars to the Kings Esarhaddon and Ashurbanipal: Volume II, Commentary and Appendices* (Winona Lake, IN).

(1983), 'Assyrian library records', *Journal of Near Eastern Studies* 42, 1–29.

(1993), *Letters from Assyrian and Babylonian Scholars*, State Archives of Assyria Cuneiform Texts 10 (Helsinki).

(1997), *The Standard Babylonian Epic of Gilgamesh*, State Archives of Assyria Cuneiform Texts 1 (Helsinki).

Parry, M. (1971), *The Making of Homeric Verse: The Collected Papers of Milman Parry* (Oxford).

Pavese, C. O. (1996), 'La iscrizione sulla *kotyle* di Nestor da Pithekoussai', *Zeitschrift für Papyrologie und Epigraphik* 114, 1–23.

Pelliccia, H. (1995), *Mind, Body and Speech in Homer and Pindar*, Hypomnemata 107 (Göttingen).

(2003), 'Two points about rhapsodes', in M. Finkelberg and G. G. Stroumsa (eds.), *Homer, the Bible, and Beyond: Literary and Religious Canons in the Ancient World* (Leiden), 97–116.

Pelling, C. (2006a), 'Educating Croesus: talking and learning in Herodotus' Lydian *logos*', *Classical Antiquity* 25, 141–77.

(2006b), 'Homer and Herodotus', in Clarke et al. (2006), 75–104.

(2013), 'East is east and west is west – or are they? National stereotypes in Herodotus', in Munson (2013), 360–79.

Penglase, R. (1994), *Greek Myths and Mesopotamia: Parallels and Influence in the Homeric Hymns and Hesiod* (London).

Perkell, C. (2008), 'Reading the laments of *Iliad* 24', in Suter (2008), 93–117.

Petrain, D. (2014), *Homer in Stone: The Tabulae Iliacae in their Roman Context* (Cambridge).

Petriconi, H. (1964), 'Das Gilgamesch-Epos als Vorbild der Ilias', in A. S. Crisafulli (ed.), *Linguistic and Literary Studies in Honor of Helmut A. Hatzfeld* (Washington, DC), 329–42.

Pilafidis-Williams, K. (2004), 'No Mycenaean centaurs yet', *Journal of Hellenic Studies* 124, 165.

Pirenne-Delforge, V. and G. Pironti (2015), 'Many vs. one', in Eidinow and Kindt (2015), 39–47.

Pironti, G. (2010), 'Rethinking Aphrodite as a goddess at work', in Smith and Pickup (2010), 113–31.

Postlethwaite, N. (1998), 'Akhilleus and Agamemnon: generalised reciprocity', in Gill et al. (1998), 93–104.

Powell, B. P. (1991), *Homer and the Origin of the Greek Alphabet* (Cambridge).

(2002), *Writing and the Origins of Greek Literature* (Cambridge).

(2003), *Homer*, 2nd edn. (Oxford).

Pratt, L. (2009), 'Diomedes, the fatherless hero of the *Iliad*', in S. M. Hübner and D. M. Ratzan (eds.), *Growing up Fatherless in Antiquity* (Cambridge), 141–61.

Pucci, P. (1987), *Odysseus Polutropos: Intertextual Readings in the* Odyssey *and the* Iliad (Ithaca, NY).

(1998), *The Song of the Sirens: Essays on Homer* (Lanham, MD).

Pulleyn, S. (ed.) (2000), Homer, *Iliad I, Edited with an Introduction, Translation and Commentary* (Oxford).

Race, W. H. (ed.) (1987), Pindar, *Poems*, 2 vols. (Loeb Classical Library) (Cambridge, MA).

Radner, J. (1982), 'Fury destroys the world: historical strategy in Ireland's Ulster Cycle', *Mankind Quarterly* 23.1, 41–60.

Radner, K., and E. Robson (eds.) (2011), *The Oxford Handbook of Cuneiform Culture* (Oxford).

Ready, J. L. (2011), *Character, Narrator and Simile in the* Iliad (Cambridge).

Redfield, J. (2001), 'The proem of the *Iliad*: Homer's art', in Cairns (2001a), 456–77 [first published in *Classical Philology* 74 (1979), 94–110].

(1994), *Nature and Culture in the* Iliad: *The Tragedy of Hector*, expanded edn. (Durham, NC, 1994).

Reden, S. von (1995), *Exchange in Ancient Greece* (London, 1995).

Reiner, E. (1961), 'The etiological myth of the "Seven Sages"', *Orientalia* 30, 1–12.

Reinhardt, K. (1997), 'The judgement of Paris', in Wright and Jones (1997), 170–191 [first published in German, 1960].

Rendu, A.-C. (2008), 'Cri ou silence: deuil des dieux et des héros dans la littérature mésopotamienne', *Revue de l' histoire des religions* 225, 199–221.

Rengakos, A. (2015), '*Aethiopis*', in Fantuzzi and Tsagalis (2015a), 306–17.

Richardson, N. (1993), *The* Iliad: *A Commentary VI: Books 21–24* (Cambridge).

(2010), *Three Homeric Hymns: To Apollo, Hermes, and Aphrodite* (Cambridge).

Rinon, Y. (2008), 'A tragic pattern in the *Iliad*', *Harvard Studies in Classical Philology* 104, 45–91.

Risch, E. (1987), 'Zum Nestorbecher aus Ischia', *Zeitschrift für Papyrologie und Epigraphik* 70, 1–9.

Robson, E. (2001), 'The Tablet House: a scribal school in Old Babylonian Nippur', *Revue d' Assyriologie et d' archéologie orientale* 95, 39–66.

(2011), 'The production and dissemination of scholarly knowledge', in Radner and Robson (2011), 557–76.

Rochberg, F. (1986), 'Personifications and metaphors in Babylonian celestial omens', *Journal of the American Oriental Society* 116, 475–86.

(2004), *The Heavenly Writing: Divination, Horoscopy, and Astronomy in Mesopotamian Culture* (Cambridge).

(2010), *In the Path of the Moon: Babylonian Celestial Divination and Its Legacy* (Leiden).

(2016), *Before Nature: Cuneiform Knowledge and the History of Science* (Chicago).

Röllig, W. (2001), 'Myths about the Netherworld in the Ancient Near East and their counterparts in Greek religion', in S. Ribichini, M. Rocchi and P. Xella (eds.), *La questione delle influenze vicino-orientali sulla religione greca* (Rome), 307–14.

Rollinger, R. (2014), 'Homer and the ancient Near East: some considerations on intercultural affairs', in I. Lindstedt, J. Hämeen-Anttila, R. Mattila and R. Rollinger (eds.), *Case Studies in Transmission: The Intellectual Heritage of the Ancient and Medieval Near East 1* (Münster), 131–42.

(2015), 'Old battles, new horizons: the ancient Near East and the Homeric epics', in Rollinger and Van Dongen (2015), 5–32.

Rollinger, R. and E. van Dongen (eds.) (2015), *Mesopotamia in the Ancient World: Impact, Continuities, Parallels*, Melammu Symposia 7 (Münster).

Romm, J. (2010), 'Continents, climates, and cultures: Greek theories of global structure', in K. A. Raaflaub and R. J. A. Talbert (eds.), *Geography and Ethnography: Perceptions of the World in Pre-Modern Societies* (Oxford), 215–35.

Rubio, G. (2006), 'Shulgi and the death of Sumerian', in Michalowski and Veldhuis (2006), 167–79.

Rumpf, A. (1927), *Chalkidische Vasen* (Berlin).

Rutherford, I. (2001), *Pindar's Paeans: A Reading of the Fragments and a Survey of the Genre* (Oxford).

(2009), 'Hesiod and the literary traditions of the Near East', in Montanari et al. (2009), 9–35.

Rutherford, R. B. (1986), 'The philosophy of the *Odyssey*', *Journal of Hellenic Studies* 106, 145–62, reprinted in Doherty (2009), 155–88.

Sallaberger, W. (2008), *Das Gilgamesch-Epos: Mythos, Werk und Tradition* (Munich).

(2010), 'Skepsis gegenüber väterlicher Weisheit: zum altbabylonischen Dialog zwischen Vater und Sohn', in Baker et al. (2010), 303–18.

Sammons, B. (2014), 'A tale of Tydeus', in C. Tsagalis (ed.), *Theban Resonances in Homeric Epic, Trends in Classics* 6.2, 297–318.

(2017), *Device and Composition in the Greek Epic Cycle* (Oxford).

Schadewaldt, W. (1997), 'Hector and Andromache', in Wright and Jones (1997), 124–42 [first published in German, 1961].

Schefold, K. (1966), *Myth and Legend in Early Greek Art* (London).

(1992), *Gods and Heroes in Late Archaic Greek Art* (Cambridge) [translated from German edition of 1978].

Schein, S. (1984), *The Mortal Hero: An Introduction to Homer's Iliad* (Berkeley).

(2016), *Homeric Epic and Its Reception: Interpretative Essays* (Oxford).

Schenkeveld, D.M. (1982), 'The structure of Plutarch's *De Audiendis Poetis*', *Mnemosyne* 35, 60–71.

Schironi, F. (2018), *The Best of the Grammarians: Aristarchus of Samothrace on the Iliad* (Ann Arbor, MI).

Schmiel, R. (1987), 'Achilles in Hades', *Classical Philology* 82, 25–37.

Schmitt, R. (1967), *Dichtung und Dichtersprache in Indogermanischer Zeit* (Wiesbaden).

Schniedewind, W. M. and J. H. Hunt (2007), *A Primer on Ugaritic* (Cambridge).

Scodel, R. (1992), 'The wits of Glaucus', *Transactions of the American Philological Association* 122, 73–84.

(2002), *Listening to Homer: Tradition, Narrative and Audience* (Ann Arbor, MI).

(2008), 'Stupid, pointless wars', *Transactions of the American Philological Association* 138, 219–35.

(2012), '*Works and Days* as performance', in E. Minchin (ed.), *Orality, Literacy and Performance in the Ancient World* (Leiden), 111–27.

Scott, W. C. (2009), *The Artistry of the Homeric Simile* (Dartmouth, NH).

Scully, S. (1990), *Homer and the Sacred City* (Ithaca, NY).

Seaford, R. (1993), 'Dionysus as destroyer of the household: Homer, tragedy and the polis', in T. H. Carpenter and C. A. Faraone (eds.), *Masks of Dionysus* (Ithaca, NY), 115–46.

(1994), *Reciprocity and Ritual: Homer and Tragedy in the Developing City-State* (Oxford).

(2004), *Money and the Early Greek Mind* (Cambridge).

Segal, C. (1994), *Singers, Heroes and Gods in the* Odyssey (Ithaca, NY).

(1997), *Dionysiac Poetics in Euripides'* Bacchae, 2nd edn. (Princeton).

Sewell-Rutter, N. J. (2007), *Guilt by Descent: Moral Inheritance and Decision-Making in Greek Tragedy* (Oxford).

Shapiro, H. A. (1993), *Personifications in Greek Art: The Representation of Abstract Concepts 600–400 BC* (Geneva).

(1994), *Myth into Art: Poet and Painter in Classical Greece* (London).

(2013), 'The François Vase: 175 years of interpretation', in Shapiro et al. (2013), 9–17.

Shapiro, H. A., M. Iozzo, and A. Lezzi-Hafter (eds.) (2013), *The François Vase: New Perspectives*, 2 vols. (Zurich).

Shear, I. M. (2002), 'Mycenaean Centaurs at Ugarit', *Journal of Hellenic Studies* 122, 147–53.

Sider, D. (2010), 'Greek verse on a vase by Douris', *Hesperia* 79, 541–54.

Sinos, D. (1980), *Achilles, Patroklos and the Meaning of* philos (Innsbruck).

Slatkin, L. M. (1991), *The Power of Thetis: Allusion and Interpretation in the* Iliad (Berkeley).

Small, J. P. (2003), *The Parallel Worlds of Classical Art and Text* (Cambridge).

Smith, A. C. (2011), *Polis and Personification in Classical Athenian Art* (Leiden).

(2012), Personification: not just a symbolic mode', in T. J. Smith and G. Plantzos (eds.), *A Companion to Greek Art* (Oxford), 2.440–55.

Smith, A. C. and S. Pickup (eds.) (2010), *Brill's Companion to Aphrodite* (Leiden).

Snodgrass, A. (1998), *Homer and the Artists: Text and Picture in Early Greek Art* (Cambridge).

Sommerstein, A.H. (ed.) (2008), Aeschylus, *Fragments* (Loeb Classical Library) (Cambridge, MA).

(2010a), *Aeschylean Tragedy*, 2nd edn. (London).

(2010b), 'The tangled ways of Zeus', in *The Tangled Ways of Zeus and Other Studies in and around Greek Tragedy* (Oxford), 164–70.

(2013), '*Atē* in Aeschylus', in D. L. Cairns (ed.), *Tragedy and Archaic Greek Thought* (Swansea), 1–15.

Sourvinou-Inwood, C. (1991), *'Reading' Greek Culture* (Oxford).

(1995), *'Reading' Greek Death* (Oxford).

Spar, I. and W. G. Lambert (eds.) (2005), *Cuneiform Texts in the Metropolitan Museum of Art II* (New York).

Spivey, N. (2018), *The Sarpedon Krater: The Life and Afterlife of a Greek Vase* (London).

Stafford, E. and J. Herrin (eds.) (2005), *Personification in the Greek World* (Aldershot).

Stamatopoulou, Z. (2013), 'Reading the *Aspis* as a Hesiodic poem', *Classical Philology* 108, 273–85.

Stansbury-O'Donnell, M. (1999), *Pictorial Narrative in Ancient Greek Art* (Cambridge).

(2006), *Vase-Painting, Gender, and Identity in Archaic Athens* (Cambridge).

Steele, L. D. (2002), 'Mesopotamian elements in the proem of Parmenides? Correspondences between the sun-gods Helios and Shamash', *Classical Quarterly* 52, 583–8.

(2007), 'Women and gender in Babylonia', in Leick (2007), 299–316.

Stefanini, R. (1969), 'Enkidu's dream in the Hittite *Gilgamesh*', *Journal of Near Eastern Studies* 28, 40–7.

Steiner, A. (2007), *Reading Greek Vases* (Cambridge).

Stewart, A. (1983), 'Stesichoros and the François Vase', in W. G. Moon (ed.), *Ancient Greek Art and Iconography* (Madison, WI), 97–118.

Steymans, H. U. (ed.) (2010), *Gilgamesch: Iconographie eines Helden/Gilgamesh: Epic and Iconography* (Göttingen).

Stinton, T. C. W. (1990), 'Euripides and the judgment of Paris', in his *Collected Papers on Greek Tragedy* (Oxford), 17–75 [first published as *Journal of Hellenic Studies* Supplement xi (1965)].

Stökl, J., 'Nebuchadnezzar: history, memory and myth-making in the Persian period', in D. V. Edelman and E. Ben Zvi (eds.) (2013), *Remembering Biblical Figures in the Late Persian and Early Hellenistic Periods: Social Memory and Imagination* (Oxford), 257–69.

Stray, C., M. Clarke and J. Katz (eds.) (forthcoming), *Liddell and Scott: Perspectives on a Lexicon* (Oxford).

Suter, A. (ed.) (2008), *Lament: Studies in the Ancient Mediterranean and Beyond* (Oxford).

Swain, S. (1988), 'A note on *Iliad* 9.524–599: the story of Meleager', *Classical Quarterly* 38, 271–6.

Symonds, J. A. (2012), 'A problem in Greek ethics', in S. Brady (ed.), *John Addington Symonds (1840–1893) and Homosexuality: A Critical Edition of Sources* (London), 39–121 [essay first published 1883].

Taplin, O. (2001), 'The Shield of Achilles within the *Iliad*', in Cairns (2001a), 342–64 [first published 1980].

Tarenzi, V. (2005), 'Patroclo *therapōn*', *Quaderni Urbinati di Cultura Classica* 80, 25–38.

Tatum, J. (2003), *The Mourner's Song: War and Remembrance from the* Iliad *to Vietnam* (Chicago).

Taylor, J. (2010), 'On the interpretation of two critical passages in *Gilgamesh and Huwawa*', in Baker et al. (2010), 351–60.

Teffeteller, A. (2010), 'The song of Ares and Aphrodite: Ashertu on Skheria', in Smith and Pickup (2010), 133–49.

Teodorsson, S. T. (2006), 'Eastern literacy, Greek alphabet, and Homer', *Mnemosyne* 59, 161–87.

Thalmann, W. G. (1984), *Conventions of Form and Thought in Early Greek Epic Poetry* (Baltimore).

Thomson, G. (ed.) (1966), *The* Oresteia *of Aeschylus* (Amsterdam).

Tigay, J. H. (1982), *The Evolution of the Gilgamesh Epic* (Philadelphia).

Tinney, S. J. (1999), 'On the curricular setting of Sumerian literature', *Iraq* 59, 159–72.

(2011), 'Tablets of schools and scholars: a portrait of the Old Babylonian corpus', in Radner and Robson (2011), 577–96.

Tomasso, V. (2016), 'Rhapsodic receptions of Homer in multiform proems of the *Iliad*', *American Journal of Philology* 137, 377–409.

Torrance, I. (2013), *Metapoetry in Euripides* (Oxford).

Torres-Guerra, J. B. (2015), '*Thebaid*', in Fantuzzi and Tsagalis (2015a), 226–43.

Tsagalis, C. (2004), 'The poetics of sorrow: Thetis' lament in *Iliad* 18.52–64', *Quaderni Urbinati di Cultura Classica* 76, 9–32.

(2006), 'Poet and audience: from Homer to Hesiod', in Montanari and Rengakos (2006), 79–134.

(2009), 'Poetry and poetics in the Hesiodic corpus', in Montanari et al. (2009), 131–78.

Turkeltaub, D. (2005), 'The syntax and semantics of Homeric glowing eyes: *Iliad* 1.200', *American Journal of Philology* 156, 157–86.

Ulf, C. (2014), 'Rethinking cultural contacts', in R. Rollinger and K. Schnegg (eds.), *Kulturkontakte in antiken Welten: vom Denkmodell zum Fallbeispiel*, Colloquia Antiqua 10 (Leuven), 507–64.

Van Brock, N. (1959), 'Substitution rituelle', *Revue hittite et asianique* 65, 117–46.

Van de Hout, T. (2010), 'The rise and fall of cuneiform script in Hittite Anatolia', in Woods (2010), 99–114.

(2011), 'The Hittite empire from textual evidence', in S. R. Steadman and G. McMahon (eds.), *The Oxford Handbook of Ancient Anatolia* (Oxford), 900–16.

Van de Mieroop, M. (1997), *The Ancient Mesopotamian City* (Oxford).

(2007), *A History of the Ancient Near East, ca. 3000–323 BC*, 2nd edn. (Oxford).

(2013), 'Beyond Babylonian literature', in Aruz et al. (2013), 276–83.

(2016), *Philosophy before the Greeks: The Pursuit of Truth in Ancient Babylonia* (Princeton).

Van Dongen, E. (2008), 'The study of Near Eastern influences on Greece: towards the point', *KASKAL: Rivista di storia, ambienti e culture del Vicino Oriente antico* 5, 233–50.

Van Erp Taalman Kip, A. M. (2000), 'The gods of the *Iliad* and the fate of Troy', *Mnemosyne* 53, 385–402.

Van Noorden, H. (2015), *Playing Hesiod: The 'Myth of the Races' in Classical Antiquity* (Cambridge).

Van Nortwick, T. (1992), *Somewhere I Have Never Travelled: The Second Self and the Hero's Journey in Ancient Epic* (Oxford).

Van Rossum-Steinbeek (1998), *Greek Readers' Digests? Studies on a Selection of Subliterary Papyri* (Leiden).

Van Thiel, H. (2000), *Scholia D in Iliadem besteht aus deutscher Einführung* (Stuttgart), www.kups.ub.uni-koeln.de/1810/.

Van Wees, H. (1992), *Status Warriors: War, Violence and Society in Homer and History* (Amsterdam).

(2006), 'From kings to demigods: epic heroes and social change, c. 750–600 BC', in Deger-Jalkotzy and Lemos (2006), 363–80.

Vanstiphout, H. (2003), *Epics of Sumerian Kings: The Matter of Aratta* (Atlanta, GA).

(2010), 'Notes on the shape of the Aratta epics', in Baker et al. (2010), 361–77.

Veldhuis, N. (2000), 'Sumerian proverbs in their curricular context', *Journal of the American Oriental Society* 120, 383–99.

(2001), 'The solution of the dream: a new interpretation of *Bilgames' Death*', *Journal of Cuneiform Studies* 53, 133–48.

Vermeule, E. (1979), *Aspects of Death in Early Greek Art and Poetry* (Berkeley).

Vernant, J.-P. (2001), 'A "beautiful death" and the disfigured corpse in Homeric epic', in Cairns (2001a), 311–41 [first published in French, 1982].

Versnel, H. (2010), *Coping with the Gods: Wayward Readings in Greek Theology* (Leiden).

Volk, K. (2002), '*Kleos aphthiton* revisited', *Classical Philology* 97, 61–8.

Vulpe, N. (1994), 'Irony and the unity of the Gilgamesh Epic', *Journal of Near Eastern Studies* 53, 275–83.

Walcot, P. (1966), *Hesiod and the Near East* (Cardiff).

Walsh, T. R. (2005), *Fighting Words and Feuding Words: Anger and the Homeric Poems* (Lanham, MD).

Wasserman, N. (2011), 'The distant voice of Gilgamesh: the circulation and reception of the Babylonian Gilgamesh Epic in ancient Mesopotamia', *Archiv für Orientforschung* 52, 1–14.

Weil, S. (2005), 'The *Iliad* or the poem of force', translated by Mary McCarthy, in C. Benfey (ed.), *War and the* Iliad: *Simone Weil and Rachel Bespaloff* (New York) [this translation of 'L'*Iliade*, ou le poème de la force' first published 1945].

Wengrow, D. (2010), *What Makes Civilization? The Ancient Near East and the Future of the West* (Oxford).

West, M. L. (ed.) (1966), Hesiod, *Theogony* (Oxford).

(ed.) (1978), Hesiod, *Works and Days* (Oxford).

(1985), *The Hesiodic Catalogue of Women* (Oxford).

(ed.) (1991), *Iambi et Elegi Graeci ante Alexandrum Cantati*, 2nd edn. (Oxford).

(1993), 'Simonides redivivus', *Zeitschrift für Papyrologie und Epigraphik* 98, 1–14.

(1997), *The East Face of Helicon: West Asiatic Elements in Greek Poetry and Myth* (Oxford).

(1999), 'The invention of Homer', *Classical Quarterly* 49, 364–82.

(2000), '*Iliad* and *Aethiopis* on the Stage: Aeschylus and Son', *Classical Quarterly* 50, 338–52.

(2001), *Studies in the Text and Transmission of the* Iliad (Munich).

(2005a), 'The new Sappho', *Zeitschrift für Papyrologie und Epigraphik* 151, 1–9.

(2005b), '*Odyssey* and *Argonautica*', *Classical Quarterly* 55, 39–64.

(2007), *Indo-European Poetry and Myth* (Oxford).

(2013), *The Epic Cycle: A Commentary on the Lost Troy Epics* (Oxford).

Westbrook, R. (1992), 'The trial scene in the *Iliad*', *Harvard Studies in Classical Philology* 94, 53–76.

Westenholz, J. G. (1997), *Legends of the Kings of Akkade: The Texts* (Winona Lake, IN).

(2007), 'Inanna and Ishtar – the dimorphic Venus goddesses', in Leick (2007), 332–47.

Whiting, R. M. (ed.) (2001), *Mythology and Mythologies: Methodological Approaches to Intercultural Influences*, Melammu Symposia II (Helsinki).

Wiggermann, F. A. M. (1992), *Mesopotamian Protective Spirits: The Ritual Texts* (Groningen).

(2000), 'Lamashtu, daughter of Anu: a profile', in M. Stol (ed.), *Birth in Babylonia and the Bible: Its Mediterranean Setting* (Groningen), 217–52.

(2007), 'The four winds and the origins of Pazuzu', in C. Wilcke (ed.), *Das geistige Erfassen der Welt im alten Orient: Beiträge zu Sprache, Religion, Kultur und Gesellschaft* (Wiesbaden), 125–66.

(2011), 'The Mesopotamian pandemonium: a provisional census', *Studi e materiali di storia delle religioni* 77, 298–322.

Willi, A. (2005), '*Kadmos anethēke*: zur Vermittlung der Alphabetschrift nach Griechenland', *Museum Helveticum* 62, 162–71.

Wilson, D. F. (2002a), *Ransom, Revenge and Heroic Identity in the* Iliad (Cambridge).

(2002b), 'Lion kings: heroes in the epic mirror', *Colby Quarterly* 38, 231–54.

Wilson, J. R. (1987), 'Non-temporal *ouketi/mēketi*', *Glotta* 65, 194–8.

Winitzer, A. (2013), 'Etana in Eden: new light on the Mesopotamian and Biblical tales in their Semitic context', *Journal of the American Oriental Society* 133, 441–65.

Woods, C. (ed.) (2010), *Visible Language: Inventions of Writing in the Ancient Middle East and Beyond* (Chicago).

Wright, G. M. and P. V. Jones (eds.) (1997), *Homer: German Scholarship in Translation* (Oxford).

Yamagata, N. (1994), *Homeric Morality* (Leiden).

 (2005), 'Disaster revisited: *Ate* and the *Litai* in Homer's *Iliad*', in Stafford and Herrin (2005), 21–8.

 (2012), 'Use of Homeric references in Plato and Xenophon', *Classical Quarterly* 62, 130–44.

Yunis, H. (2005), 'The rhetoric of law in fourth-century Athens', in M. Gagarin and D. Cohen (eds.), *The Cambridge Companion to Ancient Greek Law* (Cambridge), 191–209.

Zamalová, S. (2011), 'The education of Neo-Assyrian princes', in Radner and Robson (2011), 313–30.

Zanker, A. T. (2013), 'Decline and *parainesis* in Hesiod's Race of Iron', *Rheinisches Museum* 156, 1–19.

Zanker, G. (1994), *The Heart of Achilles: Characterisation and Personal Ethics in the Iliad* (Ann Arbor, MI).

 (1998), 'Beyond reciprocity: the Akhilleus–Priam scene in *Iliad* 24', in Gill et al. (1998), 73–92.

Ziolkowski, T. (2011), *Gilgamesh Among Us: Modern Encounters with the Ancient Epic* (Ithaca, NY).

Index of Passages Cited

Iliad (Cont.)
  19.295–300: 325
  19.326–33: 314
  19.328–33: 258
  19.362–3: 277
  20.23: 211
  20.32: 154
  20.164–75: 280
  20.204–12: 1
  20.219–29: 1
  20.248–9: 2
  21.106–13: 281
  21.275–8: 282
  21.277–8: 208
  21.386: 154
  21.522–5: 199
  21.542–3: 283
  22.261–7: 285
  22.304–5: 323
  22.345–7: 286
  22.358–66: 287
  22.360: 303
  22.363: 232
  22.418–22: 294
  22.454–9: 324
  23.33–4: 273
  23.44–47: 289
  23.61–9: 289
  23.71–4: 291
  23.80–1: 300
  23.83–92: 290
  23.91–2: 176
  23.100: 291
  23.100–7: 290
  23.346: 277
  24.25–30: 153
  24.39–49: 293
  24.63: 180
  24.85–6: 300
  24.131–2: 300
  24.184–7: 294
  24.206–8: 295
  24.212–15: 295
  24.255–8: 185
  24.478–83: 296
  24.487–8: 297
  24.503–4: 297
  24.525–6: 211, 298
  24.540: 300
  24.551: 298
  24.568–70: 299
  24.584–6: 299
  24.739: 326
  24.757–75: 326

Ludlul bēl nēmeqi
  II 39–47: 55
Lugalbanda in the Wilderness
  26–31: 57
  429–31: 58

Macrobius
  Saturnalia 6.3.1: 7

Nergal and Ereshkigal
  Late Version ii 1'–7': 253
Nothing Is of Value: 55

Odyssey
  1.1: 120
  4.563–9: 138
  4.791–3: 272
  8.43–5: 118
  8.62–75: 119
  8.523–31: 296
  11.467–70: 313
  11.484–91: 313
  11.492–503: 314
  11.510–40: 314
  11.533–64: 315
  11.547: 309
  18.129–31: 257
  18.130–7: 336
  22.347–8: 119
  24.47–59: 306
  24.71–79: 290
  24.74–75: 177

Pausanias
  1.33.7: 165
  5.19.6: 183
Pindar
  Pythian 3.80–1: 298
Plato
  Alcibiades II 149d: 154
  Apology 28e–30b: 265
  Crito 44b 1–2: 266
  Ion 535e7 ff.: 116
  Republic 383b: 180
  Symposium 178d1–180a3: 266
Plutarch
  Moralia 1.6, 23 C-E: 200

General Index

*An entry in **bold** indicates a major discussion extending over several pages*